BERLITZ®

·B·L·U·E·P·R·I·N·T·

BRITAIN

Editor
CHRISTINA JACKSON

Photography
WALTER IMBER

Layout
DORIS HALDEMANN

Cartography
HALLWAG AG, Bern

Although we make every effort to ensure the accuracy of all the information in this book, changes occur incessantly. We cannot therefore take responsibility for facts, addresses and circumstances in general that are constantly subject to alteration.

Sections of this book have appeared in slightly different form in other Berlitz publications.

Cover photo: Broadway, the Cotswolds

Additional photos: cover, pp. 6, 164, 169, 170, 173, 177, 274, 286, Erling Mandelmann; pp. 36, 94 (both), 95, 158–159 André Held, Ecublens; pp. 64, 83, 86, 91 Jeremy Grayson; pp. 246, 258, 263, 264, 266–267, 269 Roy A. Giles; p. 251 PRISMA/STROHEIM; p. 253 PRISMA/Telegraph Colour Library; p. 270 All Sport/Russell Cheyne; 285 Redfurns, London.

Maps: pp. 4, 42, 46, 57 Max Thommen

Acknowledgements
We would like to thank Martin Gostelow, Suzanne Patterson, Adrienne Farrell, Liz Brooks, Ken Bernstein and Anne-Karin Ratna for their substantial contribution to the writing and editing of this guide. We are also grateful to Eileen Harr-Kyburz and Alice Taucher for editorial assistance. We equally extend our warm thanks to the British Tourist Authority, in particular Bill Ishmael and his staff at the Zurich office and David Meurig Thomas of the Wales Tourist Board, and all the local tourist offices for their invaluable help in the preparation of this guide.

BERLITZ®

·B·L·U·E·P·R·I·N·T·

BRITAIN

By EARLEEN BRUNNER

and the Staff of Berlitz Guides

Contents

BRITAIN AND THE BRITISH	7
Facts and Figures	13
HISTORY	15
Historical Landmarks	36
WHERE TO GO	39
On the Short List	42
LEISURE ROUTES	45
LONDON AND ENVIRONS	69
London	69
Environs of London	89
BRITISH ART	94
THE SOUTH-EAST	97
Kent	97
Sussex	102
Surrey	109
THE SOUTH	111
Hampshire	111
Wiltshire	116
Dorset	120
BRITISH ARCHITECTURE	128
THE SOUTH-WEST	131
Bath	131
Bristol	134
Somerset	135
Devon	139
Cornwall	147
EAST ANGLIA AND THE FENS	153
Cambridge	153
Suffolk	155
Norfolk	160
Lincolnshire	162
CENTRAL ENGLAND	165
Oxford	165
Stratford-upon-Avon	167
The Cotswolds	174
The Midlands	178
The Peak District	185
THE ENGLISH COUNTRY TOWN	190

WALES	193
South Wales	193
Mid-Wales	202
North Wales	207
THE NORTH OF ENGLAND	219
Northern Cities	219
Yorkshire Dales and Pennine Moors	222
York	226
Lake District	236
The North-East	240
SCOTLAND	247
Edinburgh	247
Glasgow	252
Central Scotland	255
North-East Scotland	259
The Highlands	261
Islands	265
WHAT TO DO	271
Sports	271
Shopping	276
Entertainment	281
CALENDAR OF EVENTS	283
BRITISH POP CULTURE	284
EATING OUT	287
HOTELS AND RESTAURANTS	296
BERLITZ INFO	306
ROAD ATLAS SECTION	327
INDEX	348
CITY MAPS: London 74–75, Edinburgh 248	

Map coordinates next to the subheadings refer to the Road Atlas section.

Stuffed Shirts
and Stiff Upper Lips

The British are made of sterner stuff than others. They're a stoical lot, unemotional as they come, and famously laconic. A lugubrious sense of humour and a mildly lunatic streak are peculiar to the island race. Blame it on nature, nurture or nanny.

The British counter American exuberance with understatement—and French chic with eccentricity. British street fashion is the world's most inventive, and bizarre. But custom-tailored members of the Establishment also have a penchant for the unusual—startlingly coloured socks and ties, for example—and their wives wear the most outlandish hats. At Ascot it's a tradition. Yet under the skin, people are surprisingly conservative.

"How many kinds of sweet flowers grow in an English country garden?"—as the old song goes. This country garden, in a variation on British understatement, has been carefully cultivated to give an impression of nature running wild.

Change for its own sake strikes the British as a highly subversive notion. Let other Europeans drive on the right. The British refuse to conform. And there's still some grass roots resistance to metrification, initiated back in the 1970s. The drinking man, for one, has no intention of giving up his "pint".

By the same token, old buildings have a greater appeal for the British than the new. They like clutter, comfort and things with memories attached to them. Prince Charles speaks for the nation when he denounces "soulless" modern architecture, and the problem of what to replace it with is the subject of endless public debate.

Just as fraught is the issue of integration into Europe, a place that begins, in the British view, on the *other* side of the Channel. But the "Chunnel" (Channel Tunnel) will bring Britain and the Continent closer together—physically, if not mentally.

Continental sophisticates like to portray the British as a bunch of tea-drinking, dog-loving bores, conveniently forgetting that Britain was the country that unleashed the sexual revolution and

*M*oonrise over Wells
Cathedral, a great treasure for a
very small English city. Set one
above another, 293 statues stand
in the niches of the symmetrical
west façade, urging all eyes heaven-
ward. At the outset the figures,
life-sized or larger, were painted to
help identify the subjects—kings
or saints or clerics. Now they're
colourless but no less remarkable.
This cathedral, an exemplary
Gothic masterpiece, was begun
in the 12th century, when the
bishopric returned to Wells from
a temporary stay in Bath. More
than 20 bishops are buried here.

Swinging London on an unsuspecting world. "Continental people have sex lives, while the British have hot-water bottles," observed the Hungarian humorist George Mikes, perpetuating the myth.

For a tourist, Britain's many attractions are cast on an epic scale. A four-hour train journey from south to north traverses a whole continent of landscapes, from England's smoothly contoured expanses to the rugged grandeur of the Scottish Highlands.

The countryside is at its gentlest in the South-East, where millennia of cultivation have tamed the land. Orchards, vineyards, fields of hops and maize stretch across the Weald from Kent into Sussex, and flocks of sheep graze on the chalk downland.

William the Conqueror defeated the Anglo-Saxons on the South Downs above Hastings. The ruins of Battle Abbey mark the site, in open country. There's more rolling downland and rich farmland in the counties of the South—Hampshire, Wiltshire and Dorset—full of memories of Thomas Hardy's rustic characters. It's all perfectly pastoral, but you don't have to travel far to feel London's commercial and cultural pull.

Windswept moors, rocky coves and sea-battered headlands add to the appeal of the south-west peninsula. Little visited by foreigners, Somerset, Devon and westernmost Cornwall live from fishing—and British tourism. This is the nation's sunbelt, a northern Riviera warmed by the Gulf Stream.

Eastern England's wide skies and flat Fens—marshland reclaimed, like coastal areas of Holland, from the sea—inspired John Constable's art. A rural peace reigns inland, far from the container ports of Felixstowe and Lowestoft.

The River Thames flows through the country's heartland, an area that takes in Oxford and its colleges and Shakespeare's Stratford, the industrial cities of the Midlands and the (not-very-high) peaks and dales of Derbyshire. Wales, in turn, offers the contrasts of its Celtic language and customs, while castles, mountains, valleys and a 600-mile (965-km.) coastline make for a change of scene.

The craggy Pennine Mountains—England's spine—slope away to the Lake District's "bare grey dell, high wood, and pastoral cove" (in William Wordsworth's words), and to the bleak yet beautiful North York Moors. Hadrian's Wall crosses the north near the Scottish border. This coast-to-coast monument to the Roman conquest kept the warlike Celts at bay.

*L*unchtime regulars down a pint at their local. Every
pub has something that sets it apart—the clientele, the decor, the historic
associations. There are half-timbered Tudor pubs, mirrored Victorian
establishments, pubs with video games, gardens, family rooms for
children. But any pub worthy of the name offers beer—preferably hand-
pumped real ale—and conviviality.

11

Scotland's Lowlands claim the big cities of Edinburgh and Glasgow and 75 per cent of the population. But the Highland glens, lochs and snow-capped heights are wild, remote and awesomely desolate.

The British revel in the countryside (though they choose overwhelmingly to live in town), and almost everybody aspires to a country cottage, if not a country estate. You have to be a rock star or an Arab tycoon to afford the upkeep on one of the really great houses, and many hereditary owners have had to sell up—or open up. The enterprising Marquess of Bath, pioneer of the "stately homes" business, hit on the idea of opening his 16th-century Longleat House to the public shortly after World War II. Hundreds of other aristocrats followed suit. Some of them really earn their keep, managing lucrative on-site attractions, from funfairs to safari parks.

The British may not know how to commercialize their considerable technological inventiveness as dynamically as the Japanese nor do they have the industrial capability of the Germans, but they are brilliant at marketing their heritage. They've sold the Americans everything from the *Queen Mary* to London Bridge (not the original, storied, medieval structure, but a rather ugly Victorian replacement). And demand is high worldwide for second-hand black taxis and red phone boxes, for chintz, tweeds and shooting sticks—all the accoutrements of the country-house lifestyle, servants included. A school in England that specializes in training butlers can't turn them out fast enough. But most of the graduate Jeeveses go to work abroad.

"The stately homes of England," run the words of a Noël Coward song, "How beautiful they stand." But the upper classes have lost the upper hand. Money and status matter more than blood lines and the right "U" (Upperclass) accent in the modern meritocracy that is Britain. Even the royals think of themselves as working for the family "firm".

Some things never change, and the best of the past, Britain's cultural traditions and political institutions (a proud legacy that stems from the Magna Carta signing in 1215) survive intact. Life for most people still centres on the pub and local community. At least that's how it's portrayed in twice-weekly episodes of *Eastenders,* a favourite soap opera on British TV.

Old stereotypes die hard, and the warm-hearted Yorkshireman, chipper Cockney, eloquent Welshman and canny Scott live on in the popular imagination, if not in reality. As for the caricature Briton in his bowler hat, he's fast becoming an endangered species. Still, ride a commuter train (or walk the City streets) any working day and you'll see scores like him—and a representative sampling of the nation's ethnic population besides.

With more than 2 million Commonwealth and other immigrants now in residence—Indians, Pakistanis, Bangladeshis, West Indians, Cypriots, Chinese —Britain has become a truly multicultural society. The proliferation of ethnic restaurants is just one indication of the extent to which the minorities are sharing their way of life with the Anglo-Saxon majority.

The exchange works both ways. Great Britain may have lost the Empire, but the nation of Shakespeare and Dickens, the King James Bible and Oxford English Dictionary has never relinquished cultural leadership of the English-speaking world. British publishing and broadcasting set international standards of excellence. The same goes for opera, dance, theatre and cinema. And the dynamic pop scene has been evolving ever since the '60s heyday of the Beatles. At the moment, Joan Collins is probably Britain's most popular export, matched only by Andrew Lloyd Webber's current musical hit.

But nothing says Britain like "sport". A national obsession, it's virtually a British invention, though the country that taught the rest of the world to play every-

12

thing from cricket to tennis is being beaten at its own game. The West Indians and Pakistanis score most of the runs at London's international cricket grounds of Lord's and the Oval, and German, Czech and American tennis stars sweep the board at Wimbledon. The British, no longer in the first division of the economic league either, can only be philosophical. It's not whether you win or lose that counts, it's how you play the game...

FACTS AND FIGURES

Geography: The United Kingdom covers an area of 94,250 sq. mi. (244,100 sq. km.), including 12,000 sq. mi. (31,000 sq. km.) of inland waters. Mainland Britain (England, Wales and Scotland) extends 600 mi. (965 km.) from north to south and 300 mi. (483 km.) from east to west, across the widest part.

Four seas surround Britain: the North Sea, English Channel, Irish Sea and Atlantic Ocean. The island divides into a highland and a lowland zone along a line that runs from the mouth of the River Tees in the north-east to the mouth of the Exe in the south-west. Chief mountain ranges include the Pennines, England's "spine", the Cumbrian Mountains in north-west England, the Snowdon and Cambrian ranges of Wales, and Scotland's Grampian Mountains. Scotland claims Britain's highest peak: Ben Nevis, 4,406 feet (1,342 m.). Among principal rivers are the Thames, Tyne, Mersey, Severn and Humber in England, the Usk and Wye in Wales, and the Tay, Clyde and Forth in Scotland.

Population: About 55 million (some 47 million English, nearly 3 million Welsh, 5 million Scots).

Capital: London (pop. 3.5 million, metropolitan area 6.7 million)

Major Cities: Birmingham (1 million), Glasgow (730,000), Leeds (710,000), Sheffield (530,000), Liverpool (490,000), Bradford (460,000), Manchester (450,000), Edinburgh (430,000), Bristol (390,000), Coventry (312,000), Cardiff (270,000)

Climate: Largely oceanic, with cool summers and mild winters. Annual variations in temperature are relatively modest. Hot spot of the British Isles is Cornwall in the south-west, warmed by the Gulf Stream. Rainfall is heaviest between October and January, but the humidity remains high throughout the year.

Government: Constitutional monarchy. Parliament, Britain's legislative body, is made up of the directly elected House of Commons and the subordinate and largely hereditary House of Lords. The sovereign opens and closes sessions of Parliament and nominally approves all legislation.

The executive branch of government consists of the Prime Minister, leader of the majority party in the Commons, and the Cabinet, chosen by the Prime Minister from members of the Commons and Lords.

Religion: Predominantly Protestant. There are two state churches, the Anglican Church of England and the Presbyterian Church of Scotland. The Roman Catholic Church has a sizeable membership, followed by the Methodist and Baptist congregations. There are about 1 million Muslims and 350,000 Jews.

1066 and All That

Britain wasn't always an island. Until as recently as 7,000 years ago, it was joined to the rest of Europe by a land bridge. Bands of nomadic hunters had followed this route for several hundred thousand years, venturing ever farther in search of game. They wandered the tundra that was Britain's primaeval landscape, and the great forests that evolved in its place—opening a network of trackways as they went. Some of the tracks survive as footpaths to this day: Wiltshire's Ridgeway Path, for example, and Peddar's Way in East Anglia.

At the close of the Ice Age, rising seas separated Ireland from the mainland. Then the Continental connection was severed, leaving Britain high and dry. The island's subsequent history is a tale of isolation and invasion. For Celts, Romans, Saxons and Normans, Britain was the end of the line.

The transition to a settled way of life took place around 4000 B.C., with the arrival of agricultural newcomers from Europe. People began farming and breeding cattle. The skills of pottery-making and weaving developed, and trade evolved, along with a tribal organization of society. After 3000 B.C. Britain's first monuments were going up: megalithic chambered tombs, standing stones and the circular constructions known as henges.

Britain emerged from the Stone Age some time in the 2nd millennium B.C. An influx of "Beaker Folk" provided the impetus. These metal-workers from the Rhineland introduced the technology of bronze-smelting into the island. Local deposits of copper and tin were mined early on, and a lively trade grew up with the Continent.

No one profited more than the Wessex chieftains, strong men of the Salisbury Plain. They cornered the metals market and ploughed some of the proceeds into ambitious building works at Avebury and Stonehenge. The great stone circles there remain an enigma. Were they temples, burial complexes, astronomical observatories? Nobody knows for sure.

From the 8th century B.C. onwards, the primitive population of Britain was submerged in a flood of Celtic immigration. One tribe followed on the heels of another, the newcomers displacing those who had gone before. By the 5th century B.C., incoming Celts were brandishing

No mean architect, Emperor Hadrian himself designed the wall that sealed off rebellious Scotland from the north of 2nd-century Roman Britain.

15

weapons of iron. Hill forts proliferated as settlement—and conflict—spread. Two branches of the Celtic family put down roots in Britain: the Goidels or Gaels of Scotland and Ireland and the Brythons of Cornwall and Wales—the original Britons. With them came their priests, the Druids, adepts of the occult arts and human sacrifice. An underclass of labourers did the rest of the dirty work in this stratified tribal society.

A final incursion of Celts began around 200 B.C. as warriors of the Belgae tribe overran the south-east. Superior horsemanship and the skilled use of the chariot in battle ensured their success. These were troubled times for Britain. The Celts, a notoriously quarrelsome lot, fought constantly with each other. Nothing could bring them together—not even the Roman threat.

Roman Britain

Julius Caesar himself led the first Roman invasion of Britain in 55 B.C. The Belgae met his advance on the beach near Deal, but they were no match for the legionaries. After a second campaign the following year, the southern tribes submitted to Rome and made tribute payments. Caesar sailed back to Gaul in triumph. In the short term little changed for the warring Britons, but the Roman troops returned.

The Emperor Claudius mounted a large-scale invasion of Britain in A.D. 43. After some initial reluctance to cross the Channel, 40,000 soldiers came and conquered. The Romans built roads and founded cities: Camulodunum (Colchester), Londinium (London), Glevum (Gloucester), Eboracum (York)... They introduced a money economy, expanded agricultural production (sheep farming was a Roman innovation) and encouraged the leather, timber and wool industries.

Initially, imperial rule was confined to south and central England. Control of Wales and the north of England came later, after more than 30 years of military activity on the Celtic fringe. The Scottish lowlands were subdued, too, but not for long—the fiercely independent Celts saw to that. By A.D. 122 the Romans withdrew to the line marked by Hadrian's Wall, close to the present Scottish-English border.

At its peak, Roman Britain had a population of around 2 million, with 50,000 alone concentrated in the capital of London. City dwellers rejoiced in paved streets, a piped water supply and the proximity of forum, basilica, temples and public baths. The benefits of Roman civilization also reached the countryside. On hundreds of rural estates, great villas like Lullingstone and Fishbourne went up, all with central heating, piped water and suites of baths. Only in modern times would Britons live so well again.

Prosperity continued into the 4th century, a turbulent period for the rest of the empire. Many landowners from Gaul, fearful of Continental unrest, moved their assets across the Channel to Britain. And Christianity slowly gained a foothold in the island, offering solace to some.

The English Conquest

The Romans received a serious challenge to their rule in Britain in the year 367, when Picts from Scotland and Scots from Ireland breached the northern and western defences. During the century that followed, as Roman power declined and Rome itself was attacked and pillaged by northern tribes, Picts and Scots stepped up their raids. The Britons appealed for help to the Saxons, who were only too happy to oblige. They made quick work of the Picts and Scots, with a little help from their friends the Angles and Jutes. Success was so easy for the barbarians that they went on to call in other Saxons and expanded their hold on the island.

Local forces rallied to Britain's defence under the command of a leader called Artorius—model for King Arthur of Round Table fame, or so they say. But it was a lost cause. The barbarians stayed and settled on the land, mixing with what remained of the native population. Many Britons were massacred and many more fled to Cornwall, Wales and distant Brittany. The cities the Romans founded fell into decay. After a while no one even remembered who had built them.

In the 6th and 7th centuries, several Anglo-Saxon kingdoms rose to power in England. Kent in the south-east achieved an early dominance, only to be superseded by northerly Northumbria and then Mercia, King Penda's domain. Wales and Scotland meanwhile were developing along parallel lines, independent of (though often influenced by) events in England. The house of Gwynedd had begun to assert itself over the lesser kingdoms of Wales, while Picts and Scots vied for control of Scotland.

Christianity made inroads in England, thanks to the work of St. Augustine. The kingdom of Kent was the first to convert

Arthur: Man or Myth?

Yes, there really was an Arthur, though he may not have been a king. A general, perhaps, or more romantically, a resistance fighter—a hero who defended Britain to the death.

The historical facts are few and by no means indisputable. It seems a war leader named Artorius—a Briton, a Christian and a Roman citizen—raised troops to fight the pagan barbarians in the aftermath of the Anglo-Saxon invasion. He probably directed the great victory at an unidentified place called Mons Badonicus around the year 500, which stopped the Anglo-Saxon advance into England for several decades. During that brief period Artorius, Count of Britain, united the province of the Romans for one last time.

A final encounter with the Anglo-Saxons at the Battle of Camlan ended in defeat for the Britons and death for Artorius. The date, 537, appears in the history books with a question mark.

The legendary figure of the King of Camelot was the creation of the medieval writers Geoffrey of Monmouth and Chrétien de Troyes. Their tale of adultery, incest and murder has inspired many different versions of the legend, from Sir Thomas Malory's 1469 *Morte d'Arthur* to John Boorman's film *Excalibur,* released in 1982.

(597); consequently Canterbury became the seat of the archbishop. Celtic missionaries spread the gospel to the north. They founded the great monasteries of Iona, Lindisfarne and Jarrow, and by 650 or thereabouts most of the pagan Anglo-Saxons had been baptized.

Raids from northern Europe were not over yet. At the end of the 8th century, Viking sea-rovers—Norwegians and Danes—descended on Britain's coasts, creating havoc and terror in repeated attacks. The Norwegians plundered western shores from the Shetland Islands to Land's End, while the Danes concentrated on the east. They spread inland during the 9th century to establish a region known as the "Danelaw". Alfred the Great, King of Wessex, contained Danish expansion at Edington in 878. His son, Edward the Elder, and grandson, Athelstan, reconquered the Danelaw. Athelstan (d. 939) was the first king to rule all of England. Even Welsh and Scottish sovereigns swore personal allegiance to Alfred and his heirs, setting a precedent of Anglo-Saxon supremacy.

Long before the word democracy entered the vocabulary, the Anglo-Saxon kings were consulting with their nobles, or "thegns", at meetings of a council called the Witan. The kings standardized coinage and administration, dividing England into shires (precursors of today's counties), each with its own officials and courts. The villages, churches and manors of rural England took shape in Anglo-Saxon times, and merchants and artisans came together in towns.

England suffered another round of Danish raids late in the 10th century. Unprepared to fight, the ineffectual King Ethelred the Unready followed a policy of appeasement. His attempts to buy off the Danish king, Sweyn Forkbeard, bankrupted the country. Ethelred fled into exile and Sweyn briefly took over. Sweyn's son Canute subsequently became King of England (1016–35), ruling also over Denmark (from 1018) and Norway (1028).

*S*torm *clouds glower over
Britain's moodiest monument, the
stonily poetic ensemble of Stonehenge. It was built a thousand years
before the Celts settled here. The
architects of Stonehenge (starting
nearly 40 centuries ago) knew
enough astronomy to aim its axis
precisely at the sun when it rises
on the day of the summer solstice.
A bigger wonder of it all is how
6-ton stone pillars were transported
to the building site from more
than 135 miles (217 km.) away,
and, later, 50-ton behemoths from
less distant quarries. Generations
of archaeologists have been trying
to get to the bottom of the monument's myths and mysteries. It was
in ruins long before the tourists
arrived.*

But the Scandinavians lost hold when Canute died, making way for yet another invasion. In 1066 the Normans, led by William the Conqueror, stormed across the Channel and defeated the forces of Harold, England's elected king. Since the Normans' famous victory at the Battle of Hastings, no foreign power has succeeded in conquering the island kingdom.

Normans Take Over

Duke William was crowned King of England at Westminster Abbey on Christmas Day that same year. But not many people took gladly to his rule. English resistance to the Normans was fierce at Exeter, Durham, York and, last bastion to fall, Ely in East Anglia (1071). The great Saxon hero Hereward the Wake held out here against the Conqueror for months— until William built a causeway through the marshes and flushed him out.

The events of 1066 and their aftermath decimated the Anglo-Saxon aristocracy. With the Normans came a new Latin influence that profoundly affected the resilient Anglo-Saxon culture. French became the official language and remained supreme in court circles until the late 14th century. William's survey of land tenure for taxation, known as the Domesday Book, provides a unique record of the times. Success in England fuelled William's hopes of conquest in Wales. But he hadn't reckoned on the mountainous terrain and Celtic resolve. For decades Welsh princes and Norman barons struggled for control of the border territory, or Marches.

On his death, William the Conqueror entrusted England to his son and namesake, William Rufus. Normandy went to another son, Robert. Their younger brother Henry eventually ended up with both kingdom and duchy, inextricably joining England's fortunes to those of France. But Henry left no male heirs. Only after years of bitter civil war was the right to the throne of his daughter's son, another Henry, established.

House of Plantagenet

Henry II (1154–89) was not only King of England and Duke of Normandy, but also Count of Anjou, through his father Henry Plantagenet. As such he ruled all of western France down to the Pyrenees. Coupling a strong Norman monarchy with the Anglo-Saxon traditions of local rule at shire and borough level, Henry brought peace and prosperity to England.

It wasn't all easy going for Henry. There was the public outcry over Thomas Becket's murder in 1170 (see p. 22)—and the private conflict with his own family, who conspired against him. Henry weathered the Becket incident: however much he may have wished the Archbishop of Canterbury dead, he hadn't held the "dripping knife". And he went on to new popularity with the conquest of Ireland (1172). But the rebellions of his wife, Eleanor of Aquitaine, and their four sons became a source of permanent grief towards the end of his life. Henry's preference for his youngest son, John, instigated one last revolt by Richard, his oldest surviving son, in 1188. Already ill, the old king died, defeated, and Richard (the Lionheart) gained the throne.

The English developed the habit of governing themselves during Richard's ten-year reign. The king spent most of his time abroad, diverted by more pressing affairs—participation in the Third Crusade and war in France. It was almost

Before the Battle of Hastings, Duke William of Normandy vowed to build an abbey if God gave him victory over the English. Battle Abbey was consecrated in 1094. Henry VIII destroyed the church and dormitory, but the Gothic gateway survives.

inevitable that Richard would die in battle. Resentment in England ran high when his autocratic brother John took over (1199–1216). He was derided as John "Lackland", the inept king who managed to lose the Crown's Norman possessions in a series of disastrous campaigns.

Murder in the Cathedral

Thomas Becket was a worldly cleric when Henry II made him his Lord Chancellor in 1155. An old and trusted friend, Becket served the king well—so well that Henry promoted him to archbishop seven years later. The king counted on Becket's continued support, but to Henry's surprise, Becket took his new job seriously. Turning tables on the king, he became an avid champion of the Church. The specific issues involved—the king's right to try clergy who had committed civil offences in civil courts, for example—were less important than the broader principle of absolute royal authority. A power struggle between Church and state was on.

Henry never expected anyone would take him literally when he asked, "Who will rid me of this turbulent priest?" Unfortunately, four knights acted on the king's words, murdering Becket in cold blood in Canterbury Cathedral. With a few thrusts of the sword, the knights created a martyr and a saint. To this day, the date—December 29, 1170—is commemorated in the Christian calendar.

The deed sent shock waves through medieval Christendom. Henry visited the scene of the crime and did public penance. Scourging—a symbolic punishment in the king's case—didn't hurt half as much as the concessions forced on him by the pope. Overnight Canterbury turned into a place of pilgrimage. People came by the thousands to visit the martyr's tomb. Just touching it could cure disease, they said. Miracles were reported until 1547, when Henry VIII ordered the shrine destroyed.

T.S. Eliot has the last word in his play *Murder in the Cathedral,* a dramatization of Becket's assassination performed for the first time in the Chapter House at Canterbury Cathedral in 1935:

For wherever a saint has dwelt, wherever a martyr has given his blood for the blood of Christ,

There is holy ground, and sanctity shall not depart from it

Though armies trample over it, though sightseers come with guide-books looking over it.

By 1204, with only the Channel Islands left to his name, John returned to England and clashes with the Church and his barons.

Unreasonable taxes and a high-handed disregard for feudal custom endeared John to few of his subjects. Opposition to his plans for a new expedition to France led to rebellion when the expedition failed. In 1215 the king was forced to bow to the defiant noblemen assembled in the meadow of Runnymede, near Windsor, and set his seal to the Magna Carta. This historic breakthrough in the struggle against absolute power subordinated the Crown to the law. The document eventually came to be regarded as England's charter of liberties.

Parliament, that great British political institution, developed into a representative assembly during the 13th century. Under Edward I (1272–1307), a total of 45 sessions were called. Increasingly, participation was extended not only to the nobility and the Church, but also to the burghers and yeomen—the "commons", or members of the community.

It was the resourceful Edward who moved the country a step closer to becoming a United Kingdom with his conquest of Wales (1281). To control the rebellious Welsh, Edward ordered construction of a string of castles: Conwy, Caernarfon, Criccieth and Harlech. Edward's son, the young Edward, was born at Caernarfon. He became the first Prince of Wales, a title granted to the heir to the throne ever since.

Edward I brought Ireland under tighter control with the establishment of the English Pale, a military zone around Dublin. An Irish Parliament was also set up. But Scotland fought free of English domination. It was a great day for the Scots when Robert Bruce triumphed at Bannockburn (1314).

The Welsh and Scottish campaigns were the prelude to a century of conflict on the Continent. The Hundred Years' War between England and France broke out in 1337. Edward III's claim to the

French throne was the main bone of contention. Edward and his son, the Black Prince, masterminded several stunning English victories in the 1340s and '50s: Crécy, Calais, Poitiers; and Henry V and his archers turned the tide at Agincourt (1415). But the French finally won out in 1453.

More devastating than any war, the Black Death invaded Britain in the 14th century, taking an appalling toll of lives. The first epidemic of 1348 spread from the seaports in the south to Wales, Scotland and Ireland. It was followed by three more outbreaks later in the century. In a few short decades, the population of Britain fell by 40 per cent or more. Most severely affected was the peasantry.

Landowners blanched at the high wages they were forced to pay a vastly reduced work force. Never was the "servant problem" more acute than in the mid-14th century. It was bound to end in grief. The Peasant's Revolt of 1381 was suppressed, and the leader of the movement, Wat Tyler, killed—but not before the poor of England ran riot from Kent to Yorkshire.

Lancaster vs. York

Henry Bolingbroke, Duke of Lancaster, a grandson of King Edward III, deposed the tyrannical Richard II. Richard died in prison, probably on Henry's orders, and the duke ruled as Henry IV (1399–1413). Once he had gained the throne, Henry was forced to defend it by force of arms. Shakespeare immortalized Henry's struggle with the words: "Uneasy lies the head that wears a crown."

By Henry's time, people of all classes had begun to converse in English— derived from Germanic and Scandinavian dialects, with an admixture of French. John Wycliffe's translation of the Bible did much to popularize the language, along with Geoffrey Chaucer's medieval best-seller, *The Canterbury Tales*. But for a while longer, literacy would be the prerogative of the aristocracy and the Church, and it was mostly members of religious orders who benefited from an Oxford or Cambridge education.

With the accession of Prince Hal (Henry V) and his son Henry VI in turn, the Lancastrian line seemed set for a long run. But the dynasty proved as unstable as Henry VI's mental health. When Henry suffered a complete breakdown in 1453, a rival, Richard Duke of York, took the reins of power.

A bloody civil war known as the Wars of the Roses (1455–85) pitted the House of York (the white rose) against the House of Lancaster (the red rose). Richard of York died before he could gain the throne, but his son Edward continued the struggle. He imprisoned Henry in the Tower of London in 1461, and had himself crowned Edward IV.

With the old king alive and his wife and son at large, it was only a matter of time before the Lancastrians mounted a counter-coup. They managed to spring the befuddled Henry from his cell in 1470, forcing Edward into exile. The ex-king made a swift comeback the following year, and he held on to power until his death 12 years later.

When Edward IV died, his ambitious brother Richard, the Duke of Gloucester, was appointed Protector and took custody of his young nephews, Edward and Richard, the "Little Princes in the Tower". Shortly afterwards, the boys died in suspicious circumstances. The identity of their supposed murderer was never established, but most people pointed the finger at their uncle, the new Richard III.

Against a backcloth of foreign wars, plague and dynastic struggles, England grew to economic greatness. Agricultural land was fenced in for sheep-raising in Suffolk, the Cotswolds, the Welsh Marches and north of England. The wool industry generated fabulous wealth, creating a new class of rich merchants and landed gentry. Commerce in wool also contributed to the nation's developing maritime power. It was English ships that carried raw wool, and later finished cloth, from the ports of Bristol and London to markets in the Low Countries.

The two-year reign of the hunchback King Richard (known as Richard Crookback) ended with Henry Tudor's victory at Bosworth Field in Leicestershire in 1485. This Lancastrian usurper joined the red rose to the white through his marriage to Edward IV's daughter, Elizabeth of York. Their Tudor descendants would rule England and Wales for the next 118 years.

The Tudors
Henry VII (d. 1509) founded a dynasty, and more. A shrewd statesman, he forged an alliance with Spain, Europe's rising power, through the marriage of his eldest son Arthur to Catherine of Aragon, youngest daughter of King Ferdinand and Queen Isabella. Another marriage, between Henry's daughter Margaret and King James IV of Scotland, brought a thaw in relations with England's hostile neighbour to the north.

A good manager, Henry harnessed the power of the nobility and streamlined government. He also took care of business, putting both Crown and government on a sound financial footing. To his second son and namesake went the considerable fruits of Henry's labours.

Henry VIII (1509–47) was a playboy of 18 when he came to the throne, but he matured into a ruthless ruler with a talent for choosing ministers of the stature of Cardinal Wolsey, Archbishop Cranmer and Sir Thomas Cromwell. Right from the start, Henry developed a taste for power politics. He joined the Holy Alliance against France and distinguished himself in the field in 1513. The Scots, honouring their "auld alliance" with France, attacked England through the back door. The ensuing battle at Flodden saw the English under the Earl of Surrey crush the Scots. About 10,000 were killed, including King James IV himself. His wife (and Henry's sister) Margaret took over as regent for her year-old son, James V of Scotland. An uneasy peace settled on the English-Scottish border, but old enmities died hard. Wars with Scotland and France would occupy Henry VIII until the end of his days.

Henry's choice of Catherine of Aragon for a wife (the pope annulled her marriage to Arthur, who had died as a boy of 15) was as calculated as his decision to divorce her 16 years later. By 1525, it had become painfully clear that Catherine, then 42, would never provide the king with a male heir. Obsessed with the succession, and infatuated with Anne Boleyn, Henry decided to have his marriage dissolved.

Negotiations with the Church quickly foundered. It just so happened that the pope was taking orders from Catherine's nephew—and Europe's most powerful ruler—the Emperor Charles V. Alternatives to an annulment were duly proposed and forthwith rejected.

About this time, the teachings of Martin Luther began spreading to England. Precipitating events somewhat, Henry rebelled against Rome. Parliament, meeting over a seven-year period from 1529, saw to the legalities. The king was declared head of the Church of England. For members of the government, refusal to sanction the crucial Act of Supremacy was a life and death matter. The principled Lord Chancellor, Sir Thomas More, for one, was tried for treason and beheaded.

In 1536, England's monasteries began closing their doors under provisions of the Act of Suppression. Monks and nuns were pensioned off, and Church property was nationalized and sold piecemeal to pay for Henry's military adventures, unleashing a whole social revolution. Great manor houses in Tudor style rose on former abbey lands, vast tracts of which were committed to sheep pasturage.

The famous divorce was granted by Archbishop Cranmer in 1533. It came just in time. Within months Anne Boleyn gave birth to a daughter, Elizabeth.

24

Henry VIII's reign marks a watershed in English history. Suddenly, or so it would seem, people emerged from the darkness of the Middle Ages into the light of modern times. Everything was thrown into question, and the old certainties no longer held good. The intellectual ferment of the Renaissance had reached England, setting the stage for a revival of letters and the arts.

Protestant regents were the power behind the throne of the consumptive boy-king Edward VI (1547–53). One regent, Lord Northumberland, attempted to secure the succession for Lady Jane Grey, a Protestant grand-daughter of Henry VIII—and Northumberland's daughter-in-law. Edward colluded in the

The Marriage-Go-Round

Henry VIII literally moved heaven and earth to dispose of his first wife and marry his paramour, Anne Boleyn. Alas for Henry, Anne turned into a shrew once they'd tied the knot. Henry's patience with her ran out after less than three years of life together, when a miscarriage followed the birth of a daughter. Arrested on trumped-up charges in 1536, Anne ended her career on the executioner's block.

With her successor, Jane Seymour, Henry was third time lucky. Not only did she make a loving and submissive wife, she also produced the desired son, Edward, in 1537. Unfortunately, complications from the birth claimed Jane's life 11 days later. His dreams of wedded bliss shattered, the king drowned his sorrows in politics, and a political scheme brought him another wife.

Marriage number four, to Anne of Cleves, was an affair of state: Henry couldn't conceal his loathing for the "Flanders mare". By refusing to consummate the misalliance, he simplified annulment proceedings. Free again, Henry rushed the flirtatious Catherine Howard to the altar. But their love soon went sour. The king took exception to the adultery of his 22-year-old bride and ordered her beheaded.

The following year a widow named Catherine Parr came into Henry's life. She was 31 and no beauty, but by then the ageing king needed a nursemaid as much as a wife. Their marriage—her third and his sixth—may not have been made in heaven, but it lasted until his death did them part in 1547.

plot, but the rightful heir, his half-sister Mary Tudor, had the backing of the people. When Edward died, she pressed her claim and cut short Lady Jane's nine-day "reign" on the block.

A devout Catholic, "Bloody Mary" tried to turn back the clock. She restored the Roman confession and had hundreds of Protestants, including several bishops, burned at the stake. Against all advice, the queen pursued an unpopular (and loveless) marriage with a Spanish prince, the future Philip II, involving England in another costly war with France. Relief was universal when she died.

An outpouring of affection greeted Elizabeth I on her accession in 1558. The Virgin Queen was only 25 years old, but she knew how to survive. Raised in an atmosphere of political intrigue and constant peril, she looked first to security—her own and that of her country.

Elizabeth had one serious rival for the crown: her Catholic cousin Mary Stuart, the deposed Queen of Scots. Exiled in England, Mary inevitably became involved in Catholic plots to overthrow Elizabeth. Although stability was returning to religious and political life, Elizabeth wasn't taking any chances. She put Mary under permanent house arrest in 1569. Eighteen years (and several intrigues) later, with a Spanish invasion threatening, the queen reluctantly consented to the execution of her disloyal cousin. Mary's 21-year-old son, the Protestant James VI of Scotland, moved to the top of the queue of Elizabeth's potential successors.

The great struggle with Spain dominated Elizabeth's reign. Despite public denials, the queen gave tacit support to the freelance activities of England's privateers—the illegal slaving expeditions of John Hawkins and Sir Francis Drake's raids on the Spanish Main. In 1580 Drake went on to circumnavigate the globe, ending Spain's monopoly of the seas. Hawkins meanwhile was in the process of building a formidable navy.

The turning point for England came

A Stratford street artist puts the finishing touches
to a portrait of Shakespeare, ignoring Ben Jonson's advice to "looke Not
on his picture but his Booke". Instantly recognizable, this image is the
most faithful likeness of the bard. It appears on the title page of the First
Folio, published in 1623, together with Jonson's lines.

Revolution and Restoration

James VI of Scotland ascended the English throne as James I (1603–25), joining the two realms under one crown. It was only the first phase in the unification process. For another century, two separate legislatures would be maintained.

James is remembered mainly for his narrow escape from death by assassination in the abortive Gunpowder Plot (1605). Guy Fawkes was within hours of blowing up Parliament with the king in attendance when the conspiracy was uncovered. The plot was religiously motivated: Fawkes was a Catholic, but his use of violent means to further the cause won widespread censure. For a long time afterwards Catholics in Britain would be subject to persecution for their "papist treachery".

There was discrimination, too, against Protestant extremists, especially the Puritan Separatists. Escape from oppression took thousands of members of this religious splinter group to a new life in America. The *Mayflower* led the way in 1620, sailing into history from the West Country port of Plymouth, with the Pilgrim Fathers on board. About this time, Protestants from England and Scotland began moving into Ulster. They settled on land confiscated from Irish Catholics, with disastrous consequences for the future.

England was a good place to get away from in the early 17th century. Following in the footsteps of his father James, the autocratic Charles I resisted Parliament's growing power and plunged the country into civil war. In 1642 the Royalists or "Cavaliers"—supported by the aristocracy and the Church—went into battle against Parliamentary forces (the Roundheads), backed by the merchants, tradesmen and Puritans. The sympathies of the landed gentry were divided between the two.

After some early successes, Charles went down in defeat at Naseby in 1645. Four years later the country lost its monarch and the monarch lost his head. He

in 1588 with the defeat of Spain's fleet, the Invincible Armada. The outcome depended as much on adverse weather conditions as naval superiority, but it was no less decisive for that. England took on the status of a world power, and the capital, London, developed into a great commercial centre with interests in Europe, America and the Orient. A golden age of literature had already begun, marked by the achievements of Francis Bacon, Ben Jonson, Christopher Marlowe and, above all, William Shakespeare.

was publicly executed outside his palace at Whitehall. The man behind the coup, the dour Oliver Cromwell, seized power and forced the warring factions together. Dissolving Parliament, this energetic statesman proclaimed England a republic and himself Lord Protector. But the country grew disenchanted with Cromwell's dreary Puritan rule. After his death the monarchy was restored under Charles II (1660–85), the "Merry Monarch", a great theatre-goer and art collector.

Anxious not to be sent "travelling" again, Charles proved an amenable (if dissolute) king. He restored the Church of England and came down on the side of reason. After decades of strife, theological debate gave way to scientific research. Sir Isaac Newton led off with his contributions to the fields of physics, mathematics and optics.

Three successive disasters stalked England in the first decade of Charles's reign: the Great Plague, the Great Fire of London and a Dutch attack on Thames shipping. The Puritans, shocked at the moral laxity of the king and court, attributed this extraordinary run of bad luck to divine retribution. Others suggested the possibility of a papist plot. In fact, Charles *was* a closet Catholic, but he waited until he was on his deathbed to embrace the faith.

His brother James wasn't as sensible. Declaring his Roman faith and French sympathies, James II attacked the Church of England and disregarded the law of the land. This time the king didn't die: Parliament allowed him to abdicate and flee the country after only three years. The Glorious Revolution of 1688 brought the Protestant William of Orange (a grandson of Charles I) and his wife Mary Stuart (daughter of James II) jointly to the throne and gave England a stable constitutional monarchy at last. The Bill of Rights finally and officially abolished absolutism and established the supremacy of Parliament.

There was no opposition to the coup in England, though William did put down a rising of the deposed King James II's Catholic supporters in Scotland. In 1690 James sailed to Ireland from exile in France for a final showdown with his son-in-law at the Battle of the Boyne near Dublin. William and the Orangemen, aided by troops from several Protestant countries, came out the clear winners. To this day the anniversary (July 11) is celebrated by the Protestants of Northern Ireland.

Fighting broke out again when William's old enemy, Louis XIV, put his grandson on the throne of Spain (1701). William died and his successor and sister-in-law, Queen Anne (1702–14), appointed John Churchill, Duke of Marlborough, as commander-in-chief. A brilliant tactician, the duke led the Grand Alliance of several Protestant countries to an upset victory over the French in the War of the Spanish Succession (1701–13). Marlborough had won a battle but not yet the war when Queen Anne rewarded him with Blenheim Palace, named after the place in the Netherlands where the first great victory of the war took place. The capture of Gibraltar days before was another event to gratify Britain's queen.

As of 1707 Great Britain officially came into existence. The Act of Union formalized the *de facto* merger of England and Scotland accomplished a century before under James I. Henceforth there would be one flag and one parliament, with the Scots represented as a minority in the two houses in Westminster. But the Scots kept their own courts and legal system, and their national Presbyterian Church was guaranteed. Into the bargain, they accepted the Hanoverian succession.

Georgian Period

The first King George (1714–27) won the throne by virtue of his Stuart blood and Protestant faith, but Britain remained a foreign land for the German from Hanover. He never even bothered to learn English. Parliament was firmly in the driver's seat now, and party rivalries (Tory vs. Whig) dominated the political scene. The conservative Tories gambled on the restoration of the "Old Pretender", James II's son, and fell into permanent disfavour with George. The radical Whigs (the name literally means "rebel") filled the vacuum in power, claiming all the jobs in the evolving cabinet and ministries.

A Whig, Sir Robert Walpole, served as Britain's first prime minister (1721–42). He presided over an era of peace, prosperity—and corruption. Whig politicians were not averse to a bit of bribery or worse, if that was what it took to keep them in office, and graft was a constant temptation. Even the king was implicated in the South Sea Bubble scandal, the Watergate of his day, but Walpole managed to cover for the monarch, while keeping his own reputation untarnished.

There were intrigues *against* the king as well. Long after George II was crowned in 1727 the Jacobites were still working for the return to the British throne of James II's line. They had a new man for the job—James's grandson, Prince Charles Edward Stuart, better known as "Bonnie Prince Charlie". His defeat in the abortive 1745 Rebellion dashed Jacobite hopes of power.

The Georgian period was one of genteel pleasures. The British began drinking tea and taking the waters at Bath, Tunbridge Wells and Cheltenham. Sea resorts like Weymouth were all the rage, too. New wealth competed with old to build great houses in the country, complete with Adam fireplaces and Chippendale furniture. But there was also a darker side to life in Britain. The urban poor took to drink, and as gin consumption increased, the crime rate soared.

Overseas, the empire was burgeoning. The Seven Years' War with France (1756–63) brought conquests as diverse as Canada, India and Senegal. That great prime minister, William Pitt the Elder, orchestrated Britain's involvement in the conflict and saw the country emerge as the dominant world power when the fighting was over.

The American colonies were another going concern. Suppliers of valuable raw materials, the Americans were also important consumers of British manufactures. Unfortunately, a tax dispute caused a rift with the mother country that escalated into full-scale revolutionary war. To the astonishment of George III, the colonists won. In 1783 Britain formally recognized the independence of the new United States of America. Six years later came the French Revolution, an event that evoked the sympathies of the British masses.

Another sort of revolution was brewing at home: 18th-century inventions like James Watt's steam engine, Richard Arkwright's water-powered frame for spinning and Edmund Cartwright's power loom laid the foundations for the world's first mass industrial society. Thousands of miles of turnpikes and canals were constructed after the mid-century mark, improving communications between town and country, seaport and factory. Agriculture meanwhile geared up to feed an exploding population—nearly 8 million in 1790, against 5½ million in 1700. By now one Briton in three lived in town—and one town-dweller in three lived in London—the modern world's first city of a million in 1800.

Rule Britannia

Britain entered the 19th century preoccupied by the Irish problem. Irish agitation resulted not in greater independence for Ireland, but in legislative union with Britain. The Irish Parliament voted itself out of business after approving the 1801 Act of Union establishing the United Kingdom of Great Britain and Ireland. The idea was that the economic and political destinies of the two islands would become inseparable. But Irish nationalism never faded away.

Nor did French imperialism. This time the challenge came from Napoleon. Lord Nelson disposed of the French fleet at Trafalgar in 1805, assuring that Britannia would continue to rule the waves.

29

Wellington, the Iron Duke, triumphed finally over Napoleon at Waterloo in 1815. After two decades of preparations against invasion, the country could relax and celebrate a little. The territorial gains alone were cause for jubilation. They spanned the globe, from Trinidad to Ceylon to the Cape (present-day South Africa).

Oblivious of the great empire he commanded, King George III lapsed into permanent insanity by 1811. His oldest son ruled until 1830, first as Prince Regent and then in his own right as King George IV. He was not a popular figure. The decadence and conspicuous consumption of court life contrasted all too sharply with the miserable existence of the poor—perhaps a third of the population. Their lot deteriorated further when the postwar economy took a temporary nose-dive.

Unemployment and soaring food prices led to rioting in the cities. Protesters called for repeal of the protective Corn Laws which taxed imported grain in support of high domestic prices—benefiting the landowners at the expense of the urban workers. Other voices joined in, demanding liberalization of the vote and parliamentary representation.

The era of Victoria—the queen reigned from 1837 to 1901—was the great age of steam and iron, of transport, communications and commerce, of empire and reform. British engineers pioneered the steamship and railway, consuming millions of tons of coal and iron in the process. There was plenty to go around. Britain was the world's biggest producer and exporter of both commodities—until the Germans and Americans began catching up at the end of the century.

It was a hard life for workers underground and on the factory floor. From the mill towns of Yorkshire and Lancashire to the mining towns of South Wales, long hours, bad conditions, low pay and poor housing blighted the health of men, women and children. Even six and seven year olds were hauling coal and helping on the assembly line. A sub-

versive British resident named Karl Marx took note and predicted revolution in the 1848 Communist Manifesto. Instead, things looked up for the workers. They won the vote before the century was out, as well as the right to form unions and to strike. Legislation put limits on working hours and child labour.

People in the countryside fared worse, especially in the "hungry Forties", a decade of bad harvests known in Ireland as the potato famine. The move to the cities—and colonies—accelerated, and by

30

Text on the sign in the image:

A GREAT DEAL OF WORK
REMAINS TO BE DONE.
THE WHOLE OF THE FORE END
FROM THE BEAK TO JUST ABAFT
THE BREAK OF THE FO'C'SLE
IS BEING REN

A life on the ocean waves holds few perils for Sea Scouts. Not so in Nelson's day. On a ship like the Victory, *seamen (sometimes no older than the boys pictured here) faced an unremittingly harsh existence. Many more died of disease, accident or shipwreck than ever fell in the face of the enemy. Indiscipline was dealt with summararily: three or four dozen lashes with the cat o' nine tails.*

*L*ongleat's spacious Victorian kitchen has room enough
for a legion of cooks. The hierarchy below stairs was rigid, with the
butler at the top. Next came the housekeeper, lady's maid and cook,
but the life of a scullery maid was no picnic. In spite of long hours and
low wages, domestic staff considered themselves lucky. About a third
of the urban population at the time lived below the poverty line.

vice, prostitution mainly, and the thriving underworld Charles Dickens depicted in *Oliver Twist* and other novels.

With it all, the Victorians were incurable optimists. Taking their cue from Darwin (his *Origin of Species* came out in 1859), people believed that progress, like evolution, would go on and on. The poor were expected to pull themselves up by their own bootstraps. Charity was reserved for the "deserving" few.

After nearly half a century of peace, Britain took up arms to defend Turkey (and its own imperial interests) against Russian aggression in the Crimean War (1854–56). Britain and allied France barely managed to win through. The only real victory belonged to Florence Nightingale and the nursing profession.

The white man's burden was growing heavier by the year with the addition of many new colonies in Africa, Asia and the Pacific. There was mutiny in India, the "jewel in the Imperial crown", and trouble over the strategic Suez Canal, opened in 1869. Britain subsequently invaded and occupied Egypt to protect the canal and the route to India.

South Africa was another trouble spot. The original Dutch (Boer) settlers flouted British claims to the diamond- and gold-rich Transvaal and Orange Free State. In 1899, after several years of unrest, they attacked the Cape, Britain's stronghold. Winston Churchill, one of the 450,000 British soldiers who saw action in the Boer War, commented that it was "very sporting of the Boers to take on the whole British Empire". In fact, the Boers had the backing of a formidable power—the newly unified German state—and Britain's victory, after a costly three-year engagement, was hard won.

Modern Times

The death of Queen Victoria in 1901 marked the end of an era. The Industrial Revolution had run out of steam, along with an implicit belief in self-help and perpetual progress. Socialism posed new solutions to old problems. It was the

1900 four Britons in five lived in urban areas—about the same ratio as today. Many people went into "service" (domestic employment).

The high-minded Victoria set the tone for the age with her famous comment, "We are not amused." Respectability, commitment to duty and sheer hard work were the great 19th-century virtues. Family values and a strict moral code paid dividends in a falling crime rate, but appearances could be deceiving. Public morality went hand in hand with private

33

creed of the influential Fabian Society (the writers George Bernard Shaw and H.G. Wells were members) and the new Labour Party, which won 29 seats in the 1906 General Election.

Parliament laid the foundations of the modern welfare state before World War I, approving old age pensions, health and unemployment insurance and a supertax on the rich. Astonishingly, about two-thirds of the national wealth was concentrated in the hands of one per cent of the population. The Edwardian Age—King Edward VII ruled for nine years from 1901—was the last, brief golden age of that one per cent. Hordes of servants staffed the "Upstairs, Downstairs" world of London town houses and country seats from Longleat to Castle Howard.

Britain plunged into the carnage of world war with remarkable abandon in August 1914. The conflict that was supposed to be over before Christmas dragged on four years and took an unprecedented toll of lives: 750,000 dead and over a million and a half injured. A generation of young men was wiped out by the "monstrous anger of the guns". The phrase comes from "Anthem for Doomed Youth" by the war poet Wilfred Owen, who was still in his 20s when he died on the battlefield in 1918.

Life would never be the same again. Women entered the workplace during the war—and stayed there, winning the right to vote when hostilities ended. The Lost Generation wandered aimlessly through the 1920s, attempting to forget the past in a relentless social whirl.

The Irish took advantage of the war to press for independence. In the Easter Rising of 1916, radical nationalists seized the General Post Office in Dublin and symbolically proclaimed a provisional government for the Irish Republic. The British government quelled the rebellion and sent the leaders to the firing squad—shocking the Irish people and preparing the ground for a successful war of independence. In 1922 the Irish Free State was created, comprising the 26 Catholic counties of southern Ireland. The six largely Protestant counties of Ulster in the north-east remained part of the United Kingdom. Encouraged by events in Ireland, the Indians, led by Mahatma Gandhi, began to demand self-rule.

Industrial decline, unemployment and inflation came to plague Britain. While the Left (Labour and disaffected Liberals) advocated nationalization of the depressed mining industry—Britain's biggest—the Conservative government curtailed subsidies, instigating wage cuts and dismissals. The miners walked out in May 1926, and the National Trades Union Congress (TUC) called a general strike in sympathy. After nine days, the TUC gave in to government pressure and ordered members back to work, though the miners stayed out on strike for another several months. For many workers the agreement was tantamount to betrayal. Bitterness and class hatred were the legacy of 1926. The Great Depression made a bad situation worse, and the payment of unemployment benefits almost bankrupted the heavily indebted nation.

For a while in 1936, crisis in the monarchy diverted public attention from the bad economic news. Edward VIII was forced to choose between the Crown and the woman he loved, the twice-divorced American Mrs. Simpson. To the delight of modern romantics, love won the day. Edward stepped down and his brother was crowned King George VI. He would lead the country through another war.

At first, Prime Minister Neville Chamberlain's government attempted to avoid conflict through the appeasement of Germany and Italy. At the Munich Conference in 1938, Chamberlain and the French president Edouard Daladier accepted Hitler's annexation of the Sudetenland of Czechoslovakia, with the proviso that Germany would respect the independence of the rest of Czechoslovakia. Chamberlain returned to Britain claiming he had won "peace in our time". Six months later the Nazis invaded Czechoslovakia. An attack on Poland followed, and Britain went to war.

There was resolution but no militaristic fervour this time. By summer of 1940 the war had begun in earnest as Hitler's fire bombs rained down on London. The Battle of Britain was fought in the air by "the few", the legendary pilots in Spitfires and Hurricanes. They deprived the Luftwaffe of mastery of the skies and postponed the immediate threat of a German invasion. The indomitable spirit of wartime Britain was personified by Winston Churchill in his billowing "siren suit", cigar in hand, exploring the morning-after wreckage—exhorting the people to fight on. The Blitz and the flying bomb attacks of 1944 claimed 60,000 civilian lives. In all, 270,000 servicemen died in action on the Continent, in North Africa, the Eastern Mediterranean and Far East.

The rigours of war blurred class distinctions and stirred a new social consciousness which brought the Labour Party and Prime Minister Clement Attlee to power in the first post-war election. The welfare state was created to provide cradle-to-grave care for the populace. Key industries were nationalized, and the dismantling of Britain's overseas empire began. India, Pakistan, Burma and Ceylon achieved independence in the late 1940s, followed by a host of other colonies from Ghana (1957) and Malaya (1963) to the Bahamas (1973) and Belize (1981). For most of the ex-colonies, membership in the Commonwealth of Nations—a largely ceremonial organization with the British sovereign as its head—perpetuated a link with the mother country. A few far-flung outposts still fly the Union Jack, including Gibraltar, Hong Kong and the Falkland Islands (defended against Argentinian invasion in the 1982 Falklands War).

As decolonization stepped up, so did the influx of new residents from the former colonies (1 million by 1963). The presence of so many Indians, Pakistanis, Jamaicans and other Commonwealth immigrants in the capital of London and other cities has added a new dimension to British life, though not without some racial strife.

The development of North Sea oil a decade later started a stampede for Aberdeen, centre for the off-shore activities that have made Britain self-sufficient in energy. The oil industry was a bright spot in an economy that had been spiralling downwards, spawning high unemployment in a period of double-digit inflation. Wages weren't keeping up with inflation, especially in the dying coal industry. Miners went out on strike repeatedly in protest, wringing some concessions from the government. Other workers followed suit, not always so successfully.

A referendum in 1975 decided the fate of Britain's controversial 1973 entry into the European Economic Community. After long debate and heated opposition, a resounding two-thirds of the voters gave the green light to participation in Europe. It was an about-face for the insular British, wary of Continental involvement after two world wars.

Elected in 1979, Margaret Thatcher, Britain's first woman prime minister, was the new broom that swept clean: the Iron Lady stood up to the unions—and to the Russians—winning grudging respect all round. Monetarism, privatization of state-owned industries and a new emphasis on entrepreneurial skills—the ingredients of the Thatcher Revolution—have had an impact on the economy. A new prosperity has come to the south of England, parts of the Midlands, Scotland's "Silicon Glen". Even some of the old manufacturing centres like Manchester and Glasgow are experiencing revival.

With new affluence has come renewed appreciation of Britain's unique heritage: the cathedral towns, stately homes and rural villages that are the spectacular accretion of these last 2,000 years.

HISTORICAL LANDMARKS

Portrait of Henry VIII by Hans Holbein

Prehistoric Beginnings	20 000 **B.C.**	Stone Age hunters well established in Britain.
	4000	Agriculture develops.
	3000	Megalithic culture reaches the island.
	2000	Bronze Age begins. Beaker Folk arrive.
	8th–1st C	Celtic incursions. Iron technology introduced.
Roman Era	55	Julius Caesar invades Britain.
	43 **A.D.**	Romans return, build roads, found cities.
	78–80	Wales and Scotland subdued.
	128	Hadrian's Wall completed.
	4th C	Christianity takes root.
	367	Picts and Scots attack Roman Britain. Saxons, Angles and Jutes defeat them, invade in turn.
Anglo-Saxon Kingdoms	597	St. Augustine converts Saxons of Kent.
	8th–9th C	Vikings attack British coasts. "Danelaw" established.
	878	Alfred the Great of Wessex defeats Danes at Edington.
	924–939	Athelstan first king of England.
	1016–35	Canute rules.
	1066	Norman Conquest.
Middle Ages	1170	Thomas Becket murdered in Canterbury Cathedral.
	1172	Henry II conquers Ireland.
	1215	King John seals Magna Carta.

Middle Ages (cont.)	1281	Edward I subdues Wales.
	1314	Robert Bruce triumphs over English at Bannockburn.
	1337	Hundred Years' War with France begins.
	1348	Black Death epidemic spreads.
	1381	Wat Tyler leads Peasant Revolt.
	1399	Henry IV deposes Richard II.
	1455–85	Wars of the Roses.
House of Tudor	1533	Henry VIII divorces Catherine of Aragon.
	1534	England breaks with Rome.
	1558–1603	Elizabeth I rules.
	1588	English defeat Spain's Invincible Armada.
House of Stuart	1603	James I king of England and Scotland. Union of Crowns.
	1620	Pilgrims sail to America.
	1642	Civil War breaks out.
	1649	Charles I beheaded.
	1660	Monarchy restored under Charles II.
	1665	Great Plague.
	1666	Great Fire of London.
	1688	Glorious Revolution brings William and Mary to throne.
	1701–13	War of the Spanish Succession against Catholic France.
	1707	England and Scotland merge.
Georgian Period	1714	King George I accedes to throne.
	1721–42	Sir Robert Walpole serves as first prime minister.
	1745	Bonnie Prince Charlie leads Jacobite Rebellion.
	1756–63	Seven Years' War with France.
	1783	Britain formally recognizes independence of the United States of America.
	1801	United Kingdom of Great Britain and Ireland established.
	1805	Lord Nelson defeats French fleet at Trafalgar.
	1815	Wellington triumphs at Waterloo.
Victorian Britain	1837	Queen Victoria ascends the throne.
	1854–56	Crimean War.
	1869	Suez Canal opened.
	1899–1902	Boer War.
Modern Times	1901–1910	Edward VII rules.
	1914–1918	World War I.
	1922	Irish Free State created.
	1936	Edward VIII abdicates, George VI takes over.
	1939–1945	World War II.
	1947–48	India, Pakistan, Burma and Ceylon independent.
	1973	Britain enters Common Market (EEC).
	1979	Margaret Thatcher elected prime minister.
	1982	Falklands War.
	1988	Channel Tunnel begun.

The Best of Britain

A trip to Britain is like a walk in the country. You can make rapid progress towards a goal or simply meander. Obviously, it's easier to improvise outside the peak summer months, when the pressure on accommodation and transport eases. But even in the high season you can travel with relative freedom if you avoid the more heavily touristed zones. The fact is, few first-time visitors deviate from the popular London–Edinburgh trajectory, with York the natural halting place en route. Other magnets for the newcomers, Oxford, Stratford and Bath, are usually "done" as day-trips from London, which leaves the independent traveller with considerable scope.

This book includes all the important towns and regions in mainland Britain. The choice of sights is as careful and balanced as we could make it. Some of the places featured here may already be familiar to you—though we hope you'll see them in a new light—while others deserve to be better known.

We've divided the country into nine areas: London and Environs, the South-East, the South, the South-West, East Anglia and the Fens, Central England, Wales, the North of England, Scotland.

For a balanced picture of Britain, try to visit the north as well as the south of England. According to local folklore, northerners are friendlier and more open than people in the south, consequently easier to get to know. The landscape, too, is different—rugged and austere, as opposed to the gentle greenness of the south. You should also spend some time on the "Celtic fringe", in Wales or Scotland. Moodier scenery and the reputedly darker and more romantic nature of the people make for some striking contrasts with England.

Wherever you go, there will be monuments and museums, castles, cathedrals and great country houses to visit. Many attractions remain open until sunset, which means well into the evening in summer, allowing you to fit a lot into a day. You'll have to be much less ambitious if you visit Britain in winter, though, when early nightfall curtails sightseeing.

*S*talled in traffic, London bus riders rise above it all. Overleaf: spelling out the charm of Wales.

Getting Around

Detailed information about travelling around Britain appears in the Berlitz Info section at the back of the book. But before you consider the specifics, think first about how long you'll stay, how much territory you want to cover and what sort of transport you'll use.

Bear in mind that distances in Britain are relatively short. Express trains from London reach Edinburgh in about 4½ hours, Plymouth in three and York and Cardiff in under two. Driving times are somewhat longer, making rail-drive combinations an attractive alternative. Take the train to any mainline station and hire a car there, setting out in a relaxed frame of mind to explore the locale.

A word of encouragement to the wary: with the exception of London, driving in Britain doesn't require any special prowess, whatever people say. You just need a few hours to overcome your right-aiming instincts. Britain's secondary roads are well maintained, if often rather narrow, and an expanding motorway network links cities and regions.

Travelling by coach (bus) is probably the least satisfactory way to get around, at least over longer distances. You risk delays, sometimes fairly long ones, and the standard of comfort may not be quite what you'd hoped for.

You can of course fly, but it's hardly worthwhile unless you're going from London to Edinburgh (one hour) or Birmingham (40 minutes), or bound for the Channel Islands, Isle of Man or Scottish islands.

Provided you have the time and the stamina, your own two feet can be a feasible means of transport. A number of cross-country footpaths transit some eminently walkable regions of Britain, including the North and South Downs Way and Ridgeway Path in South-East England, the Cornwall Coast Path in the South-West, Central England's Cotswold Way, the Cleveland Way and Pennine Way in the North of England, and the Pembrokeshire Coastal Path in South Wales. Or consider cycling around. A bike provides more mobility, but again, you've got to be fit.

Don't leave finding a bed for the night until too late in the day. For a small fee, many tourist offices arrange accommodation in all price ranges, both locally and in other areas of Britain, through the "Book a Bed Ahead" scheme. Together with a confirmed booking, you'll be given detailed directions to your destination if you ask for them.

For a homey touch, stay at a guest house, farmhouse or bed-and-breakfast place in the country. (So-called B&Bs in the cities are impersonal budget hotels.) Pubs and inns can be pleasantly informal, too. The owners really get to know guests, especially anyone staying for several days, and they're often willing to share an insider's knowledge of an area.

At the luxury end of the price scale, the same holds true for country house hotels. Splash out for a night or two if you can, perhaps towards the end of your trip to rest up from the exertions of sightseeing. Incidentally, food at country house hotels is often quite superb.

If you're prepared to rough it in the rain, camping keeps costs down and brings you into closer contact with nature. Travelling by caravan (mobile home) or canal narrowboat (a kind of barge) is the soft option.

However you get around, wherever you stay, resist the temptation to turn a tour into a marathon, covering too many miles or sights in a day. After all, you're on holiday. Relax and enjoy the trip.

Just the Essentials

Britain's sheer wealth of tourist-worthy sights will continually keep forcing you to make choices and set priorities. So what's most important, what should you see first? Just refer to the list grouping the "musts" of British tourism region by region. It would be a shame to miss out on any of the suggestions here, as you travel around the relevant area.

London and Environs *(3-4 days)*
Buckingham Palace, Changing
of the Guard
Houses of Parliament, where the
Lords and Commons convene
Westminster Abbey, Britain's
coronation church
St. Paul's Cathedral, Wren
masterpiece
Tower of London, Crown Jewels
on display in Norman fortification
British Museum, featuring Elgin
marbles, Egyptian mummies
National Gallery, painting collection
Hampton Court Palace, royal retreat
of King Henry VIII
Windsor Castle, home of Queen

The South-East *(2 days)*
Canterbury Cathedral, medieval
pilgrimage church
Battle, 1066 site
Brighton, old seaside resort with
Royal Pavilion

The South *(3-4 days)*
Portsmouth, historic ships on view
Winchester Cathedral, England's
longest
Salisbury, market town built around
great Early English cathedral
Stonehenge, prehistoric stone circle
Longleat, stately home and safari
park
Stourhead, the last word in gardens

The South-West *(5 days)*
Bath, Georgian spa town
Bristol harbour, one-time port for
America
Wells, the town and the cathedral
Glastonbury Abbey, evocative ruin
Plymouth, from where the *May-
flower* sailed
Fowey, Cornish fishing port
St. Ives, seaside artists' community
Tintagel, King Arthur's "birthplace"

East Anglia and the Fens
(2-3 days)
Cambridge, university town on River
Cam
Ely Cathedral, of Norman
foundation
Constable Country, landscapes
immortalized in John Constable's
art
Lincoln and cathedral, dominant
feature of historic centre

Central England *(3-4 days)*
Oxford, England's oldest university
town
Stratford-upon-Avon, where
Shakespeare was born
Cotswolds, Broadway is showpiece
village in the hills
Peak District, dramatic hill scenery

Wales *(3-4 days)*
Tintern Abbey, a romantic decay
Pembrokeshire coast, holiday area
Caernarfon Castle, coastal
stronghold
Snowdonia, mountainous national
park

The North of England *(5 days)*
Yorkshire Dales, national park
Fountains Abbey, imposing remains
York and cathedral, with superb glass
North York Moors, heather-covered
uplands
Lake District, haunt of Wordsworth
and friends
Hadrian's Wall, built by the Romans

Scotland *(5-6 days)*
Edinburgh, capital city
Glasgow, city of culture and
commerce
Loch Lomond, beautiful inland lake
The Trossachs, scenic hill region
Glen Coe, brooding pass
Loch Ness, home of the monster

43

Going Places with Something Special in Mind

Britain's cultural riches are enough to overwhelm the most determined sightseer. Rather than trying vainly to see all the stately homes, cathedrals, museums and archaeological sites in a given area, why not use a theme to structure your trip? You can always make the odd digression along the way. A few suggestions:

Prehistoric Britain

The most important monuments of ancient Britain are to be found in Wiltshire. Here, in the 3rd millennium B.C., powerful chieftains began burying their dead in stone tombs. They also raised ceremonial earthworks, later amplified by huge standing stones.

AVEBURY, north-west of Devizes
Neolithic stone circle surrounded by earthworks and ditch, linked to avenue of standing stones.

WEST KENNET LONG BARROW,
south of Avebury
Well-preserved Stone Age tomb.

SILBURY HILL, west of Marlborough
Largest artificial mound in Europe, dating back to Stone or early Bronze Age. Once believed to be work of Devil.

STONEHENGE
Most famous of Britain's prehistoric monuments, circles of giant stones erected between 2200 and 1300 B.C.

*A*t Bath, steaming spring water gushes from the source.

OLD SARUM, north-west of Salisbury
Earthworks of Iron Age hill fort.

SALISBURY
Finds from Stonehenge and Old Sarum in South Wiltshire Museum.

Roman Britain

The Romans came to Britain in 55 B.C. Traces of their 400-year stay include the arrow-straight roads, defensive walls and forts that can be found throughout the country, as well as the remains of public baths and villas.

1 LONDON
Sections of city wall at Cripplegate and Tower of London. Bathhouse in Lower Thames Street. Temple of Mithras, Queen Victoria Street. British Museum: Mildenhall Treasure and other relics.

2 ST. ALBANS, Hertfordshire
Ancient Verulamium. Remains of town walls and theatre. Roman collection in Verulamium Museum.

3 FISHBOURNE ROMAN PALACE,
Chichester, West Sussex
Immense complex built for 1st-century king. Mosaic flooring and restored formal gardens. On-site museum.

4 LULLINGSTONE VILLA,
near Eynsford, Kent
Roman villa with early Christian chapel.

5 BATH
Roman baths, temple complex and adjoining
museum.

6 CAERLEON,
Gwent, Wales
Roman Isca Silurum. Ruins of Roman bar-
racks and amphitheatre.

7 CIRENCESTER, Gloucestershire
City walls, amphitheatre, collection of finds
in Corinium Museum.

8 CHEDWORTH VILLA, Chedworth,
Gloucestershire
2nd-century villa with well-preserved mosaic
pavements and bathhouse.

9 LEICESTER
Section of Roman masonry known as Jewry
Wall.

10 LINCOLN
Part of Roman gate preserved in Newport
Arch.

11 WROXETER ROMAN CITY, Shropshire
Remains of baths and exercise halls. Museum
of finds.

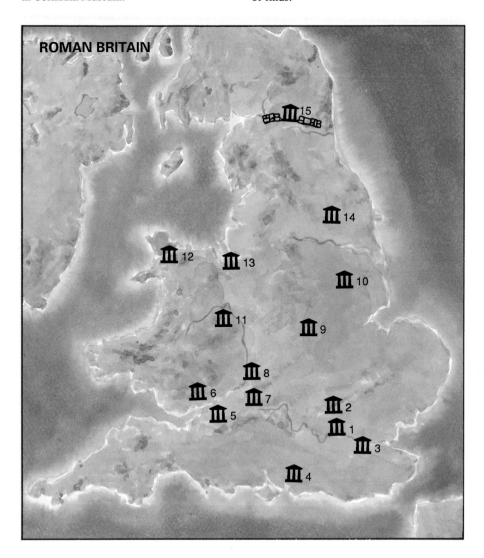

ROMAN BRITAIN

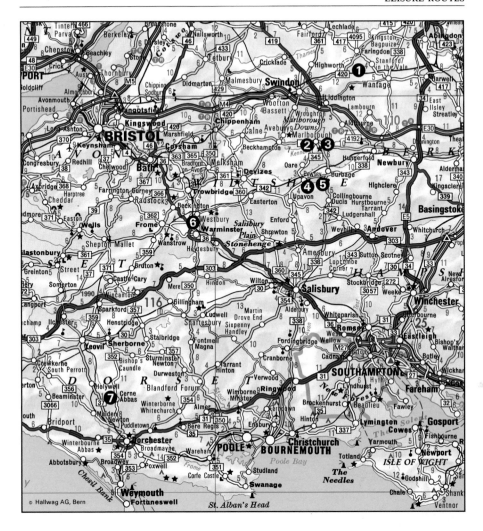

12 CAERNARFON, Gwynedd, Wales
Excavations of Roman fort.

13 CHESTER
Roman amphitheatre and ramparts. Grosvenor Museum.

14 YORK
Roman fort of Eboracum. Large collection of finds in Yorkshire Museum. Part-Roman Multangular Tower in museum gardens.

15 HADRIAN'S WALL
Roman frontier defence, built around A.D. 122, running from Solway Firth to Wallsend-on-Tyne. Museums at Carlisle and Newcastle.

Hill Figures

1 UFFINGTON WHITE HORSE, Berkshire
Oldest of hill figures. A 2,000-year-old galloping horse 365 feet (111 m.) long, cut in chalk on Berkshire Downs.

2 MARLBOROUGH HORSE, Wiltshire
Cut by local schoolboys in 1804.

3 HACPEN HORSE, Marlborough, Wiltshire
Cut for Queen Victoria's coronation in 1838.

4 ALTON BARNES HORSE, Old Adam Hill, Pewsey, Wiltshire
Figure 166 feet (50 m.) long, with huge eye.

47

5 PEWSEY NEW HORSE, Wiltshire
Carved in 1937 for coronation of George VI.

6 WESTBURY WHITE HORSE, Bratton Down, Wiltshire
Cut in 18th century on site of earlier, smaller horse.

7 CERNE GIANT, Cerne Abbas, Dorset
A 180-foot (55-m.) figure of naked man with club, possibly Hercules. Believed to date from Romano-British times.

1066

Duke William of Normandy landed on the Sussex coast in 1066. He defeated the Anglo-Saxon King Harold and seized the crown, thereby changing the course of English history.

1 PEVENSEY
Where William the Conqueror landed. Castle built by his half-brother stands within walls of old Roman fort.

2 HASTINGS
Castle ruins occupy site of William's first fortress on English soil. Embroidery depicting events from 1066 to modern times in town hall. Life-size models of people at time of Conquest in Domesday Exhibition at White Rock Theatre.

3 BATTLE, north-west of Hastings
Where Battle of Hastings took place October 14, 1066. Battle Abbey, founded by William in fulfillment of vow. Museum containing half-size copy of Bayeux Tapestry.

The Cerne Giant's creators have left no clue to their identity, nor who the chalk figure was meant to represent. Yet it remains a potent symbol of the timelessness of these rolling downs.

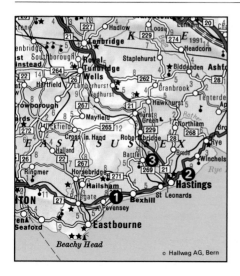

Beachy Head

© Hallwag AG, Bern

London's Historic Palaces

A tour of London's royal palaces turns the pages of England's history from the era of William the Conqueror to the present day.

TOWER OF LONDON
Begun in 1087 by William the Conqueror, it has served as palace, fortress, prison and place of execution.

PALACE OF WESTMINSTER
Principal royal palace until 15th century. Only Jewel Tower and Westminster Hall (1099) remain, incorporated into Houses of Parliament.

ELTHAM PALACE, Woolwich
Fifteenth-century palace of Plantagenet kings. Great Hall and moat bridge survive.

HAMPTON COURT PALACE,
Kingston-upon-Thames
Favourite residence of Henry VIII.

ST. JAMES'S PALACE,
St. James's Street
Tudor and Stuart palace. Charles I slept here the night before going to scaffold.

BANQUETING HOUSE, Whitehall
Where Charles I was executed; originally part of Whitehall Palace.

MARLBOROUGH HOUSE, Pall Mall
Former royal residence designed by Christopher Wren. Now Commonwealth conference centre.

SOMERSET HOUSE, The Strand
Built in 18th century on site of Elizabeth I's palace. Royal residence until George III bought Buckingham Palace. Grand setting for Courtauld Institute art galleries.

KEW PALACE, Kew Gardens
Small, Dutch-style residence of George III.

KENSINGTON PALACE,
Kensington Gardens
Queen Victoria learned here of her accession to throne.

BUCKINGHAM PALACE
Home of sovereign and royal family.

The Royal Parks

The Royal Parks, owned by the Crown but open to the public, are one of the delights of London. Cross the first four listed, a distance of 3 miles (5 km.), and you'll negotiate the busiest part of the metropolis from Bayswater to Whitehall, with only two brief encounters with traffic.

KENSINGTON GARDENS
Former grounds of William III's Kensington Palace. A children's favourite for sailing model boats on Round Pond and statue of Peter Pan.

HYDE PARK
One-time hunting preserve of Henry VIII. Bathers and boaters crowd Serpentine lake in summer.

GREEN PARK
Open parkland with massive trees, favourite of Charles II.

ST. JAMES'S PARK
Long lake and rampant shrubberies attract wild birds and relaxing civil servants.

REGENT'S PARK
Named after Prince Regent, later George IV. Vast park includes London Zoo, formal flower gardens and Open Air Theatre.

GREENWICH PARK
Former hunting grounds, site of Old Royal Observatory. Brass strip marks Meridian from which world measurements are taken.

RICHMOND PARK
Largest and wildest of royal parks. Deer still roam this one-time hunting preserve of Charles I.

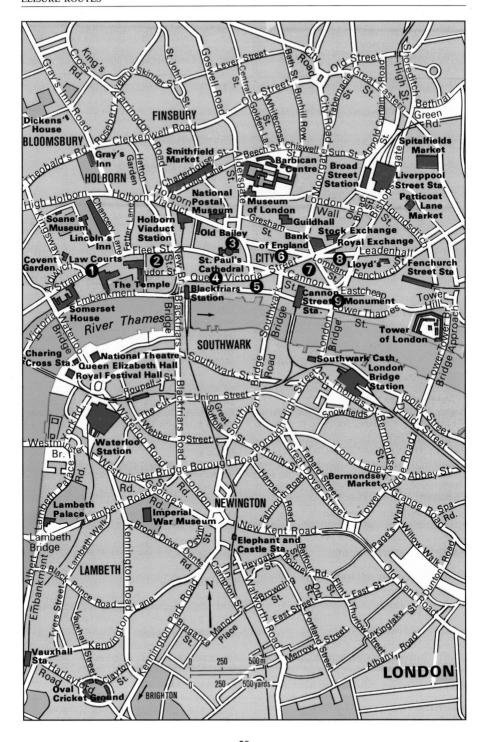

Wren's City

The Great Fire of 1666 gave London the chance to build anew in stone, embellished by the genius of Sir Christopher Wren (1632–1723). Many of his surviving churches were bombed in World War II, but they have been meticulously restored. A short walk will take you past some of Wren's best.

1 ST. CLEMENT DANES, The Strand
Isolated between streams of traffic at entrance to City of London. On site of 9th-century church built for the Danes.

2 ST. BRIDE, Fleet Street
The printers' church with "wedding cake" tower. Burned out in World War II but rebuilt.

3 ST. PAUL'S CATHEDRAL, Ludgate Hill
Wren's masterpiece topped by famous dome. Place of royal ceremonial containing tombs of the great.

4 ST. ANDREW-BY-THE-WARDROBE, Queen Victoria Street
Fine church with square tower.

5 ST. JAMES GARLICKHYTHE, Garlick Hill
Has typical, elegant Wren steeple.

6 ST. MARY-LE-BOW, Cheapside
The Bow Bells of Cockney fame ring out from its superb steeple.

7 ST. STEPHEN WALBROOK, Walbrook
One of Wren's best. Forerunner of St. Paul's, with dome, steeple and Corinthian columns.

8 ST. PETER-UPON-CORNHILL, Gracechurch Street Corner
A fine Wren church on an ancient sacred site.

9 THE MONUMENT, Monument Street
Begun by Wren in 1671 to commemorate the Great Fire.

Stately Homes

Britain's great houses count as one of the country's finest assets. Here are some of the best. All are open to the public. Confirm dates and times with tourist authorities or the National Trust before visiting.

In the London Area

KENWOOD HOUSE, Hampstead, London
Elegant mansion surrounded by parkland. Remodelled by Adam in 18th century.

SIR JOHN SOANE'S MUSEUM, Lincoln's Inn Fields, London
House of great architect, as he lived in it until his death in 1837.

APSLEY HOUSE, Hyde Park Corner, London
Adam house remodelled by Benjamin Wyatt for first Duke of Wellington. Important Old Masters, silver and porcelain.

CHISWICK HOUSE, Chiswick, London
Beautiful Neoclassical building inspired by Palladio. Built to Lord Burlington's design in 1729. Striking William Kent interior.

OSTERLEY PARK HOUSE, Isleworth, Middlesex
Elizabethan mansion, charmingly remodelled by Adam. Superb interior decoration.

HAM HOUSE, Richmond, Surrey
Imposing 17th-century house with extremely rare original Restoration furnishings.

MARBLE HILL HOUSE, Twickenham, Surrey
English Palladian villa. Lovely interior.

SYON HOUSE, Brentford, Middlesex
Old monastery modernized with characteristic style by Adam. Lavish decor.

North of London

HATFIELD HOUSE, Hatfield, Hertfordshire
Jacobean building with state apartments for royalty.

ASHRIDGE, Berkhamsted, Hertfordshire
Monastic building transformed into residence by Henry VIII. Largely rebuilt in neo-Gothic style in early 19th century.

WOBURN ABBEY, near Leighton Buzzard, Bedfordshire
Outstanding collection of paintings. Wild animal park in extensive grounds.

AUDLEY END, Saffron Walden, Essex
Jacobean house on site of Benedictine abbey. Renovated in 18th century.

South and South-East of London

CHARTWELL, Westerham, Kent
Winston Churchill's country retreat. Renovated farmhouse in attractive grounds.

KNOLE PARK, Sevenoaks, Kent
Vast home of the Sackvilles. Unique collection of Jacobean furniture with some rare silver pieces.

IGHTHAM MOTE, Ivy Hatch, Sevenoaks, Kent
Well-preserved 14th-century moated manor house and meeting place (mote).

PENSHURST PLACE, Penshurst, Kent
Battlemented 14th-century house with fine Great Hall.

HEVER CASTLE, near Edenbridge, Kent
Childhood home of Anne Boleyn. Thirteenth-century moated castle, converted into 20th-century residence for Lord Astor.

LEEDS CASTLE, near Maidstone, Kent
Fairy-tale castle built on two islands in lake.

ARUNDEL CASTLE, West Sussex
Historic seat of dukes of Norfolk for 700 years.

In Yorkshire and Humberside

HAREWOOD HOUSE, north of Leeds
Stately home in Palladian style, with Adam interiors and Chippendale furniture.

NEWBY HALL, Newby, south-west of Ripon
Graceful brick mansion with fine sculpture gallery by Robert Adam and collection of rare chamber pots.

CASTLE HOWARD, west of Malton
Grandiose house designed by Sir John Vanbrugh.

BURTON AGNES HALL, near Driffield
Jacobean red-brick house, with magnificent woodwork, mullioned windows and original staircase.

BURTON CONSTABLE, Sproatley, near Hull
Tudor house, with battlemented towers in extensive park.

Around Oxford

BLENHEIM PALACE
Stateliest of them all. Duke of Marlborough's mansion, where Winston Churchill was born.

ROUSHAM HOUSE, Steeple Aston
Tudor house, battlemented in 18th century. Landscaped garden.

COMPTON WYNYATES, Tysoe, west of Banbury
Delightful Tudor house in garden of yews.

STONOR PARK, Henley-on-Thames
Medieval house surrounded by parkland, refuge of Catholic priests during persecution.

MILTON MANOR, near Abingdon
Built to design of Inigo Jones, with addition of two Georgian wings.

In the South and South-West

COTEHELE HOUSE, St. Dominick, near Saltash, Cornwall
Romantic grey granite manor house, little changed since medieval times. Period furniture.

*A*rundel's almost toy-like appearance belies a choppy history, with a cast of characters often on the wrong side of the powers that be. The 4th earl fell foul of Richard II and was beheaded on Tower Hill; the 12th in the line spent several stays in prison for allegedly plotting against Elizabeth I. Philip Howard, the 13th earl, was also implicated in a Roman Catholic conspiracy against the queen and died in disgrace in the Tower. He was beatified in 1929. His son built up a renowned collection of marbles and statues that was donated to Oxford University after his death.

PENCARROW, Washaway,
Bodmin, Cornwall
Stuccoed Palladian house with charming Georgian decor and furniture.

BUCKLAND ABBEY,
near Yelverton, Devon
Converted Cistercian monastery, former home and museum of Sir Francis Drake.

SALTRAM HOUSE, Plympton, Devon
Elegant Georgian mansion with Adam interior.

FORDE ABBEY, Chard, Dorset
Long, low house incorporating monastic building. Notable tapestries based on Raphael cartoons.

KINGSTON LACY HOUSE, near
Wimbourne, Dorset
One of earliest classical houses in England. Fine collection of paintings.

MONTACUTE HOUSE, near Yeovil,
Somerset
Imposing Elizabethan mansion, scarcely changed since completed in 1600.

LITTLECOTE HOUSE, near Hungerford,
Wiltshire
Tudor manor. Weaponry museum in great hall. Haunted bedroom, scene of gruesome child murder in 1575.

LONGLEAT HOUSE, Warminster,
Wiltshire
Massive Renaissance mansion lit by ranks of mullioned windows. Visited by Queen Elizabeth I. Safari park with lions.

STOURHEAD, Stourton, Warminster,
Wiltshire
Palladian house with Regency interior in Italianate grounds.

WARDOUR CASTLE, Wiltshire
Palladian façade and Pantheon-style domed staircase hall. Now a school.

WILTON HOUSE, Wilton, Wiltshire
Built under supervision of Inigo Jones. Outstanding paintings include family portraits by Van Dyck. Furniture by Chippendale and William Kent.

Great Gardens

Gardening is a British national pastime. You'll see enthusiasts making the most of every tiny suburban plot, while the great stately homes in the countryside have some of the loveliest gardens to be found anywhere.

In the South

TRESCO ABBEY, Isles of Scilly
Luxuriant subtropical gardens.

KNIGHTSHAYES COURT,
Tiverton, Devon
Alpine plants and woodland garden.

EAST LAMBROOK MANOR, Somerset
Small garden of rare plants developed by gardening author Margery Fish.

COMPTON ACRES, Dorset, between
Bournemouth and Poole
Seven gardens in different styles, including Japanese and Italian.

HIDCOTE MANOR, Hidcote Bartrim,
Gloucestershire
Beautiful garden overlooking Vale of Evesham.

ROUSHAM HOUSE, Steeple Aston,
Oxfordshire
Landscaped gardens with pools and sculptures.

SISSINGHURST CASTLE, Kent
Walled gardens with different themes and colours, developed by Vita Sackville-West and Harold Nicolson.

POLESDEN LACEY, near Dorking, Surrey
Typical English garden of lawns, herbaceous borders and roses, with fine views over the Downs.

NYMANS GARDENS, West Sussex
Famous for rhododendrons, magnolias and camellias.

HATFIELD HOUSE, Hertfordshire
Jacobean-style gardens.

PUSEY HOUSE, near Faringdon,
Berkshire
Elegant gardens dipping to lake.

In Wales and the North

BODNANT, Denbigh, Gwynedd
Italian-style terraced gardens.

GWYLLT GARDENS, Portmeirion
Miles of woodland walks among rhododendrons and azaleas.

COTON MANOR, near Northampton
Old English garden with water birds.

ANGLESEY ABBEY, near Cambridge
100 acres (40 ha.) of formal gardens and parkland, embellished by statues.

STUDLEY ROYAL, south-west of Ripon
Romantic vistas of lakes, lawns and ruins.

LEVENS HALL, Cumbria
Famous for yew and box topiary.

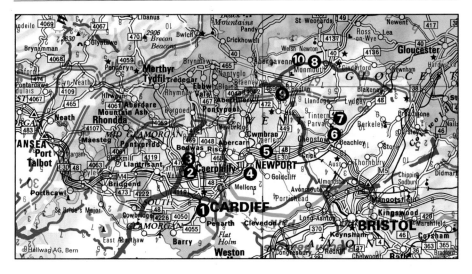

NEWBY HALL, south-east of Ripon
Rose gardens around 17th-century house overlooking river.

CRARAE GARDENS, Loch Fyne, Argyll
Exotic plants, rhododendrons, magnolias.

Castles and Ruins in South Wales

A tour of castles from Cardiff to Chepstow and Monmouth combines history with coastal scenery and the beauty of the wooded Wye Valley.

1 CARDIFF CASTLE
Norman castle on site of Roman fort, rebuilt in 19th century.

2 CASTELL COCH
Neo-Gothic remake of 13th-century structure. A William Burges fantasy.

3 CAERPHILLY CASTLE
One of greatest surviving medieval castles, ringed by towers and water defences.

4 NEWPORT CASTLE
Ruins of 15th-century fortress guarding river crossing.

5 CAERLEON ROMAN FORTRESS
Remains of barracks, baths and amphitheatre.

6 CHEPSTOW CASTLE
Britain's first stone-built fortress, guarding strategic route from England to Wales.

7 TINTERN ABBEY
Majestic ruins of Cistercian monastery in Wye Valley.

8 MONMOUTH CASTLE
Birthplace of King Henry V of Agincourt fame.

9 RAGLAN CASTLE
Impressive ruins of 15th-century castle. Tall "Yellow Tower" outside walls was destroyed by Cromwell in Civil War.

10 WHITE CASTLE
Norman fortification surrounded by steep moat.

Castles and Mountains in North Wales

England's Edward I built several massive fortresses on the north-west coast of Wales to subjugate the newly conquered Welsh. Their rebellious spirit is epitomized by the majestic peak of Snowdon.

1 HARLECH CASTLE
One of Edward's forts. Here Henry V besieged Welsh hero Owain Glyndwr.

2 CAERNARFON CASTLE
Edward's spectacular fortress and palace, scene of investiture of Princes of Wales.

3 SNOWDONIA NATIONAL PARK
Scenery on a grand scale around Snowdon, highest mountain in Wales.

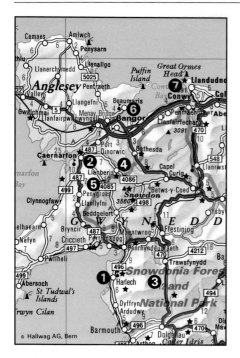

HOPETOUN HOUSE, near Queensferry
Eighteenth-century mansion with Adam interior, set in beautiful park on south shore of Firth of Forth.

FALKLAND PALACE
Stuart castle with French-style façade.

SCONE PALACE, near Perth
Neo-Gothic house built on site where early Scottish kings were crowned. Collection of furniture and china.

CULROSS PALACE,
south-east of Stirling
Royal palace where Charles I was born.

4 SNOWDON MOUNTAIN RAILWAY
In operation since 1896. Runs 5 miles (8 km.) from Llanberis to summit of Snowdon.

5 DOLBADARN CASTLE
Ruined 13th-century castle of Welsh princes guards Llanberis pass.

6 BEAUMARIS, Isle of Anglesey
Castle noted for its concentric walls, turrets and moat. Built by Edward to guard Menai Strait.

7 CONWY CASTLE
Built by Edward. A formidable fortress with eight massive towers.

Historic Scottish Castles

Several of Scotland's most famous castles and historic houses lie within the Edinburgh area.

EDINBURGH CASTLE
Imposing fortress on rocky summit, stronghold site for more than 1,000 years.

PALACE OF HOLYROODHOUSE,
Edinburgh
Home of Mary Queen of Scots. Official residence in Scotland of British sovereign.

Great Cathedrals

The 27 great cathedrals of England and Wales illustrate among them the whole development of medieval architectural style, from Norman (1066–1180) to the three subdivisions of Gothic: Early English (1189–1307), Decorated (1307–77) and Perpendicular (1377–1485). Here is a selection of the finest examples.

1 WINCHESTER
Norman transepts and crypt date from 1079, when Winchester was capital of England. Striking Perpendicular nave is Europe's longest.

2 SALISBURY
Early English style throughout. Only English cathedral designed to single concept. Begun in 1220, completed 1280. Tower and soaring spire added in 14th century.

3 WELLS
First English cathedral to be constructed in Gothic style (1175–1260). Superbly carved west front.

4 EXETER
Retains Norman transept towers. Remainder rebuilt in Decorated style in 13th and 14th centuries.

5 CANTERBURY
Founded 1070. Eastern end magnificently rebuilt in Early English style after a disastrous fire in 1174. Perpendicular nave and Bell Harry Tower.

6 ELY
Norman nave and tower (begun 1083). Early English and Decorated additions. Unique octagonal lantern in Decorated style.

7 GLOUCESTER
Norman core (1089), rebuilt in Perpendicular style. Holds alabaster tomb of Edward II.

8 LINCOLN
Supreme example of Early English style, with Norman west front preserved. Some Decorated and Perpendicular elements.

9 YORK MINSTER
Britain's largest cathedral, with massive central tower and fine stained glass.

10 DURHAM
Finest example of Norman architecture in Britain (1093). Beautifully proportioned nave with massive, incised columns.

Ruined Abbeys of Yorkshire

Only magnificent ruins remain of England's great medieval abbeys, suppressed by Henry VIII. But their extensive lands and wealth passed to the nobility and rich merchants and indirectly gave rise to many of the country's stately homes.

BOLTON ABBEY, north of Ilkley
Ruined Augustinian priory on banks of River Wharfe. Nave now serves as parish church.

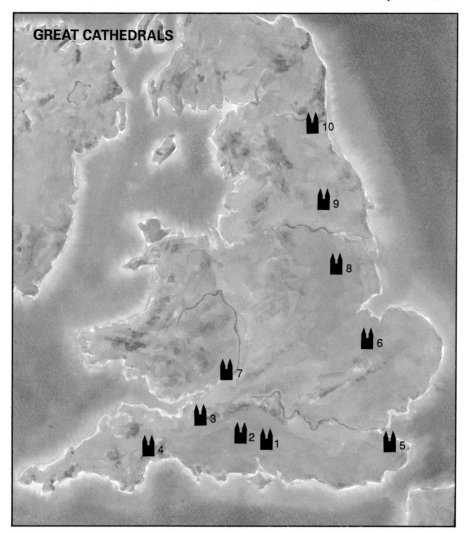

GREAT CATHEDRALS

FOUNTAINS ABBEY, south-west of Ripon
Well-preserved, romantic ruins of 12th-century Cistercian monastery, once richest in England.

BYLAND ABBEY, south-west of Thirsk
Cistercian abbey of which west front remains.

RIEVAULX ABBEY, north-west of Helmsley
Ruins of 12th-century Cistercian monastery in Rye Valley.

WHITBY ABBEY
Picturesque 13th-century ruins on site of monastery founded by St. Hilda in 657.

King Arthur's Cornwall

Pursuit of the legendary 6th-century hero King Arthur and his Knights of the Round Table is as good a reason as any to explore the rugged coast of Cornwall.

1 TINTAGEL
Ruins claimed to be of Arthur's castle, where king was born and lived with Queen Guinevere. Cave of magician Merlin. King Arthur's Hall, built in 1933, with stained-glass windows of knights.

2 BODMIN MOOR
Site of King Arthur's last battle against his evil nephew Prince Mordred at Camlann on river Camel. Magic sword Excalibur was flung into Dozmary Pool on moor.

3 LAND'S END
View towards Isles of Scilly, "Islands of the Blessed", where mortally wounded Arthur took refuge with his knights after seas rose up to bar Mordred's way.

4 MOUSEHOLE
Merlin lived on rock below village.

5 FOWEY
Eight-foot (2.5-m.) Tristan Stone, a mile to north, commemorates one of Arthur's knights; Castle Dore, overgrown Iron Age mound a couple of miles further on, once held castle of Tristan's uncle, King Mark.

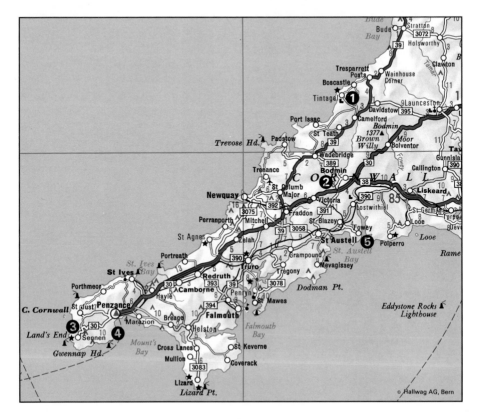

58

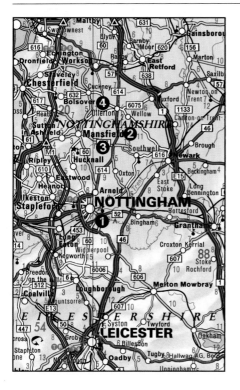

Shakespeare Country

The memory of William Shakespeare (1564–1616) lives on in his home town of Stratford and the villages around it. See the sights that launched England's original tourist industry more than two centuries ago:

1 STRATFORD-UPON-AVON
Shakespeare's birthplace. Holy Trinity Church, burial place of the bard.

2 SHOTTERY, west of Stratford
Anne Hathaway's Cottage, childhood home of Shakespeare's wife.

3 WILMCOTE, north-west of Stratford
Mary Arden's House. Sixteenth-century farmhouse where Shakespeare's mother grew up.

4 ASTON CANTLOW, north-west of Stratford
Church where Shakespeare's parents are said to have been married.

5 CHARLECOTE PARK, Wellesbourne
Elizabethan house typical of Shakespeare's time, extensively restored. According to tradition, Shakespeare was caught poaching a deer in the park and was brought before the owner, Sir Thomas Lucy, to be fined.

Robin Hood Country

The story of Robin Hood has become an integral part of Nottingham's folklore. The 13th-century outlaw of Sherwood Forest, who robbed the rich to feed the poor and tricked the Sheriff of Nottingham, helped King Richard regain his throne from his usurping brother John.

1 NOTTINGHAM
The castle, fortress of King John; statue of Robin Hood.

2 SHERWOOD FOREST
Ancient oak woodlands north of Nottingham, once royal hunting grounds and domain of Robin Hood and his Merry Men.

3 EDWINSTOWE
Church where Robin Hood wed Maid Marion. Robin Hood Exhibition at Visitor Centre. Major Oak, a thousand years old, where outlaws hid.

4 BLIDWORTH, west of Sherwood Forest
Tomb of Robin's henchman, Will Scarlett.

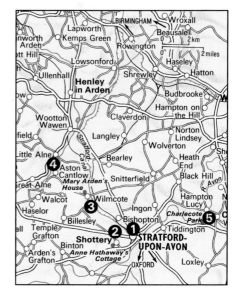

For Love of the Landscape

The Trossachs

The Trossachs compress within a small picturesque area a microcosm of the Scottish Highlands—lochs, glens, peaks and waterfalls at their most romantic.

CALLANDER
Starting point for tour. Small Regency town.

LOCH VENACHAR
Long lake beneath peak of Ben Ledi (2,873 ft./876 m.), highest point in Trossachs.

LOCH ACHRAY
Mile-long pass leading to head of Loch Katrine.

LOCH KATRINE
Most beautiful and romantic of Scottish lakes, inspiration for Sir Walter Scott's poems *Rob Roy* and *The Lady of the Lake*.

LOCH ARD FOREST
Woods of oak, birch and mountain ash, part of Queen Elizabeth Forest Park.

Peaks and Dales of Derbyshire

Derbyshire's Peak District, easily reached from Manchester, Sheffield or Derby, offers magnificent scenery of wooded hills and limestone gorges, protected as a national park.

MATLOCK BATH
Former spa in beautiful Derwent Valley. Grottoes and caves. Wooded Heights of Abraham accessible by cable car.

HADDON HALL, between Matlock and Bakewell
Medieval house with priceless tapestries.

CHATSWORTH HOUSE, north-east of Bakewell
Immense Baroque mansion.

TIDESWELL
Notable 14th-century church of St. John. Annual "well-dressing" ceremony.

BUXTON
Spa since Roman times. Mary Queen of Scots, as a prisoner, was treated for rheumatism here.

DOVEDALE GORGE
Twisted rocks along peaceful river valley. Caves at Dove Holes.

CASTLETON
Peveril Castle, setting for Sir Walter Scott's *Peveril of the Peak*. Underground caverns.

Dartmoor

Dartmoor National Park covers 365 square miles (945 sq. km.) of open moor-

*O*n Dartmoor, walkers revel in miles of open,
heather-clad moorland, interspersed with cob and thatch villages, sparkling
streams and weathered granite tors. But there is also a vaguely sinister,
haunting quality to the place. The grey walls of the notorious prison
for hardened criminals loom menacingly over the landscape.
And here, in a swirl of fog, Sherlock Holmes had his spine-chilling
confrontation with the Hound of the Baskervilles.

land and wooded valleys. A 50-mile (80-km.) tour starting from Buckfastleigh will take you through a variety of Devon landscapes.

BUCKFASTLEIGH
Terminus of picturesque Dart Valley Railway from Totnes.

BUCKFAST ABBEY
Modern abbey built by Benedictine monks.

ASHBURTON
Former wool town and slate-mining centre.

BUCKLAND-IN-THE-MOOR
Romantic Devon village of thatched stone houses.

WIDECOMBE-IN-THE-MOOR
Famous for fair immortalized in song, held on second Tuesday in September.

MANATON
Fifteenth-century moorland church.

POSTBRIDGE
Granite "clapper bridge" over East Dart River.

TWO BRIDGES
Medieval "clapper bridge" over West Dart.

tre's grounds Swiss chalet, removed from Gad's Hill Place, in which Dickens wrote *A Tale of Two Cities.*

COBHAM, west of Rochester
Leather Bottle Inn, described in *The Pickwick Papers.*

COOLING (7 mi./11 km. from Rochester)
Children's graves, which Pip in *Great Expectations* claims are of his family.

CHALK (5 mi./8 km. from Rochester)
House where Dickens and wife Catherine spent honeymoon. Forge on which Dickens modelled Pip's childhood home.

GAD'S HILL PLACE
Bought by Dickens in 1856 and where he died, now girls' school.

BROADSTAIRS
Dickens's favourite seaside resort. Annual Dickens Festival. Bleak House, where he wrote part of *David Copperfield,* contains personal mementos. Dickens House Museum was original of Miss Betsey Trotwood's house in *David Copperfield.* Royal Albion Hotel, where Dickens wrote part of *Nicholas Nickleby.*

SARRE, near Canterbury
Crown Inn, frequented by Dickens.

Charles Dickens in Kent

From the age of five to ten, Charles Dickens (1812–1870) lived with his family in Chatham. These were the happiest years of a rather difficult childhood. Later, as a famous novelist, he bought Gad's Hill Place near Rochester, a house he had admired since he was a boy. This area of Kent inspired scenes in many of his books.

CHATHAM
The Dickens' family house was at No. 2 (now No. 11) Ordnance Terrace.

ROCHESTER
Cathedral appears in *The Mystery of Edwin Drood* and Jasper's Gate was home of drug addict John Jasper in that novel. Restoration House was model for Miss Havisham's home in *Great Expectations.* Royal Victoria and Bull Inn was scene of meetings of fictitious Pickwick Club. Charles Dickens Centre (Eastgate House, High Street) contains waxwork displays and mementoes. Also in Cen-

Hardy's Dorset

Thomas Hardy (1840–1928) lived most of his life in the county of Dorset, immortalized as Wessex in his novels. A tour of places associated with the writer takes you through some lovely countryside. Names in parentheses are those used by Hardy in the novels.

1 DORCHESTER (Casterbridge)
Featured prominently in Hardy novels. Thomas Hardy statue at Top o' Town. Hardy's study in County Museum. Max Gate, house on Dorchester outskirts, where writer lived for 43 years till his death. Maiden Castle and Maumbury Rings, featured in *The Mayor of Casterbridge.*

2 STINSFORD (Mellstock)
Hardy's heart buried in churchyard (but his ashes are in Westminster Abbey).

3 PUDDLETOWN (Weatherbury)
Waterston Manor was model for Bathsheba's Weatherbury Farm in *Far from the Madding Crowd.*

4 HIGHER BOCKHAMPTON (Upper Mellstock)
Hardy's Cottage, his birthplace and early home, where he wrote *Under the Greenwood Tree* and *Far from the Madding Crowd*.

5 PUDDLETOWN HEATH (Egdon Heath)
Featured in *The Return of the Native*.

6 WEST STAFFORD
Church in *Tess of the D'Urbervilles,* where Tess and Angel Clare were married.

7 LULWORTH COVE (Lulstead Cove)
Troy swam out from here and was believed drowned in *Far from the Madding Crowd*.

8 WOOL
Woolbridge Manor Hotel (Wellbridge Manor), where Tess and Angel Clare spent blighted honeymoon.

9 BERE REGIS (King's Bere)
In *Tess of the D'Urbervilles,* Tess and her family camped out on a four-poster bed outside church, under stained-glass Turberville window in south wall.

10 SHAFTESBURY (Shaston)
Background to *Jude the Obscure*.

11 MARNHULL (Marlott)
Tess Cottage, believed original of Durbeyfields' home.

12 SHERBORNE (Sherton Abbas)
Old town little changed since it figured in *The Woodlanders*.

13 WEYMOUTH (Budmouth)
Hardy worked for a Weymouth architect and stayed here again while writing *The Trumpet Major*.

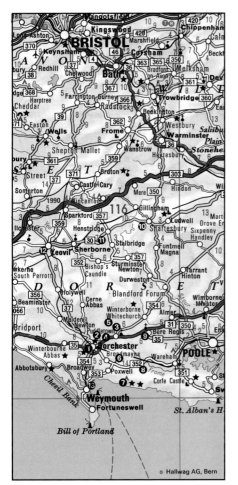

© Hallwag AG, Bern

Constable Country

John Constable (1776–1837) excelled as a painter of his native Suffolk and its river, the Stour. Constable's naturalistic portrayal of the countryside, the blown clouds and vibrant sunlight, made him the father of modern landscape painting. Some of the scenes remain just as Constable painted them.

DEDHAM
Picturesque old centre of wool trade. Constable attended village grammar school. Painted 15th-century church and former water mill. Dedham Vale beside Stour was one of artist's favourite subjects.

STRATFORD ST. MARY, near Dedham
Village of timber and pink Suffolk plaster. Former water mills survive in Constable's art.

EAST BERGHOLT, near Dedham
Pleasant cloth-making village. Plaque marks site of house where Constable was born, son of local miller. Memorials in parish church to artist and wife Maria.

FLATFORD, near East Bergholt
Flatford Mill on River Stour inspired some of painter's greatest works. Nearby, Willy Lott's house, also featured in paintings.

STOKE-BY-NAYLAND, near East Bergholt
In the heart of Constable country. Painter captured essence of village, with 15th-century church and half-timbered Guildhall.

In the Steps of Bonnie Prince Charlie

The 23-year-old Stuart Pretender, Prince Charles Edward, "Bonnie Prince Charlie" (1720–88), sailed on a French ship to the Hebridean island of Eriskay in 1745 to try to win back the British throne for his father. You can trace his tragic odyssey from his landing on the mainland to his final defeat and abandonment of Scottish soil.

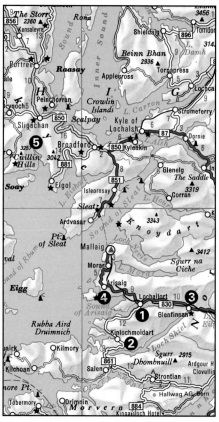

1 LOCH NAN UAMH, north of Lochailort
Where Bonnie Prince Charlie landed in June 1745. Footpath leads to cave where he spent first night. And in September 1746 a French boat took the defeated prince from here to France, after five months in hiding in the Highlands and islands.

2 KINLOCHMOIDART
Row of seven beech trees commemorates seven followers who landed with prince. Ruined castle of Tioram belonging to Clanranald, one of the seven, lies on island in Loch Moidart.

3 GLENFINNAN
Where prince raised his standard at gathering of clans on August 19, 1745, and proclaimed his father king. Memorial tower surmounted by kilted Highlander stands at head of Loch Shiel.

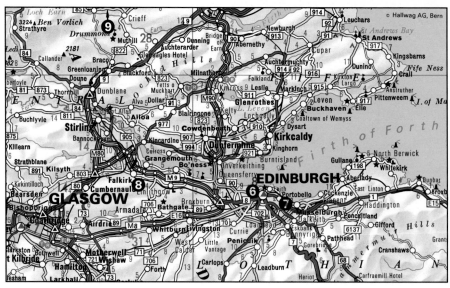

4 ARISAIG, north of Lochailort
Where hunted prince lay hidden in hut on July 18, 1746, with price of £30,000 on his head.

5 SKYE
On the run in islands of Outer Hebrides, prince crossed to Isle of Skye. He was disguised as maid of young woman supporter, Flora Macdonald. From Skye he returned to mainland.

6 EDINBURGH
Captured by prince, who held court in Holyroodhouse.

7 PRESTONPANS, east of Edinburgh
Where prince's forces decisively defeated government troops on September 21 in 10-minute battle. Southward push into England followed.

8 FALKIRK
On the retreat, prince's generals gained one last victory over government army here on January 17, 1746.

9 CULLODEN MOOR, east of Inverness
Where prince's Highlanders, pursued by Duke of Cumberland and his men, gave battle on April 16, 1746. Highlanders were annihilated in less than an hour. Battlefield museum in old farmhouse. Cairns mark spot where Highlanders fell.

The Whisky Trail

Scotland claims the world's only Malt Whisky Trail, calling in at distilleries of seven world-famous brews in a 70-mile (113-km.) tour through the foothills of the Grampian Mountains, north-west of Aberdeen. The word whisky, incidentally, comes from the Gaelic *uisge-beatha,* meaning "water of life".

STRATHISLA, Keith
Strathisla whisky distillery marks starting point of tour.

GLENFIDDICH, Dufftown
Museum attached to distillery shows history of Scotch whisky.

TAMNAVULIN
Best time to visit this and other distilleries is from April to October.

THE GLENLIVET
Here, as at all the distilleries, you can watch malting of barley and mashing, fermentation and distillation process.

GLENFARCLAS
At this distillery, as at others, you get guided tour and opportunity to purchase products at distillery shop.

TAMDHU
Distillery in valley of River Spey. Quality of water and smoky flavour from peat over which barley is dried play important part in whisky production.

GLEN GRANT, Rothes
Last distillery on tour. Traditional quality and flavour of this and other brands depend largely on the skill of the stillman at distilling stage.

Bird-watching in Norfolk

Norfolk has some of the finest bird-watching areas in Britain, with a variety of coastal, marsh, fen and meadow habitats attracting migrating waders in spring and autumn, ducks and geese in winter and song birds in summer. Full information from Royal Society for the Protection of Birds, The Lodge, Sandy, Bedfordshire.

HOLME NATURE RESERVE, north-east of Hunstanton
Dune, woodland and shore are a magnet for migrant passerines and waders.

SCOLT HEAD ISLAND
National Nature Reserve with breeding colonies of terns, accessible by boat from Brancaster Staithe.

CLEY AND SALTHOUSE
Bird-watchers' paradise of marshes, lagoons and shore. Many different species can be seen, including rare migrants.

THE BROADS
Large expanse of freshwater lakes, reedbeds and islands. Ideal for birds, especially Hickling Broad National Nature Reserve and Horsey Mere. Motorboats to cruise the Broads can be rented at off-season rates in spring and autumn, the best time for bird-watching.

BREYDON WATER, behind Yarmouth
Estuary lake, frequented by geese, duck, spoonbills and waders.

NORFOLK WILDLIFE PARK AND ORNAMENTAL PHEASANT TRUST, Great Witchingham
One of largest pheasant collections in world.

Pilgrim Country

American roots lie deep in English history, and many places have strong American associations. But nowhere more than East Anglia and the Fens. So many of the Founding Fathers of the United States came from the area that it's known as "Pilgrim Country".

GAINSBOROUGH, Lincolnshire
Medieval Old Hall, where the Puritans (then called Separatists) met towards end of 16th century. John Robinson Memorial Church, built in 1896, commemorates the Separatist pastor who intended to sail on *Mayflower*, but died before it left.

SCROOBY, Nottinghamshire
Reverend Richard Clyfton brought his followers here after a split in Gainsborough Puritan congregation. They met in William Brewster's Manor House. Under persecution, the Puritans tried to flee to the Netherlands in 1607, but were seized on board boat in Boston. They eventually went to Leyden in 1609 and sailed on *Mayflower* in 1620.

AUSTERFIELD, South Yorkshire
William Bradford, leader of the Pilgrims and second governor of Plymouth Colony was born here. His *History of Plimouth Plantation* recorded Pilgrim Fathers' odyssey. North aisle of church was restored in Bradford's memory by Society of Mayflower Descendants.

BOSTON, Lincolnshire
Pilgrim Fathers were arrested here when they first tried to flee religious persecution in 1607. Cells in Guildhall where they were imprisoned were restored by Bostonian Society of Massachusetts. Column at Scotia Creek marks spot where group of Puritans led by John Winthrop sailed for New World in 1630. St. Botolph's Church, a major American shrine, was restored by American Bostonians in 1857 in memory of John Cotton. Cotton sailed for Massachusetts in 1633 after being ousted as vicar because of his Puritan beliefs. Church tower, known as the Boston Stump, was rebuilt by Americans after World War II. Fydell House contains an American Room, opened by Ambassador Joseph Kennedy in 1938.

LINCOLN
Stained-glass window in cathedral honours Captain John Smith, leader of colony at Jamestown, Virginia, who was released from Indian captivity by the chief's daughter, Pocahontas. Another window commemorates pilgrim ship *Arbella* on which John Winthrop, first governor of Plymouth colony, sailed in 1630.

Industrial Britain

The Industrial Revolution began in Britain, transforming it from a rural to an urban society in less than a century. Historic mills, mines, factories and other installations across the country have been preserved as monuments to the early days of the machine age. A number of museums also highlight Britain's great industrial heritage.

BATH
Camden Museum, displays of Victorian engineering tools.

BIRMINGHAM
Museum of Science and Industry in one of the world's original industrial cities.

BLAENAVON, Wales
Big Pit Mining Museum, until recently a working pit.

BRADFORD
Industrial Museum at Moorside Mills.

BURTON-ON-TRENT
Bass Museum of 200 years of brewing.

CORNWALL
Geevor Museum of tin mining at Penzance. Poldark mine at Wendron.

GLASGOW
Summerlee Heritage Park at Coatbridge Sunnyside, with displays of engineering equipment from Victorian times.

IRON-BRIDGE, Shropshire
World's first cast-iron bridge, spanning River Severn; Iron-Bridge Gorge Museum, open-air site includes blast furnaces, beam engines, tile and china works, mine and printing works.

MANCHESTER
Greater Manchester Museum of Science and Technology, including 1830 Liverpool Road Station, oldest railway passenger station in world. Castlefield Visitor Centre, Deansgate, an urban heritage park with displays on area's industrial past.

NEWCASTLE-UPON-TYNE
Museum of Science and Technology features cases Tyneside shipbuilding, mining and engineering.

66

NOTTINGHAM
Industrial Museum at Wollaton Hall has displays on local printing and lace works. Canal Museum in warehouse on Beeston Canal. Lace Hall, depicting history of lace-making from 1850 to today.

STANLEY, near Durham
Beamish North of England Open Air Museum, featuring coal miners' cottages and pit machinery.

SWANSEA, Wales
Industrial Maritime Museum. Trostre Tinplate Works at Llanelli, still functioning.

STOURBRIDGE, West Midlands
Glassworks, exhibits and demonstrations.

WOLVERHAMPTON
Bilston Museum of copper work, displaying decorative, machine-made boxes, candleholders and plaques.

*P*int-sized relic of the Age of Steam at New Romney offers nostalgics a ride back into the past.

Railway Nostalgia

Britain's railways have been modernized, but you can still make wonderfully scenic trips by old-time steam trains in the land that gave birth to the railway.

BLUEBELL RAILWAY,
Horsted Keynes, Sussex
Runs 5 miles (8 km.) to Sheffield Park station.

BRECON MOUNTAIN RAILWAY,
Merthyr Tydfil, Wales
Travel a four-mile (6-km.) trajectory through Brecon Beacons National Park.

DART VALLEY RAILWAY, Devon
Scenic trip along River Dart from Buckfastleigh to Totnes.

KEIGHLEY AND WORTH VALLEY LIGHT RAILWAY, North Yorkshire
Five-mile (8-km.) trip from Keighley to Oxenholme, stopping at Haworth.

ROMNEY, HYTHE AND DYMCHURCH RAILWAY, Kent
Thirteen-mile (21-km.) run from New Romney to Dungeness lighthouse.

TALYLLYN RAILWAY, Wales
From Tywyn to Nant Gwernol, past waterfalls of Fathew Valley.

A Capital Place

London has more of everything—more traffic, more people, more litter, more contrasts, more variety, more excitement. Londoners revel in the cosmopolitanism, the ethnic diversity, the pace. For an Englishman "up" from the country, the capital is the place for shopping, the theatre, eating out. Tourists, of course, enthuse about London's Englishness, the historic aura, the civility, the quiet charm of garden squares and terraces. You'll probably start your trip in London, and if you don't you should. You'll gain valuable insights into Britain's past and present that will help you to put your subsequent travels into perspective. There's also a logistical reason for beginning here: road, rail and air routes all radiate from the capital.

It is perfectly possible to visit attractions in the South-East and parts of the South, East Anglia, Central England and the South-West from a base in London—Stonehenge, Bath, and Constable Country, for example. But don't do too many of these long day-trips. You'll find it more pleasant and less tiring to lodge locally and really get to know an area.

Big Ben is the name of the bell heard round the world, marking the hours in Greenwich Mean Time (or British Summer Time, in season). Beneath the belfry sprawls the Mother of Parliaments.

London
6 B–C2

London's role as Britain's capital is a relatively new one—the merger of England and Scotland did not occur till 1707—though the city has always had a certain importance. It developed from a Celtic outpost into the largest town in Roman Britain, becoming England's capital with the Norman Conquest in 1066. Even today, London retains a commercial, financial and cultural prominence out of all proportion to Britain's diminished post-imperial status.

The sheer size of London, the irregular pattern of the streets and the fact that so many sights are hidden from view make the city a difficult place to get to know. Try to find time your first day in town for an introductory bus tour. Once you've taken in the larger picture, you can set out to explore the different districts of London on foot.

Extravagant in every way, London has

not one but three distinct "centres". Westminster claims the Houses of Parliament and the abbey. The West End embraces theatreland, the exclusive shops of Mayfair and St. James's, Chinatown and Soho. And The City, London's business and financial hub, is the site of St. Paul's Cathedral and the Tower.

Westminster

London's hub is **Trafalgar Square,** a vast gathering place for tourists and pigeons. The name recalls the 1805 Battle of Trafalgar in which Lord Nelson defeated Napoleon's fleet off the Spanish coast. Nelson's statue tops the very tall Corinthian column in the centre of the square, his tricorne a sky-high perch for the birds.

Grand public buildings front onto the square. On the north side stands the **National Gallery,** Britain's great collection of European art (see p. 88), with the fine Baroque Church of St. Martin-in-the-Fields to the east. And on the south side, Admiralty Arch frames a magnificent view of **The Mall** (pronounced to rhyme with "pal"), the sweeping boulevard that edges **St. James's Park.** On a sunny day this patch of green lures civil servants from the neighbouring ministries of Whitehall.

Overlooking the park is a series of elegant houses: Carlton House Terrace, incorporating the Institute of Contemporary Arts; Marlborough House, where Commonwealth officials meet in conference; Clarence House, home of Queen Elizabeth the Queen Mother.

Clarence House adjoins the much older **St. James's Palace,** a maze of passages and courtyards reconstructed many times. From 1698 to 1837 this was a royal residence. Queen Victoria preferred Buckingham Palace, but even today foreign ambassadors are officially accredited to the Court of St. James.

Buckingham Palace, behind high iron railings, seems as solid and durable as the monarchy itself. Every palace should look like this, columned, porticoed,

expansive, with sentries at the gate. Constructed in 1703 for the Duke of Buckingham, the palace was remodelled by John Nash in 1825. The imposing façade clad in white Portland stone dates from 1913. When the sovereign is in residence, the royal standard flies overhead.

The palace proper is out of bounds to tourists, but you can visit the **Queen's Gallery,** where changing exhibitions highlight works of art from the fabulous royal collections. Enter from Buckingham Palace Road. Further up the street,

*T*he Changing of the Guard at Buckingham Palace
is the best free show in London. For a good view of the ceremony, take up
a position on the steps of the Victoria Memorial, opposite the palace gates.

the **Royal Mews** provides opulent stabling for the queen's horses. The ceremonial carriages they draw are on display in the Coach House.

Palace of Westminster

The Houses of Parliament occupy the building known as the Palace of Westminster, after the medieval royal residence that stood on this site. The original palace went up in flames in 1834, making way for the neo-Gothic extravaganza you see today. Sir Charles Barry (knighted for his efforts here) provided the bold rectangular plan, while the medieval detail inside and out is the inspired work of A.W.N. Pugin, Victorian apostle of the Gothic.

In the interests of security, tours of the complex have been suspended. However, the public is admitted to debates in the Commons and Lords. Join the queue after 6 p.m. Monday to Thursday and from 9.30 a.m. to 3 p.m. Friday.

Parliament meets from November to July, recessing at Christmas and Easter. The House of Commons sits from early afternoon to late evening Monday to Thursday (late morning to early afternoon Friday). The prime minister is on hand to answer members' questions on Tuesday and Thursday afternoons.

The House of Lords sits every afternoon, winding up earlier than the Commons. The Royal Gallery is reserved for the queen when she visits the Lords; the sovereign doesn't have the right to enter the Commons.

From Parliament Square you have a good view of **Westminster Hall,** a surviving element of the old Palace of Westminster masterfully grafted on to the new. (In this hall, former seat of the Law Courts, Guy Fawkes and Charles I stood trial.) But even more impressive is the river elevation, a counterpoint of pinnacles and spires, the square bulk of Victoria Tower balanced by the belfry that houses **Big Ben.** This 13½-ton bell strikes the hours with a chime known around the world. Strictly speaking, only the bell, and not the clock or the tower, is referred to as "Big Ben". The name recalls the rotund Sir Benjamin Hall, Commissioner of Works at the time the bell was cast in 1859.

Westminster Abbey

The abbey is Britain's coronation church, a royal mausoleum and a national shrine. Kings and queens lie buried here alongside eminent statesmen, soldiers and scientists, musicians and men of letters. The high altar has been the scene of every coronation for the last 900 years— and many a royal wedding. Westminster Abbey remains a house of worship: regular services take place on Sundays, when the highly regarded boys' choir sings.

There may have been an abbey at Westminster as early as the 7th century, but it was Edward the Confessor who laid the foundations for the church as we know it. In 1245, Henry III took Edward's creation and built it anew in grand Gothic style. Henry VII contributed the chapel that bears his name.

The West Door leads directly into the **nave,** a soaring stone vault that reaches impossibly high overhead. Moving down the aisle, you pass the tomb of that nameless World War I hero, the Unknown Warrior. Memorials to men of science— Faraday, Darwin and others—cluster around the tomb of Isaac Newton, nearby. **Statesmen's Aisle** in the north transept is the province of Disraeli, Peel

---

Changing of the Guard

Everyone should see London's premier tourist spectacular at least once. The guard changes year-round, weather permitting, in two different locations:

- At Buckingham Palace, in front of the main entrance, daily at 11.30 a.m. (alternate days in winter). The 30-minute show features a military band which parades from St. James's Palace down the Mall.
- In Whitehall, at the Horse Guards. The Household Cavalry, astride sleek black mounts, changes guard at 11 a.m. weekdays and 10 a.m. Sundays.

---

and Gladstone, while across the way in **Poet's Corner** lie Chaucer and Spencer, Dickens, Hardy and Browning.

The royal tombs lie apart in the area beyond the high altar. The **Chapel of Edward the Confessor** contains the shrine of the king-saint, canonized in 1161. Until the Reformation, pilgrims came here to meditate and confess their sins. On view in the chapel between enthronement ceremonies, the **Coronation Chair** gathers dust as casually as a family heirloom in an attic. Since 1308, every monarch has been crowned on this battered oak throne. Beneath the seat is the ancient Stone of Scone, a block of Scottish sandstone identified by romantics with Jacob's pillow. Edward I filched it from the Scots, whose coronation stone it was (see p. 257).

Further along, the **Chapel of Henry VII** is simply magnificent. Henry, the first Tudor king, commissioned this last great masterpiece of the Gothic as his final resting place. The uniquely English "Perpendicular" style of the architecture stresses the vertical, as the name suggests. At the head of the chapel repose Henry and his queen, Elizabeth of York. A constellation of royalty surrounds them: Elizabeth I, James I and his mother, Mary Queen of Scots, Charles II, William and Mary, Queen Anne.

Whitehall

This area of government buildings extends from Parliament Square to Trafalgar Square. The name derives from Henry VIII's defunct Palace of Whitehall and applies equally to the neighbourhood, its main thoroughfare, the civil servants who work here and the bureaucracy to which they belong.

Heading up Parliament Street from Parliament Square, you pass the imposing late 19th-century headquarters of the Treasury. Here, some 10 feet (3 m.) below ground, sprawl the **Cabinet War Rooms,** Churchill's high command post from 1940 (entrance at Clive Steps in

The Oldest Parliament

England had a parliament long before the country became a parliamentary democracy. As early as the 13th century, representatives of the whole country—nobles and burghers alike—came together to consult with the king, either at the Palace of Westminster or in the abbey opposite. By 1529, when Parliament took up permanent quarters at Westminster, the body had already divided into the Commons (spokesmen for the communes or shires) and Lords.

Today there are 650 Members of Parliament, elected to the Commons by universal suffrage. The House of Lords consists of about 1,100 members, both hereditary and life peers. The chamber reviews, and sometimes revises, bills sent up from the Commons. Peers also hold limited veto powers. Although there are occasional demands for abolition of the Lords, these have so far been rejected by the tradition-loving public.

King Charles Street). With the surrender of Japan, the door was literally closed on this chapter of British history, and the labyrinth of blast-proof rooms survived intact. You'll see the Transatlantic Telephone Room, where scramblers coded Churchill's calls to Roosevelt, and the Map Room, with charts plotting troop movements on the Russian front and developments in the Pacific theatre.

A few steps away is an address known around the world: **No. 10 Downing Street,** office and residence of Britain's prime ministers since 1735. Only visitors on official business may approach the unassuming doorway of No. 10.

Beyond this point, Parliament Street continues as Whitehall. Outstanding on this stretch, the **Banqueting House** of 1619 provides a gilded setting for court ceremony. The **Horse Guards,** opposite, maintain their traditional sentry posts at the entrance to the royal domain of St. James's. Housed in 18th-century elegance next door, the **Admiralty** commanded the world's greatest fleet.

East of Trafalgar Square, the **Strand** links Westminster to The City along a route opened in Edward the Confessor's time. It's a busy street of hotels, theatres

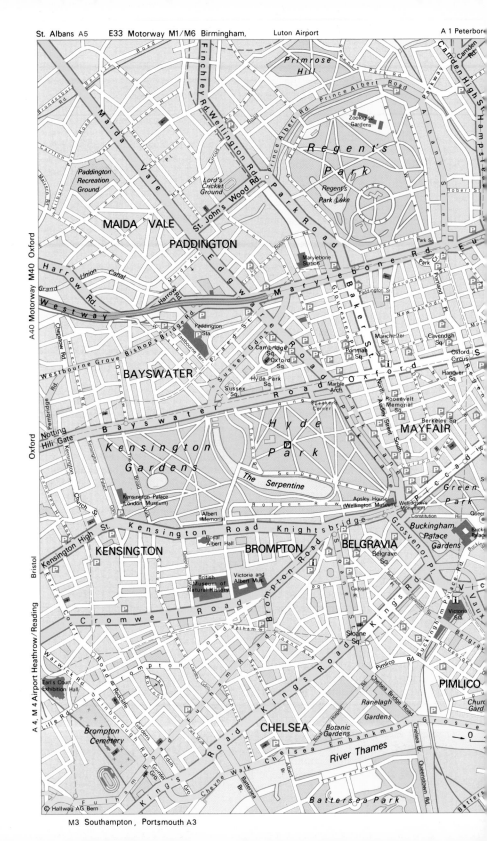

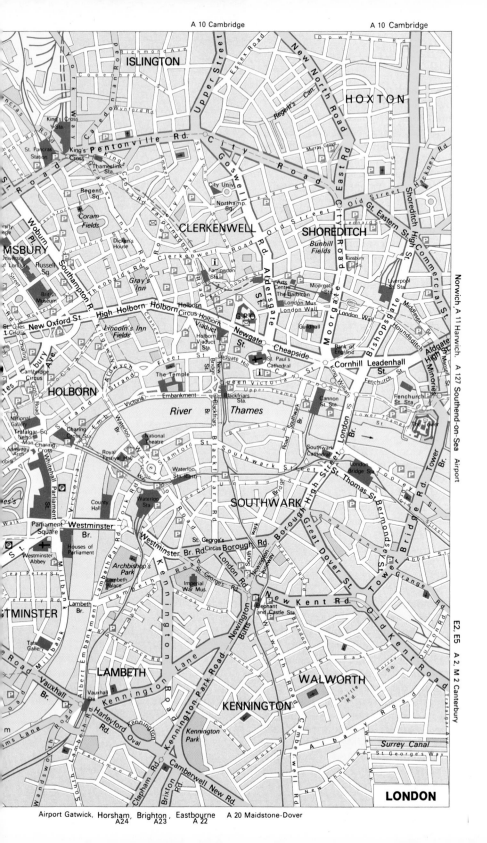

ISLINGTON

HOXTON

Richmond Ave.

Copenhagen

Wynford Rd.

King's Cross Sta.

St. Pancras Station

King's Cross

Pentonville Rd.

Thameslink Sta.

City Road

Regent Sq.

City Univ.

Northamp. Sq.

Coram Fields

Dickens House

CLERKENWELL

SHOREDITCH

Bunhill Fields

Gt. Eastern St.

Shoreditch High St.

Liverpool St. Sta.

MSBURY

University of London

Russell Sq.

British Museum

Southampton R.

Gray's Inn

Farringdon Sta.

Clerkenwell Road

Arts Centre

The Barbican

London Mus.

London Wall

Moorgate Sta.

Finsbury Sq.

New Oxford St.

High Holborn

Holborn Circus

Holborn

Viaduct

Newgate St.

Cheapside

Guildhall

London Wall

Moorgate

Bishopsgate

Houndsditch

Middlesex St.

Aldgate High St.

Minories

St. Giles Circus

Lincoln's Inn Fields

Holborn Viaduct Sta.

G.P.O.

St. Paul's Cathedral

Bank of England

Cornhill

Leadenhall St.

Fenchurch St.

Fenchurch St. Sta.

Cambridge Circus

HOLBORN

The Temple

Ludgate Hill

Queen Victoria

Upper Thames

King William

Cannon St. Sta.

London Bridge

Lower Thames St.

The Tower

National Gallery

Trafalgar Sq.

Nelson Mon.

Charing Cross

Charing Cross Sta.

Embankment

Blackfriars Sta.

River   Thames

Blackfriars Br.

Southwark Br.

Southwark Cathedral

London Bridge Sta.

Tooley St.

Tower Br.

Admiralty Arch

Whitehall

Royal Festival Hall

National Theatre

Waterloo Sta. (East)

St.

Southwark Street

Borough High St.

Bermondsey St.

County Hall

Waterloo Sta.

SOUTHWARK

St. Thomas St.

Grange Rd.

Parliament Square

Westminster Br.

St. George's

Borough Circus

Borough Rd.

Gt. Dover St.

Abbey St.

Houses of Parliament

Westminster Abbey

Westminster Br. Rd.

London Rd.

New Kent Rd.

Old Kent Rd.

TMINSTER

Archbishop's Park

Lambeth Palace

Imperial War Mus.

Elephant and Castle Sta.

Tate Gallery

Lambeth Br.

Kennington Lane

St. George's Rd.

Newington Butts

Walworth Road

Surrey Rd.

Vauxhall Br.

Vauxhall

Kennington Road

Kennington Park Road

LAMBETH

WALWORTH

Harleyford Rd.

Kennington Oval

Kennington

KENNINGTON

Kennington Park

Camberwell New Rd.

Clapham Rd.

Brixton Rd.

Albany Rd.

Surrey Canal

St. Georges Way

Norwich A 11 Harwich.   A 127 Southend-on-Sea   Airport

E2, E5   A 2, M 2 Canterbury

LONDON

and commercial premises, not a place for strolling. Watch the sights go by from the window of a bus: the smart Savoy Hotel, a monument to Art Deco, and 18th-century Somerset House, home of the **Courtauld Institute Galleries,** the small but select study collections of London University's prestigious school of art history.

Down on the Thames embankment, raised benches offer unimpeded views of the river, muddy and sluggish here. The obelisk by the water's edge is a 3,000-year-old Egyptian original from Heliopolis, dubbed **Cleopatra's Needle.** Hungerford Footbridge takes you across the Thames to the **South Bank** complex, a forbidding fortress of the arts. Don't let the grim exterior keep you away from the exhibitions at the Hayward Gallery or the Museum of the Moving Image, the National Film Theatre's retrospectives, the concerts at Festival Hall or the best of British theatre at the National Theatre.

The City of London
The City takes care of business—insurance, banking, commodities trading. Every working day, half a million commuters descend on London's compact commercial centre, an overnight ghost town of 5,000. The "Square Mile" extends from the boundary stone of Temple Bar in the Strand to the Tower of London, and from the Thames to the Barbican—the area originally within the Roman wall. Beyond Temple Bar, begins Fleet Street, an extension of the Strand.

Legal London
Hidden from view on either side of Fleet Street are the Inns of Court: the Temple, Lincoln's Inn and Gray's Inn. For members of the bar these venerable societies are a professional home for life.

Access to the **Temple** is through two narrow gatehouses near Temple Bar, one leading to Middle Temple and the other to Inner Temple. Originally the headquarters of the crusading Knights Templar (hence the name), the Temple has been associated with the legal profession

since the 14th century, first as a school of law and then as a professional society. Like the other Inns of Court, the complex comprises dining hall, chapel, gardens, offices and judges' lodgings.

Anyone may enter the Temple precinct, but most of the buildings are closed to sightseers. One exception is the round Norman Templar church, put up in 1185. In the old days, lawyers met their clients in the crypt.

Chancery Lane takes you past the Public Records Office to the gatehouse

76

*B*y river through Docklands, downstream from Tower
Bridge. Once the world's busiest port, Docklands is now Europe's biggest
building site. The old warehouses are being converted into residential
and commercial space and scores of new office complexes are shooting up,
along with property values.

77

of **Lincoln's Inn**, older even than the Temple. Notice the medieval diamond-patterned brickwork of the late 15th-century Old Hall, the oldest surviving structure in the compound. If you look into the windows of the New Buildings (a mere three centuries old), you'll see stacks of legal documents on the ledges, bound with the "red tape" that has become a synonym for bureaucracy in the English language.

At the bottom of Chancery Lane, across High Holborn, **Gray's Inn** is famous mainly for its gardens.

Make your way back to **Fleet Street,** a name that lives on as a metaphor for British journalism. None of the big national newspapers have offices here now. They've all transferred to new premises east of The City in Wapping. Not that the historical associations have gone

away. You can visit **Dr. Johnson's House** in Gough Square, and climb up to the attic room where the original Fleet Street hack compiled the first *Dictionary*. A museum in the crypt of **St. Bride's,** the old printers' church, chronicles the rise—and fall —of the industry in Fleet Street. Famous in its own right is the Wren sanctuary and wedding-cake steeple of St. Bride's.

Fleet Street comes to an end at Ludgate Circus. Ahead lies St. Paul's, a very visible landmark atop Ludgate Hill.

St. Paul's Cathedral
Christopher Wren had the privilege rarely granted a cathedral builder: after more than three decades of work on St. Paul's, he saw his design realized in 1708. The architect, then 75, lived on till the age of 90, to be buried at last inside the walls of the cathedral. The Latin epitaph on his tomb translates: "Reader, if you seek his monument, look around you."

Wren's cathedral is the third or fourth on this site. The even larger Gothic structure that came before it was destroyed in the 1666 Great Fire. Known as Old St. Paul's, it was preceded by a Romanesque house of worship that grew from Bishop Mellitus' church of 604.

Balance and clarity distinguish Wren's design for St. Paul's. The Gothic plan of a Latin cross harmonizes with the Classical dome and Baroque west towers. Among the outstanding elements: Grinling Gibbons' beautifully carved choir stalls, Jean Tijou's wrought-iron choir screen and gates, and the scenes from the life of St. Paul that cover the dome, painted by Sir James Thornhill.

St. Paul's has its quota of monuments and famous tombs: the outsize

*F*ire *destroyed Old St. Paul's, and Wren's masterpiece would have burned, too, but for the volunteers who kept a nightly vigil during the Blitz. On the night of December 29, 1940, buildings around St. Paul's were levelled, but the bucket brigade saved the cathedral.*

Wellington memorial, in the aisle to your left as you go in; the effigy of John Donne, in the choir aisle; and Nelson's monument, in the south transept. You'll see the stairs to the soaring dome nearby. It's an easy climb to the Whispering Gallery at the base of the drum. Put one ear to the wall and you can hear a whisper as it travels from the other side of the gallery, more than 100 feet (30 m.) away.

North of St. Paul's stands that concrete and brick colossus, the Barbican Arts and Conference Centre. The complex houses concert and exhibition halls, theatres, cinemas, a library and art gallery on eight levels—half of them underground. Not everyone raves about the architecture, but the standard of cultural offerings is high. Try to get tickets for a performance of the resident London Symphony Orchestra or Royal Shakespeare Company.

Approaching from St. Martin's le Grand, you enter the Barbican via the striking modern Museum of London. One of the largest exhibits stands outside in the grounds: a section of the medieval town wall, built on Roman foundations.

The Bank

The heart of London's financial district, referred to as "The Bank", centres on the complex of eight streets that converge outside the Bank of England, impregnable behind high, windowless walls. Security is of the essence: vaults within hold the nation's gold reserves. Needless to say, tourists are barred from the bank, but they are welcome in the museum adjacent, with historical exhibits and video displays (enter from Bartholomew Lane).

The Lord Mayor's official residence is Mansion House, the Renaissance-style palace across the way. A law court and prison cells are part of the original fixtures and fittings. North-west of the Bank, off Gresham Street, Guildhall is the town hall of The City. This resilient building of 1411 has withstood every disaster from the Great Fire to the Blitz.

Step inside (during office hours) for a look at the ancient Great Hall with its minstrel's gallery and Gothic stonework.

Shirtsleeves are replacing top hats at the computerized Stock Exchange, just east of the Bank in Throgmorton Street. The business has come a long way since its urbane beginnings in the 18th century. Guides initiate visitors into the mysteries of securities trading at "the House", as the exchange is known to insiders. In the visitor's gallery, an informative film is screened—like the deals made here—continuously.

Lloyd's of London, the international insurance underwriters, originated in a coffee house—Edward Lloyd's establishment near the Tower of London. Three centuries on, the society has expanded to high-tech premises in Leadenhall Street, designed by Richard Rogers of Pompidou Centre fame. Any working day, visitors are welcome to look the building over and observe members at work in the Underwriting Room.

The Tower

The Tower of London has been a fortress, palace, prison and place of execution for more than a thousand years. Among the celebrated victims: the sons of Edward IV (the "Little Princes in the Tower"), Henry VI, Anne Boleyn, Catherine Howard, Sir Thomas More, Sir Walter Raleigh... The fortifications are defended by Yeomen Warders—about 40 men in Tudor costume, halberds at the ready. Also known as Beefeaters, members of this detachment of royal bodyguards conduct free guided tours of the Tower (weather permitting).

Crossing the moat, grassed over last century, you pass into the outer enclosure with its display of cannon. The gloomy river entrance is known as Traitors' Gate. In the Bloody Tower opposite, the little Princes died and Raleigh languished. A passageway through the Bloody Tower opens onto the inner enclosure. Look for the scaffold site on the emerald lawn of Tower Green. The ravens you'll see flapping about have always nested within the walls. According to legend, the tower would collapse were they to fly away.

Straight ahead is the queue for the **Jewel House.** The line may seem dauntingly long, but it usually moves fairly quickly. Railings channel sightseers past displays of ceremonial silver and vestments—notice the splendid coronation robe—to the vault containing the **Crown Jewels.** Look out for St. Edward's Crown; the Imperial State Crown, paved with diamonds and precious stones; and the royal sceptre, set with the largest cut diamond in the world, the 530-carat *Star of Africa.*

Moving across the yard to the **White Tower,** you enter the oldest part of the fortification—now housing the **Royal Armouries,** one of the world's definitive collections of arms and armour. On an upper floor, **St. John's Chapel** has the distinction of being London's oldest church (1080) and its only Norman sanctuary.

East of the Tower is one of London's trademarks, **Tower Bridge.** This marvel of Victorian engineering in mock Gothic style conforms to every tourist's expectations of how old London town should look. Until the 1970s, the original hydraulic engines powered the control gear. You may want to have a look at the machinery in the **Engine Room Museum,** but the outstanding attraction is the **panorama** from the walkways—a vast view of the wide, smooth river and the high-rise City beside it.

East again, **St. Katharine Docks,** so hard hit by the Blitz, have reopened as a marina. The complex is part of the reviving **Docklands** area, an 8½-square-mile (22-sq.-km.) enterprise zone that extends along both banks of the Thames from the Tower to Greenwich. Once derelict, Docklands has become a desirable place to work, shop and live—in a converted warehouse, perhaps, or one of the futuristic tower blocks that are shooting up all over. New developments include Tobacco Dock and Butler's Wharf with shops, restaurants, offices and flats; the London Arena sports and entertainment centre; and London City Airport. Get there via Thames Line riverbus or the Docklands Light Railway.

West End

For suburbanites, visiting the West End is "going up to town". Focus for theatre, shopping and entertainment, this somewhat diffuse district claims the smart hotels, restaurants and clubs, with Piccadilly and Oxford Street for its main thoroughfares.

West End sightseeing begins in **Piccadilly Circus,** where city lights shine brightest. The celebrated traffic circle has been abolished to ease circulation into Shaftesbury Avenue and on to The City, and a pedestrian zone surrounds the Shaftesbury Memorial, improving access to the famous statue of **Eros** (1893) on its fountain pedestal.

Piccadilly Circus has always been a great gathering place. Now all the people have somewhere to go: the **London Pavilion,** a shopping and leisure centre on the north side of the Circus (home of Madame Tussaud's Rock and Pop attraction), and the neighbouring **Trocadero,** incorporating the "London Experience" multi-vision show, the Guinness World of Records exhibition, a Brass Rubbing Centre and the Imperial Collection of facsimile crown jewels. A few steps away in **Leicester Square** (pronounced "lester"), the big West End cinemas screen all the first-run hits, competing with 40 or more theatres scattered throughout the neighbourhood.

Busy **Piccadilly** links the Circus to Hyde Park Corner, exactly one mile (1½ km.) away. Among all the airline offices, restaurants, shops and hotels, the square brick tower of **St. James's, Piccadilly** stands out. Yet another Wren church—some would say his best—St. James's has a quiet dignity. It's the parish church of the **Royal Academy of Arts,** installed in Burlington House just across the way. The avant-garde may regret the

81

conservative stance of this august body, but everybody agrees that the Royal Academy puts on some of the best exhibitions in town.

Shopping is a consuming activity in Piccadilly's elegant arcades and department stores. Beadles in livery guard the entrance to **Burlington Arcade,** among the oldest (1819) and most exclusive of the capital's covered shopping promenades. Over the road at **Fortnum & Mason,** shop assistants in tail coats preside over purchases of caviar and quail's eggs in what must be the grandest grocery department in the world.

Beyond the arcades of the Ritz Hotel, **Green Park** parallels the south side of Piccadilly. On a Sunday, London's street artists make this stretch their pitch.

Piccadilly ends in greater style than it begins at Hyde Park Corner. **Apsley House,** the lone town house by the park, was once the westernmost residence in the city, known simply as No. 1, London. The Duke of Wellington moved in two years after Waterloo, and his descendants still keep a *pied-à-terre* here—so convenient for the West End. The lower floors house the **Wellington Museum** of Napoleonic memorabilia, with some exceptional Old Masters from the Wellesley family collections on view.

Across the way lie the crescents and squares of **Belgravia.** Not everyone can afford the rates (taxes) in this stately district, and many of the cream stucco houses now belong to foreign embassies and legations.

Mayfair

The aristocrat of London neighbourhoods, posh Mayfair lies to the north of Piccadilly, between Park Lane and Regent Street. All the elegant shops are here and the most exclusive clubs and casinos. **Bond Street,** Old and New, is the place to buy cashmeres, furs, jewellery, Old Masters, fine antiques. Bond Street leads London's art and antiques trade, bolstered by the presence of **Sotheby's,** the prestigious auction house. Galleries spill over into the surrounding streets—Cork, Albemarle, Grafton, Dover. And Mayfair's own **Museum of Mankind** is near at hand in Burlington Gardens. Running north from here, **Savile Row** outfits Britain's best-dressed men of affairs.

Of course, Mayfair also has its secluded residential streets—and a Mayfair address has undeniable cachet—but the squares are not the patrician compounds they were. Mostly modern buildings surround Berkeley (pronounced

*S*ummer in the city: suits and ties are no impediment
to a spot of sunbathing beside the Serpentine in London's Hyde Park.
And there's always a deck chair for hire.

"barkly") Square, where the cream of London society lived, and the United States has colonized Grosvenor (say "grovener") Square, site of the stridently modern American Embassy.

The large luxury hotels line **Park Lane**, no longer a lane but a very busy boulevard. West-facing rooms have a million-pound view of **Hyde Park** across the road, accessible by subway (pedestrian underpass). A path leads diagonally across the park to the Serpentine, an artificial lake, and Lido bathing beach. Another path parallel to Park Lane takes you to **Speaker's Corner**. This open space near Marble Arch echoes to unbounded eloquence on Sunday afternoons. Any orator who has a message—philosophical, religious, ideological, but rarely dull—can face the hecklers here.

Just behind Park Lane, an enclave of 18th-century Mayfair survives in **Shepherd Market**, an area of outdoor cafés, antique shops and boutiques. **Marble Arch**, at the north end of Park Lane, is the gateway to Oxford Street. John Nash designed the Neoclassical portal for Buckingham Palace in 1828. But Nash got his measurements wrong. Too narrow to admit the royal coach of state, Marble Arch had to be scrapped. Eventually it was set up here, on the site of Tyburn Tree, a place of public execution from the 12th to the 18th centuries.

Run the gauntlet of **Oxford Street** only if you're in the mood for some serious shopping in the big stores. Chain outlets show the way to Oxford Circus and the smart shopping precinct of **Regent Street**, with Garrard's, the crown jewellers, Hamley's giant toy emporium and Liberty's, renowned for its floral fabrics and half-timbered façade, a charming 1920s pastiche of the Tudor style. Regent Street continues north to Portland Place and **Regent's Park**, with its lake, canal and open-air theatre. **London Zoo** (see p. 89) occupies a triangle of land in the park.

The lower end of Regent Street curves east to Piccadilly Circus, following John Nash's stately street plan.

St. James's

Officers and gentlemen frequent St. James's, the area south of Piccadilly. Here in the heart of clubland you'll find the centuries-old wine merchants, barbers, hatters, shirtmakers and cobblers that cater to the most discerning masculine tastes.

The famous **clubs** line St. James's Street and Pall Mall. Don't look for a placard on the door—White's, Boodles, Brooks's and others turn an anonymous face to the world. The concept of an exclusive male meeting place evolved from the coffee house of the 18th century. Once there were as many as 150 clubs in St. James's, but the number has declined sharply this century. An anachronism in a modern world, the clubs still ban women by and large.

St. James's remains very much a male preserve. Even the art and antique dealers put the accent on the masculine, featuring sporting pictures, outsize leather armchairs and old meerschaum pipes. Focus for the art trade is Christie's, the auctioneers in King Street.

Soho

What the Pigalle area is to Paris, Soho is to London. Hard-drinking, hard-living, hard-core Soho is famous for its bohemian pubs, jazz clubs, ethnic restaurants, food shops and sex shops. You are, on the whole, relatively safe here—just use discretion in choosing the establishments you enter, especially after dark.

Cosmopolitan Soho developed in the 17th century, when Huguenot and Greek refugees flooded into London. A contingent of Frenchmen followed after the Revolution. Then came the Italians, Spanish and Chinese. The name "Soho" is an old hunting cry that goes back to the days when Londoners rode to hounds across the fields of Leicester. Now Leicester Square marks the southern boundary of the district.

Adjacent to the square is **Chinatown**, recently furnished with bilingual street signs, oriental gateways and pagoda-style phone boxes. Oblivious to the tourist trappings, the local community goes about its business—queueing up at the Hong Kong Cinema, dining out at the local restaurants. Have a meal at one of the busy establishments in Gerrard or Wardour streets to experience the neighbourhood at its authentic best.

Following Wardour Street across Shaftesbury Avenue into the heart of Soho, you pass the moody ruin of **St. Anne's Church** (1680), bombed in the Blitz and never restored. Continental bakeries, food shops and restaurants are scattered through the surrounding streets: Brewer, Old Compton, Frith and Greek.

Not far from Oxford Street and the book shops of Charing Cross Road, peaceful **Soho Square** isolates itself from the excitement, while **Carnaby Street**—that faded '60s mecca—stands aloof on the western fringes, just behind Regent Street. Fashion moved on a long time ago, but the tourists still keep coming.

Covent Garden

The new Covent Garden offers buskers (street entertainers) and bustle around the old market buildings vacated by London's fruit and vegetable sellers. Trendy shops have invaded the **Central Market** and surrounding streets, with stalls for crafts and clothing under cover and out on the Piazza. This is one area where you can browse and buy in the evenings and on Sundays. The wine bars and restaurants keep late hours, too, making Covent Garden a popular after-theatre rendezvous. The name is a corruption of "convent" garden, a reminder that the land was once cultivated by the monks of Westminster Abbey.

Inigo Jones's striking **St. Paul's** holds down the east side of the Piazza, the forecourt of the church an arena for street theatre. To the west, the former Flower Market accommodates the vintage tube trains and buses of the **London Transport Museum,** with room to spare for the exhibits of the **Theatre Museum.** Of course, the great cultural institution here is the

Royal Opera House, showcase for the Royal Opera and Ballet companies (box office in Floral Street).

Bloomsbury

This district evokes memories of London's early 20th-century literary life. Between the wars, the novelist Virginia Woolf, historian Lytton Strachey and art critic Roger Fry all lived and worked here. There are many pleasant squares and two internationally renowned institutions—the **British Museum** (see p. 88) and University of London.

London's Villages

Hundreds of villages have been woven into the urban fabric of London, each with its own high street and village green, its shops, pubs and local characters. We concentrate on three every tourist will want to explore.

Knightsbridge

Shoppers queueing for the bus by Knightsbridge Green, near Harrods, may not take that triangle of grass for the old common of Brompton village. The humble hamlet of 150 years ago has become one of London's most desirable residential neighbourhoods and a leading shopping centre.

Harrods, biggest of the big stores, grew up with Knightsbridge. Henry Charles Harrod opened his Brompton Road grocery business in 1849, building the present terracotta palace at the turn of the century. Much more than a store, Harrods is a national institution. The range of services is simply phenomenal: pharmacy, kennels, bank, pub, undertakers—Harrods has them all.

Beyond Harrods and its several fashion floors is diminutive **Beauchamp Place** (pronounced "beechum"), the former village high street—now a street of high-fashion shops. Brompton Road and Sloane Street, the main shopping arteries, converge beyond the green with Knightsbridge, the wide avenue that parallels Hyde Park.

*P*otted plants relish the wintry sun in a Chelsea
mews. A generation ago, only Bohemians lived in these converted stables
or garages. Now lavish renovations make mews houses fashionably
unaffordable, especially in the alleys of the best neighbourhoods.

The tumult of **Kensington High Street** begins beyond the palace gates. Chain stores dominate the high street, with white stucco terraces and gardens of tangled greenery behind. There's only one avenue to explore: **Kensington Church Street,** an address known to antique collectors the world over.

Down in South Kensington—"South Ken" for short—a complex of four major **museums** draws the crowds to the busy junction of Exhibition, Brompton and Cromwell roads. The decorative arts collections of the **Victoria and Albert Museum** occupy the Renaissance-style brick building, with the Natural History Museum in all its neo-Romanesque splendour opposite, adjacent to the more functional premises of the Science and Geological museums. These temples to the Victorian gods of Art and Science are larger than any cathedral. Even in a less reverent age, they still inspire awe.

Chelsea

This is London's global village. Chelsea sets the trends and the world follows. The mod look, the punk craze, the romantic revival—whatever's next, you'll see it first in the **King's Road,** main street of Chelsea. Tourists beat a path from Sloane Square to the river by way of Christopher Wren's sprawling **Royal Hospital,** a dominant Chelsea landmark since the 17th century. Charles II founded this retirement home for old and disabled soldiers with veterans of the Civil War in mind. Some 400 pensioners live here today. The hospital's vaulted chapel and Great Hall (the pensioners' mess hall) are open to visitors most mornings and afternoons. A small museum in the grounds traces the history of the institution.

Between the hospital and Chelsea Embankment, the well-tended lawns of Ranelagh Gardens provide the setting for Britain's most fashionable flower show every spring, while the modern building on the far side of the hospital houses the **National Army Museum.**

Kensington

Genteel Kensington skirts the rambling red brick palace where the Prince and Princess of Wales reside. And the "Royal Borough of Kensington and Chelsea" lets the fact be known. **Kensington Palace** is one royal establishment open to the public. You can tour the historic State Apartments, occupied by kings and queens from William and Mary to Victoria, and walk out around the grounds, a pleasant expanse of public parkland better known as **Kensington Gardens.**

Museums

British Museum
(Great Russell Street, WC1).
This vast storehouse of culture originated in Sir Hans Sloane's 18th-century "Cabinet of Curiosities", with its fossils, coins and classical antiquities. The collection divides into eight sections: the art of classical Greece, ancient Egypt and Western Asia, treasures from Roman Britain and medieval Europe, oriental objects, coins and medals, prints and drawings. Don't even attempt to cover every area; concentrate on two or three—or simply seek out the following highlights:

Elgin Marbles, 5th century B.C. Friezes and figures from the Parthenon in Athens.

Portland Vase, 1st century B.C. Roman cameo glass.

Khorsabad Entrance. Colossal gateway of 710 B.C. from the royal citadel of the Assyrian King Sargon II.

Rosetta Stone. Key to the deciphering of Egyptian hieroglyphics.

Mummies. Humans *and* animals, from crocodiles to cats.

Sutton Hoo Treasure, 7th century. Treasures from the burial ship of King Raedwald of the Angles.

Prints and Drawings. The complete engraved and etched works of Schongauer, Dürer, Rembrandt. Drawings by Michelangelo, Rubens, Watteau.

Manuscripts and Printed Books. Magna Carta, Gütenberg Bible, Shakespeare's First Folio.

Reading Room. Where Karl Marx wrote *Das Kapital.*

National Gallery
(Trafalgar Square)
From a group of 38 paintings purchased for the nation from the estate of the banker John Julius Angerstein in 1824, the collection has grown to more than 2,000, including many landmarks in the history of Western European art. Some highlights:

Masaccio. His very human *Virgin and Child* of 1426.

Piero della Francesca. The timeless *Baptism of Christ* and joyous *Nativity,* an unfinished late work.

Botticelli. The *Mystic Nativity* of 1500, so full of grace and movement.

Leonardo da Vinci. *Virgin of the Rocks* and cartoon of the *Virgin and Child with St. Anne and St. John the Baptist*—shot at by a madman and expertly restored.

Giovanni Bellini. A striking portrait of *Doge Leonardo Loredano.*

Titian. *Noli Me Tangere, Portrait of a Man* and the wonderfully stagey *Bacchus and Ariadne.*

Peter Paul Rubens. The *Judgment of Paris,* all rosy, rippling, opalescent flesh.

Jan van Eyck. That minutely observed portrait of a marriage, *Giovanni Arnolfini and his Wife.*

Hans Holbein the Younger. *The Ambassadors,* a complex allegorical work.

Rembrandt. Two self-portraits, painted three decades apart, and a loving portrayal of Hendrickje Stoffels as the *Woman Bathing in a Stream.*

Thomas Gainsborough. *Mr. and Mrs. Andrews,* a masterpiece of 18th-century portraiture, and *Morning Walk.*

John Constable. His *Haywain, Cornfield* and *Salisbury Cathedral* capture the very essence of the countryside.

Turner. The great *Rain, Steam and Speed.*

Diego Velázquez. *Rokeby Venus,* the artist's only nude.

Tate Gallery
(Millbank, SW1)
The Tate is several museums in one: a collection of British art, a Turner museum, gallery of modern painting and sculpture, and showcase for "new art".

Some **British** highlights: the Hogarths, especially *Painter and His Pug;* the sporting pictures of George Stubbs; Blake's colour prints for the *Divine Comedy* and *Job;* Constable's virtuoso landscape prints; the Pre-Raphaelites.

The **Turners** (on show in the Clore Gallery): *Snow Storm: Hannibal and his*

Army Crossing the Alps; Venice with Salute; Norham Castle.

The **moderns**, from Picasso's *Three Dancers* of 1925 to Carl Andre's *Equivalent VIII* (1966).

Attractions

Madame Tussaud's
(Marylebone Road, NW1)
A London tradition since 1835, the ever-popular waxworks offers some enjoyable moments of high kitsch. You'll see the diarist Samuel Pepys at his desk, Mary Queen of Scots preparing for her execution, and a startling Sleeping Beauty on her bed. Photo opportunities abound in the Gallery of the Famous, where you're invited to "picture yourself" with celebrities from Picasso to Gaddafi. The famous Chamber of Horrors is very dark and very crowded. Hang on to your money in the mob.

Highgate Cemetery
(Swain's Lane. Tube to Archway, then bus 271 or 210)
To visit the historic western section, the "Valhalla of the Victorians", you have to join one of the free, hour-long tours run every day. Guides lead the way to the graves of personalities as diverse as George Cruft, founder of London's annual dog show, and Robert Addis, the toothbrush tycoon. The most famous grave, that of Karl Marx, lies across the road in the modern eastern part, open all day long. Inevitably, his monument urges: "Workers of all Lands Unite".

London Zoo
(Regent's Park, NW1)
About 8,000 animals live and breed here. Deer and antelope roam an open paddock, and lions stalk modern moated terraces, while rhinos and elephants are at home in a spacious free-form brick pavilion. Have a look, too, at some of the historic installations: the original Regency camel house with its square clock tower, now an information centre, and the 1930s penguin pool.

Environs of London

Greenwich
(London SE10)   7 C2
Approaching from the water you see Greenwich at its best, the twin domes of the Royal Naval College framing the white cube of Queen's House. Hard by the pier rises the spindly mast of the clipper *Cutty Sark* (1869). Nearby is *Gypsy Moth IV*, the ketch that took Sir Francis Chichester on his solo journey around the world in the 1960s.

It's an uphill climb from the pier to the **Old Royal Observatory**. Established in 1675, the observatory functioned here until smog and city lights forced the scientists out into the countryside in the 1930s. They left behind a historic collection of instruments, including the telescope used by Edmund Halley to sight his comet. A strip of brass in the courtyard marks 0° Longitude. The Greenwich Meridian was officially adopted in 1884 as the prime meridian.

Downhill, the **National Maritime Museum** presents the history of British seafaring from sail to steam. The West Wing has the most interesting exhibits, including a flotilla of **royal barges** (the boats that slipped down the Thames to the strains of Handel's *Water Music*) and the **Nelson relics,** above all the blood-stained uniform from Trafalgar.

An arcade runs from the West Wing past **Queen's House** (notable for its Palladian architecture) to the East Wing, where you'll find exhibits on Britain's navy and life at sea.

The **Royal Naval College** occupies the historic Baroque buildings of the Royal Naval Hospital, set dramatically at the water's edge. Both Prince Charles and Prince Andrew attended this training school for officers.

Kew Gardens
(Kew, Surrey)
A visit here is a delight in or out of lilac time. Officially the Royal Botanic Gar-

dens, with 50,000 species of plants from all over the world, Kew fulfills its scientific purpose in a setting of sheer beauty. It was thanks to the pioneering botanists of Kew that the breadfruit took root in the West Indies, and the rubber plant in Malaysia. Even today Kew remains one of the world's major experimental centres. Whatever your botanical interests, you'll want to see the period glasshouses: John Nash's classical **Aroid House,** enclosing a mini tropical rainforest, and Decimus Burton's mid-19th-century **Palm House,** damaged in a freak 1987 hurricane and now restored. That storm toppled some of Kew's rarest hardwood trees, including specimens dating back to the gardens' early 18th-century beginnings. But the scars are slowly healing, and the rhododendron dell, bamboo and azalea gardens are as lovely as ever.

Hampton Court Palace
(Hampton Court, Middlesex)
This red-brick Tudor mansion lies 12 miles (20 km.) upstream from London. Built in 1515 by Cardinal Wolsey, it was appropriated by Henry VIII 15 years later when Wolsey fell from favour. Henry liked Hampton Court so much that he spent all his honeymoons here but one—the first. Catherine of Aragon got a look in all the same. She and Henry were Wolsey's first guests.

Among later monarchs, only William and Mary shared Henry's enthusiasm for the place. They asked Wren to build a new suite of rooms—but the popularity of their creation ended with George II. Queen Victoria finally opened Hampton Court to the public in 1838. In the meantime, crown pensioners had begun to occupy "grace and favour" accommodation on the premises. It was one such lodger who started the fire that spread unchecked in 1985, devastating the Wren wing, including the King's Audience Chamber, Cartoon Gallery and adjacent rooms—all closed for long-term restoration.

You enter the palace through the Great

Gatehouse, leading to Base Court and Anne Boleyn's Gateway. Continue into Clock Court, where the sun revolves briskly around the earth in Nicolas Oursin's astronomical clock of 1540—oblivious to the Copernican revolution. From here you go inside, your route through the palace depending on the building works in progress.

The interior offers the contrast of William and Mary's carved, gilded and upholstered **State Apartments** (separate but equal), with the timber-and-plaster

*P*rincess Augusta, mother of George III, set aside part
of the grounds of Kew Palace to encourage experiments in cultivation.
From 18th-century beginnings the Botanical Gardens grew. Today, some
300 acres (121 ha.) contain more than 25,000 species of trees and plants.
Something beautiful is always blooming all year round.

91

Tudor rooms: **Wolsey's Closet,** a study faced with fine linenfold panelling; Henry VIII's Haunted Gallery (haunted by the ghost of Catherine Howard); and the **Great Hall,** where king and court ate, drank and made merry.

⚑ Windsor Castle
(Windsor, Berks.)   6 B2

Picturesque in the extreme, the world's largest occupied castle sprawls atop a bluff beside the Thames. The walled precinct divides into a lower, middle and upper ward, dominated by the chess-piece Round Tower of 1170. Additions were made piecemeal through the centuries, notably St. George's Chapel (1478-1511) and the luxurious State Apartments, begun by Charles II.

As you enter the complex through the main gateway, **St. George's Chapel** lies straight ahead. This triumphant example of the Perpendicular style ranks on a par with Henry VII's Chapel in Westminster Abbey. The West Window (1509) portrays kings and queens of England in a blaze of stained glass, including the reigning monarch, King Henry VIII. On his death in 1547, Henry was buried in a vault below the floor of the chapel. Edward IV and Charles I are also entombed here, as well as more recent kings and queens, beginning with George III.

A garden grows in the moat encircling the Round Tower. Further on is a passage leading to the **State Apartments** in the upper ward. Official functions still take place in St. George's Hall, the Waterloo Chamber and certain other rooms —decorated throughout with carved and gilded furniture from England and France, Gobelins tapestries, exceptional paintings by Rubens and Van Dyck, and Antonio Verrio's ceiling scenes.

This section of the palace is closed when the queen is in residence, but it doesn't really spoil a visit if you can't go in, there's so much else to see at Windsor—**Queen Mary's Dolls' House,** to start with. Don't dismiss this charming period piece as a thoroughbred toy. Con-ceived specifically to raise money for a children's charity, the house was commissioned by the queen from the outstanding architect of her day, Sir Edwin Lutyens, and its contents from the leading manufacturers and designers, including the Wedgwood china and Hoover—a tiny working model. The **Exhibition of Drawings** next door features art from the queen's comprehensive collection of Old Masters—Michelangelos, Leonardos, Holbeins.

The small shops near Castle Hill are worth a wander, and there's the neighbouring township of Eton to see. A footbridge leads from Thames Street across the river to the quadrangles of **Eton College,** the most private of England's public schools.

Whipsnade Park Zoo
(near Dunstable, Beds.)   6 B1

A pioneering institution run by London Zoo, Whipsnade was one of the first zoos to dispense with cages. The animals here—wild horses, white rhinos, deer, gazelle—have the freedom of expansive modern paddocks and enclosures. Ride through the African section on the narrow-gauge Whipsnade and Umfolozi Steam Railway, a vintage train that originally operated in Zululand.

Woburn Abbey
(Woburn, Beds.)   8 B3

Commercialization detracts only a little from Woburn's stately appeal. Designed by Henry Flitcroft with additions by Henry Holland, the 18th-century house occupies the site of a Cistercian monastery. Three wings surround a central courtyard, echoing the layout of the old cloisters. A fourth wing of the building was lost to dry rot in 1950, an event that inspired the Duke of Bedford's entry into the stately home business. A tour of the house is only the beginning of a visit to Woburn, a vast leisure complex incorporating a safari park, the **Wild Animal Kingdom.** Various restaurants, gift shops and an antiques centre (nominal admission fee) generate the additional revenue needed to keep Woburn in trim.

The Marquess of Tavistock, the Duke of Bedford's heir, makes his home at Woburn. He and his family occupy the **Private Apartments** in the north wing, closed to the public when the family is in residence. The Tavistocks live in the grand manner, dining in style in the **Canaletto Room** when they number more than six. The china is Sèvres (a gift to a ducal ancestor from Louis XVI), and the 21 views of Venice are priceless Canalettos.

The **State Rooms** (west wing) have gilded Rococo ceilings, silk wall coverings and, in the Chinese Room, wallpaper imported from China some 250 years ago. Reserved for royal visits—Queen Victoria and Prince Albert came to stay in 1841—these rooms were hardly ever used, which explains the superb condition of the upholstery and decoration.

Focal point of the remaining wing is Henry Holland's sumptuous **library** of 1790. Above the bookcases hang portraits—by Rembrandt and Van Dyck, no less.

Luton Hoo

(Luton, Beds.) 6 B1

A succession of distinguished architects worked on this house, beginning with Robert Adam and ending with Robert Smirke. And the park bears the stamp of the ubiquitous Capability Brown. But it's the contents that steal the show. South African diamond magnate Sir Julius Wernher and his son, Sir Harold, assembled most of the art objects on display: medieval ivories, Limoges enamels and some exceptional paintings by Franz Hals, Hobbema, Memling and Bartolomé Bermejo (an earthy *St. Michael*). Among many impressive Italian Renaissance bronze statuettes, a *St. John the Baptist* by Sansovino stands out. The superb Fabergé jewellery came to Luton Hoo through Sir Julius's marriage to a Russian aristocrat, the granddaughter of Alexander Pushkin.

Waddesdon Manor

(near Aylesbury, Bucks.) 6 B1

Baron Ferdinand de Rothschild fulfilled a life-long ambition when he built his dream house, a Renaissance-style château, levelling a hill and importing half-grown trees to plant on the site. The architecture, the setting and the interior, with authentic Rococo *boiseries* (carved wood panelling) couldn't be more French. The furniture bears the maker's marks of the incomparable Cresson and Riesener, there's some magnificent Sèvres porcelain and paintings by Watteau and Boucher. The baron never ran out of energy or money as a collector. Consequently his house overflows with furniture and objects. There's far too much for an ordinary mortal to take in on a first visit. Sooner or later you'll feel like escaping into the grounds for fresh air and a view of uncluttered horizons. Look out for the 19th-century aviary stocked with rare birds, and the small herd of Japanese Sika deer.

Hatfield House

(Hatfield, Herts.) 6 B1

Queen Elizabeth I was reading under an oak tree in the park at Hatfield when she received the news of her accession to the throne. Only a section of Old Palace, her childhood home, survives. Robert Cecil, 1st Earl of Salisbury and prime minister to King James I, demolished most of the building in 1608 to make way for a new house in the fashionable Jacobean style. A visit to Hatfield concentrates on the imposing residence of the Cecils, with its wood-panelled **Great Hall,** grand Renaissance **staircase** and separate **state apartments** for the king and queen. Mementoes of Elizabeth I range from two famous portraits to the queen's silk stockings and gardening hat.

The remaining wing of the Elizabethan Old Palace, situated in what are now known as the West Gardens, provides a suitably historic venue for **medieval banquets,** complete with minstrel, serving wenches and mead.

BRITISH ART

Turner's Music Party

Millais' An Enemy Sowing Tares

European art at the time of the Tudors was an international affair, with painters travelling from one country to work for the kings and courts of others. A number of foreign artists found employment in England, among them **Hans Holbein the Younger** (1407–1543). But Holbein's art had its roots in the German realist tradition. More distinctively English was the work of miniaturist **Nicholas Hilliard** (1547–1619), who painted tiny, jewel-like portraits of courtly gentlemen in a country setting.

Little more than a hundred years later, England in the period of *The Beggar's Opera* combined an elegance and squalor that **William Hogarth** (1697–1764) catches perfectly. Genuine moral outrage informs the grisly black humour of *Gin Lane, Marriage à la Mode* (National Gallery, London) and other Hogarth works, including his masterpiece, *The Rake's Progress* (Sir John Soane's Museum, London). Designed to be engraved, Hogarth's incisive Neoclassical pictures belong to a tradition of English satirical graphics that continues through the florid lampoons of **James Gillray** (1757–1815) and the Dickensian quirkiness of **George Cruikshank** (1792–1879).

After the cynical polish of the 18th century, the years around 1800 saw the rise of Romanticism. The poetry of Wordsworth and Coleridge exemplifies the more spiritual and rural tendencies of the movement, which found artistic expression in the sublime landscape—evocative paintings of lakes, cliffs and mountains by James Ward, John Martin and others. But perhaps the greatest Romantic artist was the highly individual visionary, **William Blake** (1757–1827). As much a poet as a painter, Blake used his mastery of dynamic line and colour to illustrate his own hand-made books of poetry (of which the Tate Gallery, London, has a beautifully displayed collection). His art features such subjects as roses, fruit trees, lambs and angels in a pastoral setting. Yet despite this typical Romanticism—for Romanticism was in part a reaction against the increasingly ugly and prosaic world of the Industrial Revolution—Blake himself was a confirmed Londoner who lived in Soho and rarely travelled outside the city. He turned back, on one famous outing, when he reached the spot where London Zoo now is, believing that the country air would do him harm.

John Constable (1776–1837) and the

idea of the English countryside are inextricably linked. Constable's pictures of Suffolk were boldly revolutionary in their attempt to show the natural world as it actually looks—a celebrated example is *The Haywain* of 1821 (National Gallery, London)—capturing the light and feel of the English countryside, just as the French Impressionists would do for their own landscape several decades later. His practice of using points and dabs of white paint to create light effects—the sparkle of a brook or wet foliage, for example—is absolutely faithful to the eye's experience of the outdoors, but it was ridiculed in his day as "Constable's Snow".

The work of **J.M.W. Turner** (1775–1851), on the other hand, is much more Romantic than Constable's, and his magnificent symphonies of colour and light, sometimes only loosely and inspirationally based on a recognizable scene, have something of the grandeur of Beethoven. The *Fighting Téméraire, 1838* (National Gallery, London) conveys an airy and dramatic nostalgia as the sun sets on a great timber ship, symbol of an earlier age, brought to its last berth by a stocky little steam tug.

Later in the 19th century a continuing idealism prevailed among the painters of the Pre-Raphaelite Brotherhood, most notably **John Everett Millais** (1829–96), **Dante Gabriel Rossetti** (1828–82) and **William Holman Hunt** (1827–1910). These painters sought to counter the harsh and often shoddy aspects of the age of Dickens with a purity, beauty and fidelity to nature that they believed existed in the Middle Ages and the early Renaissance (before Raphael (before the 16th century), from which they took their inspiration and their name. The hyper-real and finely detailed pictures, such as Millais' *Ophelia* of 1852 and Holman Hunt's *Our English Coasts* of the same year (both Tate Gallery, London), typically focussing on women and nature, show the same arduous attention to detail which characterized Britain in the reign of Victoria—here turned to the pursuit of aesthetic excellence.

Unlike the French, the British are not by temperament theoretical or intellectual. Thus 20th-century British art has stayed slightly outside such prevailing movements as Cubism or international abstraction, concentrating rather, as it always has, on the human body and the real world, especially the countryside.

Henry Moore (1898–1986), a Yorkshire miner's son, united both preoccupations in his monolithic sculptures of the female nude, which may go some way towards accounting for his phenomenal success. The harsh and unruly landscapes of his childhood gave him a deep respect for the integrity of his materials, and he even verges on abstraction in his relentless pursuit of their true nature.

The 20th-century painter with the most uncompromising vision of the body must be **Francis Bacon** (born 1909), leading member of the figurative and physical School of London, whose work lives up to the meatiness of his name. His awesomely raw and howling pictures (*Three Figures and a Portrait,* 1975, Tate Gallery, London), like the plays of Samuel Beckett, express all the despair of the human condition.

In contrast to Bacon, **David Hockney** (born 1937) has been accused by some critics of blandness. After the Pop-Art irony of his early output, the more recent work of this flamboyant and colourful character seems highly civilized in a distinctly contemporary way *(A Bigger Splash,* 1967, Tate Gallery, London). Hockney wears his considerable technical skill and knowledge of art history lightly to create a vision of a modern good life without national boundaries.

Figure I *by Francis Bacon*

White Cliffs Country

The South-East has always been Britain's gateway. The English Channel is at its narrowest here, tempting swimmers—and invaders—across. Celts and Romans, Angles, Saxons and Normans all made it to shore, but Napoleon and Hitler only dreamed about storming the island fortress. The motorway and rail lines linking London to the coast extend like tentacles from the octopus of the capital. Head out of the city on any route to discover peaceful countryside and the rolling beauty of the Downs. The hills end abruptly at the Kent and Sussex shorelines, where high chalk cliffs drop down to the sea. The white cliffs are still a potent symbol, not only of the South-East, but of all England. Sighting them, Eurotourists know they've arrived.

Kent

The county takes its name and boundaries from the 6th-century Saxon kingdom. This is the "Garden of England", an area of orchards, vineyards and the hop plants essential to beer-making. Kent also encompasses a historic coastline, where resorts and ports alternate with castles and forts.

Canterbury has been a tourist town since the days of Chaucer's pilgrims. Cradle of English Christianity, the medieval cathedral is still the focal point of a visit.

Canterbury   7 D2

In the Middle Ages, all roads led to Canterbury and its cathedral, the site of St. Thomas Becket's shrine. Chaucer's pilgrims made the journey from Southwark, now a borough of London, nearly 60 miles (100 km.) away. Other penitents followed the Pilgrim's Way across the North Downs from Winchester.

The cathedral is the centrepiece of the old town, still partially enclosed by medieval walls. Though wartime bombs tore the heart out of the city, many ancient buildings survive. Were the Wife of Bath to return today she would be able to find her way from **West Gate** along the cobblestones of St. Peter's and High streets to narrow **Mercery Lane,** the traditional approach to the cathedral precinct. Modern pilgrims enter through the archway of **Christ Church Gate,** built of the same buff-coloured stone as the cathedral.

Canterbury (Durovernum Cantiacorum to the Romans) looks back on at least 2,000 years of history. This was a royal capital of the Saxons long before Thomas the Martyr brought the city fame and wealth (see p. 22). Even had Becket never lived, Canterbury would have been revered as the cradle of English Christianity. In 597 a monk called Augustine landed here to convert the people. He established his see and founded **Canterbury Cathedral.**

This great example of the Gothic illustrates the evolution of the style, from the earthbound magnificence of the Early English choir to the lofty grace of the Perpendicular nave and Bell Harry tower. Like the architecture, the stained-glass windows are outstanding, but it's the Becket connection that brings most people to Canterbury.

Everybody wants to see the **martyrdom site,** directly across from the cathedral entrance in the north-west transept. A stone slab marks the place where the archbishop fell. His shrine at the cathedral's east end was destroyed on Henry VIII's orders in 1538. Now a lighted candle in Trinity Chapel keeps the memory of St. Thomas alive.

The old houses and inns around the cathedral recall the heyday of the pilgrimage circuit, when Chaucer's band set out. And that's the theme of the Pilgrim's Way tourist "experience" (St. Margaret's Street), touted all over the city.

A short drive east takes you to **Whitstable** and the sea. Try to visit this fishing town in a month with an "r": Whitstable means oysters and the harbourfront pubs that serve them. Canterbury's historic port, Whitstable occupied a strategic site on the stretch of coast known to the Romans as the Saxon Shore. The ruined Roman fort at nearby **Reculver** is a landmark on Kent's coastal footpath, the Saxon Shore Way.

Margate doesn't make the best introduction to the British seaside. The wide sand beach, seafront hotels and "prom" (promenade) are all here, along with the traditional fun fair on the "front". But the crowds have been diverted—by package flights to Greece and the costas of Spain. Local residents are looking for ways and means of enhancing Margate's appeal: watch this space for future developments.

Charles Dickens' **Bleak House** puts neighbouring **Broadstairs** on the tourist map. The cliff-top house, one of several holiday residences rented by the writer, was named after the book and not the other way around. But the name is apt all the same, since the house inspired the novel. A competing attraction, the **Dickens House Museum** on the seafront displays a small collection of Dickensiana.

Cinque Ports 7 D2

Attractive **Sandwich** has enough old world charm for two towns. The streets are narrow and medieval and the houses suitably half-timbered. Sandwich's designation as a Cinque (pronounced "sink") Port dates back to the 13th-century reign of Edward I, when five towns on the south-east coast received special privileges from the Crown in exchange for "ship service"—the provision of warships and men. Sandwich's harbour later silted up, and 2 miles (3 km.) now intervene between the sea and the town's riverside quay.

The Big Bore

Bridge, causeway, tunnel—you name it and someone has proposed to build it across the English Channel between Britain and France. So many projects have failed to get off the ground over the years that people seem to be waiting for the latest scheme to come to nothing. Can the "Chunnel" succeed? The Eurotunnel consortium of British and French companies clearly thinks so.

The system they're constructing will ferry cars on trains in dual tunnels, one for east- and the other for west-bound traffic. Travel time between Folkestone, England, and Sangatte, France, is estimated at 35 minutes. Claustrophobes and short-haul ferry operators are already beginning to put a brave face on the future. With a projected completion date of 1993 on the horizon, it's beginning to look like "when" rather than "if".

Inland, too, is **Richborough**, the place where the invading Romans probably landed in A.D. 43. The conquerors knew the importance of fortifying the site: **Richborough Castle** incorporates the remains of formidable Roman defences.

By the 14th century, most of the towns between Sandwich and Hastings had joined the Cinque Ports confederation. Waterfront **Deal** was no exception. Once famous for its dockyard, Deal has a strip of steeply shelving beach but no harbour: ships drop anchor in the sheltered Downs offshore. It was here that Julius Caesar's historic raiding party reconnoitred in 55 B.C. The Romans finally waded to shore somewhere in the vicinity of Deal.

It's an easy walk to **Walmer Castle**, a couple of miles south along the Saxon Shore Way. The Tudor fort is the official residence of the Lord Warden of the Cinque Ports, an honorary post held since 1980 by Queen Elizabeth, the Queen Mother. Recently the Queen Mum remarked that she had yet to receive the spoils of shipwreck that traditionally accompany the title. In the old days the Lords Warden grew rich on booty, so many ships broke up on the treacherous shoals of Goodwin Sands, 4 miles (6 km.) out.

Have you been wondering where those long-distance swimmers start their cross-Channel marathons? **St. Margaret's Bay**, off the Dover Road at the end of the B2058, is the time-honoured spot. Here, at the Strait of Dover, the English Channel narrows to a mere 17 miles (27 km.), bringing England and France within firing range. During World War II, German buzz bombs launched from the Boulogne coast homed in on targets around **Dover.** Though the city suffered extensive damage in this and other attacks, the Norman castle, adjacent Saxon church and Roman lighthouse still stand, and there are, as the wartime song promised, "bluebirds over the White Cliffs of Dover". At low tide you can walk west along the beach to **Shakespeare Cliff,** a 350-foot (107-m.) shaft of chalk identified with a scene from *King Lear.* Or head out across the heights any time, suspended between sea and sky.

The main business of Dover and neighbouring **Folkestone** is ferrying passengers across the Channel. Business on the boats will decline sharply come 1993, when the Channel Tunnel is due to open (see box). For a sneak preview of the world's longest undersea passage, visit the **Eurotunnel Exhibition Centre** on the western outskirts of Folkestone, near Junction 12 of the M20. A viewing platform overlooks the hectic building site.

Six miles (10 km.) from Folkestone's construction crews, **Hythe** is another old Cinque Port with charm. Go for a ride on the pint-sized Romney, Hythe and Dymchurch Railway—one-third the size of a normal train. The miniature line skirts the moody, misty (but no longer marshy) **Romney Marsh.** Sheep by the thousands graze the flatlands, planted with a dozen villages and as many stone-built churches. New Romney's Norman and Early English **St. Nicholas** is just one of them.

A 14th-century latecomer to the Cinque Ports confederation, the appealing "Ancient Town" of **Rye** is landlocked now. Two miles (3 km.) separate the forest of masts in Rye Harbour from the steep, cobbled streets of the historic centre. Walk uphill past all the tea shops, sweet shops and antique shops to the parish church and **Ypres Tower,** remnant of a 13th-century fort. The museum within highlights Rye's Cinque Ports connection. The association with Henry James is just as strong. The writer spent the last two decades of his life in the Georgian elegance of **Lamb House** (West Street), a National Trust property open to the public a couple of days a week.

James rated **Winchelsea** as highly as Rye, commenting, "The great thing is if you live at Rye you have Winchelsea to show." Chief sight today: the 14th-century **parish church,** dedicated to St. Thomas Becket.

*A*uthentic in every respect, the Mermaid Inn in Rye
looks no different from any other of the town's Tudor buildings.
You could even have a drink in the lounge and still miss a singular feature
of this historic establishment: the smugglers' tunnels that run underground to the coast. Ask the manager to show you the entrance, inside,
next to the fireplace.

The Mermaid.

Orchard Country   7 C2

Inland from Rye, a network of small country roads penetrates a fertile plain known as the Weald of Kent. Apples, pears and cherries are the big crops, followed by grapes and hops. Fields and farmland surround a clutch of appealing villages: tile-hung **Goudhurst** on its hill; half-timbered old **Biddenden,** a medieval centre of the cloth trade; and little **Smarden** (pop. 1,000), a charming collection of black-and-white timberwork and weather-board (clapboard) cottages.

Half-way between Goudhurst and Biddenden, stop off at **Sissinghurst Castle** to see the great garden created by writer Vita Sackville-West and her husband, diplomat Sir Harold Nicolson. Enthusiasts rave about the walled White Garden.

"Jewel of the Weald", **Tenterden,** south-east of Biddenden, is terminus of the nostalgic steam-powered **Kent & East Sussex Railway.** The line ends just over the Sussex county line at **Bodiam,** noted for its moated 14th-century castle, roofless but entire.

Scotney Castle, near Lamberhurst, is another romantic ruin in landscaped grounds. A third variation on the theme, **Leeds Castle** (north of Biddenden) stands astride two islands in a mirror lake. You could easily spend a couple of days exploring this small area of Kent, basing yourself at a farmhouse (look for the roadside signs advertising vacancies) or village inns.

Royal Tunbridge Wells also makes a good touring centre. Kent's answer to Bath, the town developed as a spa in the 17th century. Don't miss the arcaded pedestrian street called the **Pantiles** (southwest of the modern centre), heart of the one-time spa. The Georgian shopfronts —displaying jewellery, clothes, bibelots— have an unselfconscious period charm.

Kent's Historic Houses   7 C2

You could see all of them, but it might be too much of a good thing. The homes lie quite close together, within minutes by car of Tunbridge Wells.

Penshurst Place, Penshurst. This battlemented, crenellated house is the ancestral seat of the Sidneys. The most famous family member was the Elizabethan soldier-poet Sir Philip Sidney. His direct descendant, William Philip Sidney, Lord De L'Isle, lives at Penshurst today. Architectural highlight of a visit is the open-beamed Great Hall of 1350, one of the oldest in the land, complete with the dais for the lord of the manor. In the wood-panelled Long Gallery, a Renaissance addition, look for the death mask of

Queen Elizabeth I, displayed on a table beneath a portrait of the "Virgin Queen".

Hever Castle, near Edenbridge. A frequent overnight guest, Henry VIII courted Anne Boleyn at this, her family home. Wax tableaux in the Long Gallery recreate scenes from the heady early days of their love, symbolized by a replica of Henry's wedding gift to Anne: the clock on the mantelpiece in the Inner Hall. Another poignant souvenir is on display in Anne's old bedroom: the illuminated Book of Hours she carried to her execution on Tower Green (see p. 25).

It was love at first sight all over again when the expatriate American millionaire William Waldorf Astor (later Lord Astor) first set eyes on Hever in 1903. Merely acquiring the property wasn't enough. A practical romantic, Astor installed efficient central heating and plumbing that worked. The Tudor "village" behind the castle was his 100-room guest wing, disguised as a cluster of individual dwellings.

Chartwell, Westerham. The Astors' near neighbour, Winston Churchill lived with relative modesty in the 14th-century farmhouse he purchased in 1922. Administered by the National Trust, a private charity, the house remains as it was when the Churchills were in residence. Five rooms are on view to the public: the dining room, drawing room, library, Clementine Churchill's bedroom and the study where Winston Churchill habitually worked until four in the morning—at his father's Georgian desk or his own stand-up table. There's a small collection of memorabilia on display, mainly uniforms, decorations and awards. You can also see the garden studio where the 20th century's most famous amateur artist pottered away at his landscapes and still lifes.

Knole Park, Sevenoaks. "It looked a town rather than a house." So begins Virginia Woolf's description of Knole in her novel *Orlando*. She grew to know the place through her friendship with Vita Sackville-West, one of the Sackvilles of Knole. The family connection goes back to 1566, when Queen Elizabeth I gave this 14th-century manor to her cousin, Thomas Sackville.

For eight generations now, Sackvilles have been living with the same velvet and damask hangings and walnut and ebony furniture. Much of it was royal cast-offs, magnificent but outmoded Restoration pieces discarded by William of Orange after the Glorious Revolution—and acquired as a right of office by his Lord Chamberlain, Charles Sackville, the 6th Earl of Dorset. Undervalued by William—and beyond price today—are the silver table, candlestands and pier glass made for King Charles II in 1680.

Sussex

Bucket-and-spade holidaymakers and, increasingly, conference-goers patronize the traditional resorts along the coast, from Hastings to Brighton. But the real Sussex lies inland, in the rural Weald and downland villages. This has been corn and sheep country since the Romans first developed the agricultural potential of the area. Nowadays there are fewer sheep and more commuters, but a county identity still holds.

Hastings   *7 C2*

Hastings is the self-proclaimed capital of "1066 Country". Bypass the pier and mini-golf pitch, the old town and ruined castle (William the Conqueror's first English fort) for the evocative site of the Battle of Hastings, in open country 6 miles (10 km.) to the north-west.

The town of **Battle** grew up beside the field where King Harold's English army met Duke William's Norman knights in 1066. The ruins of **Battle Abbey**, destroyed in the Dissolution, mark the site. Walk through the massive entrance gate, past the crumbling monastic buildings and out onto the ridge held by the axe-wielding English infantrymen. Signs posted around the battlefield explain the events of October 14 as they unfolded: the Norman cavalry attacked repeatedly and were repeatedly repulsed—until William feigned retreat. Drawing Harold's soldiers to lower ground, he rounded on them, decimating the Anglo-Saxons. Symbolically enough, Harold died at dusk, shot through the eye with an arrow. A modern stone slab marks the place where the king was slain. Here, for five centuries, stood the high altar of the abbey church founded by William to commemorate the conquest.

Eastbourne   7 C2
Like the crowds on the pier and Grand Parade, Eastbourne is somewhat past its prime. You probably won't want to stay the night in the resort, but there's some superb scenery in the surrounding area. A cliff-top path takes walkers out around **Beachy Head** (keep away from the edge!) and the **Seven Sisters,** a rippling wall of chalk with seven distinct summits. Sea birds nest on the heights and there are vertiginous views of the coast and countryside. Look east beyond Eastbourne to William the Conqueror's 1066 landing place at **Pevensey Bay**—and west past the Seven Sisters towards Brighton. Completely built up now, the coastline developed during Rudyard Kipling's lifetime, and the writer found it "of great horror". Turn away from the sea for a while and set your sights inland, where the South Downs villages offer appealing rural contrasts.

South Downs Detour   7 C2
The South Downs Way—footpath, bridle path and cycleway—follows the line of hills west to the Hampshire border. Walkers prepared to go the distance should allow about a week to cover the full 80 miles (129 km.), but there's a lot to see right around the starting point of Eastbourne.

First landmark on the Way is the 226-foot (69-m.) **Wilmington Long Man,** near Wilmington village. This outline figure carved into the chalk flank of Windover

Hill holds what looks like a staff in each hand. He may represent a medieval pilgrim, Saxon cult figure or Roman god—no one can say for sure. An early date is certainly conceivable: man has been walking the Downs since the Stone Age (see p. 15).

In neighbouring **Alfriston** village, directly on the South Downs Way, you'll see large boulders which may have marked the original prehistoric footpath. Some of the stones lie on the Tye, the impossibly picturesque village green. Here, too, stands St. Andrews, "Cathedral of the Downs", and the church's thatched medieval **Clergy House,** home of the priest and, latterly, the parson. It was the first building to be acquired by the National Trust in 1896.

This corner of Sussex found favour with artist Duncan Grant (1885-1978), who lived at **Charleston Farmhouse,** near Firle village, for 60 years. A breath of Bohemia survives at Charleston (open to the public several afternoons a week), decorated by Grant and the painter and designer Vanessa Bell in idiosyncratic "Bloomsbury" style.

Vanessa Bell's sister, the novelist Virginia Woolf, summered close by at **Monk's House** in Rodmell, on the River Ouse, and it was in the Ouse that Virginia Woolf drowned herself in 1941. The National Trust opens Monk's House as a shrine to the author of *Orlando* and *The Years.*

Yet another reason to linger in the area: the opera house at **Glyndebourne,** famous for its summer productions. Performances begin in the late afternoon, allowing time for a leisurely champagne supper on the lawn during the interval (intermission). You have to book tickets—and accommodation—well ahead: hotels and inns for miles around are full up during the Glyndebourne season. The county town of **Lewes** is the obvious place to stay, and a "must" for sightseers. Civic monuments sum up 1,000 years of Sussex history, beginning with the Norman castle.

Brighton 6 B2

Gently decaying now, Brighton has an antiquated charm that may not be to everyone's taste. But the Regency architecture *is* unique, if somewhat faded. And there's a concentration of interesting antique shops in **The Lanes,** the area of pedestrian streets near the seafront.

It was the future George IV who catapulted the developing resort of Brighthelmstone to fame and fashion in the 1780s. He leased a farmhouse in Brighton, as he called the place, and elegant society followed. An adventurous few had paved the way 30 years before. Taking the advice of a local doctor, they came here to breathe sea air and bathe in—even drink—sea water. Thus was born the notion of a holiday by the sea. But that's all history now as Brighton turns from the resort business to the conference and tourist trade.

First stop for a tourist is the ultimate in holiday houses, the Prince Regent's **Royal Pavilion,** bordering on The Lanes. John Nash designed this domed and

104

*T*he South Downs end with a flourish at the Seven
Sisters, chalk cliffs 500 feet (150 m.) high. This stretch of coast and the
downland above make up the Seven Sisters Country Park, popular
with walkers. But you need sturdy legs and lungs to follow the trail
across the rollercoaster summits of the Sisters.

turreted "Hindoo" fantasy in 1815, transforming an earlier palace that in turn incorporated the original farmhouse leased by the prince in the 1780s. No expense was spared—and no holds were barred—in the construction and decoration of the palace (still under wraps as major structural restoration work continues).

A lingering smell of damp adds a touch of poignancy to the extravagant exoticism of the interior, featuring Chinese motifs—flying dragons, writhing serpents and costumed oriental figures. Follow the arrows to view the drawing rooms, Banqueting Room, library and bedrooms in sequence. Even the kitchen has an eastern look, with rows of cast-iron palm-tree columns.

Former royal stables house the **Brighton Museum and Art Gallery** in Church Street, noted for its modern British paintings and 20th-century decorative arts collection.

Down by the water, the Victorian **Palace Pier** echoes the architecture of the Pavilion in wood and cast iron. All the traditional amenities are on offer to a dwindling public, including deck chairs, souvenir shops, fruit machines and a pub. Across from the pier, the **Aquarium and Dolphinarium** has been "somewhere to take the children" for a century now. Some other classic Brighton-area sights lie inland.

Devil's Dyke, a natural beauty spot several miles to the north-west, has long attracted excursionists. As the story goes, the devil made this gash in the Downs to flood the churches of Sussex. But, confusing the light of a candle for daybreak,

*B*righton used to have rather a raffish reputation; the Prince Regent entertained his mistresses here, under the pleasure domes of the Royal Pavilion. "Prinny's" infatuations with women never lasted long, but he kept up a lifetime love affair with the resort.

he stopped work before he'd finished the job. Legend aside, the view from the crest of the dyke is memorable. A way inland lies the Sussex Weald, the undulating continuation of Kent's fertile agricultural land.

The perennially popular **House of Pipes** in the nearby village of Bramber displays one man's collection of smoking material, from meerschaum pipes to tobacco tins. Items date back to that innocent period in the history of tobacco use, before government health warnings robbed a smoke of its pleasure.

Arundel   6 B2
The town rises from its peaceful river, the Arun, to hilltop **Arundel Castle,** a picturesque jumble of battlements and towers. In its present incarnation, Arundel dates from the late 19th century, though the keep and drawbridge go back to the castle's 11th-century beginnings. Fine furniture, tapestries and Old Masters by Holbein the Younger, Van Dyck, Gainsborough and Reynolds enhance the neo-Gothic interior.

This has always been the home of the Earl of Arundel, a title that passed with the castle to the Howard family in 1580. The Howards, like the Fitzalans before them, are staunch Roman Catholics. They had their family chapel partitioned off from the Anglican parish church after the Reformation, financing Arundel's Gothic-style Catholic **cathedral** some 300 years later. It's dedicated to a 16th-century forebear, St. Philip Howard, who died a martyr's death in the Tower of London, where he was imprisoned for allegedly having had a mass said for the success of the Spanish Armada.

Amberley
This thatched village on the banks of the Arun attracts weekend artists and anglers in droves. Even the old industrial site to the south is scenic: the Amberley Chalk Pits, now an award-winning open-air **museum** highlighting the industrial heritage of the Downs. Local craftsmen dem-

onstrate bygone trades (boatbuilding to brickmaking), and there are collections of vintage tools and vehicles on show. The quarry itself may just look familiar. It was a location for the James Bond thriller, *A View to a Kill.*

Petworth   6 B2
Imposing 17th-century **Petworth House** inspired numerous Turner masterpieces, including the luminous landscapes on display in Petworth's Turner Room. Other Turner works hang in the North Gallery, a private museum created by the 2nd Earl of Egremont in 1824. But Turner isn't the whole story here. Take in the state rooms, with an impressive collection of Old Masters, the Carved Room (carved by Grinling Gibbons), painted Staircase Hall and artfully contrived garden (a Capability Brown design).

Dominated by the house, pretty **Petworth village** has rural charm and some well-stocked antique shops.

Chichester   6 B2
An inland town strictly speaking, Chichester adjoins its **harbour,** 50 superb miles (80 km.) of indented shoreline, with 17 miles (27 km.) of navigable channels. Harbour **cruises** start from Itchenor, and sailing boats and sailboards (windsurfboards) can be rented there and at several other towns in the area. Harbourside **Bosham** (pronounced "bozem"), a picturesque huddle of wood and brick cottages, is another likely place.

Chichester proper retains its grid-like Roman street plan. The Gothic **Market Cross** stands at the junction of the four main streets, named after the cardinal points. Off West Street rises the **cathedral,** its spire visible out to sea. Two fires in the 12th century damaged the original Norman structure, but many Norman features survive, along with Early English additions—and some contemporary pieces: a Graham Sutherland altarpiece (1962), John Piper tapestry (1966) and Marc Chagall window (1980).

In the south-east quadrant of the city,

an area called the Pallants preserves some exceptional 18th- and 19th-century houses. The **Queen Anne Pallant House Gallery** contains furniture, porcelain and glass from that gracious era.

It's an easy walk or bus ride to **Fishbourne Roman Villa** (on the west side of the city), one of the largest buildings of the period discovered outside Italy. A British chieftain called Cogidubnus lived in unparalleled luxury here. There are many fine mosaics and a "Roman" garden, replanted according to archaeological information.

In the close environs, **Goodwood House** contains the French furniture, Gobelins tapestries and Sèvres porcelain acquired by the 3rd Duke of Richmond, an ambassador to the court of Louis XV. The architect James Wyatt designed the house specifically to complement the collection, which it does with appropriate Neoclassical restraint. Wyatt's Tapestry Room, hung with scenes from *Don Quixote,* holds some of the best pieces.

Goodwood Park, the racecourse in the grounds, is the scene of "meetings" from May to the end of September.

The **Weald and Downland Open-air Museum** at Singleton resembles a real little village, with its farmhouses, barns, market hall, artisans' workshops and village school. Of timber, flint or brick, the buildings exemplify the rural architectural traditions of the South-East. All were rescued from demolition and set up on this wooded 60-acre (24-ha.) South Downs site.

Surrey

Greater London long ago engulfed the northern fringes of the county, but the green belt of protected fields and forests around the metropolis has effectively halted further urbanization. Dominated by the North Downs and Thames Valley, the Surrey countryside is as lovely as any you'll see. Breathe deeply: the air smells of cut grass and roses.

Guildford 6 B2

Londoners are deserting the capital for cities like Guildford (pop. 60,000)—old enough and small enough to have a sense of history and community, in the heart of the countryside, yet within easy commuting range of the West End and City. The attractive high street climbs a hill past the 17th-century **Guildhall,** or town hall (the building with the projecting clock), to the **Grammar School,** Guildford's upper school since 1557. The modern cathedral of 1936, in a spare Gothic style, brings the urban landscape up to date. And all around lie the natural attractions of the North Downs.

Loseley Park *(near Guildford)*
The popular dairy and cereal products made here carry the logo of Loseley's many-gabled façade. The house was built during Elizabeth I's reign, and the queen herself was a guest at Loseley on several occasions. Stones for its construction were plundered from nearby Waverley Abbey. The More-Molyneux family (descendants of Sir Thomas) open the house and grounds to visitors. Guides show you around the Great Hall, Library, Drawing Room and bedrooms. There are some important pictures, mainly portraits, and fine period furniture and objects, but the overall impression is of a (quite grand) family home, rather than a museum. The farm, in 1,400 acres (567 ha.), very nearly upstages the house. To join a guided farm walk you have to book in advance. Call (0483) 571881 to make arrangements.

Ripley 6 B2
Gardeners amateur and professional consider a visit to the Royal Horticultural Society's **Wisley Garden** on the order of a pilgrimage. The display of azaleas and rhododendrons is justly famous, but you'll also want to have a look at the laboratories, glasshouses, rock garden and pinetum included in Wisley's 300-acre (122-ha.) tract.

From Historic Ships to Megaliths

The nautical South takes in Portsmouth's naval installations, historic and modern, and Southampton's docks, as well as the exhilarating yachting waters of the Solent and Channel. Bays, coves and headlands punctuate a long and eventful coast, backed by Dorset's downland cliffs and the oak and beech woods of Hampshire's New Forest. Timber from the forest built Nelson's fleet, and his flagship, *Victory,* is Portsmouth's unique tourist attraction. But Trafalgar counts as recent history on the time scale of the South. The cathedrals of Salisbury and Winchester take you back six to eight centuries before that. And another four to five millennia separate them from Maiden Castle and the oldest megaliths at Stonehenge.

Hampshire

The county is as richly agricultural as ever—if you discount the urban sprawl around Portsmouth and Southampton. Listen out for the local accent, with its distinctive burr.

Portsmouth   6 B2

This is the Royal Navy's town. Lord Nelson sailed from Portsmouth to victory—and death—at Trafalgar in 1805. The D-Day invasion force assembled here in 1944, followed by the Falklands Task Force in 1982. Morale in the city has

H MS Victory *is the world's last remaining ship of the line. The old sailing warship has 104 cannon ranged on three decks.*

been high ever since the South Atlantic campaign.

There's a lot to see in the harbourfront **Royal Dockyard,** focus for a visit. Start with the most visible landmark around, the three-masted **HMS Victory,** Lord Nelson's ship, in dry dock near the entrance. To go on board you have to join one of the guided tours run at frequent intervals throughout the day, every day except Christmas.

Black rigging and red and black painted trim give the *Victory* a suitably martial look. The 2,100-ton man-of-war carried 104 guns and 850 men—300 officers, 550 crew. The young sailors from today's navy who serve as guides take evident satisfaction in describing conditions on board 200 years ago, when leg irons and flogging kept the men in line, and a daily ration of rum kept them quiet. While the crew endured squalor and privations below decks, the admiral lived in considerable style above. His sleeping cabin (with silk upholstered cot) and wood-panelled day and dining cabins have all the elegance of a Georgian town house. And the furniture bears comparison with the period's best—except for the fact that these pieces could be folded and stowed away to clear the decks for action.

The fateful encounter at Trafalgar began at about 12.40 in the afternoon of October 21. Less than an hour later, Nelson sank to the Quarter Deck, mortally wounded by a French sniper. A plaque marks the place where the admiral fell. He was taken below decks to the cockpit, where he learned the outcome of the battle before he died. (The Trafalgar diorama in the **Royal Naval Museum** adjacent to the *Victory* puts you in the thick of the action.)

Touring a second ship would be a letdown if it were any other than Henry VIII's **Mary Rose,** salvaged in 1982. Wait your turn to enter the ship hall (a few steps from the *Victory*), where you can watch restorers at work on the hull in a special temperature- and humidity-controlled environment. On display in the neighbouring exhibition hall are objects recovered with the ship, from cutlery, tools and clothing to pocket sundials.

Two other vessels to visit: the iron-clad **HMS Warrior** (1860), berthed at a pier near the dockyard gate, and the submarine **Alliance,** across the harbour at the Royal Naval Submarine Museum in Gosport. Get there via the Portsmouth Harbour Ferry. Or board a launch for a spin around the **harbour,** an expansive 4 miles (6 km.) long and 2 miles (3 km.) across, narrowing to 300 yards (274 m.) at the mouth.

Old Portsmouth, the area bordering on the dockyard, is more new than old, thanks to wartime air raids.

Isle of Wight   6 A2

The trip across Spithead to Ryde takes just seven minutes by hovercraft from Southsea (the fastest way to go), twice as long by catamaran from Portsmouth,

longer still by ferry. A chip off the "old block" of the mainland, this holiday isle has miniature downs and chalk cliffs, beaches, resorts and piers, and a relatively mild climate that places it squarely in Britain's sunbelt. If the Victorians had colonized California, it would probably look like the Isle of Wight—full of flower beds, promenades and parish churches.

The sheltered east coast has the popular **resorts:** Ryde, Bembridge, Sandown, Shanklin, Ventnor. Yarmouth, in the west, and Cowes are famous yachting centres.

Southampton   6 A2

Post-war reconstruction has given the city a deceptively modern appearance. It may not look the part, but Southampton is the port that launched the *Mayflower* in 1620 and the *Titanic* in 1912. Not many tourists come here, unless they've just arrived on a transatlantic liner or continental ferry. But if you are passing through, you'll want to spend some time around the waterfront, cruising the harbour and seeing the docks, having a drink at a pub or wine bar in Town Quay or the Ocean Village complex (the "Covent Garden of the South").

The **Southampton Art Gallery** in the Civic Centre ranks among the best of Britain's provincial museums, with exceptional displays of historic and contemporary British works.

New Forest   6 A2

New in William the Conqueror's day, the forest embraces 145 square miles (375 sq. km.) of woods, heath and farmland between Southampton Water and Hampshire's River Avon. Then, as now, there was a scattering of villages here. **Lyndhurst,** the largest of them (pop. 3,000), has the most shops and the biggest traffic jams, as well as the museum and **Visitor Centre.** Pick up the excellent Forestry Commission map of suggested itineraries, and ask about guided walks and other activities.

Walking is the best way to see the flora and fauna of the New Forest—from red deer and the ubiquitous semi-tame ponies to rare wild orchids and gladioli. But you can get a good general impression by car, especially via the **Rhinefeld** and **Bolderwood ornamental drives** (signposted off the A35, Lyndhurst–Bournemouth road). Banks of fern colour the roadside deep green in high summer, russet and gold in autumn, and there are ancient stands of oak and beech trees. The sky opens over the moors, where the cream, grey and brown New Forest ponies run. The car park at **Stoney Cross Plain** is a good place to observe the ponies at close range. The **Rufus Stone**, nearby, marks the spot where William Rufus (King William II) met his death, out hunting in 1100. The arrow that killed him allegedly rebounded off a tree. There's no longer any hunting in the forest, but camping, picnicking, horse riding and fishing are all permitted in designated areas. That makes it very popular with British holidaymakers, and a great place for a tourist to observe the British at ease.

Beaulieu
6 A2

The theme attractions at Beaulieu (pronounced "bewlee") in the heart of the New Forest keep Lord Montagu's bank balance in the black. Not every peer of the realm has a monorail at his doorstep, or enough vintage cars to fill a museum, though these days many wish they did.

Palace House, the Montagu family home (13th-century core with Victorian additions), is open to the public—like the rides, amusements and theme exhibits—364 days a year. By way of added attractions, there are ruins of a Cistercian abbey to visit in the grounds.

Entrepreneurship must run in the Montagu family. An 18th-century ancestor set up the shipyard at **Buckler's Hard,** a couple of miles away, and proceeded to build the "wooden walls" of England with New Forest timber. The Maritime Museum here documents that erstwhile industry.

Romsey
6 A2

This market town grew up around the Norman **Abbey Church,** a particularly pure example of the style. Lord Mountbatten's burial place, the church is a shrine to the memory of Britain's wartime First Sea Lord, who was killed by IRA terrorists in 1979.

Exiting the A31 at Romsey, you see the main entrance to **Broadlands,** Lord Mountbatten's Hampshire home. His grandson, Lord Romsey, resides here now. A tour of the property includes the Mountbatten Exhibition in the old stables, where a film show recaps Lord Mountbatten's 60-year career as sailor, statesman and commander. The Neoclassical house is interesting in its own right. The furnishings and fittings commissioned by the 18th-century statesman, Lord Palmerston, the original owner, provide a dignified setting for the family collections of Lord Mountbatten, who inherited Broadlands in his youth—lock, stock and barrel.

Winchester
6 A2

One of England's most historic cities, Winchester predates even the Romans. Later on, this was the capital of King Alfred's Wessex and, for a time after the Norman conquest, co-capital (with London) of England. Centuries of prosperity have given Winchester the attractive medieval, Georgian and

Rain Man
St. Swithin was buried, at his own request, in the churchyard of Winchester Cathedral. He wanted to lie outdoors, where the rain would fall on his grave. But in 971, as Swithin's cult grew, it was decided to move the saint's body to a shrine of gold inside the church. An attempt was made to open the grave on July 15, but rain halted the work. It continued to rain for 40 days—a sign of St. Swithin's holy displeasure. His extraordinary control over the elements made Swithin patron saint of weather. Even today, rain on St. Swithin's Day (July 15) means 40 consecutive days of drizzle—not an unlikely prediction in soggy Britain.

Victorian buildings that make the compact city centre such a pleasant place to visit. Notice especially the charming bow-windowed façade of the *Hampshire Chronicle* in the High Street and, further along, the slender Perpendicular Civic Cross of 1450.

A passageway beside the cross leads to Winchester's **cathedral** in its peaceful close. Here, in earlier times, stood the Roman forum. The original Saxon Old Minster was dedicated to a trio of saints that included the 9th-century Bishop of Winchester, St. Swithin (see p. 113). The present cathedral—England's longest—is mainly Gothic, though the original Norman style prevails in the transepts and crypt. Tour the crypt (summer months only) and you'll hear the story of William Walker, the diver who shored up the cathedral's flooded foundations early in the century, saving the church from collapse.

The high, wide Perpendicular nave makes a tremendous impact, the bays repeating themselves into a seeming infinity. Look for the graves of Jane Austen (north aisle), marked by an inscribed stone slab, and Compleat Angler Izaak Walton, who lies in Silkstede Chapel. A marble tomb under the central tower holds the remains of William Rufus (King William II). No religious ceremony accompanied his interment, a hurried affair that took place within a day of his death (see p. 113). The rumours, barely voiced, that the king was a heretic and a practitioner of the occult arts could explain his "accidental" demise and unceremonious, unchristian burial.

The voluntary guides on hand in the cathedral will be happy to point out these and other monuments, including St. Swithin's shrine (a modern replacement), Mary Tudor's chair (left behind after her ill-fated wedding to Philip II of Spain) and the wooden mortuary chests that contain the bones of England's early kings (Egbert, Egwyn and the Dane Canute). Visit the library before you leave, if only to see the 12th-century **Winchester**

Bible, a masterpiece of the medieval illuminator's art.

South of the cathedral, through King's Gate, is **Winchester College,** one of the oldest (1382) and toughest of England's public schools. "Learn, Leave or Be Licked" remains the byword here. South again, via the riverside footpath, you come to the **Hospital of St. Cross,** an almshouse of 12th-century foundation. Ask for the Wayfarer's Dole and you'll be given age-old sustenance—a horn of ale and some bread.

They've been farming Salisbury Plain since the Stone Age, when the first agriculturalists settled here. Traditionally the plain is unfenced, with vast open fields, which simplifies harvesting. There are no real towns on the plain, but the military presence is pervasive. The high downland makes a great place for manoeuvres.

Jane Austen

Ordinary people living ordinary lives were the subject of Jane Austen's novels. The modest daughter of a country clergyman, Jane opposed a healthy realism to the melodrama that was the 19th-century novelist's stock in trade.

Trips to Bath and London, and frequent visits to friends and relatives in the neighbourhood of Steventon, the Hampshire village where Jane grew up, informed her writing. Though she returned time and again to the themes of courtship and marriage in her novels, Jane herself remained single. Evidence suggests that her great love—probably a military officer or clergyman—died.

In keeping with the convention of the times, Jane Austen did not sign her books. *Sense and Sensibility* came out anonymously in 1811, followed rapidly by *Pride and Prejudice,* and *Mansfield Park.* When *Emma* appeared in 1815, the novel carried a dedication to the Prince Regent, a great fan, from the still nameless author. Only after her death, with the posthumous publication of *Northanger Abbey* and *Persuasion,* was Jane Austen's identity revealed.

Chawton   6 B2

Anyone who has read *Mansfield Park, Emma* or *Persuasion* will want to visit **Chawton Cottage,** the red-brick house where Jane Austen (1775–1817) wrote her most accomplished novels. She must have had, in addition to her other gifts, an incredible power of concentration. Jane did all of her writing in the busy sitting room of the house she shared with her mother, sister and a family friend.

Wiltshire

There's something eternal about the Wiltshire landscape—the undulating open spaces of Salisbury Plain, the oblique light and the silence. Not even the tour buses can disturb the rural peace of the countryside, scattered with sheep and scores of prehistoric sites.

Salisbury   6 A2

This archetypal market town has substantial houses of timber and brick, historic inns with names like "The Pheasant" and "Haunch of Venison", and a tree-lined central market square where traders have been setting up their stalls for close to 800 years. (Tuesdays and Saturdays are market days—the optimum time for a visit.)

On the south side of the city, the cathedral distances itself from commerce behind the walls of the close. There's nothing haphazard about the arrangement: purpose-built, town and cathedral took shape during a few short years of the 13th century. New Sarum, as Salisbury was then known, replaced the ancient hilltop city of **Old Sarum,** a couple of miles away. The new town was built from the old—the abandoned site was quarried for its stone—and all trace of habitation there has vanished, though the earthworks retain the imprint of the citadel and original cathedral.

The foundations of the new riverside **cathedral** were laid in 1220. The choir, transepts and nave went up in record time—38 years—and by 1265 the magnificent west front was completed. A splendid afterthought, the soaring spire was added a century later. It's very tall (over 400 ft./120 m.) and very heavy (more than 6,000 tons)—so heavy that the cathedral staggers under the weight. The columns carrying the tower have actually buckled, causing the spire to lean. A brass pin in the floor of the crossing documents the tilt: 2 feet 6 inches (75 cm.) from the vertical.

Beautifully proportioned, in Early English style throughout, Salisbury is the most harmonious of England's medieval cathedrals. And it's the architecture itself—the strength of line and interplay of form—that impresses here.

By way of curiosities, the cathedral displays one of the four surviving copies of Magna Carta (on view in the Chapter House) and, in the north aisle, what is said to be the world's oldest working clock (1386). Designed to be heard, rather than seen, it has no face but sounds the hours.

Wilton
6 A2

If you've seen one stately home, you *haven't* seen them all. **Wilton House** (2½ miles [4 km.] west of Salisbury) is another of the really great ones. The property fell to the Herbert family through a bit of old-fashioned, 16th-century nepotism: William Herbert, the first Earl of Pembroke, just happened to be the brother-in-law of Henry VIII's sixth wife, Catherine Parr. The original Tudor house (incorporating the remains of a medieval monastery) was remodelled along classical lines by Inigo Jones after a devastating 1647 fire.

An architectural tour de force, the eight state rooms created by Jones culminate in the theatrical extravagance of the **Double Cube Room** (60 by 30 by 30 ft./18 by 9 by 9 m.). Apart from John Webb's opulent carved and gilded decoration, there are choice pictures by Van Dyck, and the bold furniture designed by William Kent a century later specifically to complement this setting.

Herbert family tradition maintains that Shakespeare acted in *As You Like It* here, but the visits of Marlowe, Spenser and Ben Jonson are better documented.

Stonehenge
6 A2

Visible from afar, the grey-green monoliths look deceptively small, even fragile in the immensity of Salisbury Plain. Half-toppled now, they lie in partial disarray, like abandoned pieces from an outsize game of building blocks.

On average, 7,000 people a day visit Britain's most famous prehistoric monument. Pay the entrance fee at the turnstile in the car park opposite and join the inevitable queue that snakes its way through the passage under the roadway. The pressure of tourism is such that sightseers are no longer allowed to wander among the stones. You circle them, instead, at a distance.

Stonehenge evolved over a period of more than a thousand years, in three distinct phases. A Neolithic people laid claim to the site in about 2800 B.C. They created the circular earthworks (very apparent still) and positioned what are now known as the Station Stones, Heel Stone and Aubrey Holes.

With the advent of the Beaker Folk around 2100 B.C., concentric rings of bluestones went up and a stone entrance avenue began to take shape. But this scheme was completely transformed a hundred years later by a Bronze Age people descended from the Beaker Folk. Regarded as the real builders of Stonehenge, they exchanged the outer circle of bluestones for the now incomplete ring of tall sarsen stones. Inside it they erected five huge trilithons—pairs of giant stones topped with a lintel, of which three remain in place—and 19 smaller bluestones (now 11), both arranged in a U-formation opening towards the entrance.

What actually went on here remains the subject of intense speculation. The alignment of the Heel Stone and sarsens to the sun points to Stonehenge's function as a solar temple, a theory that has gained almost universal acceptance. Other orientations to the moon and heavenly bodies would indicate that Stonehenge also served as an astronomical observatory or calendar, but these orientations may be coincidental—controversy rages. A strong case can however be made for the funerary or ritual signifi-

Secular Order of Druids

Larger than you'd think, membership in Britain's twelve Druid orders numbers over 100,000. There's no direct connection with the original priestly caste. That died out a couple of millennia ago, along with an insistence on human sacrifice. Modern Druids aren't even all Celts. They merely practise the rituals of the old Celtic nature religion, with its New Age emphasis on harmony between man and the universe.

The Midsummer gatherings at Stonehenge used to be the culmination of the Druid ritual year. However, the number of people attending got out of hand. The wear and tear on the site was considered too great, and the stones have been closed to celebrants.

The redoubtable Lady Bankes was at home alone, holding the fort, when strategic Corfe Castle came under Parliamentary attack during the Civil War. Commanding a small garrison, she succeeded in staving off a force of 600 for six weeks in 1643. When the Roundheads finally took the castle three years later, they blew it apart with gunpowder by way of revenge.

of country houses. England's first significant Renaissance building (completed 1580), it was the first house to open its doors to the public (1949) and the first to develop a commercial attraction: Longleat's famous lions, installed in the Capability Brown-designed park in 1966. Single and combined tickets are available for admission to the house, safari park and other points of interest— the VIP Vehicles display, Dr. Who Exhibition, Butterfly Garden, miniature railway and so on. The considerable profits from these many sidelines are channelled back into the house, the *raison d'être* of it all.

Longleat is open daily, year-round except for Christmas. It's still very much a family home, though the Thynne family no longer occupies the area on show to the public. An era ended when Longleat's Bath Bedroom, the original bedroom with adjoining bath, went into retirement in 1946—after more than a century of use by three generations of Thynne men, coincidentally marquesses of Bath.

Apart from the Elizabethan Great Hall, most of the rooms you'll see have a 19th-century Italianate look. However, some earlier features survive, like the 17th-century Cordoba leather wall covering in the State Dining Room and the Flemish tapestries and Boulle furniture in the Saloon. The firm of W.G. Crace did the redecorating, with a little help from the 4th Marchioness of Bath. It was her idea to dye the red and gold Persian carpet in the State Drawing Room green— to match the lawn outside.

cance of the site. The Aubrey Holes, from the earliest phase of occupation, were found to contain cremated human remains.

As for the Druids, they were mere upstarts, appropriating Stonehenge for their shrine in the 3rd century B.C., hundreds of years after it had fallen into disuse.

Longleat House
(Warminster)   5 D2
A series of startling innovations sets Longleat apart from the rank and file

Stourhead
(near Mere)   5 D2
Banking money built Stourhead (pronounced "stirhead") in the 18th century. Henry Hoare I ("Henry the Good") put up the Palladian house in the 1720s, and the second Henry ("the Magnificent") laid the groundwork for the extraordinary landscape garden in the 1740s. See the house first or you risk a disappointing anticlimax after a tour of the grounds.

Fire destroyed the central part of the building in 1902, but the contents were salvaged and the impressive Regency library was spared. The scholar and antiquarian Richard Colt Hoare, grandson of Henry Hoare II, wrote his 13-part *History of Modern Wiltshire* in this quiet, carpeted retreat. Thomas Chippendale supplied the furniture—including the massive "Egyptian" desk and library steps. More Chippendale pieces decorate the Picture Gallery in the opposite wing, displaying the kind of classical landscapes that inspired the incomparable garden.

It may look natural, but every detail at Stourhead is contrived, from the undulating shoreline of the lake to the distant vistas of massed trees and buildings. An amateur of genius, Henry Hoare II collaborated with Henry Flitcroft on the architectural focal points of his scheme: the Temple of Flora, grotto, dominant Pantheon (a replica of Rome's), Temple of Apollo and other follies. Even the church of Stourton village, on the estate, has been drawn into the design by the careful positioning of the Gothic high cross that stands on lower ground, closer to the water.

"Village" is a big word for Stourton's handful of buildings. Apart from the church and National Trust shop, the Spread Eagle Inn, originally Stourhead's guest annexe, is the only visible structure. A National Trust establishment now, it makes a welcome refreshment stop.

Dorset

The pastoral spirit of Thomas Hardy's novels lives on in the thatched cottages, lanes and fields of Dorset. The region formed part of Alfred the Great's kingdom of Wessex, a name that Hardy revived in his writing. Dorset is Wessex, and Wessex is Hardy Country.

Bournemouth   6 A2

Thomas Hardy's name for the resort was Sandbourne, and as such it figured in several of the novels, including *The Hand of Ethelberta* and *Jude the Obscure*. But little remains of the Victorian atmosphere Hardy knew: modern blocks of flats have replaced many of the grand hotels from Bournemouth's 19th-century heyday, and the streamlined Bournemouth International Centre signals the town's commitment to the developing conference trade. The "Mediterranean-look" pine trees, incidentally, were all imported back in the 1840s.

Two museums attract sightseers to the East Cliff section of the city: the **Rothesay Museum,** an astonishing miscellany of ceramics, typewriters, hand guns and more; and the **Russell-Cotes Art Gallery and Museum,** the former home of Sir Merton Russell-Cotes, an Edwardian hotelier with a taste for exotic art with erotic overtones (a Rossetti *Venus,* nudes by William Etty). Ken Russell couldn't have found a better location for his film *Valentino*.

There's good swimming—and fossiling—at Lulworth Cove, a famous beauty spot on the Dorset coast. Fossilers search the crumbling cliff faces behind the beach for the remains of prehistoric sea life trapped in the rock. West along the foot of the cliffs is a fossil "forest", with some impressive specimens.

Poole and the Purbecks   6 A2/5 D2

Three miles (5 km.) of sandy beaches link Bournemouth to the historic port of **Poole,** Dorset's yachting centre. For local colour, make for **The Quay,** a busy marine scene of sailing boats and fishing trawlers, ships' chandlers, shipyards, pubs and inns. The handsome buildings on the waterfront and in the **Old Town** just behind it date mainly from the Georgian period, when Poole's lucrative fishing industry was at its peak. Prior to that, wool brought Poole prosperity. **Scaplen's Court,** a medieval merchant's house in the High Street, recalls the good old days of the cloth trade.

Poole has a great natural attraction in its **harbour,** one of the world's largest, with seven islands and countless coves, creeks and inlets around its 60-mile (100-km.) rim. Ferries connect Poole Quay to the isles and harbourside towns. The most popular spot for an outing is **Brownsea Island,** a National Trust nature reserve at the mouth of the harbour. Waterfowl, peacocks, red squirrels and sika deer are the protected species here. Go for a swim or a picnic, or join one of the guided tours of the island (afternoons only in the tourist season). On the southwest side, Baden-Powell Stone offers a classic panorama of the Purbecks, with Corfe Castle on its high hill.

Back on the mainland, the landscaped gardens of **Compton Acres** (Canford Cliffs Road, near Sandbanks) provide more scenic beauty and distant views of Poole and the Purbeck Hills.

Wareham, across the harbour from Poole, dominated Dorset trade between the 9th and 13th centuries—Poole gradually taking over as Wareham's port silted up. The Saxon **Church of St. Martin** is one of the few early buildings to survive a devastating 1762 fire. But Wareham (Hardy's Anglebury) was charmingly rebuilt in harmonious Georgian style.

To the south-east lies the **Isle of Purbeck,** a peninsula that encompasses hills, moors and a rugged coastline. **Corfe Castle,** or what is left of it, commands the only break in the smoothly contoured, 12-mile (19-km.) Purbeck range. The Norman fortifications were blown apart by Parliamentary forces during the Civil War. Hardy, sensitive to the sinister quality of the ruins, called the castle Corusgate. With the Restoration, the royalist Bankes family recovered the title to the property, but rather than rebuild, they decided to construct a new house, Kingston Lacy, near Wimborne Minster. The key to the castle hangs there still. The village of Corfe Castle—an attractive cluster of shops and houses at the foot of the castle hill—survived the war intact. Buildings are of the local limestone, a hard, fine-grained variety known as Purbeck marble.

Swanage, the quarry town, was a quiet backwater when Thomas Hardy lived here (1875–76). He named the place Knollsea, which he described as "a seaside village lying snug within two headlands, as between a finger and thumb". But by the end of the century Swanage had developed into a popular resort. Some of the most prominent civic monuments arrived as ballast on the sailing ships that carried Purbeck stone from Swanage to London: the Wellington Clock Tower (from Waterloo Bridge) and Town Hall façade (originally the front of a City guildhall).

The **Dorset Coast Path** follows the contours of the Purbeck peninsula from Studland (great views to Poole) round to Kimmeridge. **Lulworth Cove,** a sandfringed circle of blue, and the natural rock formation of **Durdle Door** add interest to the Weymouth leg of the path. (Most weekdays, a short section west of Kimmeridge is closed to walkers for military manoeuvres.)

Dorchester   5 D2

The town is as venerable as they come, with an important Neolithic site and the odd Roman relic (a section of wall, the remains of an amphitheatre). But it was Thomas Hardy who really brought Dorchester fame. The writer studied, worked and eventually lived here, from 1883 until his death in 1928 (see box). The local Tourist Information Centre at 7 Acland Road stocks an impressive range of literature on Hardy Country, and the staff there can advise you about any special tours and activities (tel. [0305] 67992). Keen readers of Hardy will want to visit some of the places identified with scenes in the novels. We propose a 13-point itinerary in the Leisure Routes chapter of this guide, pages 62–63.

Red-brick **Max Gate**, the house Hardy designed for himself in Dorchester proper, is closed to the public, but you can see a reconstruction of his study at the **Dorset County Museum** (High West Street). Apart from extensive Hardy material (manuscripts, notebooks and the like), the museum exhibits a collection of fossils and some fascinating artefacts from Maiden Castle. Don't omit a visit to the site itself, only a couple of miles outside town on Dorchester's southern outskirts.

Hardy appropriated the archaic name for **Maiden Castle:** Mai-Dun ("Strong Fort"). The hilltop was first occupied some 3,000 years before the Roman invasion of A.D. 43, though the defences you see today were constructed much later, around the middle of the 4th century B.C. Iron Age chiefs lived with their dependents on the heights, surrounded by a buffer zone of farms and tribal settlements. They were kings of the mountain until the legionaries attacked, led by a future emperor, Vespasian. A footpath climbs up through the grass-grown ramparts to the summit. From the top, there's a great view back towards Dorchester, an elipse of stone surrounded by downland.

Cerne Abbas   *5 D2*
The thatched village (Hardy's Abbot's Cernel) preserves the remnants of a 10th-century Benedictine Abbey and, on the hillside above the abbey, the startlingly nude image of a fertility god, the **Cerne Giant,** cut into the chalk between 1,500

Thomas Hardy
Britain's greatest regional novelist, Hardy (1840-1928) maintained strong links to his native Dorset in his art as in his life. Hardy was born in Higher Bockhampton village, to a stonemason and his wife, a former serving maid. He was educated there and in neighbouring Dorchester, where he served a five-year architectural apprenticeship. Work and travel subsequently took him to London and the Continent, but Hardy always returned to Dorset, the inspiration of *Under the Greenwood Tree* (1872), the first of the Wessex novels, and *Far From the Madding Crowd,* his first success, published serially in 1874. A decade later, he settled permanently in Dorchester. The powerful late novels followed: *Tess of the D'Urbervilles* and *Jude the Obscure* (1895), as well as numerous volumes of poetry.

Hardy wrote about what he knew best, the simple people and rural scenes around him, but his work transcends time and place to deal with the human condition. He treated the themes of adultery, immorality, even murder in a nonjudgemental manner that shocked Victorian morality. Hardy neither condemns nor condones, but understands, a point of view that makes him seem such a modern writer today.

and 2,000 years ago. Archaeologists speculate that the 180-foot (55-m.) outline figure represents Hercules, complete with signature club. To a casual observer, though, the giant may look more like a comic-strip caveman than a god.

Sherborne   *5 D2*
This is Dorset's most beautiful country town, with an abbey, two castles and a medieval centre. The magnificent **Abbey Church** incorporates Saxon, Norman, and Early English features, but it is the fan vaulting of the Perpendicular choir and nave that stands out. Horizontal mirrors allow you to inspect the carved stone in detail, especially the decorated bosses at the intersections of the ribs. The old monastery school survives as Sherborne, one of the elite public schools. According to tradition, King Alfred the Great was educated by the monks of Sherborne.

As for the castles, they occupy a

Capability Brown park: Old Castle, a Norman ruin, and Sir Walter Raleigh's **Sherborne Castle** (1594). Elizabeth I "gave" Raleigh the property when he presented her with a hint and a jewel of equivalent value. The explorer initially attempted to restore the Old Castle, but he ended up by building the new. It wasn't his to enjoy for long. Raleigh ended up in the Tower of London, and his house reverted to the Crown. A diplomat, Sir John Digby, subsequently purchased it, and Digbys live here still.

Weymouth   *5 D2*
The resort will forever be associated with King George III, whose seaside holidays in Dorset made history. Prior to George's first visit in 1789, royals had never gone on vacation. The king enjoyed the experience so much that he made an annual habit of it, returning to Weymouth every time. The stingy Hardy character, Uncle Benjy, complained about high Weymouth (Budmouth Regis) prices in *The Trumpet Major*. "King George hev ruined the town for other folks", he concluded. Spending money with abandon, fashionable 18th-century holidaymakers built the terraced Georgian houses that still line the seafront **Esplanade,** now a more plebeian tangle of deck chairs, sun-worshippers and souvenir sellers.

South of Weymouth lies the barren **Isle of Portland,** a peninsula Hardy characterized as the "Gibraltar of Wessex". This is another important stone quarrying area, the source of rugged, white Portland stone. Hardy locations are thick on the ground here: the ruins of Tudor **Sandsfoot Castle,** where sculptor Jocelyn Pierston trysted over the years with a mother, daughter and grand-daughter called Avice (read *The Well-Beloved)*; 19th-century **Pennsylvania Castle** (built for a local governor named Penn), where Pierston lived in the novel; and **"Avice's Cottage",** now a museum of Portland life.

Pulpit Rock at Portland Bill, the tip of

the peninsula, offers the ultimate Dorset vantage point. The surf crashes dramatically underfoot as you look out towards the churning water of Portland Race. Fair weather or foul, this can be a treacherous stretch of coast. The 1906 **Portland Bill Lighthouse,** fourth on the site, keeps shipping a safe distance from shore. A second, non-operational lighthouse serves as a **Bird Observatory and Field Centre**—for a rare, bird's-eye view of the birds: auks, kittiwake, fulmar and passarines, according to season.

*W*alking the ramparts of Maiden Castle, the Iron Age
earthworks that are one of Europe's oldest fortifications. To reach
the summit, attackers had to penetrate a labyrinth of narrow passages,
with sharp turns between deep ditches and high inner ramparts. When the
Romans arrived in Britain in the 1st century A.D., Celtic chieftains
mounted a last valiant stand at hill forts like this.

Chesil Bank, a wall of shingle 18 miles (29 km.) long, joins Portland to the mainland, and continues west up the coast as far as Abbotsbury. On the lee side of the bank, the **Fleet Lagoon** is the protected haunt of sea birds, mainly cormorants, terns and swans. Abbotsbury's medieval **Swannery** was founded some six centuries ago by monks, who raised the birds for their meat. Once there were thousands of swans on the Fleet. Now they number in the hundreds. Also by the lagoon, the **Subtropical Gardens** of Abbotsbury are the unique legacy of an 18th-century landowner. The abbey ruins and 15th-century tithe barn built by the monks can still be seen in the village centre.

Bridport   5 D2

This venerable river port lies a mile inland from good swimming, fishing and sailing at **West Bay.** The fabrication of fish nets is the big local industry, an outgrowth of Bridport's original rope and cord manufacture. For centuries, Bridport had the rope business all sewed up, supplying sailors—and hangmen—countrywide. A "Bridport dagger", as everybody knew, was a hangman's noose.

Despite its Saxon foundation, Bridport has a mainly Georgian aspect. The especially wide streets once accommodated the rope-makers, who worked outside. Visit the Perpendicular **parish church** and the little **museum,** a cornucopia of vintage rope-making paraphernalia.

A 5-mile (8-km.) detour inland takes you to **Parnham,** a stately home with a difference. This Elizabethan manor provides a timeless setting for the unique furniture designs of John Makepeace, a latter-day Chippendale, who lives and works here. Makepeace creates both one-of-a-kind pieces and limited editions in the Furniture Workshops on the premises (open to the public on Wednesdays). Many articles are on sale—for a price. Makepeace also supervises the influential School for Craftsmen in Wood, based at Parnham.

Lyme Regis   5 D2

As picturesque as you'd expect, with cliffs to either side and hills behind, this small fishing port and resort has inspired novelists from Jane Austen *(Persuasion)* to John Fowles *(The French Lieutenant's Woman).* The Regency bustle of **Broad Street** swoops down to **Marine Parade** and the sea. At the western end of the parade, an ancient breakwater, the **Cobb,** protects the harbour.

Cliff walks are particularly exhilarating in the area of Lyme. Head east 4 miles (6 km.) to **Golden Cap,** at 619 feet (189 m.) the highest cliff on this stretch of the coast. Or walk the rugged **landslip,** a landslide chasm west of town that opened on an eventful Christmas Day last century. To east or west, fossiling is good along the foot of the cliffs, though you can't expect to unearth an ichthyosaurus or pterodactyl as Mary Anning did. Her famous 19th-century finds are displayed at the **museum** in Bridge Street.

Sherborne Abbey's fan-vaulted ceiling reveals a fascinating symbolism. Look for the carving of a long-haired mermaid holding a comb, on one of the bosses over the nave. By coincidence, the abbey occupies the site of a pagan shrine, dedicated to the water spirit that inhabited a nearby stream.

BRITISH ARCHITECTURE

The buildings of Britain—the cathedrals, thatched cottages, Victorian pubs and imposing 19th-century railway terminals—are as varied as its ways of life.

So-called **Norman** architecture (1050–1150)—the British equivalent of Romanesque—survives in various churches, cathedrals and castles: Durham Cathedral, the crypts of Canterbury and Winchester cathedrals, St. John's Chapel and the White Tower in the Tower of London, and Dover Castle, Kent. This solid, ponderous style features simple, geometric decoration and the plain round arch.

Britain's medieval cathedrals show that great architectural achievement of north European Christianity, the **Gothic** style (1150–1550), at its peak. Spires and steeples give churches a fantastic skyward thrust, enhanced by pointed arches and flying buttresses, stained glass and richly carved ornament. Small details—the figure of a toothache sufferer at Wells Cathedral and the famous Lincoln Imp—display a crude medieval humanity.

As on the Continent, the Gothic style divides into three distinct phases. Salisbury Cathedral exemplifies the initial **Early English** phase (to 1280). Also known as the "pointed" style, it has the lancet window as its hallmark. Bristol and Wells cathedrals are typical of the slightly later Decorated style (to 1380). Ogee curves and naturalistic plant forms adorn capitals, corbels and pinnacles. And Bath Abbey and St. George's Chapel, Windsor illustrate the more austere **Perpendicular Gothic** (to 1540), characterized by simpler vertical forms and the panel motif.

Meanwhile, secular buildings across the land—manor houses, guild halls, alms houses—went up in half-timbered "vernacular" style. Perennially popular vernacular architecture (with dark wooden beams and white or buff plaster) remained in favour well beyond the Tudor and Elizabethan eras.

The **Renaissance** manner didn't catch on at first in Britain, though crude classical motifs appear on buildings as diverse as Hampton Court Palace in Middlesex (begun 1514) and Longleat House in Wiltshire (under construction from 1572–80). The real rebirth of British architecture came at the beginning of the 1600s, when Inigo Jones (1573–1652) introduced the use of the dome and classical orders. He derived his **classicism** from a study of Palladio, the 16th-century Italian architect, who in turn was influenced by the writings of the Roman architect Vitruvius. There's a down-to-earth, secular grandeur to Jones's work: the Queen's House at Greenwich, the Banqueting House in Whitehall, London, and the church of St. Paul's, Covent Garden, London. In the last, an example of classicism at its simplest, the primitive Tuscan order reflects the simplicity of the Reformed Church.

Towards the end of the 17th century, architects such as Sir Christopher Wren (1632–1723), Sir John Vanbrugh (1664–1726) and Nicholas Hawksmoor (1661–1736) began to mix classical with Gothic and **Baroque** elements. Wren's St. Paul's Cathedral in London, based on a Gothic plan, with Baroque towers and a magnificent classical dome, is the crowning achievement of the age. Among secular buildings, Blenheim Palace, designed by Vanbrugh with Hawksmoor, stands out. Hawksmoor remains a more shadowy figure. There's a vaguely sinister quality to some of his designs, notably St. Mary Woolnoth in the City of London, and the Mausoleum at Castle Howard in Yorkshire.

In the 18th century, classicism was domesticated to produce the **Georgian** style (1720–1790), which many people consider the most civilized and practical ever. Robert Adam (1728–92), the leading exponent, also produced refined designs for furniture and interiors (Harewood House, near Leeds; Kenwood, London). Georgian elegance is best appreciated not in single buildings but via an entire ensemble. The planned crescents, squares and terraces of Bath by John Wood the Elder (1704–54) and Younger (1728–81) are the supreme example.

A generation later, John Nash (1752–1835) carried the architectural ensemble into a grander, **Regency** mode (1790–1830) with his designs for London's Carlton House Terrace and the terraces adjoining Regent's Park. Regency architecture of a very different kind can be seen in the Royal Pavilion at Brighton, remodelled in 1815 by the versatile Nash for the future King George IV. This ornate piece of orientalism displays Indian and Chinese motifs. It was great fun while it lasted, but Queen Victoria wasn't amused.

Blenheim Palace, Oxfordshire

Victorian architecture (1830–1900) combines high-minded historicism with unprecedented technical know-how. A taste for the Gothic had never really gone away. Sir Charles Barry's (1795–1860) cathedral-like styling of the Houses of Parliament revived it again. Still in his twenties, A.W.N. Pugin (1812–52) collaborated, designing the Gothic details of the façade and interior, including the furniture and fittings. Another example of Victorian historicism in brick and terracotta, the Natural History Museum by Alfred Waterhouse (1830–1905), harks back to a kind of Romanesque. Not everyone was a Medievalist, however, and something of a battle ensued between adherents of the Gothic and classical styles. Sir Robert Smirke (1780–1867), architect of the British Museum — a particularly plain and monumental classical building — took a Greek temple as his model.

New technology made possible such proud Victorian achievements as the tunnels and suspension bridges of Isambard Kingdom Brunel (1806–59) and the magnificent but now vanished Crystal Palace by Sir Joseph Paxton (1801–65), who designed the prefabricated glass and iron structure. for the 1851 Great Exhibition. The huge greenhouses at Kew Gardens, London, give some idea of what it was like.

By the end of the 19th century, a reaction to Victorian excess set in, in the person of Charles Rennie Mackintosh (1868–1928). His spare, angular **Art Nouveau** designs for buildings (the Glasgow School of Art, Sauchiehall Street, Glasgow) and furniture foreshadow the Modernist style.

But the British didn't really take to metal and glass **Modernism.** Suburbia provided the most typical 20th-century form: houses in half-timbered "stockbroker Tudor", complete with stained glass in the hallway and roses in the garden — kitsch or cosy, depending on your point of view. Of course Britain (and the City of London in particular) has its high-rise complexes. Richard Rogers' Lloyd's Building in the City, begun in 1980, shows British Modernism at its best.

The streamlined style has many critics, none more outspoken than Prince Charles, who likened a proposed high-rise extension to the National Gallery to "a carbuncle on the face of an old friend". The nation seems to echo the prince's sentiments. As the Post-Modern 1990s get under way, the trend is towards neo-Georgianism and nostalgia.

129

Cheddar, Cider and Cream Teas

You're never far from the sea—the open Atlantic or English Channel—in the West Country, England's south-westerly extension. The counties of Somerset, Devon and Cornwall share the peninsula and its long coastline, rugged to the north and west, gentler along the southern, Channel shore. The South-West is relatively remote from the rest of Britain, with a distinct regional character. In the old days, the West Country drank more cider than beer (and still drinks plenty), the visitors consumed a lot of cream teas (and still do). Accents are softer and slower, and outsiders have sometimes assumed that wits are, too—to their cost, often enough.

Bath   *5 D2*

The Romans could never resist a hot spring. When they found one here in A.D. 44, they established a settlement, calling it Aquae Sulis (the "waters of Sul", the local Celtic deity). Their baths can still be seen today near the abbey in the city centre. After the Romans left, no one went in much for bathing until the early 18th century, when a Dr. William Oliver built a bath here for sufferers from gout. (His name and his face appear on crunchy Bath Olivers—crackers invented by the good doctor—which some people insist are the best accompaniment to Cheddar or Stilton cheese.) Quite suddenly, taking the waters at Bath became all the rage with fashionable London society, though socializing at soirées, theatre and balls generally took precedence over bathing in, or drinking, the metallic-tasting spa water. Richard "Beau" Nash was appointed Master of Ceremonies in 1704 and dictated for decades the manners and styles of the Bath season. Everybody who was anybody got into a coach and came here, buying houses or taking apartments in the magnificent new Georgian terraces. Bath's reign at the pinnacle of fashion lasted fully a hundred years. Jane Austen writes about it in *Northanger Abbey* from her own youthful experience at the end of the 18th century.

The **abbey** in late Perpendicular style seems to warm rather than dominate the centre. Notice the great west window and the stone-carving on the towers. The angels climbing ladders to heaven commemorate a dream in which God commanded a bishop of Bath to restore the church.

The **Pump Room,** opposite, was one of

Hampers at the ready—and not a folding chair in sight—day-trippers on Dartmoor picnic British style, lounging on the grass.

*D*on't take the plunge: the Roman Great Bath that gave Bath its name is strictly a tourist attraction. But it's still in perfect working order. Water gushes from the source at the rate of ¼ million gallons (nearly a million litres) a day. The temperature is a steaming 46 °C (115 °F).

Taking the Cure
Did it work—immersing yourself up to the neck for hours in the warm waters of Bath? Eighteenth-century doctors' records show that 70 to 80 per cent of patients had their aches and pains much relieved. Sceptics might respond "they would, wouldn't they?" But space-age research backs up the old claims. Weightlessness speeds up excretion of liquid from the body, carrying toxins with it, and near-immersion in baths has the same effect. Many of those coming for treatment were suffering from the high lead content of drinks such as the cider of the time, and the cure helped to wash lead compounds out of the body. Then, no doubt, the satisfied customers went home and carried on drinking as before.

spring. Finds from the adjacent temple complex, revealed in 1983, are on view in a small, on-site museum.

The chief monuments of Georgian Bath lie up the hill from the centre. John Wood the Elder built the terraced houses of **Queen Square** (1728) and the **Circus** (1754) as entities, giving the occupants the feeling of living in something larger. His son, John Wood the Younger, designed the 30 houses of the **Royal Crescent** (1767) to look like a very grand single residence. Now a museum, No. 1 Royal Crescent has been restored and redecorated in late 18th-century style.

The **Assembly Rooms** (1771) near the Circus were *the* place to drink tea, play cards and dance. Now they house a costume museum. Other fine examples of Georgian elegance include the terraces of **Duke Street** and **Great Pulteney Street,** but you can wander at will and discover many more. Like Florence's Ponte Vecchio, Robert Adam's little **Pulteney Bridge** incorporates small shops. At the east end of Great Pulteney Street, the **Holburne of Menstrie Museum** displays superb collections of ceramics and silver from Britain and the Continent. There are many fine paintings on view, too, especially British portraits from the 18th and 19th centuries.

the gathering places for society when Bath was at its zenith. Now all the tourists queue up to have lunch or tea to the strains of the Pump Room trio. On the far side of the room, spa water is dispensed by the glass, still warm from the source. The windows overlook the **King's Bath**, a medieval installation that was the only section of the complex known to Georgian curists.

Excavated in 1878, the **Roman Baths,** below Pump Room level, include the steaming Great Bath and gushing sacred

On a hill to the south, **Prior Park** was

built by John Wood the Elder for Ralph Allen. He owned important quarries of the "Bath stone" from which all those Georgian houses were built. It is still insisted on today, at least for the facing. Three miles (5 km.) east, **Claverton Manor** is the home of the **American Museum in Britain**, featuring rooms furnished with the crafts and antiques of many periods and areas, from colonial New England and French New Orleans to Spanish New Mexico and the Old West. There are comprehensive displays of American Indian and folk art, as well.

Bradford-on-Avon   *5 D2*

This pretty little town of narrow streets and stone houses has three claims to fame. One is the 10th-century **Saxon church**, as well preserved as any in the country and very little altered. That was paradoxically due to the fact that it was turned to other uses when the 12th-century parish church went up. The second highlight is a small, domed **chapel** on the old stone bridge, where pilgrims used to pray. Later it became the town lock-up. And across the bridge at Barton Farm, look for the third: a great 14th-century **Tithe Barn**, 168 feet (51 m.) long with massive timbers supporting the roof.

⚓ *Bristol*   *5 D2*

"All ship-shape and Bristol fashion", goes the old approving phrase. The city is now one of Britain's largest (over half a million if you include the vast suburbs). It all started around the harbour on the River Avon, several miles from the sea and secure against invaders and storms. Bristol's ships dominated the wine trade with France and Spain, and gave the city's name to a type of sherry. John Cabot of Genoa and his Bristol-born son Sebastian sailed from here, reaching mainland North America in 1497. Wool exports, then tobacco imports, brought prosperity and the attendant elegant houses and fine public buildings. In the 20th century, Bristol aircraft and engines led the way from the beginnings of aviation to the supersonic era.

The oldest part of the city lies between Bristol Bridge and Quay Street. Look for the classical **Exchange** building by John Wood the Elder. The brass pillars outside, called the Nails, were used as tables for cash payment: hence, "cash on the nail". What happened to the quay at Quay Street? In the last century this arm of the harbour was partially filled in. The oval **Centre**, a small park, is built on part of it. Just south lies what's left of the channel, with the lively **Watershed** leisure complex on one side and the Arnolfini arts centre on the other.

From the Centre, walk along King Street to the 1766 **Theatre Royal**, which miraculously preserves its original layout. It's the home of the renowned Bristol Old Vic. Across the **Floating Harbour** (the main waterway through the city), you'll see the 292-foot (89-m.) spire on the tower of **St. Mary Redcliffe**, "the fairest, goodliest and most famous parish church in England" (and who would argue with Queen Elizabeth I?). It was founded in the 12th century, and completed in the 19th. Bristol also has a **cathedral**, a fine church in its own right. You'll notice how much of the city is on two levels: old streets below, bridged by newer ones, with steps between. And World War II bombing left some obvious scars; the shopping area of Broadmead is built on the worst-hit part.

Bristol claims two masterpieces of the great engineer Isambard Kingdom Brunel. His 1845 *Great Britain,* the first ocean-going, propellor-driven iron ship, was brought back here in 1970 from the Falkland Islands, where she was abandoned in 1886. You can board the ship, under restoration in the dry dock at the far end of Princes Wharf. Up in the fashionable suburb of Clifton, Brunel's still awe-inspiring **Clifton Suspension Bridge** spans the 250-foot-deep (76-m.) gorge of the Avon. It's been the scene of countless stunts and jumps and daredevil flights.

Somerset

The county name comes from the Saxon word for "lake dwellers". An area of marsh and swamp, the Somerset Levels are England's most extensive wetlands. But Somerset also takes in moorland and hills like the Mendips and Quantocks.

Wells 5 D2

From the busy little high street and marketplace, just pass through the gateway into the precinct of the **cathedral** and you're in a different world. You could almost be across the Channel, for the cathedral's astonishing **west front** is more like the finest in France than any other in England. Imagine this supreme example of the Decorated style when it was finished, in about 1235, with its 400 figures of apostles and saints, angels and prophets all painted in full colour. Wind and weather, Puritan idol-smashers and ill-judged cleaning have taken their toll, so that some statues are missing and some unrecognizable. Recent restoration has tried to protect the survivors and, controversially, put in some replicas. Be sure to walk around the outside to the **east end** as well.

Inside, the Early English austerity of the nave makes a strong first impression, enhanced by the bold scissor-shaped arches in the crossing. They represent an unusual solution to a problem: the tower had threatened to collapse when a spire was added in the 14th century. There's a feast of stained glass, woodcarving and modern embroidery in the choir and, in the north transept, a 14th-century **clock** with model axemen striking the quarter hours and knights jousting every hour. Worn steps lead up to the octagonal **Chapter House,** considered to be the most beautiful of its period (around 1300).

Across the green stands the crenellated **Bishop's Palace.** Swans still circle the moat, but not the famous bell-ringing pair, alas. One of them was run over by a car, and its mate ran away in despair. It's been impossible to train new birds to ring the gatehouse bell at meal times; the tourists keep them all too well fed.

Wookey Hole

North and west of Wells, the limestone Mendip Hills may look solid, but they're honeycombed with holes—Roman lead mines, ancient coal mines and countless caverns cut by rivers and streams that dissolved the rock. Wookey Hole is a group of caves formed where the underground River Axe comes to the surface. Bones found in the caves show they were occupied by Stone Age hunters, when bears, rhinos and mammoths roamed the Mendips. Three caves are open to visitors, and some finds can be seen in the Museum of the Caves. The site has been commercialized for a long time—there's a Madame Tussaud's waxworks exhibition, among other ancillary attractions—but you can get away from the crowds by walking up nearby **Ebbor Gorge.**

Cheddar 5 D2

Spectacular **Cheddar Gorge,** over a mile long and up to 450 feet (137 m.) deep, winds down from the ridge of the Mendips through a dramatic gash in the rocks. Several caverns leading off the gorge can be visited. Attractions include stalactites and stalagmites and Stone Age relics. Cheese from the farms around Cheddar village was so widely imitated that now it's made all over Britain and as far away as North America and New Zealand. The original, wrapped in cloth and matured for months at Somerset farms, is worth searching for.

Glastonbury 5 D2

The town is surrounded by a halo of legend so old that lack of evidence hardly matters. One very ancient belief holds that Joseph of Arimathea came here after the Crucifixion, carrying the Holy Grail —the chalice used at the Last Supper— which he buried under the steep hill called the Glastonbury Tor. When he

Thatchers' Britain: keeping alive ancient skills, artisans affix nature's own roofing material to a house in Exmoor. Thatched roofs, ever rarer in Britain, have fallen victim to exorbitant insurance premiums and the dwindling number of trained workmen.

In the early days, the land all around Glastonbury would have been marsh and lakes. The second great legend identifies the city as the sacred isle of Avalon, where King Arthur came, and where his body was brought after his death. A plaque marks the supposed burial site before what was once the high altar of the abbey church.

Stroll in the town to see several 14th- and 15th-century buildings, including the handsome **George and Pilgrims Inn**, where the more prosperous pilgrims used to stay. The **Abbot's Tribunal** is now a museum with local finds from Iron Age villages that once hid among the surrounding swamps and lakes.

A walk up the **Tor** is worth it for the superb view. At the summit stands the tower of a ruined chapel. **Chalice Well**, in gardens at the foot of the Tor, marks the site where the Holy Grail was buried.

Cadbury Castle

If you're fascinated by Arthurian legend, you'll want to climb the flat-topped hill crowned with an earthwork called Cadbury Castle, near the village of South Cadbury. Some claim this to be the site of Camelot itself. Excavations revealed the remains of a 5th-century timber hall, so someone of importance lived here.

You could spend a whole holiday in the South-West visiting sights with an Arthurian connection. If the idea appeals, see p. 58 in our Leisure Routes section for a detailed itinerary.

leaned on his staff on nearby Wirrall ("Weary-all") Hill, it took root and grew into the Glastonbury Thorn. (This particular tree was chopped down in the Civil War, but a thorn tree in the abbey grounds is said to have grown from a cutting.) Joseph went on to found Britain's first Christian church in Glastonbury, or so the story continues, and the town became a magnet for pilgrims. **Glastonbury Abbey** is today a romantic ruin set amid beautiful grounds.

Montacute House

(near Yeovil) 5 D2

Gabled Montacute, in exemplary Elizabethan style, is one of the most beautiful of England's stately homes. The local Ham Hill stone has weathered to the same honey-gold that gives such warmth to the nearby villages. Montacute narrowly escaped demolition in the 1930s, before the National Trust took the property over. None of the original furniture remains, but a number of valuable period pieces have been loaned or given to the house. And the top-floor **Long Gallery** displays a fine collection of pictures of 16th- and 17th-century notables from the National Portrait Gallery in London, including some portraits of Queen Elizabeth I in magnificently frothy dresses.

Muchelney

This village was once an island in the marshes. In fact, Muchelney means "big island". Benedictine monks founded a monastery here in the 7th century. It was destroyed by Viking raiders in the 9th century, refounded in the 10th and reconstructed in the 15th. Only ruins survive, but the village seems to be built of its stones. Look at the unusual painted ceiling of the parish church, with angels dressed like plump Tudor ladies of the day, around 1600.

Barrington Court

(Ilminster) 5 D2

This fascinating early Tudor house has famous spiral chimneys. The sugar baron, Colonel Lyle, who lived here in the 1920s, avidly collected old wood panelling and fittings from all over Europe and installed them in his house, giving the place a uniquely eccentric quality. Lovers of gardens will want to see Gertrude Jekyll's formal design. The Lyle family now occupy the former stable buildings.

Taunton 5 D2

Somerset's lively county town lies in the rich farmland of the Vale of Taunton or Taunton Deane, famous for cider apples and dairy herds. Don't be put off by modern expansion and traffic: there are special flavours to be sampled. Stubborn independence put Taunton on the "wrong" side in several English rebellions. The Duke of Monmouth was proclaimed king here in 1685 before marching off to defeat at Sedgemoor. Ghastly retribution in the form of Judge Jeffreys' Bloody Assize in the Great Hall of the **Norman castle** sent hundreds to the gallows or the plantations of the West Indies. The castle now houses the **County Museum**. Try to get to the Saturday market, and in summer to the County Ground for the cricket—it's a religion here. Search out the tiny side streets of Georgian houses and bow-windowed shops, and the **Church of St. Mary Magdalene**, with its beautiful slim tower and striking interior.

The rolling, wooded Quantock Hills north-west of Taunton are a maze of hidden hamlets which have been the home of writers from Wordsworth to Evelyn Waugh. **Nether Stowey** has a fine old manor house, but it was in the little cottage at 35 Lime Street that Coleridge wrote *The Rime of the Ancient Mariner*.

The Bristol Channel Coast 5 C-D2

For more than 100 miles (160 km.), the coastline of Somerset and North Devon alternates holiday camps and resorts with some dramatic scenery. **Weston-super-Mare** is the biggest seaside town, with summer throngs and all the traditional entertainments from donkey rides on the beach and Punch and Judy shows to golf and concerts. **Burnham-on-Sea** has extensive sands—the tide seems to go almost out of sight—and a church with a leaning tower: biblical advice was ignored and it was built on sand. There's a strange history to the reredos. Designed for Whitehall Chapel by Inigo Jones and carved by Grinling Gibbons, it was installed instead in Westminster Abbey, discarded, and set up here.

Minehead is noisy and cheerful, with an old quay and harbour, more vast beaches at low tide and good cliff and coastal walks. Not far away lies **Selworthy**, a lovely village of thatched cob cottages. Cob, a cunning blend of chalk rubble, clay, cow manure and even hair, was once widely used to make walls. The walls had to be built up slowly, over months or even years, on a plinth of flint—an early damp-proof course, in fact. These days, central heating in the houses dries the cob, so it cracks, and few know how to make a mixture to patch it

138

up. Climb up to Dunkery and Selworthy beacons for breathtaking views to seaward and inland, over Exmoor.

Exmoor National Park 5 C2
Small is beautiful in this favourite of England's many stretches of moorland. Only about 21 miles (34 km.) from east to west, and no more than 12 miles (19 km.) north to south, it's nevertheless a region of infinite variety. Red deer, wild ponies and grouse make their home on the high heath and in the hidden valleys. Hardy sheep graze the uplands, and little villages nestle amid the softer cow pastures. This is walking country, but keep an eye on the weather, which can turn bleak.

Exmoor is the memorable setting of R.D. Blackmore's fateful novel *Lorna Doone,* and fans of the book like to identify the places on Exmoor that it refers to: Doone Valley itself is placed a few miles north of Simonsbath. **Dulverton** makes a good centre for exploration of the southern part. **Watersmeet,** naturally enough the place where two rivers join in a picturesque valley, is the best starting point for walks in the north of the park. Don't miss the little town of **Dunster,** with its 17th-century octagonal Yarn Market and dramatic castle (though the romantic look is the result of 19th-century additions).

The high ground of Exmoor meets the sea in some of the finest coastal scenery in Britain. The best way to see it is by walking the Somerset and Devon Coast Path, where cliffs and promontories alternate with headlong descents. But the road west from Minehead is spectacular enough. The one-in-four ascents out of **Porlock** and **Countisbury** were considered a great test for cars in the early days of motoring.

Exmoor straddles the county boundary. At clifftop **Lynton,** with **Lynmouth** hundreds of feet below it on the sea, you're in Devon. Torrential rains on the moor in 1952 sent disastrous floods through Lynmouth, causing severe loss of life.

Devon
The county's charms are no secret to the British holidaymakers who crowd the resorts and villages of Devon in the summer season. Take care on the roads: driving can be difficult in the narrow lanes.

North Devon 4-5 B-C2
Ilfracombe is a breezy resort with an old harbour, dozens of shingle beaches and the bonus of **Torrs Walk,** a winding path that seems to hang over the sea. Further west, the more sheltered waters of the Bristol Channel give way at **Woolacombe** to Atlantic swells, to the joy of all surfers. Don't mix up the two old towns of **Barnstaple** and **Bideford,** unless you want to annoy the inhabitants. They were rival ports until silt in the River Taw kept ships from reaching Barnstaple, the main market town of North Devon. Some of England's greatest sea captains came from Devon, and the men of Bideford sailed with the best.

You can take a voyage, too, from Bideford (or Ilfracombe in summer) to **Lundy Island.** The 20-mile (32-km.) trip can be choppy, so don't forget to take precautions if you're susceptible to seasickness. The island, only 3 miles (5 km.) long and roughly half a mile (1 km.) wide, is a bird sanctuary and perfect for walking. In fact there aren't any cars, and not many beds either, so make a reservation if you want to stay overnight.

Back on the mainland, **Appledore** is a charming little fishing port and yacht harbour, with steep narrow streets of Tudor cottages climbing from the quayside. But when it comes to steep streets, **Clovelly** takes the medal. Its stepped and cobbled alleys would be quite impossible for cars, so they have to be left in the huge park (lot) at the top. So picturesque and celebrated is Clovelly that the tide of visitors sometimes threatens to swamp it. As an antidote, watch the white foam fly where roaring surf pounds grim, jagged rocks at **Hartland Point.**

Exeter Cathedral's west front displays an impressive array of 14th-century sculpted figures. But they survived only by sheer luck. When, during a night-time air raid in World War II, the Germans mistook Exeter for Plymouth and thoroughly bombed the place, most of the city's medieval town centre was destroyed. A walk down today's modern High Street reveals little that's exceptional. But step into the Cathedral Close and you enter another world: the great Gothic edifice flanked by Norman towers occupies a green oasis of calm. Around the close, some of Exeter's few remaining half-timbered houses now serve as coffee houses and craft shops.

Exeter 5 C2

Devon's capital was Roman Isca, and the 1st-century walls are still visible along Southernhay and Northernhay. They were uncovered, bizarrely, by the same bombing raid of World War II that burned so much of the old city around the **cathedral**. By some miracle, this, Exeter's glory, was almost unscathed. The two towers are true survivors—having been retained from an earlier Norman building. The main body of the cathedral dates from the 14th century, with wonderful rib vaulting, a minstrel's gallery and massive, canopied bishop's throne. Nearby in Cathedral Close, **Mol's Coffee House** (now an art shop) was once the haunt of Elizabethan captains—Drake, Raleigh and others. They must have felt as if they were at sea in the stern of a great galleon.

From Princesshay, you can enter the underground passages which supplied Exeter, luckier than most medieval cities, with pure spring water. Ask about guided tours at the Tourist Information Centre in the Civic Centre.

Down at the quay by the River Exe, the **Maritime Museum** features a fascinating collection of 100 boats—coracles to sampans—many afloat on the river and the adjoining canal basin.

North of Exeter, the road leads to Exmoor (see p. 139), but first, at **Bickleigh,** you'll find an old-world village of thatch and cob cottages.

Tiverton was once famous for wool, then for lace; now it's quite industrial. Nearby **Knightshayes Court** is worth a visit. William Burges designed this triumph of Victorian Gothic architecture for John Heathcoat-Amory, 19th-century heir to the Tiverton lace fortune. The garden is one of Devon's finest. Hounds chase foxes across the amusing topiary hedges.

South Devon Resorts 5 C2-3

The sheltered south coast dresses itself up as an "English Riviera", with palm trees and rows of white-painted hotels. It got a

boost every time there was a European war, from Napoleonic times onwards, when it was difficult to travel abroad. The fashion grew for retiring here, so some of the resorts are pretty sleepy.

Beer has the last chalk cliffs on the Channel coast, with caves that were once used by smugglers, and **Branscombe** (pop. 500) is an exceptionally appealing little village of cob and thatch houses. Queen Victoria lived at **Sidmouth** as a baby, and the town retains an air of respectability.

*Rows of identical terraced houses are not unique
to the little Devon town of Beer. They are everywhere to be found. Look
carefully, though; each house has its own individual touch—with gates
in different styles, no two door knockers alike and front gardens trim
or tangled. Such housing is particularly conducive to neighbourliness—
you can't help but know what's going on next door.*

143

The red cliffs and pebble beach of **Budleigh Salterton** were the setting for *The Boyhood of Raleigh* (the Millais painting and the actuality). The South Devon Coast Path crosses the clifftops from here to **Exmouth,** the oldest resort in the county. People first came to Exmouth for sea bathing early in the 18th century. It's not far to **Teignmouth** from the 1,700-foot-long (518-m.) estuary bridge: the former fishing port has been transformed into a vast yacht harbour, as an old resort keeps up with the times.

That's even more true of the biggest and showiest, the Queen of the Coast, **Torquay,** where facilities operate all the year round, and estate agents advertise time-share apartments, just as they do in the Algarve. For contrast, look into **Kent's Cavern** (Ilsham Road), which Stone Age remains show to be one of the oldest inhabited sites in Britain. In Torbay Road, the ruins of 12th-century **Torre Abbey** merit a look; the later house on the site is the local art gallery.

Together with Torquay, Paignton and Brixham border beautiful Torbay. At **Paignton's** little port they still bring in crabs and lobsters, but the fish market to see is at **Brixham** in the early morning. The catch there includes the fish you'll eat for dinner in restaurants throughout the South-West.

A few miles inland, **Totnes** has one of the most attractive old town centres in England. A host of 15th- to 19th-century buildings line the main street as it climbs from the River Dart, past the Tudor East Gate to the hilltop Norman castle. Craft and antiques shops are a Totnes speciality. Some of the best of them have a **Butterwalk** address.

The name of **Dartmouth** has become synonymous with the Royal Naval College, but there's also much of tourist interest. As you walk in the old town, keep an eye out for **St. Saviour's Church** (1372), noted for its carved stone and woodwork, and **Agincourt House,** the home of a 15th-century merchant. The river estuary is beautifully sheltered,

and guarded by two castles: they used to haul up a chain between them to keep out enemy ships.

At the southernmost point of Devon, **Salcombe's** protected waters are perfect for sailing. The locals boast about the mild climate and grow orange and lemon trees to prove it.

Plymouth   4 B3

The waters of its Sound count as one of the finest natural harbours in the world. No wonder Plymouth has seen so many famous ships and sailors put to sea in peace and war: Sir Francis Drake, finishing his legendary game of bowls on the Hoe before engaging the Spanish Armada in 1588; the *Mayflower* Pilgrims voyaging to the New World in 1620; Captain Cook setting out on his three-year journey around the world in 1768; and the battalions joining the D-Day landings and the 1982 Falklands task force. The city centre was comprehensively smashed in World War II bombing, so buildings are modern rather than historic. The panorama from the top of the high-rise Civic Centre gives you an idea of the layout of this big city, dwarfing any other west of Bristol.

Some of the old atmosphere survives in the **Barbican** area, between the 17th-century citadel and Sutton Pool, the original harbour that Drake knew. Fishing boats tie up here now. Look for **Island House,** where the Pilgrim Fathers spent their last night in England, and **Mayflower Steps** on the pier, where they embarked. Plaques nearby commemorate other colonial voyages: the departure of Bermuda's

Top of the pops; bands and groupies come and go, but Britain dominates the international music scene.

first settlers in 1609, and New Zealand's 230 years later. The Old Customs House by the quay, and taverns like the Ship Inn and Green Lantern, date from Plymouth's Elizabethan heyday.

Take in the view of the Sound, its inlets and headlands from the green expanse of the **Hoe**. Or, better still, go for a harbour cruise. Circular trips take you out past Drake's Island and the dockyard at **Devonport,** home to the grey ships of the Royal Navy.

When Drake got back from his voyage around the world in 1581, he used some of his store of gold to buy **Buckland Abbey,** 6 miles (9 km.) north of Plymouth. The Great Hall and wood-panelled drawing room look as they did in Drake's day. On the upper floor, naval displays feature relics of Drake, including the celebrated drum that he took with him to sea. A legend claims that the drum will beat if England is ever in danger, and that its sound will bring Drake's spirit to the rescue.

Stately homes are scattered around the shores of the Sound. **Saltram House,** 3 miles (5 km.) east of Plymouth, is a magnificent Georgian remodelling of a Tudor mansion, with rooms by Robert Adam and many Reynolds portraits. **Antony House** lies across the Tamar, near the Torpoint ferry. This classical early Georgian residence in silvery granite has the original furnishings, pictures and famous needlework of the Carew family, whose descendants still live here. You can reach Tudor **Cotehele,** up the Tamar from Plymouth, by boat as well as road. It's a remarkable survival: the Edgecumbe family moved into a newer house (Mount Edgecumbe on Plymouth Sound) and didn't modernize this one. The collections of armour and furniture are outstanding, and there's a branch of the National Maritime Museum here, too.

Dartmoor 5 C2-3

When you've had enough of cities, beaches and summer crowds, retreat inland to the wilderness. Dartmoor (a national park) is the least inhabited tract of land in southern England, though it's dotted with traces of medieval tin workings and prehistoric stone circles.

Dartmoor is superb pony-trekking and walking country, but if you go on your own, check the weather forecast: mists can roll in and it's notoriously easy to get lost. The granite outcrops called "tors" that rear up out of the moor are great landmarks—if you can tell which is which. And beware of bogs, dangerously marshy areas that aren't always obvious.

Information is available year-round at the park headquarters in **Bovey Tracey.** In spring and summer, branches are open at **Okehampton,** a good base for the northern moor, and **Tavistock,** the market town to the south-west. The Bronze Age village of **Grimspound** is ringed by a huge wall to keep out wild animals. That's near **Widecombe-in-the-Moor,** known for the September fair that "Uncle Tom Cobbleigh and all" were heading for in the old folk song. When you see the crowd there, you'll think they've arrived.

Say "Dartmoor" in a word-association game and most British people will respond "prison". High on the bleakest part of the moor, the famous gaol (jail) originally held POWs from the Napoleonic Wars. Now it's for criminals, and

---

Naughty but Nice

Anywhere west of Stonehenge they start, the "Cream Teas" signs. What should you get? A pot of tea, of course, not just a cup. Maybe some little sandwiches, maybe some cakes, too. But definitely scones, with butter, jam (preferably home-made strawberry) and *cream.* Thick yellow cream, it should be. Not runny, certainly not runny. Devotees will argue till the cows come home whether Devonshire or Cornish (clotted) cream is more toothsome. Devonshire is made by gently heating the milk (not boiling it) so that the cream concentrates on top to be skimmed off. Cornish has itself been heated to concentrate it still further, to the consistency of slightly crumbly butter. Spread the scones with butter, jam and a liberal blob of the calorific, cholesterolic cream—and enjoy. You can always skip dinner.

Princetown has grown up around it to house the staff. It all looks depressing and you won't want to linger. **Dartmeet** is far more attractive: an ancient, rough stone "clapper" bridge crosses the bubbling East Dart just north of the modern road bridge.

The unique **Castle Drogo,** built between 1910 and 1930 is the remarkable work of Lutyens. It's set high over the gorge of the River Teign, so its views of the moor are superb. You feel like a game of croquet on the lawn? No problem, they have equipment for hire.

Cornwall

The River Tamar almost severs Cornwall from the rest of England. Practically an island, it was always a place apart, looking more to the sea than to neighbouring but very different Devon. The separate Cornish language died out, though it's been revived by a few enthusiasts; relics remain in the soft dialect that rolls like the sea swell.

The South Coast   *4 A–B3*
The railway bridge across the Tamar brought the first wave of tourists to Cornwall (1859), but they were as nothing compared with the summer migrations of motorists that followed. **Looe** was the first of the picturesque fishing villages to net a huge catch of visitors. It's still one of the most crowded, and the headquarters of English shark fishing. (Sharks? Don't worry, "Jaws" has never been spotted; swimming is perfectly safe, though it might be cold.)

Polperro's little harbour is so narrow at the mouth that it used to be shut off in bad weather. The narrow streets are closed to cars and some of the fishermen's cottages seem to stand right in the water. In the Middle Ages, the men of neigbouring **Fowey** (pronounced "foy") used to go in for private enterprise raids on the coast of France. Cross on the ferry to Polruan for the best view of the old

waterfront. These days Fowey engages in the peaceful export of china clay from the diggings near **St. Austell,** where spoil heaps pile up like miniature alps. (Britain is one of the world's main producers of the clay, used in paper and cosmetics as well as porcelain.) Inland from Fowey, near Lostwithiel, you'll find the romantic ruins of the Norman castle of **Restormel.**

Mevagissey, one of the prettiest of Cornwall's fishing villages, used to export thousands of tons of salted pilchards a year to the Catholic countries of Europe, especially Italy. Now the fishermen take tourists out after sharks.

In **Veryan,** a bit inland, are some curious round houses that were supposed to deny the devil any corner in which to hide. The village is the gateway to **Roseland,** which has nothing to do with roses (the word means "spur" or "heath" in Cornish). But this stretch of coast does have one of the gentlest climates in all England and some have dubbed it the "Cornish Riviera".

The superb harbour of **Falmouth** is a yachting centre and it's still an important port. Being the first and last call in England once made it the place where urgent transatlantic mail was transferred between ship and shore. Dominating the bay, **Pendennis Castle** formed part of Henry VIII's chain of coastal defences. Continental invasion never came, but the fort saw action in the Civil War: the Roundheads finally captured it after a six-month siege.

The 18th-century merchants of Falmouth who aspired to more genteel surroundings went to live in **Truro,** which soon boasted the most elegant Georgian terraces west of Bath. Fine Regency and Victorian houses were added, though a Georgian aura survives along Boscawen and Lemon streets. The town also claims Cornwall's cathedral, a Gothic-revival building begun in 1880, four years after Cornwall gained ecclesiastical independence from Devon. Truro **museum** is Cornwall's best, noted especially for its display of minerals.

*T*rying *his luck in a choppy sea at Newquay, a surfer attempts to overrule the law of gravity. On a fine summer day, Newquay's spacious sand beach can become crowded, but there's always plenty of room in the ocean.*

Mont-Saint-Michel in Normandy. Later, defence-minded kings decided it would make a fine spot for a castle. You can reach the site for three hours at low tide by a stone causeway. Otherwise take a boat from Marazion or from **Penzance,** end of the railway line from London and an early seaside resort. Just south, the little fishing harbour of **Mousehole** (pronounced "mowsal") attracts visitors by virtue of its name as much as its charm.

Finally, at the most westerly point of England (though not of Britain), comes the end of the road, the vast car park, worn paths and granite cliffs of **Land's End.** Millions go, just for a geographical fact, though various facilities have now been built to give them something to "do".

Next stop America? Not quite, for 28 miles (45 km.) south-west of Land's End, the **Isles of Scilly** lie scattered across the sea like jewels. You reach **St. Mary's,** the largest (and that's only 4 sq. mi./ 10 sq. km.), by boat or helicopter from Penzance. Launches can take you on to the other inhabited islands: **Tresco** noted for its semi-tropical gardens and two castles (one was put in the wrong place so they had to build another); **St. Martin's,** with more open heathland and fine walks; tiny **Bryher** and southerly **St. Agnes.** Rare birds that have been blown off course alight on the Scillies, bringing a rush of "twitchers" (bird-spotters) to log them. Four miles (6 km.) out from St. Agnes, **Bishop Rock Lighthouse** signals ships to keep away from treacherous reefs that wrecked so many in the past and now bring divers lured by relics—and by Spanish gold.

North Cornwall   4 A3–B2

The north Cornish coast has few harbours to compare with the south. Instead, Atlantic rollers crash onto open sandy beaches or at the foot of dramatic cliffs. **St. Just,** near Land's End, was a centre of tin mining: some of the workings, like Botallack, ran far out under the sea. Now the old engine houses make romantic

Most southerly point on the English mainland, the pinnacles of the **Lizard** have looked down on countless shipwrecks. The multicoloured serpentine rock here is polished into souvenirs, but you should see it in its natural state—in the cliffs of **Kynance Cove** and around the old smugglers' harbour of **Mullion Cove.**

The extraordinary **St. Michael's Mount,** rising out of the sea like a vision, was once crowned by an abbey founded by monks from the remarkably similar ruins. Geevor, at **Boscaswell,** the last mine to operate in Cornwall, houses a tin mining museum. There's another at **Pool** near Redruth.

St. Ives was once a tin and fishing port, but as these trades declined in the 19th century, a wave of artists, and then a flood of tourists, discovered it. St. Ives has survived, almost as pretty as ever, though many cottages have been turned into gift shops and restaurants. The potter Bernard Leach worked here, and his studio still functions in the tradition he established. Barbara Hepworth's house is now a museum of her life and sculpture.

Newquay is the main resort, with great sandy beaches that bring surfers from as far as Australia and Hawaii. On the cliff-tops, you'll see huers' huts, a relic of the Cornish fishing industry. It was a huer's job to spot shoals of pilchards and signal to the fishing boats. **Padstow**'s old fishermen's cottages cluster around the quaysides, but the river mouth has silted up. Consequently the harbour is much less important than it was when Sir Walter Raleigh presided at the **Court House** on the South Quay as Warden of Cornwall.

Crowds are drawn to **Tintagel** by the magic name of King Arthur, accepting the legend that this was his birthplace. Not by the village, which is worth seeing only for the 14th-century house which served as the Old Post Office. Nor the 12th-century castle ruins on the promontory linking Tintagel Head to the mainland. They're several hundred years too late. And yet, these black cliffs and caves may persuade you.

Boscastle harbour—now sanded up—had such a tricky entrance that vessels had to be "warped through" (towed by rope). The cliffs and country around are magnificent for walks. At **Bude,** north Cornwall signs off with more spectacular scenery, 500-foot (150-m.) cliffs and sandy surf beaches.

Inland, the market towns of **Bodmin** and **Launceston,** once dreaded bottle-

necks for traffic, are now by-passed, but worth a detour. Bodmin has a fine 15th-century church, St. Petroc's, and Launceston a hilltop Norman castle and the 16th-century church of St. Mary Magdelene, almost covered with stone carving. Between the two towns lies the wild upland region of **Bodmin Moor,** most of it only accessible to walkers. It's dotted with prehistoric standing stones and circles. Here, too, is Dozmary Pool, supposed by some to be the lake into which Sir Bedivere threw the sword Excalibur.

150

*N*ear Land's End the breeze arriving from across the
Atlantic can add wings to a golf ball—or anything else not battened down.
Many of the houses here seem to crouch, as if waiting for the next
sou'wester to blow.

Rich in Farmlands, Rich in Spirit

The eastern lowlands are like nowhere else in Britain. There are no big cities, no mountains either, no sense of connection to the rest of the country. Isolated for centuries by a barrier of marshland and fen, the people of East Anglia have developed a sturdy independence of mind and freedom of spirit.

Strictly speaking, three counties make up Britain's eastern bulge: Essex, Suffolk and Norfolk. But the two neighbouring counties of Cambridgeshire and Lincolnshire have a similar pastoral landscape of sprawling farmlands under boundless skies.

Cambridge
9 C3

The "other place" is smaller than Oxford, and more compact in its charm. More serious, too. Let Oxford nurture prime ministers and literary men; Cambridge produces physicists, economists and medical researchers. And whereas Oxford is tainted with industry, in Cambridge the town is the university is the town.

Much of the character of the place comes from the River Cam, which flows silently behind the medieval colleges, between green lawns overhung by willows. Take a punt along the delightful stretch of river and garden known as **The Backs** and you'll slide slowly past Queen's and King's colleges, under ancient Clare Bridge and the Venetian-style Bridge of Sighs. The boatyards at Mill Lane (off Trumpington Street) and Quayside (off Magdalene Street) have punts for hire. But you may find it difficult to propel yourself along: poling is not one of those skills you acquire immediately. "Chauffeurpunt" (in Silver Street, behind Queen's College) offers the easy way out, for about the price of a taxi.

Cambridge University began with a handful of students attached to religious and lay teachers. The first college, Peterhouse, was founded in 1284 by the Bishop of Ely. And the newest, Robinson, came into being in 1979, bringing the total to 25. As at Oxford, the colleges follow a monastic design, with buildings grouped around courts (the equivalent of the Oxford quad). Women were not admitted to the university until the mid-19th century, when Girton, the first women's college, was founded. Today the university has 10,000 undergraduates, more than a third women, and most of the colleges are open to both sexes.

Reflections of far-off Venice in Cambridge: pole-propelled punts and even a romantic Bridge of Sighs.

The colleges lie fairly close together— off the main street known, variously, as St. John's, Trinity, King's Parade and Trumpington. Make your way past the old houses, coffee bars and shops (Heffer's for books is a major landmark) to "K.P.", King's Parade, in the heart of Cambridge. **King's College Chapel** dominates this stretch, magnificent in its setting of green lawns. A masterpiece of the Perpendicular style, the chapel is bold, structurally simple, yet richly decorated within. Light pouring through the stained-glass windows (there are 25 in all) tints the stone red, violet and gold. Behind the altar, *The Adoration of the Magi* by Rubens swirls with colour, too, while the fan vaulting overhead adds to the overall elaboration. Attend the evensong service at 5.30 p.m. to hear the college choir sing.

Narrow King's Lane takes you to **Queens' College.** The name pays tribute to the two founding queens: Margaret, wife of Henry VI, and Elizabeth, wife of Edward IV. Notice the complicated **sundial** in Pump Court, incorporating one of the rare moondials in existence. Erasmus, the Renaissance scholar and theologian, lodged in the Tower here during a three-year stint as Greek professor from 1510. The half-timbered building by Cloister Court is the President's Lodge. Queens' College extends to the opposite bank of the Cam. Take the **Mathematical Bridge** across. This matchstick construction was made without nails (according to "mathematical" principles) in the 18th century. A hundred years later, curious students took it apart to see how it was done and couldn't put it back together again, so it's now bolted.

North of King's College Chapel, at Gonville and Caius College, that is **Caius** (pronounced "keys"), you can pass through the three gates of student life: the Gate of Humility, the Gate of Virtue and, finally, the Gate of Honour, which leads to **Senate House.** Degree ceremonies take place in this Palladian auditorium designed by James Gibbs.

Trinity is the largest college in the university, with 1,000 students. As you pass through the gateway, look up at the statue of the founder, King Henry VIII. In one hand he holds an orb and in the other, a chair leg—the result of a student prank. The **Great Court** is the largest in Cambridge. Traditionally, students try to run the circuit of this 2-acre (½-ha.) expanse while the clock in the chapel tower chimes out the strokes of 12.

Trinity's most distinguished building, the **Wren Library,** stands in Nevile's Court. An arcade runs underneath, giving a view of the river and the Backs—a stroke of genius on the part of the architect, Sir Christopher Wren. Books published before 1820 are kept in the library, along with Sir Isaac Newton's notebook of his Trinity expenses and Lord Byron's college admissions book, recording his pledge of good behaviour. Prince Charles, first member of the royal family to attend university, was a Trinity man.

Neighbouring **St. John's** was the college of William Wordsworth and Cecil Beaton. At the entrance stands a three-storey Tudor gatehouse, decorated with heraldic beasts and Tudor emblems in honour of Lady Margaret Beaufort, mother of Henry VII and patron of the college. The Norman **Round Church** at the top of St. John's Street was built by the Knights Templar around 1130.

A student at Cambridge in his day, Samuel Pepys left his library to his old college, **Magdelene** (pronounced "maudlin"), when he died in 1707. Among the books (kept on the original shelves in the original order) was his famous coded diary.

Venerable **Jesus College** (off Jesus Lane) incorporates buildings of the 12th-century nunnery of St. Radegund. The old cloister, slightly enlarged, survives as Cloister Court, and the church where the nuns worshipped serves, with subsequent additions, as the college chapel. The stained-glass windows in medieval spirit were designed by Edward Burne-Jones and others for Morris and Co.

Two other colleges to look for: **Christ's**, in St. Andrew's Street, famous for its gardens (though there is nothing to substantiate the claim that John Milton planted the legendary mulberry tree); and neighbouring **Emmanuel**, with its Wren chapel and colonnade, where 21 of the Pilgrim Fathers studied.

The university museum, the **Fitzwilliam** (Trumpington Street), admirably fulfills its didactic purpose with wide-ranging collections of Egyptian, Greek and Roman antiquities, European porcelain, rare books, coins and medals and paintings from the Italian Renaissance to the 19th- and 20th-century British school. The **Kettle's Yard Art Gallery** (Northampton Street) features paintings and sculpture of the 1920s and '30s in a domestic setting.

Around Cambridge   *9 C3*

Literary pilgrims head a couple of miles south of town to the Old Vicarage at **Grantchester**, home of World War I poet Rupert Brooke. The village war memorial commemorates his death.

South again is the market town of **Saffron Walden**, famed from medieval times as a centre of the saffron trade. Enjoy the half-timbered charm of the High Street, a quaint medley of old houses and inns like the Cross Keys, inaugurated in 1450. The curious earth maze in the vicinity probably had something to do with pre-Christian fertility rites.

Nearby **Audley End** is the largest Jacobean house ever built. This flagrant example of *folie de grandeur* bankrupted Thomas Howard, Lord Treasurer to James I. James remarked rather pointedly that the house was "too large for a king"—but that didn't stop his grandson Charles from buying it several decades later. Audley End eventually reverted to the Howard family, who spent 40 years cutting it down to size. Two wings were demolished, but what remains is very grand indeed. The Great Hall is decorated with fine wood and plaster work, and the drawing room, done over by Robert Adam, preserves its original furnishings.

North-east of Cambridge, **Anglesey Abbey** has been rebuilt so many times the house holds little intrinsic interest. But Lord Fairhaven's collection of clocks, furniture, paintings and coins is worth seeing, as are the grounds—over a hundred landscaped acres (40 ha.), with a working watermill that grinds corn.

The A10 takes you the 15 short miles (24 km.) north of Cambridge to **Ely** (the old Isle of Eels). Treacherous marshland surrounded the island, where Hereward the Wake, "last of the English", held out against William the Conqueror until 1071. While most of the marshland has been drained, the small National Trust reserve called **Wicken Fen** is much as it was in Hereward's day—half open water, half marsh and often shrouded in mist.

The silhouette of Ely's massive **cathedral** is visible for miles across the flat fenland. Construction began in 1083 on the site of an abbey founded by St. Etheldreda. In 1322, the central tower fell, destroying the Norman choir. The choir was rebuilt in Decorated style, and an octagonal lantern tower, the great **Octagon**, was raised. Eight 64-foot (19-m.) oak posts support this tour de force of medieval engineering of haunting beauty. All England was searched for trees of sufficient size.

Suffolk

With its pink-washed, half-timbered villages, Suffolk is the gentle face of East Anglia, a county of tall churches, broad fields and placid rivers. But the coast is busy with ferries and shipping.

Aldeburgh   *9 D3*

This small fishing town provided the inspiration for Sir Benjamin Britten's 1945 opera *Peter Grimes,* based on a poem by a local writer. Sir Benjamin, a native of Aldeburgh himself, returned the compliment. The Aldeburgh Festival

he founded for the première of *Peter Grimes* has gone from strength to strength. But you have to book tickets months ahead for the main June season. The opera house is actually in Snape, a few miles inland.

Constable Country
The country around Dedham Vale is gently undulating and human in scale, planted with sturdy oak trees and slender church towers. This is the terrain that inspired John Constable, son of a mill owner, to paint some of the most enduring images of the English countryside. "I associate my careless boyhood with all that lies on the banks of the Stour," he wrote. "Those scenes made me a painter."

Constable tourism focuses on the village of **Dedham,** largest and most attractive in the Vale, with colour-washed Georgian houses and a 15th-century church that Constable painted time and again. Detailed maps on sale locally pinpoint Constable sights and viewpoints featured in the paintings. A detailed itinerary appears in the Leisure Routes section of this guide, p. 63.

A footpath meanders through the fields from Dedham to the hamlet of **Flatford,** the inspiration of some of Constable's greatest works (*Flatford Mill* [1817], *The Haywain* [1821]). The mill Constable's father owned is now on private land, but the National Trust opens the adjacent Bridge Cottage to the public. There's a small Constable exhibition, a book shop and a tea garden by the Stour—all very pleasant.

Some 800 tons of wood and lead, the octagon and lantern of Ely Cathedral are a feat of medieval engineering.

It's just a mile to **East Bergholt,** the parish where Constable was born in 1776 and spent much of his youth. Even without so notable a son, it would be worth visiting for its pink half-timbered houses, dating from the time of the Flemish weavers. The church of **St. Mary** hasn't changed since the Constable family worshipped here. Money to complete the tower ran out long before John Constable was born and it still stands unfinished.

The Wool Towns   *9 C3*
Beyond Dedham Vale the landscape changes subtly. Follow the B1070 road as it weaves through fields and in and out of a series of small towns. Every time you use the car horn, flocks of birds, startled, fly up.

Around **Hadleigh,** you'll see men on tractors hard at work, and the token flock of sheep. But it's nothing like it was in the old days when this one-time wool centre was one of the most prosperous towns in the country. The medieval heart of Hadleigh contains the 14th-century **Church of St. Mary;** the turreted Tudor gatehouse known as the **Deanery;** and the **Guildhall,** spectacularly overhung by two upper storeys.

Kersey is a typical medieval Suffolk weaving village. Modest weavers' cottages and pastel-tinted, half-timbered dwellings line The Street, as the main thoroughfare is called. It dips down to a ford across a small stream and uphill again to the Perpendicular **Church of St. Mary.**

One of the most visited little towns in Suffolk, **Lavenham** has as complete a collection of half-timbered houses as you'll find anywhere in England. It's all eminently photographable, from the **Church of St. Peter and St. Paul,** on its hill, to the old **Guildhall** the clothmakers built. Lavenham was famous for its blue cloth, tinted with woad, the favourite dye of the ancient Picts.

For a village, **Long Melford** really is long—2½ miles (4 km.) from end to end.

157

*D*edham Vale has changed little since John Constable painted this scene in 1808. Walk through the fields from Dedham village to Flatford and you can revel in the same rural landscape, the vivid greens of the water meadow and the ephemeral effects of light and cloud.

Buildings range from the heyday of wool, when the crenellated parish church went up, to prosperous Victorian times. Turreted **Melford Hall**, the Tudor mansion to the east of the central green, has a good collection of porcelain, period furniture and paintings. There's also a room devoted to Beatrix Potter, who often came to stay.

The painter Thomas Gainsborough was born at **Sudbury** in 1727. **Gainsborough's House**, in Gainsborough Street—where else?—is the tourist mecca here. The father of the painter joined two Tudor houses and added a Georgian façade. There are some examples of Gainsborough's art on view, all minor works.

Bury St. Edmunds 9 C3

St. Edmund is literally buried in Bury, as the locals call the town. Edmund, the young Saxon king of East Anglia, was beheaded by the Danes in 869 for refusing to renounce Christianity. According to tradition, searchers found his head guarded by a wolf, a scene featured on the municipal coat of arms. The abbey which sheltered the martyr's remains was originally founded in 636, rebuilt to take his body in 903, and enlarged in the 11th century as it became a centre for pilgrims from all over Europe.

After the Dissolution, the abbey fell into ruin. Public gardens surround what remains of the refectory and abbot's house. Two of the gate towers survive intact, the great 14th-century Abbey Gateway, at the entrance to the gardens, and the **Norman Tower**, now the belfry of Bury's Perpendicular Gothic cathedral.

Norfolk

In Norfolk, fields and pheasant-breeding woodlands give way to flat fens (reclaimed inland swamps) and coastal marshes, interspersed with stretches of open water known as the Broads.

Norwich 9 D2

The university town of Norwich is a fairly quiet place today. Odd to think that in the 17th century it was second in size to London. The cathedral is the main sight. The Norman castle (clad in Bath stone a century and a half ago) runs a distant second, with a boat trip through the Broads an added attraction.

The **cathedral's** slender Perpendicular spire is the trademark of Norwich. It's the second highest in England after Salisbury's. Massive Norman pillars in the nave soar into Gothic vaulting, ornamented with intricately carved bosses.

You can enter the Cathedral Close from the old Saxon marketplace, known as **Tombland**, through either of two medieval gates, Erpingham or St. Ethelbert's. The grounds run down to the River Wensum at the old watergate of **Pulls Ferry**.

Norwich's town centre includes a network of old alleys, cobbled streets and arcades. **Elm House Street** is one of the finest medieval thoroughfares in Britain. Unusual facing of patterned square flint distinguishes the **Guildhall** on the main Market Square. You'll find similar facing on the **Bridewell Museum**, a 14th-century merchant's house, now a museum of craft and industry. But the most interesting museum is installed in the **castle.** Paintings and watercolours by members of the late 18th-century Norwich School (Crome, Cotman and others) are on view.

On the south side of the marketplace stands the **Church of St. Peter Mancroft**, one of the finest of more than 30 medieval churches in the city, and a particularly good example of the Norfolk style of Perpendicular Gothic.

Blickling Hall
(near Aylsham) 9 D2

Built of mellow rose-coloured brick, with imposing corner towers and Dutch-style gables over the windows, Blickling was designed to impress. With its completion in 1625, the Lord Treasurer, Sir Henry

Hobart, announced he'd "arrived". The house is set in a vast park, including formal gardens and a crescent lake. Henry VIII's wife, Anne Boleyn, spent her childhood in an earlier house on the site.

The Broads   *9 D2*

Between Norwich and the sea extends an area of lagoons, rivers and marshlands known as the Norfolk Broads. The Broads are stretches of open water created in medieval times by villagers digging for peat. Linked by streams, rivers and canals, the Broads provide more than 200 miles (320 km.) of navigable waterways for sailing, angling and wildlife observation.

Wroxham, self-styled capital of the Broads, is the centre of the holiday boating industry. Other notable (and quieter) villages in the area include **Ranworth,** whose 15th-century church, St. Helen's, is known as the Cathedral of the Broads, and **Horning,** which organizes a summer boat race and regatta. Near Ranworth, the **Broadlands Conservation Centre** maintains a raised walkway through woodland and fens.

King's Lynn   *9 C2*

The locals shorten the name of their town to Lynn. This busy old port stands on the River Ouse, 30 miles (45 km.) above its outflow in the great bay known as the Wash. It was near here that King John lost his baggage train, crown jewels and all, when overtaken on the sands of the Wash by an unexpectedly high tide.

The richly decorated chalice known as King John's cup, on view in **Holy Trinity Guildhall,** may have been part of the treasure. Interesting in itself, the Medieval Guildhall is an attractive building faced with chequered stone and flintwork.

There's a concentration of houses from the medieval to Georgian periods in the streets near the quay. Of particular interest are the **Hanseatic Warehouse** (1428), a reminder of the days when Lynn had the Hansa cities for trading partners, and classical **Custom House** (1683), built down by the sands of King Staithe (staithe being a Norfolk word for wharf). Just south, a few steps from the Ouse, **Hampton Court** is a courtyard of half-timbered merchants' homes and warehouses.

Of the several churches in the town, **St. Margaret's** (in the Saturday Market Square) is the most imposing, with massive west towers.

Sandringham House   *9 C2*

The royal family has houses in the most scenic areas of Britain. The estate of Sandringham, purchased by Queen Victoria for her son and heir Edward, is no different. You can visit the house and gardens in summer, when the royal family are not in residence. There's nothing remarkable about the Victorian architecture—it's the aura of royalty that draws the crowds. Look for the vintage car museum in the grounds, and a big game museum of hunting trophies.

Holkham Hall

(near Wells-next-the-Sea)   *9 C2*

This severe Palladian mansion rises unexpectedly out of a landscape of dunes and salt marshes. And that's only the first surprise, for the stark exterior conceals some of the most opulent rooms in Britain. The great Marble Hall with its vaulted ceiling and grand staircase sets the tone.

William Kent designed the house for Thomas Coke, Earl of Leicester, in collaboration with the great Palladian, Lord Burlington, an architect by avocation. Everything here rates superlatives, including Thomas Coke's magnificent collection of paintings, numerous Poussins and Dughets, as well as works by Rubens, Van Dyck and others.

Another Thomas Coke (1752–1842) of Holkham, great-nephew of the original owner, conducted his pioneering experiments in soil improvement, crop rotation and sheep breeding on the estate.

Lincolnshire

You might think you were in Holland, what with all the windmills and tulip fields. There's almost no high ground, but the great bulk of Lincoln Cathedral provides a bit of dramatic incidence, rising as it does from the flat landscape.

Lincoln   8 B2

Historic, unspoiled, untouristic—Lincoln is well and truly off the beaten path. But it wasn't always so: two great highways, Ermine Street and Fosse Way, met here in Roman times. The street called Bailgate ends at **Newport Arch**, the only Roman gateway in England to straddle a roadway.

The triple-towered **cathedral** is the dominating feature. An earthquake shattered the original Norman structure in 1185, but the great Norman west front remains, decorated with statues, including those of 11 kings from William the Conqueror to Edward III. The rest is Early English and Decorated, scarcely touched since it was completed in 1311. Inside the church, the decorative rib vaults and canopied choir stalls are superbly carved. Beyond the high altar, 30 angels support the roof of the **Angel Choir**. On the last complete column on the north side you'll see the legendary Lincoln Imp, said to have been turned to stone for his mischief. Two beautiful rose windows light the west transept, the Bishop's Eye and the Dean's Eye.

William the Conqueror gave Lincoln its other landmark, the huge **castle**, in 1068—only two years after he came to power. A 13th-century bastion known as Cobb's tower housed a prison and gallows until the middle of the last century.

Jews were encouraged by the Normans to settle in Lincoln in the 12th century, so that they could help to finance trade. Two stone-built houses, among the oldest Norman dwellings to survive in England, testify to the importance of the Jews at this period. One is the **House of Aaron the Jew**, just below the castle. The other, lower down the hill, is simply known as the **Jew's House**.

Boston   9 C2

Not only did Boston generate a transatlantic namesake, it produced a whole new breed of nation-builders to populate it. Those pillars of the Puritan faith, the Pilgrim Fathers, came from Boston and neighbouring towns, but they dreamed of a better life in the New World. In 1607, a group of potential colonists was prevented from making a break for America. They were arrested in Boston and imprisoned in the Guildhall, 13 years before the party in the *Mayflower* made history. A number of sights in the Boston area are associated with the founding of the United States. See p. 66 in our Leisure Routes section for a detailed itinerary through Pilgrim Country.

The 272-foot (83-m.) steeple of the **Church of St. Botolph** is the town's most inspiring landmark. They call it the Boston Stump because it was never finished, but even without the intended spire it's impressive enough.

*I*n Lincoln, class convenes in the open air. Not much has changed in windmill design since the Middle Ages, when Britain first utilized wind power to grind corn. Of the few windmills still standing, most have been converted into fanciful houses.

Dreaming Spires and Dark Satanic Mills

Here you have the essence of England, the country's very heart. You'll find it in the thatched villages of Shakespeare Country and in Oxford's "dreaming spires", in the rolling Cotswold Hills and the adventurous, rugged moorlands of the Peak District. Essentially English, too, are the big cities of the Midlands—Birmingham, Nottingham, Derby, Stoke-on-Trent and the rest—the cities that fuelled the expansion of empire. These days the Midlands are still hard at work. But micro-chips turn the wheels of industry now, and the "dark Satanic mills" of the poet Blake are museums of industrial history.

⚑ Oxford
6 A1

You can't help but be aware that this is the oldest English-speaking university in the world. Its colleges lie timelessly encapsuled within the modern city, their Gothic spires and pinnacles soaring above cream stone buildings and green quadrangles.

Oxford's origins go back to 1167, when English students from Paris's Sorbonne joined other scholars in this town at the junction of the rivers Cherwell and Thames (here known as the Isis). Originally, college life was based on monastic models, complete with rules and discipline, refectory, cloisters and chapels. Over the subsequent 800 years of learning the number of colleges has increased to 35 and the students to more than 10,000, but the aura of hallowed antiquity and hushed scholarship remains.

If you're making only a short visit to Oxford, concentrate on just a few of the great buildings and try to catch the feel of student life and traditions. Most of the colleges lie off the long curving **High Street**, known as "the High". At Carfax, the main crossroads, stands the 14th-century **Carfax Tower**, once part of St. Martin's Church. Climb to the top for a great view of all of Oxford.

A short way down St. Aldate's from Carfax you come to **Christ Church College,** founded by Cardinal Wolsey in 1515. **Great Tom**, the bell in the tower above the St. Aldate's entrance, still chimes 101 times at 9.05 each evening, when the gates closed on the original 101 students.

It's jubilation all round as Oxford students in full regalia receive their degrees.

Pass through the gateway into Tom Quad and two other interconnecting "quads", or quadrangles, that make Christ Church one of the biggest colleges: the middle quad, Peckwater or Peck, is traditionally the haunt of Britain's aristocracy. A mathematics professor named Charles Dodgson (better known as Lewis Carroll) lodged in Canterbury Quad. Between tutorials he dreamed up *Alice in Wonderland,* inspired by Alice Liddell, the young daughter of the dean of the college. Rather embarrassed by the fame of his whimsical book, Dodgson had fan mail addressed to "Lewis Carroll" at the college returned to the sender stamped "unknown".

In the impressive 16th-century dining hall hang portraits of the famous who once ate here as humble undergraduates. John Locke, John Wesley and W.H. Auden were all "members" of the college, which has educated countless politicians as well. Students covet rooms overlooking Christ Church Meadow, an expanse of green that runs down to the Isis.

The **Church of Christ**, entered from Tom Quad, has been Oxford's Anglican cathedral since the time of Henry VIII. Parts of the structure date back even further to the 12th century, when the Priory of St. Frideswide, nucleus of the university, stood on this site.

Take the High Street as far as Magpie Lane to visit **University College**, one of the earliest. Its origins go back as far as King Alfred the Great in the 10th century, or so college officials claim, though the formal founding date is 1280. The majority of the buildings are 17th-century Gothic. Look for a memorial to the poet Shelley, who was expelled for writing an atheist pamphlet.

Two distinguished colleges are hidden off the High in Merton Street. **Merton College**, dating from 1264, is one of Oxford's oldest, and its library, one of England's earliest. The 14th-century Mob Quad was the first college quadrangle.

Peer through the gateway of **Corpus Christi College** (1517), opposite Merton, into the handsome Front Quad. The pelican that tops the 16th-century sundial here has been the college mascot for over three and a half centuries.

Continue down the High to **Magdalen** (pronounced "maudlin"), founded in 1458. Not only does the college have a reputation for flamboyance (Oscar Wilde and Dudley Moore belonged to Magdalen), it is also considered the most beautiful, with extensive lawns, gardens and a deer park, a serene Gothic cloister and Perpendicular bell tower. On May Day, college choristers gather at 6 a.m. to sing a Latin hymn of praise from the tower. The River Cherwell flows past the college and through its water meadows.

North of the High you'll find **New College**. The Perpendicular buildings are outstanding, above all the chapel. Just as interesting as the architecture are the works of art within: an El Greco painting of *St. James,* Sir Joshua Reynolds's stained-glass design for the West Window; and the tortured statue of *Lazarus,* sculpted by Sir Jacob Epstein in 1951. The beautiful college gardens contain a section of Oxford's 13th-century city wall.

New College Lane has its own "Bridge of Sighs"—a modern copy of the one in Venice—but Oxford's bridge merely joins two buildings belonging to **Hertford College**.

Pass under the bridge and make your way to Broad Street, the heart of academic Oxford. The major landmark here is the Neoclassical **Sheldonian Theatre**, inspired by Rome's Theatre of Marcellus. Designed by the young Christopher Wren (it was his first building), the Sheldonian provides a distinguished venue for academic ceremonies and concerts.

Nearby you'll find Oxford's world-famous library, the **Bodleian**. A magnificent old room holds the 15th-century collection of Humphrey, Duke of Gloucester, which forms the nucleus of the Bodleian's present reserve of 3 million volumes. The Bodleian is entitled to a copy of every book printed in

166

England. Rare books, including a Shakespeare First Folio, can be seen in the adjoining Perpendicular Gothic building known as the **Divinity School**.

Standing alone on a patch of grass, the circular **Radcliffe Camera** (Chamber), originally a science library, now serves as an offshoot reading room of the Bodleian. James Gibb provided the handsome Baroque design.

The "souls" of **All Souls College**, opposite, belong to the soldiers who died in the Hundred Years' War between England and France. This is the only college that restricts its membership to Fellows, who have teaching or research appointments.

Outside **Balliol College** (famous for classical scholars and statesmen) stands the **Martyrs' Memorial** to the Protestant bishops Cranmer, Latimer and Ridley, who were burned at the stake in Queen Mary's reign.

An important stop on any tour of Oxford is the **Ashmolean Museum**. A Greek-Revival building houses the art and archaeological treasures donated to the university over the centuries, in particular fine works by Tintoretto, Rubens, Poussin, Hogarth and Reynolds. Anglo-Saxon antiquities include the **Alfred Jewel**, a rare portrait in enamel of King Alfred. Some of the spectacular finds from Sir Arthur Evans' excavations at Knossus in Crete and Sir Flinders Petrie's digs in Egypt have also made their way to the Ashmolean.

Blenheim Palace   6 A1

A residence grand enough for royalty, Blenheim symbolizes England's greatness in the time of Queen Anne. The nation gave the palace to John Churchill, 1st Duke of Marlborough, in gratitude for his victory over the French in the crucial Battle of Blenheim. The duke never saw the place in its finished state, but he chose Sir John Vanbrugh as architect and approved the massive, colonnaded Baroque design.

References to Blenheim crop up everywhere: in the **Great Hall**, where a paint-

ing shows John Churchill presenting a plan of the Battle of Blenheim to Britannia, in other paintings and tapestries, even in the **park**, where trees were planted according to the disposition of French and English troops on the field. Sweeping vistas extend across landscaped grounds to a towering victory column, monumental bridge and serenely beautiful lake, a Capability Brown creation.

Stratford-upon-Avon   8 A3

The birthplace of England's greatest poet and playwright stands at the heart of what has come to be known as Shakespeare Country. The area is overrun with—but not really spoiled by—tourists, who have made the old market town of Stratford a centre of pilgrimage for more than two centuries now.

You can't miss **Shakespeare's Birthplace** in Henley Street: the modern Shakespeare Centre alongside is the most prominent building in town. You enter the Birthplace through the Centre, which houses a library and archives. Nothing

William Shakespeare

Shakespeare was born in Stratford on April 23, 1564. His father, John Shakespeare, was a farmer who had moved from the countryside to seek a better life. John turned to glove making and dealing in wool, and soon grew rich enough to buy the house in Henley Street where his son was born.

In 1582, at the age of 19, William married Anne Hathaway, a woman six years older, with whom he had three children.

By the 1590s, Shakespeare's career as a playwright in London was well on its way. Success brought prosperity as well as fame, and in 1597 the poet bought a rather grand house in Stratford which he named New Place. He also acquired a ten per cent share in the company that built the legendary Globe Theatre in London two years later.

During the last years of his life, Shakespeare was regarded as England's foremost dramatist. He spent most of his time in Stratford and died here on April 23, 1616, at the age of 52.

more substantial than long tradition maintains that William Shakespeare was born in the bedroom on the upper floor. But it's a tradition that has captured the imagination of writers from Charles Dickens and Sir Walter Scott to Victor Hugo and Herman Melville. Look for their names, scratched into the glass of one of the windows.

The Shakespeare trail leads on to **Judith Shakespeare House,** at the corner of Bridge and High streets. Now Stratford's Tourist Information Centre, this was the home of William Shakespeare's daughter, who married one Thomas Quiney, a wine merchant by trade.

The foundations of William Shakespeare's own house, **New Place,** are visible at the corner of Chapel Street and Chapel Lane. The house would have been the focus of Stratford tourism today had it not been for a Reverend Francis Gastrell, who bought the house from Shakespeare's descendants in the 18th century. Something of a crank, he got so fed up with souvenir hunters that he actually burned the place down. But the tourists still kept coming. All that remains is **Great Garden,** planted with "daisies pied and violets blue".

Nash House, next door on Chapel Street, belonged to Shakespeare's granddaughter, Elizabeth Hall Nash, and her husband Thomas Nash. Of interest here is a collection of 18th-century souvenirs of Stratford: jugs and seals decorated with portraits of the bard.

Near the corner of Chapel Lane, the **Guildhall** of 1417 houses the Grammar School where young Will is thought to have learned his "small Latin and less Greek". Still in use as a school, it's off-limits to tourists. The **Chapel of the Guild of the Holy Cross,** connected to the Guildhall in the 1400s, serves as the school's chapel.

Hall's Croft, in the street named Old Town, is one of the more charming and authentic of the Elizabethan houses preserved by the Birthplace Trust. Susanna Shakespeare, William's elder daughter, lived here after her marriage to Dr. John Hall. The house is decorated as it would have been when the Halls occupied it 400 years ago. Be sure to have a look at the dispensary, furnished in the style of an Elizabethan consulting room. On view is a medical treatise written by Dr. Hall, and the type of primitive surgical tools he used to treat "desperate diseases".

Shakespeare remained attached to Stratford all his life, and it was here that he died in 1616. The poet and playwright lies buried in **Holy Trinity Church,** approached down an avenue of trees. A visit to his tomb in the chancel, marked by a simple stone slab, is an obligatory stop for literary pilgrims.

The 1,500-seat **Royal Shakespeare Theatre** in Waterside is another. People book tickets for one of the plays months in advance, though a limited number are available at the box office on the day of the performance. For details write to the RST, Stratford-upon-Avon, Warwickshire CV37 6BB. Call (0789) 69191 for 24-hour booking information. Credit card bookings can be made on (0789) 295623. Even if you don't manage to see a performance, you can join one

*S*wept by fire in 1694, Lord Leycester's Hospital in Warwick, a fine set of medieval timber-framed buildings, survived more or less intact. In 1571, Robert Dudley, 1st Earl of Leicester, converted the old Merchants' Guild House into a rest-home for veteran soldiers, a mission it still serves today for ex-servicemen and their wives.

all + men   Love + the + brotherhood   Fear + God

*F*rom the courtyard of Warwick Castle, Queen Elizabeth watched a firework display in 1572. The centrepiece, a flying dragon, ran amok and almost set the town ablaze. Continuously occupied for nearly seven centuries, Warwick Castle, like so many great English houses, bears the mark of many different owners.

of the backstage tours, available most days. Don't miss the **RST Picture Gallery and Museum**, a fascinating collection of Shakespeariana. And don't overlook the smaller venues, adjacent to the RST in Waterside: the **Swan Theatre**, built in the style of a Jacobean playhouse, stages works by Shakespeare's contemporaries, while The Other Place is a small venue for classical and contemporary productions. Contact the RST for programmes and tickets.

Shottery

The most photographed of Shakespearean landmarks is undoubtedly **Anne Hathaway's Cottage**. The thatched farmhouse has a worldwide reputation for picturesque charm. A highlight for many is the "courting settle" by the fire, where William Shakespeare may well have popped the question. In their day, fields and forests intervened between Stratford and the village of Shottery, site of the cottage. Now a street of detached and semi-detached mock Tudor houses leads the way. It's more pleasant to walk than drive: follow the well-marked footpath that begins at Evesham Place. You can make it there and back in half an hour.

Only fragments remain of the **Forest of Arden**, north-west of Stratford, the setting for Shakespeare's *As You Like It*.

Warwick Castle   8 A3

A cast of characters from any of Shakespeare's historical plays would have felt at home in **Warwick Castle**, "the finest medieval castle in England". The battlements dominate the town of Warwick from a steep cliff beside the Avon, north of Stratford. The Beauchamps, the wealthy and powerful medieval earls of Warwick, installed themselves here in the 14th century. Shakespeare described one of them as a "proud setter-up and puller-down of kings". But the reign of the earls came to an end in 1978, when Madame Tussauds acquired the title to the property. Already a fixture on the tourist circuit, the castle has gained in popularity as its tourist potential has been exploited. Wax figures positioned throughout the **private apartments** recreate "A Royal Weekend Party 1898"—an amusing gimmick. Works of art are the big attraction in the carved and gilded **state apartments:** a celebrated equestrian portrait of Charles I by Van Dyck and a painting of two lions by Rubens.

Warwick even has a ghost, the spirit of Sir Fulke Greville, a 17th-century earl, who was murdered by his valet in 1628.

Sulgrave Manor   8 A3

Not every American knows that the ancestral home of George Washington lies near Banbury. The manor was built on land purchased by Lawrence Washington from Henry VIII in 1539. The fine period furnishings on display, assembled when the house was restored, include a Gilbert Stuart portrait of George Washington. It was George's great-grandfather, Colonel John Washington, who left here for America in 1656 as mate on a small English ship.

*W*ere boaters designed with alfresco lessons in mind? The British educational system may frown on individual differences in appearance, but children are encouraged to study—and think—independently.

Kenilworth Castle   8 A3

This awesome ruin recalls 500 years of turbulent history. The thick-walled Norman keep, known as **Caesar's Tower**, went up in 1160, before King John made the fortress his stronghold. Subsequently the castle passed to the dukes of Lancaster. John of Gaunt built the **Strong Tower** and great **Banqueting Hall**, while the Earl of Leicester, one of Elizabeth I's favourites, added the **Gatehouse** and formal gardens and turned the castle into a palace fit for the queen he hoped to wed. Some of Cromwell's soldiers dismantled the castle in 1649, at the end of the Civil War, though most of the massive red sandstone walls and towers were left standing. After the war, the artificial lake and moat were drained.

↟ *The Cotswolds*

The rolling Cotswold hills, between the Thames and Severn valleys, cover an area scarcely 55 miles (88 km.) long by 25 miles (40 km.) wide. Acres of pasture alternate with beech woodlands and medieval villages of honey-coloured Cotswold stone.

Farming the thin topsoil was difficult, and agriculture was abandoned in the 13th century in favour of sheep raising. Merchants grew rich in the wool and cloth trades, spending their money to build "wool churches" and country estates. Decline of the wool trade in the 19th century brought an end to prosperity, but the villages managed to preserve their character and charm, almost untouched by the Industrial Revolution.

Northleach   8 A3

Flocks of black birds pepper the sky above Northleach, and a quilting of green fields surrounds the town—a fairly sleepy, friendly sort of place. There's a collection of pleasant pubs, some small shops that cater to local trade, and the grand Perpendicular church all the tourists come to see. Rubbings from North-

leach's brass plaques of wool merchants are popular souvenirs. Make your own with paper and crayons from the Cotswold pharmacy in the market square. Look for the monument to John Fortey, whose wealth paid for the nave with its vaulted roof. At the west end of town, across the highway, the **Cotswold Countryside Collection** takes a nostalgic look at local farm life.

Chedworth Roman Villa

This lavish country estate was occupied from the 2nd to 4th centuries A.D. by prosperous Roman landowners. The best-preserved Roman villa in Britain, it has been partially restored to give an impression of the sophisticated whole—the central heating and sewage systems, elaborate bath complex and dining room, both with fine mosaic pavements. A small **museum** houses artefacts unearthed on the site.

Cirencester   8 A3

Those Romans who lived in luxury at Chedworth may have made their fortunes in nearby Cirencester, or Corinium Dobunnorum, as it was known. Anglo-Saxon warriors sacked the town in the 6th century, but you can still see the amphitheatre and foundations of the forum and basilica. Roman sculptures and frescoes are displayed in the **Corinium Museum** in Park Street.

The affluent Middle Ages endowed Cirencester with its substantial wool church, **St. John the Baptist**, focal point of the central Market Place. The unusual three-storied south porch draws your eye up. Other notable features include the brasses in Trinity Chapel and the elaborate fan vaulting in St. Catherine's chapel.

A third age of prosperity in the 18th century provided this capital of the Cotswolds with another asset—direct access into **Cirencester Park**, the extensive grounds of the stately home of the Earl of Bathurst. The park's chest-nut-lined avenues, footpaths and picnic sites remain open to the public year-round.

Bourton-on-the-Water

Visit Bourton in the peak of the tourist season and you may find yourself caught in a tail-back of traffic. People inundate the village—it's just another attraction now, albeit a very beautiful one. The River Windrush flows slowly through the centre, straddled by low-arched bridges of Cotswold stone and flanked by a wide green sward and ancient mellow houses. Where do all the people go? Over to the Motor Museum, Aquarium, old mill and Model Village, and to Birdland (home of 600 exotic species) and the Butterfly Exhibition.

The Slaughters

There's nothing murderous about the name: it simply comes from the original Norman landowner, de Scoltre. In Upper Slaughter, a farming village with a medieval look, a cluster of houses is set in rich meadow land. A trout stream favoured by ducks flows through Lower Slaughter, and there's a picturesque manor house, once a convent, now a hotel, and a steepled church.

Stow-on-the-Wold   *8 A3*

"Stow-on-the-Wold where the wind blows the cold" perches high on a hill at the junction of several important roads. Gabled shops and inns enclose the spacious **market square**, site of an annual sheep market. Stocks, once used to shame offenders, still stand in the shadow of the steepled **Town Hall** and venerable parish **Church of St. Edward.**

Cheltenham   *8 A3*

To the British mind, Cheltenham symbolizes propriety. Nothing seems amiss in this attractive Regency city. Fame came to Cheltenham in 1715, when an alkaline spring was discovered on the banks of the River Chelt. Visits by Dr. Johnson, Handel and King George III, Lord Byron and the Duke of Wellington (who was cured of a liver complaint) gave the spa undeniable cachet. Early in the 19th century, a new town plan created wide avenues and plenty of parks and gardens for exercise—an important part of the cure. Trees shade the pedestrian **Promenade**, Cheltenham's main shopping thoroughfare, lined with terraced buildings that were private residences in Cheltenham's Regency heyday. Just off the Promenade are the **Imperial Gardens** and **Town Hall**, a venue for concerts during the Cheltenham Music Festival in July.

Further uphill, the shops of **Montpellier Walk**, separated by caryatids, are a highlight of the town's elegant architecture. At the bottom of the Walk stands the **Montpellier Rotunda**, a former pump room where spa water was taken.

Winchcombe   *8 A3*

Look down on Winchcombe from the surrounding hills and you'll see a huddle of stone roof tops in a green and wooded valley. The terraced medieval houses of Cotswold stone date from the 16th century, when Winchcombe thrived on tobacco growing. Although the town was originally capital of the powerful Saxon kingdom of Mercia, only the ruins of an abbey founded by King Kenulf remain. Today, artisans make Winchcombe a centre of creative activity. There's also a small railway museum, with displays of old tickets, uniform buttons, track components and the like. The Perpendicular **Church of St. Peter** features 40 grotesque gargoyles.

Sudeley Castle

King Ethelred the Unready was the first owner of the Sudeley estate, just outside Winchcombe, and an admiral in the Hundred Years' War built the present castle around 1450. But the most famous owner was fictional: Bertie Wooster, known to readers of P. G. Wodehouse's novels. His house, Blandings, bears a strong similarity to Sudeley. Sudeley's hour of glory and tragedy came in Tudor times. Catherine Parr, Henry VIII's last wife, became the mistress of Sudeley on her marriage to Sir Thomas Seymour, but she died after only a year in the castle, giving birth to her first child. Catherine's wood-panelled bedroom has been re-decorated as it might have been in her time, and her prayer book and a love letter to Sir Thomas have been preserved.

Queen Elizabeth I visited the castle several times, but the Banqueting Hall where she was lavishly entertained stands in ruins. It was destroyed in the Civil War, along with the chapel and Catherine Parr's tomb. The Dent family restored the castle, chapel and tomb; their descendants live in the castle today.

Sudeley's notable collection of paintings includes works by Van Dyck, Rubens, Turner, Hogarth and others.

Broadway 8 A3

This perfect Cotswold town is the enterprising centre of Cotswold tourism, but unlike some of the villages, Broadway is big enough to contain the crowds. And crowds there are, walking the broad **High Street,** and spilling out of all the tea shops and pubs, antique shops and art galleries—open seven days a week in the tourist season. One of the outstanding buildings, the **Lygon Arms Inn** in the High, served as headquarters at different times during the Civil War for both Charles I and Oliver Cromwell. Other Broadway landmarks include 18th-century Fish Inn, on Fish Hill, and the 12th-century Church of St. Eadburgha.

Snowshill Manor

A 20th-century romantic, architect Charles Paget Wade lived in 16th-century fashion here, working at traditional crafts, and reading by lamplight. He was a flamboyant character by all accounts—a photograph in the hall shows him with flowing hair and a bow tie—and an insatiable collector. Snowshill contains an incredible clutter of objects that range from Chinese lacquered cabinets to Japanese samurai armour, African musical instruments, old craftmen's tools, clocks and penny-farthing bicycles.

Chipping Campden 8 A3

The old market ("chipping") town of Chipping Campden calls itself "The Gem of the Cotswold Wool Towns". The curving High Street is terraced with old stone houses, their doors painted a showy blue, yellow, black or white. Chipping Campden's woolstaplers (dealers in wool) were among the richest men in England during the 14th and 15th centuries. They sold their fleece at **Woolstaplers' Hall,** centrepiece of the market square since 1340. An eccentric museum of bygones (jelly moulds to mantraps) is housed here today.

The Perpendicular **parish church** contains a brace of monuments to those pillars of the local community, the Grevel, Hicks and Noel families.

There's nothing like a rousing brass band. Concerts take place all over in the summer months—in city parks and stately homes, like Sudeley Castle, near Winchcombe. They're well attended, too. "The English may not like music," as conductor Sir Thomas Beecham observed "but they absolutely love the noise it makes."

Gloucester   *11 D3*

The Romans called it Glevum (but you should say "gloster"). This manufacturing centre and busy inland port is attractive in parts. The four main streets still form a cross at the centre of town, following the Roman plan. Gloucester claims a variety of historic features, but the glorious **cathedral** remains the chief attraction.

The Perpendicular spire is the most recent addition to this Norman building, which started off as an abbey church. The miracle-working tomb of the murdered King Edward II brought medieval pilgrims to Gloucester. It lies under a pinnacled canopy in the north choir aisle. The alabaster effigy, an idealized portrait, is a masterpiece of 14th-century sculpture.

Henry III was crowned in the cathedral, and the great **east window**—a 72-foot (22-m.) wall of glass—commemorates the Battle of Crécy, fought by his great-grandson, Edward III. Beautiful fan vaulting, the earliest in the country, decorates the **cloister** and the lavatorium, where the monks washed their hands.

Berkeley Castle

Berkeleys have been living in feudal style here for centuries. There's been a moated fortress at Berkeley since the 12th century, though most of what you see today dated from two hundred years later. Don't miss the grim cell where Edward II was killed in 1327 by a red-hot poker thrust, in revenge for his dependence on court favourites. England's barons met in the **Great Hall** on their way to Runnymede to seal the Magna Carta in 1215.

Slimbridge

The Severn Estuary is famous for migrating wildfowl. At Slimbridge, the Wildfowl Trust, founded by the late Sir Peter Scott, maintains the world's largest and most varied collection of water fowl—literally thousands of wild swans, geese, eiders and others. Observation towers and water-level hides give you several different perspectives on the birds.

The Midlands

England's industrial achievements are now as much a part of its history as the cathedrals and castles. And here is where it all began, when the Darby family of Coalbrookdale started smelting iron with coke in the 18th century. But there's plenty of pastoral beauty, too. To the west, on the border with Wales, lie the fascinating Marches, an area rich in fine Norman castles and half-timbered villages.

*A*sk *an Englishman what his ideal home would be, and chances are he'll come up with something resembling this cottage in the Midlands. Cottages are sometimes draughty and impractical, with low beams and impossibly shaped rooms, but their charm and cosiness are legendary.*

179

Gloucester guarded the lowest crossing over the River Severn; from here the Roman legions launched their—relatively unsuccessful—incursions into Wales in the 1st century A.D. Above the town rises the glorious Norman cathedral, known for its cloisters and tomb of Edward II, murdered in 1327.

legacies of the years of Victorian prosperity. But urban development has changed the look of the city, bringing Birmingham the Bull Ring Centre shops and New Street Station, Inner Ring Road and infamous Spaghetti Junction.

Main stop for a tourist is the **Museum and Art Gallery**, one of the country's best, with a famous pre-Raphaelite collection. The **Barber Institute of Fine Arts**, a distinguished gallery attached to the university, features European painting and sculpture, classical antiquities and oriental and Asian art. Interesting, too, is the **Museum of Science and Industry**, full of the engines that powered the Industrial Revolution. The setting, a converted canalside factory building, couldn't be more appropriate. Another big attraction for industrial history enthusiasts: the **Gas Street Canal Basin**, in the heart of the city, starting point for a canalside walk.

Dudley 8 A2

In the old days, factory towns like Dudley produced a "plague of smoke" (as Charles Dickens put it) that stained everything black. The open-air **Black Country Museum** brings together period buildings of the industrial era and reconstructed workshops (glass cutters' and chain makers'). The replica of one of the first steam engines built at Dudley is fully operational. Take a narrowboat along the canal and try "legging it" through Dudley tunnel as the bargemen did, propelling the boat with your feet against the tunnel wall.

Birmingham 8 A2-3

The Victorians called the city the "workshop of the world": if it was made of metal, Birmingham made it, from pins to guns to railway engines.

World War II bombing and the loss of colonial markets plunged Birmingham into recession. They still manufacture textiles, chocolate and motor parts here, though the service sector seems to be the wave of the future.

Birmingham's Town Hall, its canals, museums and symphony orchestra are all

Iron-Bridge Gorge 11 D2

The Industrial Revolution started here, along the idyllic banks of the River Severn, when Abraham Darby first smelted iron using coke as fuel in place of charcoal. Darby's original blast furnace of 1709 is just one of the historic industrial sites that make up the 6-square-mile (15-sq.-km.) **Iron-Bridge Gorge Museum.** You may also want to see the world's first iron bridge, cast at Iron-bridge in 1779, the old blast furnaces at Coalbrookdale and Blists Hill and the Coalport bone china factory, in operation from the 1790s to the 1920s.

Coventry   *8 A3*

Coventry today is predominantly modern, a steel-and-concrete replacement of the city devastated by German bombs in 1940. The poignant shell of the old 14th-century Gothic cathedral stands at the entrance of the new St. Michael's, which rose Phoenix-like out of the rubble. Sir Basil Spence provided the angular design in the early 1950s.

For the generation that lived through the war, the rebuilding of the **cathedral** symbolized hope in the future. Some of Britain's best modern artists were involved in the project: John Piper designed the immense **stained-glass window** in the baptistry, while Graham Sutherland contributed the moving *Christ in Glory* tapestry behind the altar. The **Spirit of Coventry** exhibit in the undercroft traces the city's history, using special effects, including laser holographs.

Broadgate garden, traditional centre of the city, preserves a tenuous link with the obliterated past in the 1949 equestrian **statue** of Lady Godiva. Coventry's history began with the Benedictine abbey her husband founded in her honour in 1043.

Was the Lady a Tramp?
Everybody has heard of Lady Godiva, history's first streaker, but the story behind her famous ride is less well known. As legend would have it, she implored her husband, Leofric, Earl of Mercia, to reduce the high taxes he'd levied on the people of Coventry. Unwilling to say no to his wife, he agreed—provided she rode naked through the town. No one was more astonished than Leofric when Godiva took up the challenge. The townspeople, warned in advance of Godiva's intentions, all closed their shutters, except for Peeping Tom, or so the legend continues, and he was struck blind.

The **Museum of British Road Transport** celebrates the city's more recent history. This notable collection highlights Coventry-made cars, bicycles and motorcycles from the Daimler, Jaguar and Triumph plants.

Northampton   *8 B3*

Boots and shoes have made Northampton famous since the days when it kept Cromwell's army on the march. The **Central Museum** displays a comprehensive collection of footwear from all over the world, from Roman times to the present day. Queen Victoria's diminutive wedding shoes make a hilarious contrast with a pair of outsize boots worn by an elephant on a Hannibal-style expedition through the Alps.

A 1675 fire left Northampton with little to show for its Norman and Saxon past, but that doesn't deter the sightseers. Most of them are just passing through—on their way to **Althrop,** childhood home of a certain Lady Diana Spencer.

Nottingham   *8 A2*

Robin Hood, the outlaw of Sherwood Forest, is Nottingham's main claim to fame. What a shame so little of Robin's Nottingham remains. The old castle went by the board during the Civil War, and 19th-century industrialization and 20th-century redevelopment have taken their toll.

If you find yourself in Nottingham, you could visit the museums of lace and textiles (Nottingham's industrial speciality) or the Tales of Robin Hood attraction in the city centre. But don't go for a walk down Maid Marian Way—it's part of an urban ring road. There's not much of Sherwood Forest left either, alas. The last remnants of the woodlands surround the **Sherwood Forest Visitor Centre** at Edwinstowe.

Newstead Abbey

Lord Byron's ancestral home preserves a romantic aura befitting the poet. A 12th-century priory, it was converted in 1540 into a house, incorporating the façade of the abbey church. Newstead Abbey was in an advanced state of decay when Lord Byron inherited it. But he was infatuated with the place and put a lot of money and energy into restoring it. Mounting debts forced Byron to sell out in 1818. When he left Newstead, he also abandoned England for ever. Ironically, the house has become a Byron shrine. You can see the table where the poet wrote *Childe Harold* and the memorial to his dog Botswain, inscribed with Byron's lines.

Hardwick Hall
(near Chesterfield)   *8 A2*
Elizabeth, Countess of Shrewsbury, aged 70 and four times a widow, began building a house in 1590. The magnificent result reflected the wealth of the second-richest woman in the land—Bess of Hardwick, they called her. Her initials, ES, stand out along the roofline of the house. The windows grow taller with every storey, culminating in the lofty High Great Chamber on the top floor. The room was designed to accommodate the huge tapestries that hang there.

Grantham   *8 B2*
The birthplace of Margaret Thatcher is also famous for sausages and gingerbread. But its buildings embody more ancient history. The **Church of St. Wulfram**, with its tall spire, has an old chained library, and there are some historic inns, like the **Angel and Royal Hotel,** where King John held court in 1213. Isaac Newton and Britain's first woman prime minister both studied in the local grammar school.

Belvoir Castle
The name of the castle is pronounced, perversely enough, "beaver". Seat of the Dukes of Rutland, this crenellated mock-Gothic extravaganza is famous for its picture gallery. The paintings on display include works by Rembrandt, Rubens, Holbein, Poussin and Gainsborough—none of them second rate.

Derby   *8 A2*
"Darby" is the home of Royal Crown Derby porcelain and Rolls Royce aero-engines. It's also the place where Bonnie Prince Charlie broke off his march on London in the 1745 Jacobite rebellion. **Derby Museum** has a room commemorating his visit, with panelling from the house where he stayed.

The Industrial Revolution brought considerable expansion to Derby, and it's still an important manufacturing centre. The **Royal Crown Derby Works** in Osmaston Road opens its doors to visitors, by prior request. A museum on the premises displays pieces from the company's 18th-century beginnings.

Kedleston Hall
Ostentatious was the word Dr. Johnson used to describe Kedleston in the century it was built, and Dr. Johnson knew a thing or two about words. Robert Adam designed the house on a grand scale: the pavilions alone are larger than many stately homes. But Adam, characteristically, kept things under control, and the effect in the end is awesome, but never vulgar. John Linnell, the cabinet-maker, extemporized on Adam's designs to produce the extraordinary mermaid sofas in the State Drawing Room.

Stoke-on-Trent   *8 A2*
They've been making pottery here since the 16th century, but it was Josiah Wedgwood who put the manufacture of tableware on an industrial footing. He opened the first factory in "The Potteries" in 1769. And the region has never looked back.

The **Stoke Art Gallery and Museum** has a fine collection of Spode, Minton, Copeland and, especially, Wedgwood pieces on display. For a comprehensive look at the industry, visit the enormous **Wedgwood Potters Visitors' Centre** in the factory at Barlaston. The **Gladstone Pottery Museum** at Longton gives a lively explanation of the traditional firing method, using bottle kilns.

Shrewsbury 11 D2

If it's medieval charm you're looking for, look no further than the cobbled streets and Tudor houses of Shrewsbury (pronounced "shrozebry"), enclosed in a loop of the River Severn. Typical of the local architectural style is the half-timbered warehouse called **Rowley's House** in Baker Street. Now a museum of local history, this nostalgic landmark dates from the days of the flax and wool trade. Taking you back even further, exhibits include artefacts from the excavations at nearby Wroxeter (Roman Viroconium).

The Normans saw Shrewsbury's value as a border fortress near the frontier with Wales and built the castle on a rise above the town. There are two outstanding churches: 12th-century **St. Mary's** and **Shrewsbury Abbey Church** (Norman to 19th century).

Hereford and the Marches 11 D3

This is an area of pastoral beauty, home of cattle and cider. Tranquil half-timbered villages surround the old city of Hereford, but it hasn't always been so peaceful here. William the Conqueror appointed the Earl of Hereford one of three barons to quell the turbulent Marches, the borderlands running towards the mountains of Wales. Today you can tour the border castles, hills and towns north-west of Hereford or walk part of the 140-mile (224-km.) **Offa's Dyke Path,** which parallels the ancient rampart and ditch built by the Saxons to contain the Welsh tribes (see p. 193).

The main sight of **Hereford** city is the **cathedral**, part Norman, part Decorated, with a massive 14th-century tower and unique **chained library** of 1,500 books, "chained" so that particularly valuable and irreplaceable volumes could not be taken away. Hereford's famous **Mappa Mundi**, a huge 13th-century map of the medieval world, shows Jerusalem at the centre and Paradise at the top. A public outcry foiled a recent bid by cathedral administrators to sell the map to pay for the upkeep of the church.

Worcester 11 D3

This cathedral city is famous for gloves, fine porcelain and bottled Worcestershire sauce. The name of the sauce and the town are pronounced alike: "wooster".

Worcester has many attractive faces, none more so than the **cathedral**, built on the banks of the Severn. Once part of a Benedictine abbey, the church has a Norman core overlaid with successive styles of Gothic. The **tomb** of King John (of Magna Carta fame) stands in the chancel. Take a close look at the marble effigy, the earliest existing of any English king. The lion biting the end of John's sword is said to represent the barons curbing his royal power. Near the high altar is the tomb of the Tudor Prince Arthur, who died at the age of 15—already a married man. His widow, Catherine of Aragon, went on to marry his younger brother, Henry VIII.

You can tell Worcester was a Royalist city by the **Guildhall** statues of Charles I and Charles II (and by the head of Cromwell nailed by the ears). Worcester was the last town in England to surrender to Cromwell. Visit the **Commandery**, the Royalist headquarters, for an interesting replay of Civil War history. Charles II hid in nearby **King Charles House** after his decisive defeat at the Battle of Worcester in 1651.

The **Dyson Perrins Museum** (Severn Street, adjoining the porcelain factory) is the showcase for an inclusive collection of antique Royal Worcester pieces.

Chester 11 D2

The continuity of history that you find in so many British cities is clearest of all in Chester. Here, on the banks of the River Dee, the Romans established their major military base of Deva in A.D. 79. They stayed for more than three centuries, guarding the fertile lands of Cheshire from raiders, whether from the Welsh hills or the Irish Sea. Later, this was a Norman stronghold and a launching pad for invasions of North Wales—and it's still a natural gateway if you're heading that way today.

There's no better introduction to Chester than to walk along the top of the best-preserved **ramparts** of any English city. The full circuit is 2 miles (3 km.), and well worth doing if you can, perhaps dropping down to street level at various points to see some of the sights. Even if you don't go all the way round, be sure to cover part of the northern and eastern stretches where a lot of the original Roman stonework is to be seen. The west and south walls were probably built by the Normans to extend the enclosed area.

If you start at **Eastgate** and head north past the cathedral, you'll reach King Charles's Tower, at the north-east corner of the ramparts. Charles I is said to have watched from here as his army was defeated at the Battle of Rowton Moor, several miles to the east. Between the tower and **Northgate**, there are stretches of Roman wall as much as 17 feet (5 m.) high. Walk on, and you can look out over the locks of the Shropshire Union Canal —and beyond, to the green hills of North Wales. The west wall overlooks a great open space by the river where the Romans had their harbour. Called the Roodee, the site has served as Chester's racecourse since 1540.

The south-west corner of the wall incorporates **Chester Castle**, largely a Georgian restoration, except for the Norman tower. A military museum is housed within. The wall continues along the banks of the Dee to **Bridgegate**, which leads directly to the Old Dee Bridge. For centuries this was the only dry crossing to the south and to Wales, and the scene of many skirmishes. Look out from **Wolf Gate** over the remains of the largest Roman amphitheatre found to date in Britain, an oval over 310 feet (96 m.) long.

Inside the walled city, the **Rows** are highly unusual shopping arcades one storey up from ground level. The idea seems to date from the 13th century, and it may have developed as townspeople attempted to bypass the Roman rubble in the streets below. That can't have been unique to Chester, but in other places they generally smoothed off the debris and built on top. Perhaps here the remains of Roman stonework were so substantial that it was easier to make new walkways above. Although some of the houses in the Rows have been restored, many 14th- to early 17th-century structures preserve their original timber frames. Sometimes the exposed wood is richly carved. Look for Bishop Lloyd's House and Leche House among the many fine buildings along **Watergate Street**.

Chester's rather unassuming **cathedral** is the church of the former Benedictine abbey, founded in 1092. There's something from every century, though, including the 19th. The superb carving on the **choir stalls** (c. 1390) includes an elaborate Tree of Jesse, displaying the genealogy of Christ.

The Peak District

Right on the doorstep of industrial Manchester, Derby and Sheffield, the Peak District offers a dramatic change of scenery. The wild landscape of moorland crags and rushing trout streams constitutes England's original national park, covering some 450 square miles (1,165 sq. km.). This is prime holiday country for fishing, climbing, potholing, walking or cycling, its attractions remarkably unspoilt.

Ashbourne   8 A2

Gateway to the Peak District, Ashbourne retains much of the quiet charm it must have had when Izaak Walton fished the waters of the River Dove for trout. Except, that is, on Shrove Tuesday every year when the inhabitants turn the town into a football field and play an all-day no-rules game with goals 3 miles (4½ km.) apart.

In the heart of the rolling farmlands between Ashbourne and Leek, the pretty village of **Tissington** is one of several that still go in for the old custom of "well-dressing". Using flower petals and leaves, villagers create a series of designs around the fonts, as they have every year in May since 1348, when Tissington escaped from a severe outbreak of the Black Death.

Matlock
8 A2

Matlock and its spa at Matlock Bath lie in the narrow wooded gorge of the River Derwent. The setting is beautiful, as Roman and Regency curists appreciated, but the Matlocks have been commercialized.

A couple of attractions that might appeal to Derwent Valley visitors: cable car rides to the **Heights of Abraham** and the Gulliver's Kingdom and Royal Cave theme amusements. The **Riber Castle Fauna Reserve and Wildlife Park** specializes in rare breeds, both British and European.

Bakewell
8 A2

A pleasant market town on the River Wye, and the only town within the confines of the Peak District National Park, Bakewell makes a good centre for touring the Peaks. The five-arched medieval bridge over the river is one of the oldest in England. Stop by The Old House museum of country exhibits—and sample the famous Bakewell tart, made with ground almonds.

Chatsworth
(Bakewell)
8 A2

Home of the dukes of Devonshire, palatial Chatsworth is England's answer to Versailles. You can stay on the grounds in the Devonshire Hotel, one of the Duchess's projects. There's also an adventure playground, and farming and forestry exhibitions.

William Talman, a contemporary of Wren's, designed the Baroque mansion for the 1st Duke of Devonshire in the 1680s. At the beginning of the 19th century, Jeffery Wyatville added a new library, sculpture gallery, ballroom and

theatre. At the same time, Joseph Paxton was at work in the garden, creating his innovative waterworks and glasshouses. Highlight of a visit to Chatsworth is Talman's **Painted Hall** (decorated with vigorous scenes from the life of Julius Caesar by Laguerre) and his marble and cedar-panelled **chapel.** Through the 1930s, the entire household gathered weekly to pray before the monumental alabaster altar.

The most splendid furniture and decorative objects fill the house, but some of

*Chatsworth has always been open to visitors.
In the old days, anyone who asked was given a free tour of the house
and gardens, complete with a demonstration of the waterworks.*

*W*ild and remote, the Peak District is all the more surprising for its proximity to the large urban conglomerations of Manchester and Sheffield. Within the confines of the national park, running the length of the Pennines, the landscape varies from the harsh moorland of millstone-grit country in the north to the limestone hills of the south.

the more important paintings may not be on view. The collection of Old Master drawings is accessible only to scholars.

Haddon Hall
(Bakewell)   *8 A2*
Perfect of its type, medieval Haddon Hall is smaller and less thronged than Chatsworth, but equally well worth visiting. The dukes of Rutland, whose house this is, moved to the much grander Belvoir Castle in the 17th century. Haddon Hall was left empty, and intact. The galleried banqueting hall and medieval

kitchen are virtually unchanged in 600 years. And the house is beautifully set off by its terraced and balustraded Elizabethan rose garden.

Buxton   *8 A2*
At 1,000 feet (305 m.), Buxton is one of England's highest spa towns. The place came into its own in the 18th century, when the 5th Duke of Devonshire commissioned the stately **Crescent**, built in columned Palladian style by John Carr. The one-time Pump Room houses the "Micrarium", where microscope images of insects and plants are projected onto larger screens.

Scenic roads branch out in all directions to cross the Peak District. Fans of the Brontë sisters will head west out of Chapel-en-le Frith to the attractive little village of **Heathersage**, the setting for Morton in *Jane Eyre*.

Castleton   *8 A2*
From commercialized Castleton, a popular touring centre, you can visit **Peveril Castle's** massive 11th-century keep, as well as a whole range of caves and potholes. Among them are the **Peak Cavern** (in Castletown proper), Derbyshire's largest natural cave, traversed by rope-walks; **Blue John Cavern,** west of town, source of the region's semi-precious Blue John fluorspar stone; and **Speedwell Cavern,** west again, where a short walk and underground boat trip take you to where the waters tumble into the abyss of a huge pothole.

North of Castleton you reach the bleaker part of the Peak District, known as the High or Dark Peak—with vast tracts of moorland, few villages and still fewer people. This awesome area is traversed by the **Pennine Way**, a challenging footpath that starts at **Edale,** below Mam Tor ("Shivering Mountain"), and extends over beautiful but rough terrain for 250 miles (400 km.) to the borders of Scotland. Stop at Edale's National Park Information Centre for advice about prevailing conditions before you set out.

A SENSE OF PLACE: THE ENGLISH COUNTRY TOWN

The English country town is instantly recognizable but hard to define. Even the name is a contradiction in terms, although this might never occur to the people who live there. The country towns embody the very essence of England: the traditional values of neighbourliness, courtesy and civic pride which somehow continue to thrive amid the pressures of modern life. Hardly any planning went into the creation of the country town, and the haphazard tangle of roads at its heart offers the driver no favours. It's often preferable to arrive by coach (bus) or train and discover the location on foot. Railway stations are typically situated a little outside the town centre. Many of them preserve their original Victorian architecture: a neat wooden awning with elaborate eaves over the platform, and a squat red-brick station house, at the top of a street called, not unreasonably, Station Road.

Street names are a wonderful introduction to a town. Every town plan tells a story of the pattern of influences that make up its history: medieval guilds (Weavers' Row, Coopers' Lane), the pub (White Hart Lane, Red Lion Street), the church (Rectory Road, Bishop's Walk) and the marketplace. But walking, for its own sake, is rather alien to English town life. There is a great saying in Yorkshire: "Never stand when you can sit", which sums up a whole attitude to life, but is also meant literally. After 5.30 p.m., when the shops close, there is a definite lull in activity, and the empty streets leave the visitor free to explore the town at leisure. This is not to say

Castle Combe, Wiltshire

that people stay at home. A busy life goes on behind closed doors in the clubs, classes, voluntary societies and, of course, the pubs.

The pub, alehouse or inn is a presence in town life almost as ancient as the church or monastery. The current holder of the title Oldest Pub in England, the "Talbot" in the Northamptonshire town of Oundle, can trace its origins back to a hostel founded by a group of monks in A.D. 638. The claim is strong, but it could actually be applied to any number of inns. For the pub owes its very existence to the charitable hostelries set up by religious houses. The Hospital of St. Cross in Winchester uniquely maintains this tradition, giving the customary Wayfarer's Dole of bread and ale to all who request it.

English towns may appear picturesque, but they were almost invariably constructed on sound pragmatic principles. Until canal transport made it feasible to import raw materials, most towns had to rely on local resources. This has given them the distinctive character that still shines through the motley textures of modern development. In the south, timber and packed earth were the principal building materials. Flint and brick were used in the east, and stone in the north and south-west. But within these major groups there are myriad subtle distinctions between various tones of brick, different ways of using timber, and assorted qualities of stone. Compare, for example, the Yorkshire town of Haworth, home of the Brontës, with Chester. Haworth uses a warm, red sandstone—making for an atmosphere that's far more appealing, if less inspirational to the romantic imagination.

From the low huddle of all these approachable, often ramshackle buildings, one more exalted structure invariably soars up to catch the eye: the church spire. Despite the old saying, a cathedral does not make a city. Many towns have beautiful cathedrals, set in the middle of that great invention of the English church, the cathedral close. On a more human scale are the smaller churches, often built by local subscription. As communally owned property, they were put to all kinds of uses that today would be regarded as sacrilegious: shelter, celebration and even wassailing. The churchyards, in turn, doubled as a marketplace. However, this practice was prohibited in the reign of Edward I, and it was at this time, around 1285, that many of England's market squares were founded. The tradesmen, it seems, missed the religious atmosphere, and in many of the market-places they put up small monuments to hold

Pub signs—and names—can be plain or fanciful

the crucifix, essential for the sealing of contracts and agreements. These "butter crosses", or market crosses, also served as pulpits. Wymondham, in Norfolk, has a very special cross, where miracles were said to have taken place, while Ludlow's Butter Cross is a complete classical building whose upper floor was used as a charity school. And in Bury St. Edmunds, the market cross doubled as the local theatre.

Every town has its own character and sense of place, a memorable individuality acquired gradually over time. No urban planner in his wildest imagination could ever have invented the unique ensemble of buildings of different styles and periods that is the country town.

Beyond the Celtic Fringe

The Welsh are different, and proud of it. The distinction crystallized when the Celtic people of Wales fought off the Anglo-Saxons who had taken over England, and the 8th-century Saxon king Offa tried to wall off the recalcitrant Welsh behind a massive earthwork rampart and ditch. You can still see Offa's Dyke stretching for many miles near the present border with England.

Freelance Norman lords came next, licensed by William the Conqueror to keep what they could capture. Some won a foothold around the motte-and-bailey castles they put up across the country, but again the Welsh kept their language and their culture largely intact. Edward I finally broke the power of the Welsh princes in the 13th century. He built a chain of massive castles, using the latest technology learned in the Crusades, to hold the people down. Paradoxically, it's these "Welsh", really English, castles that are some of today's biggest attractions for visitors.

The last great rebellion, of Owain Glyndwr around the year 1400, gave Wales a national hero, but its failure left the country shattered. Then, with Welsh fortunes at their lowest ebb, the twisted patterns of history brought a Welsh-born prince to the English throne as Henry VII, first of the Tudor kings.

Poetry in stone: roofless now, the shell of Tintern Abbey is just as beautiful in ruin as in its 12th-century Cistercian heyday.

The Welsh tongue survives from before the Roman conquest, though it absorbed many Latin words. Only a minority speak Welsh today, but hear it used by a poet and you'll appreciate the power a spellbinding leader could wield. No doubt it's the music of their language that explains the number of great actors, writers and orators who have come from Wales. Perhaps the marvellous choirs, too, and even the national passion for rugby football, which the Welsh see as a form of poetry.

South Wales

If you think only of coal mines, steel works and tin plate, think again. From the green valleys of the Severn, Wye and Usk to the rocky headlands and sandy bays of Pembrokeshire in the south-west, you journey through a land of extraordinary variety.

Wye Valley   5 D1/11 D3
The border between England and Wales follows the deep, wooded valley of the River Wye. Sections of **Offa's Dyke**, up to 30 feet (9 m.) high, mark the eastern bank, and the sudden onset of bilingual

road signs tells you you've crossed into Wales.

Whether you come from the north-east by the old Roman road, or cross the Severn by the graceful suspension bridge, take a look at **Chepstow**'s mighty Norman castle. It was probably the first to be built in stone after the conquest, with lines of red Roman tiles robbed from ancient sites nearby. The town still has some of its medieval walls, the 16th-century gate (which houses a museum), and steep, winding streets with little bow-fronted shops.

Up the Wye in a setting of green meadows and wooded cliffs, the eloquent ruins of **Tintern Abbey** moved William Wordsworth to write a poem. Vaulted by the sky, they look as if they were always meant to be like this. Not only the abbey church but parts of many other buildings survive, abandoned when Henry VIII dissolved the monastery in 1536.

Not much remains of the castle at **Monmouth**, where Henry V was born. Longbowmen from the vicinity brought him victory at Crécy and Agincourt, and you'll see his statue in Agincourt Square beside one of local son Charles Rolls, pioneer aviator and co-founder of Rolls-Royce. The gated bridge over the River Monnow was already a venerable landmark in Henry's day: it's the only Norman bridge still standing in Britain. Lord Nelson stayed for a time in Monmouth during his 1801 progress around the country: the Nelson Museum commemorates the fact.

To the south-west, the nondescript town of **Raglan** is separated from its castle by a busy motorway, the A40. You'll have to cross it (use the pedestrian walkway) for a closer look. The 15th-century lords of Raglan had social pretensions to satisfy, and their castle puts as much emphasis on decorative effect as invulnerability. Still, Raglan held out for months against Parliament in the Civil War. When Cromwell's troops finally broke through the defences, they took the castle apart in vengeance.

Abergavenny 11 D3

Lying where the River Usk breaks out of the mountains, Abergavenny is a bleak yet busy market town that likes to call itself the Gateway to Wales. In fact you have a choice of routes. Northward stand the peaceful **Black Mountains**: they're actually red sandstone, covered with green gorse and purple heather, but some trick of light makes them look black.

To the west, the Heads of the Valleys road cuts right across the top end of the South Wales coalfield. The grey towns with their tightly packed houses fill the dozen famous mining valleys from Ebbw Vale to the Rhondda. Here you'll see the impact of the Industrial Revolution, and its aftermath, as the rundown in coal and steel production is forcing a search for new roles. Landscaping and tree planting on former tips (dumps) and slagheaps—and the cleaner air—are transforming the environment.

Blaenavon 11 D3

The **Big Pit Mining Museum,** in a scarred landscape of lumpy hills, offers a grim look at life in a Welsh coal mine. Until the early 1980s, 1,300 men were still at work here, in continuous shifts. And even now, the mine, a cooperatively run tourist attraction, is Blaenavon's biggest employer. Former miners take you 300 feet (90 m.) down to the old seams, for a look at the boring and haulage equipment, roadways and stables (pit ponies toiled in the mine until the 1970s). Don't be startled when you're asked to leave your battery-powered watch above ground, at the start of the tour. It's a safety precaution, not a tourist scam: dry cell batteries can cause the methane gas naturally present in the mine to explode.

Crickhowell Area 11 D3

Carry on up the green vale of the Usk to **Crickhowell**, a little town with fragments of a castle and fine Georgian houses. **Agen Allwedd,** in the hills to the south-west, is a target for cave explorers: the caverns are 14 miles (22 km.) long.

The round tower that gave the little village of **Tretower** its name still looks out over a medieval street. Over the gatehouse of Tretower Court you'll see not only pistol loops but ducts for pouring something horrible on would-be attackers. The 14th-century house itself has been well restored, especially the woodwork. Sliding wooden shutters seem such a good idea they ought to make a comeback.

Brecon   *11 C3*
There's quite an array of craft and antique shops here, in narrow streets dominated by a fine **cathedral**. Notice the chapel dedicated to the shoemakers guild, and the ancient cresset stone whose oil-filled cups used to light the building. The town's wonderful setting, ringed by mountains, makes it a great centre for exploring the **Brecon Beacons National Park** to the south and west, splendid hillwalking country. Four miles (6 km.) west of Brecon, there's a mountain information centre just off the A470 D road. The peak of the range at Pen-y-Fan, 2,906 feet (887 m.), involves a vigorous walk rather than a real climb, and the views are superb—weather permitting. In the south of the Beacons, **Ystradfellte,** a village in a famously pretty area of streams, caves and waterfalls, offers an escape from the industrial landscapes so near to the south.

Newport   *5 D1*
The River Usk reaches the sea, or rather the mouth of the Severn, at busy Newport. Roman **Caerleon**, where 6,000 soldiers of the 2nd Legion Augusta were based, lies just upstream. Some 50 acres (20 ha.) of remains have been excavated, none more atmospheric than the oval amphitheatre. It was built around A.D. 90, at about the same time as the Coliseum in Rome. Tradition, if no hard evidence, links Caerleon with King Arthur, and it's easy to believe the town could have stood against the Saxons after the legions left Britain.

Cardiff   *5 C2*
The biggest city in Wales is now its capital, despite rival claims. The docks area used to have a wild reputation and its people, descended from the world's sailors, were the most cosmopolitan in Britain. Now there's an air of respectability about the place, especially the spacious centre.

Cardiff Castle may be the best thing in a rather dull town, architecturally speaking. It's mostly a 19th-century confection—William Burges designed the fantastical interiors—with a separate, magnificent moated Norman keep.

The **National Museum of Wales,** an institution of national stature, puts Welsh cultural achievements into a British, and European, context. It takes a certain pride in reminding you that Richard Wilson, Edward Burne-Jones and Augustus John were Welsh. Note the remarkable collection of Roman and Romano-British standing stones, some inscribed with the strange Celtic Ogham script.

Llandaff Cathedral, in the north-west of the city, has had its ups and downs. The building was already in an advanced state of decay when Cromwell's soldiers drank in the nave and fed their pigs in the font during the Civil War. Twice restored after that, the cathedral was hit in a World War II air raid and reconstructed by 1957. See how you react to the modern concrete arch and Epstein's great aluminium figure of Christ.

A near-religion, rugby has its "cathedral" in Cardiff at the Arms Park National Stadium. Try to get a ticket for a big game: nothing can match the atmosphere, and the crowd's singing can equal any opera chorus.

The **Welsh Folk Museum** at St. Fagans celebrates the Welsh way of life. In extensive, wooded grounds west of town, they've set up a truly unique collection of buildings from all over Wales: cottages and farmhouses, complete with pigsty, a chapel, tannery, smithy, even a woollen mill. Don't miss the little tollhouse with its list of charges.

*Intent on the day's catch,
young anglers seem oblivious
of their historic surroundings.
The lake they're fishing forms part
of Caerphilly Castle's formidable
defence system. Water and walls
created a complex obstacle course
designed to foil even the most
persistent attacker. During a siege,
archers took up their stations
on the concentric walls, each one
higher than the last, launching
arrows on the unfortunate
intruders below. Caerphilly boasts
a tower that out-leans
Pisa (9 feet [just under 3 m.] off
the perpendicular). The tilt
has been blamed on the marshy
ground—with a little help
from Cromwell's troops.*

Caerphilly 5 C1

Caerphilly Castle is the biggest in all Britain (not counting stately Windsor). It represented the "state of the art" of defence around 1300, with a lake *and* a moat formed by a dam to the east that was itself a massive curtain wall. The concentric walls of the main fortification were so devised that even if attackers took the outer wall, they were still dominated by the inner one, and if they got between the two, they could be sealed off and dealt with.

Caerphilly's other claim to fame is a mild, white crumbly cheese that's now made in many other places.

Castell Coch

Landowner and coal baron, the 3rd Marquess of Bute restored Caerphilly Castle, and ordered the Victorian additions to Cardiff Castle. Then, on the site of a small ruin by the River Taff, he had his architect, William Burges, create a castle to surpass them all, Castell Coch. Complete with a dungeon and working drawbridge, it's a Romantic dream of the Age of Chivalry, brilliantly executed. The painted murals throughout are astonishing for their detail and meticulous finish. See the drawing room with scenes from Aesop's fables and the whole world of nature.

Swansea 5 C1

The second city of Wales in numbers (and not only in numbers by its own account) has a certain spaciousness to it, partly because World War II bombs cleared the centre. Decline of the once massive steel and tin plate industries and the coal export trade has left this a cleaner, quieter place. The Guildhall (1934) has huge and riotous murals by Welsh artist Frank Brangwyn that were intended as a World War I memorial for the House of Lords, but rejected as too strong meat for their lordships. Rather than show scenes of horror, Brangwyn depicted the good life Britain's peers had died to preserve—a novel approach. Majority opinion in the House considered the result more appropriate to a nightclub. London's loss was Swansea's gain.

Gower Peninsula 4-5 B-C1

This stretch of land west of Swansea is miraculously unbuilt in spite of the pressures on the area from the industrial valleys and towns. Where better to escape the gloom of the valleys than by the sea? Limestone cliffs, sandy bays, marshes that are a haven for birds, caves where the bones of extinct animals have been found: all attract walkers and, of course, cars. The traffic on the few roads can be daunting at weekends.

Oystermouth and The Mumbles, on the bay nearest to Swansea, have all the Victorian paraphernalia of old resorts. The railway built round the bay, horse-drawn at first, carried passengers as far back as 1807, making it a world first.

Oxwich has a sandy beach, two castles and a nature reserve—all very pleasant. But the village is too charming for its own good: people, traffic and caravans threaten to overwhelm it. The Gower Society does its best to protect the peninsula, and publishes a full guide to its sights.

Carmarthen Area 10 B3

Ancient tradition places the cave of the wizard Merlin near the market town of Llandeilo, and castle collectors won't want to miss nearby Carreg Cennen. If King Arthur and his knights ever rode out of a fortress, it would have looked like this, you'll think. Further down the Tywi valley you come to Carmarthen, whose Welsh name, Caerfyrddin, actually means "Merlin's City". An ancient tree stump in Priory Street is reputed to be the one in his prophecy:

When Merlin's oak shall tumble down,
Then shall fall Carmarthen town.

The citizens aren't taking chances: the tree is held up with iron bands and concrete. One thing is sure, apart from all the legends: this was Roman Moridunum, most westerly of the major British bases. Carmarthen was the scene, too, of "Rebecca riots" in 1843, a protest against extortionate charges at the all-too-numerous toll gates.

Laugharne (pronounced "larn") has some attractive Georgian houses and a romantic ruin of a castle, but these days its fame depends on the memory of the rumbustious poet Dylan Thomas. He lived here with his family in the Georgian house called the Boathouse, on and off from 1948 to 1953, working in the garden shed. Thomas died on a tour of the United States and was brought back for burial in the hillside graveyard of St. Martin's Church. He swore that Laugharne was not the model for Llareggub in *Under Milk Wood,* but that hasn't stopped the search for resemblances.

Five miles (8 km.) of firm sand at **Pendine** made it the site for world land speed challenges in the 1920s. Sir Malcolm Campbell set successive records of up to 180 miles per hour (290 k.p.h.), and Welsh ace Parry-Thomas was killed here. His car was buried in the sand, but later exhumed and put on display.

Pembrokeshire   *10 B3*

The rich farmland of the south-western peninsula of Wales looks not unlike England's West Country. It was settled, too, by English-speakers and used to be a separate county, Pembrokeshire, known as "Little England beyond Wales". Almost the whole of the coast falls within the boundaries of a national park. The 167-mile (269-km.) Pembrokeshire Coast Path takes you out along the cliffs. The sandy beach of Amroth is the starting point; here at low tide you can see the stumps of a 1,000-year-old sunken forest.

A fashionable watering place early in the 19th century, when bay-windowed Regency hotels rose above the little harbour and along the cliffs, **Tenby** is still popular for holidays. You'll soon see why: the original town inside the best-preserved old walls in Wales; the choice of beaches (North Sands, Castle Beach and South Sands); and plenty to see and do in the vicinity.

Less than 3 miles (5 km.) offshore, **Caldey Island** has been the site of a Cistercian monastery since 1929. The order actually revived an ancient abbey, which stood here for many centuries up to the Dissolution of 1534. Take a launch trip and see how the monks have put the ancient buildings back into use, how they farm their tiny island and produce scents from the island's flowers.

Along the coast in the castle at **Manorbier**, about the year 1146, was born one of the greatest scholars, travellers and, above all, writers of his time: Giraldus Cambrensis ("Gerald of Wales"), half-Norman, half-Welsh. The record of his travels is the best account we have of what the country was like in the Middle Ages.

Mighty **Pembroke Castle**, with water on three sides, dominates the town of Pembroke. Climb the keep for the view and look inside at the great stone domed roof. A spiral staircase leads down from the North Hall into a great cave called "the Wogan", which must have been a shelter for narrow boats. The defences were designed by William Marshall, who once unhorsed Richard the Lionheart but spared his life. Harri Twdwr (better known as King Henry VII, first of the Tudor dynasty) was born here in 1457.

Intriguingly, the port of **Pembroke Dock** was built with money acquired by one man (Charles Francis Greville) through trading away his mistress to another (his uncle, Sir William Hamilton). The woman in question was Emma Hart, later Lady Hamilton, who was to return to Wales with Lord Nelson on his 1801 tour. The natural harbour of **Milford Haven**, across the water, is one of the best in Britain. The town of the same name grew up after Sir William Hamilton got permission from Parliament to build the docks.

Haverfordwest ("harford", as the locals say it) was the centre of English settlement in these parts and, in one of those fascinating anomalies, used to be a county all by itself. Its castle is "one of

the ruins that Cromwell knocked about a bit", as the old song goes. A building within the walls has been restored as a museum of local history.

It's worth making for the end of the neck of land at **Dale**, a sheltered yachting centre with beaches on either side of the peninsula. It was on the sandy western shore that Henry Tudor landed in 1485, so near his childhood home of Pembroke, to begin the triumphal march that led to Bosworth Field, victory over Richard III and the crown.

Marloes has much older memories: you can clamber over Iron Age ramparts and see, offshore, the islet of Gatehold, with traces of a hundred prehistoric huts. A mile or two out to sea lie the islands of **Skomer** and **Skokholm**, the former with more mysterious relics of an old settlement, both with squadrons of seabirds. Boats to the isles set sail from Dale or Martin's Haven.

Follow the sweep of St. Bride's Bay to **St. David's**—a cathedral city, but one no bigger than many villages. **St. David's Cathedral** almost hides in a hollow, probably on the site chosen by the patron saint of Wales himself in the 6th century. (The concealment was intentional in the days when raiders usually arrived by sea.) In contrast to the severe exterior, there's plenty of decorative detail within the Norman church. Look out for the humorously carved misericords on the 15th-century choir stalls: laughter was a weapon against the devil.

More boat trips beckon: sail to **Ramsey Island,** a nature reserve just offshore, or **Grassholm** (12 mi. [19 km.] out to sea), home to thousands of gannets.

Up the coast, **Fishguard** is the ferry port for sailings to Rosslare in Ireland. If you think the docks look oversized for the purpose, you're right. There were hopes, long ago, of attracting Atlantic liners and whisking the passengers to London by train. Still earlier excitements included a raid by the American John Paul Jones during the War of Independence, and the "French invasion" of 1797, when a ragtag force led by the Irish-American Colonel Tate landed in the hope of igniting a peasants' revolt. It was the last notable hostile landing on the British mainland, and it's said the raiders first got drunk and then surrendered to Welsh women, mistaking them in their red dresses for redcoats of the army.

Inland, the rolling uplands of **Mynydd Preseli** were the source of the massive "bluestones" that Bronze Age Britons set up at Stonehenge, all of 240 miles (386 km.) away.

*Q*uiet days on the Welsh Riviera:
old-fashioned relaxation is on offer at scenic Tenby, the prime resort
of the Pembrokeshire Coast.

201

Cardigan Area
10 B3

Aberteifi ("Mouth of the Teifi") is the Welsh name for **Cardigan,** a dynamic little town. An old bridge spans the river that once brought sea-going ships to the harbour, before it silted up. There's memorable fishing along the Teifi: salmon make the run upriver to spawn.

A few miles inland, **Cilgerran** is a fishing centre for salmon and trout. You may still see coracles on this stretch of the river. The small wickerwork and canvas boats were traditionally used by local fishermen, and every August Cilgerran holds a coracle regatta. The ruin of Cilgerran's Norman castle looms above the gorge of the river.

Mid-Wales

Genteel spas and gentle hills merge almost imperceptibly with rural England to the east; lovely valleys drop to meet the long curve of Cardigan Bay to the west. In between, on the remote and empty moors and hills, you'll see more sheep than people. This narrow waist of Wales has its own personality and an atmosphere more restful than the heavyweights of north and south.

Aberystwyth
11 C3

Far from other big towns, the Queen of Cardigan Bay cultivates her independence. Victorian railway-builders made it

202

*C*hoir practice in St. David's Cathedral. Singing comes naturally to the Welsh, and it's not just reserved for Sundays. There's plenty of vocalizing at soccer and rugby matches. And the Welsh National Opera, renowned for its innovation, has produced international stars.

*Y*ou'll see more sheep than people on the hillsides
around Builth. The old spa town is also a centre for the centuries-old local
weaving industry. Country mills turn out high-quality produce bearing
the red dragon symbol of Wales.

merly in splendid isolation on a hill above the town, the library is surrounded by the new buildings of the greatly expanded university.

On a promontory by the sea, only fragments remain of another of Edward I's many powerful castles.

Vale of the Rheidol   *11 C2*

The journey is half the fun on the narrow-gauge steam railway that runs up the wooded valley of the Rheidol to **Mynach Falls**. The River Mynach meets the Rheidol in spectacular waterfalls hundreds of feet high, and three bridges stand one above the other over a vertiginous gorge. The lowermost, Devil's Bridge, dates from the 12th century and, far from being built by the devil, ought to be credited to the monks of Strata Florida Abbey (which lies in ruins to the south).

The **Plynlimon** range looks deceptively gentle. In fact, the hills rise to over 2,400 feet (732 m.). Trek to the top for some superb views over Cardigan Bay. But first check the weather forecast, and stay on firm tracks: boggy morasses lurk beneath innocent-looking green moss and reeds, and thick mists can roll in and mystify even those who know these moors. On the south-west face of the hills, the Wye and the Severn start their serpentine paths to the Bristol Channel.

Rhayader   *11 C3*

It's water, water, everywhere if you head down the Wye to Rhayader and on to a chain of nostalgic spas in the heart of mid-Wales. Rhayader's a good centre for fishing, walking, pony-trekking and antiquing. Search in craft and antique shops for the Welsh dresser you've always wanted.

The **Elan Valley** has long been flooded as a reservoir for Birmingham. If the water level is not too high it's eerie to look down on the few remaining stones of Shelley's cottage in Elan Village, remembering that the poet's first wife, and in the end he, too, drowned in boating accidents.

easy to get here, and package-holiday pioneer Thomas Savin made it cheap, providing a week's free board for the price of a ticket in the 1860s. He lost a fortune, and his grand hotel on the promenade was a failure, but it provided the University of Wales with its original building. A **museum** of decorative and folk art is housed here now.

Welsh scholars do their research at Aberystwyth's **National Library of Wales** *(Llyfrgell Genedlaethol Cymru),* the largest collection in Welsh in the world. For-

Spa Towns
11 C3

Now for that test of your Welsh pronunciation: Llandrindod Wells, Builth Wells, Llangammarch Wells and Llanwrtyd Wells came to be fashionable in the 18th century in the manner of Bath. People arrived to take the waters, and pump rooms, hotels, even gaming rooms sprang up. **Llandrindod**, the largest, remains a spa but adds golf and fishing. It also makes a convenient touring centre for the whole area. So does **Builth**, a market town on a beautiful stretch of the Wye. **Llangammarch** waters contain barium, said to be good for the heart, and **Llanwrtyd**'s were thought to be invigorating after an 18th-century vicar claimed the local frogs to be exceptional jumpers.

New Radnor
11 D3

The town is anything but new: the question is whether it was founded by Saxon King Harold when he was Earl of Hereford or by the Normans. Don't assume that Radnor Forest had many trees, either—though there are plantations now. It was a forest in the old sense, meaning moorland used for hunting, and it's still rich in wildlife.

Hay-on-Wye
11 D3

Hay's old toll bridge straddles the border with England, a remarkably tranquil landscape of green hills, though the castle ruins revive memories of the days when this was a hostile frontier. But it's for literary pursuits, not past disputes, that Hay is remembered. The town hosts an annual literary festival of national stature, and local bookshops (mainly concentrated in the area of Castle Street) just happen to stock the *world's* biggest selection of second-hand books. Collectors come from far afield to browse through hundreds of thousands of volumes on sale.

Llandovery to the Coast
11 C3

The busy market town of **Llandovery** can be your base for forays to the Black Mountain (not to be confused with the Black Mountains—plural—to the east). Tough mountain walkers head for the crest between two lakes that look as lovely as their names sound, Llyn y Fan Fawr and Llyn y Fan Fach.

If you walk in the hills, you'll be able to take old drovers' tracks by which sheep and cattle were herded to English markets. In places they follow even more ancient paths paved by Roman legionaries. The Romans weren't just empire-building: it was gold that lured them here. You can visit authentic Roman gold mines at **Dolaucothi** near Pumpsaint. The Visitor Centre sets out the history of the mines in background displays. But the most exciting thing is to go underground into the Roman adits, or tunnels, which honeycomb the slope—though it's not for the less agile or sufferers from claustrophobia.

A few miles south, **Talley Abbey** is a peaceful ruin of graceful arches and walls set among lakes and woods. There's some beautiful country around **Lampeter,** a small market and college town, and **Tregaron,** the starting point for hiking and pony-trekking excursions into the Cambrian Hills.

From here you can return to the coast, to the sailing centre of **Aberaeron**, a planned port and town built by newly rich Thomas and Susannah Jones: it gives away its age by the street names—Waterloo Street, Regent Street.

South along the coast lies the one-time shipbuilding harbour of **New Quay**, which now hosts only pleasure craft and a few lobster fishermen.

Machynlleth
11 C2

Up the Dyfi valley, Machynlleth stood at a major coaching crossroads. All of 24 inns clustered around the market cross where the Victorian clock tower stands today. Most of the inns have been converted to other uses, but it's not hard to identify them. Walk down Doll (Toll) Street to see a table of the charges that had to be paid in the days of turnpike roads. Even sheep weren't exempt, as this was, and still is, a sheep market town. The days of glory, though, are long gone; Machynlleth was once the capital of Wales, and here in 1404, at the height of his success, Owain Glyndwr was proclaimed king.

Welshpool   *11 D2*
An evocative title for border lands, the Marches bring echoes of raid and counter-raid, but Welshpool (Trallwng in Welsh) is peaceful enough now. Nearby **Powis Castle**, once a bastion, was turned into a Georgian palace. Capability Brown's lush gardens around it are reckoned a national treasure, and if you're interested in India, you'll revel in the Clive Museum in the castle.

In the hills that beckon to the northwest, **Lake Vyrnwy** (Llyn Efyrnwy) looks natural enough now, but it's man-made. Created in the 1880s, the lake provides the city of Liverpool with water. Llanwddyn village near the dam is equally new, built for the people whose houses were submerged as the waters rose. Take a boat trip (you can hire a rod, and the fishing's excellent) or walk in the forests and on the moors.

North Wales

To climbers and lovers of mountains, this part of Wales means Snowdonia National Park, with some of Britain's most challenging rock climbing and wild scenery. Railway buffs want to ride the historic narrow-gauge railways, and an increasing number of visitors are fascinated by the industrial history on view in the slate quarries.

Llangollen   *11 D2*
Song and dance fill every corner of the valley in July when the International Musical Eisteddfod attracts choirs and folk groups from around the world. Competitors wear their national costume. Above the town, engineering genius Thomas Telford tamed the falls of the River Dee to feed his Shropshire Union Canal. The canal swoops over the river on a 1,000-foot (300-m.) aqueduct of cast iron, some 120 feet (37 m.) up.

Spare a glance for **Plas Newydd** (New Place), home for 50 years of the scandalous "Ladies of Llangollen". These two Irish aristocrats ran away together and bought a cottage here in 1778, eventually expanding it into this long black-and-white timbered curiosity. Polite society cut the odd couple, and their respective families disinherited them. But less conventional acquaintances came to call—including William Wordsworth and the Duke of Wellington. Their guests were expected to bring a gift of carved oak. The result is on view inside.

Right on the border, with Offa's Dyke passing through the grounds, massive **Chirk Castle** was an archetypal fortress of the Marcher lords. It seems to have been an unlucky place, six owners being hanged or beheaded in medieval times. Then by changing sides at the wrong time in the Civil War, yet another owner managed to fall foul of the Roundheads and the Cavaliers: Chirk was wrecked by both. The castle itself was turned into a magnificent Georgian stately home. The elaborate wrought-iron gates, as intricately fashioned as lace, took the local Davies brothers 15 years to make.

Walkers will head south-west along the lovely Vale of Ceiriog and into the Berwyn hills.

Erddig
(Near Wrexham)   *11 D2*
When the National Trust acquired this great house, built around 1700, it was something like a time capsule. Rooms had been left unchanged for a hundred years, some storerooms and outbuildings for even longer. The laundry, for example, retained all the original 18th-century equipment, including a hand-cranked box mangle. And farming on the estate used traditional techniques that had died out elsewhere.

North from Ruthin *11 C2*

At the hilltop market town of **Ruthin,** where Owain Glyndwr's uprising began in 1400, you'll see fine half-timbered buildings that would have been standing even then. You can stay in the castle: this 19th-century construction on the site of the old fortress is now a hotel.

Nearby in **Denbigh**, the museum inside the ruined castle has some relics of the explorer H.M. Stanley, who was born in a cottage below the walls in 1841.

Down the valley of the River Clwyd, **St. Asaph** rivals St. David's for the title of Britain's smallest cathedral city, and the mainly 15th-century cathedral itself is no larger than many village churches. But it does mark the site of one of the earliest monasteries in Wales, founded in 537.

North Coast *11 C2*

Holiday crowds flock to brash **Prestatyn** and **Rhyl** from Liverpool across the bay, attracted by the flat sandy beaches and the funfairs.

Three miles (5 km.) upriver at still-impressive **Rhuddlan Castle**, Edward I of England, after years of campaigns intended to crush their independence, announced to Welsh leaders that he was naming as their prince one who was "born in Wales and could speak never a word of English". He was referring to his baby son, whose birth had just occurred at Caernarfon.

Colwyn Bay has no such echoes of history: it grew up as a rather ordinary resort with a long sandy beach and promenade. On a hill above the town, you can see free-flying birds of prey at the Welsh Mountain Zoo.

Llandudno is the giant among Welsh seaside spots, with a traditional sweep of hotels and guest houses along the north shore sands. A cable railway and toll road lead to the top of 679-foot (207-m.) **Great Orme Head,** west of town, for vast views of Anglesey and Snowdonia. Little Orme Head to the east is lower, with cliffs a rugged 400 feet (122 m.) high.

In his master plan to subdue the Welsh,

Edward I had to secure the crossing of the River Conwy, and his **Conwy Castle** survives as a perfect example of medieval fortification. Take a walk around the battlements and the walls of the town, which developed as a dependency of the castle. Telford's suspension bridge of 1826 leading to the castle gate is a graceful addition, paralleled by Robert Stephenson's 1848 railway bridge.

Facing Anglesey across the Menai Strait, **Bangor** is home to a branch of the University of Wales. The venerable look

*Sarah Ponsonby and Eleanor Butler caused quite
a stir when they set up home together at the manor of Plas Newydd in
Llangollen. Not many women in the 18th century stepped out in top
hats and masculine attire. It was enough to keep the neighbours gossiping
for the next fifty years.*

*P*alace and fortress, Caernarfon has seen two princely
investitures this century. In 1911, Prince Edward, later Edward VIII,
and in 1969, Prince Charles, were invested with the insignia of the Prin-
cipality of Wales—a sword, coronet, gold ring and gold rod. After
the ceremony, the new prince greets his subjects from the castle balcony.

of the cathedral is deceptive: it's mainly the result of 19th-century restoration.

Nearby **Penrhyn Castle** is no restoration, it's a complete fake. As if there were not enough Norman castles in Wales already, sugar and slate baron Lord Penrhyn had another built in the 1820s and '30s. His architect, Hopper, went in for the colossal, both in scale and quantity of decoration. These days the castle belongs to the National Trust. It's home not only to the original "Norman" furniture (don't miss the outsize, slate state bed— Queen Victoria slept here), but to the most disparate collections (locomotives to dolls).

The **Penrhyn slate quarries** lie a few miles inland at Bethesda, a village that took the name of its Nonconformist chapel in place of the original Glan Ogwen. You can tour the quarry and see how the "queens", "duchesses" and other fine "ladies" (the different slate sizes) in blue, red and green are cut from a 1,000-foot-deep (300-m.) gash in the mountainside.

Anglesey
10-11 B-C2

Ynys Môn in Welsh, Mona to the Romans, the island is flatter than any other part of Wales, but with rugged cliffs and sandy beaches. The tireless Thomas Telford built the 1826 **Menai Bridge** from the mainland. It was the first practical, heavy-duty suspension bridge ever constructed—579 feet (177 m.) from pier to pier, and 100 feet (30 m.) above the water at the highest tide (by order of the Admiralty, to let navy ships through).

Llanfair P.G. is the short form for a 58-letter name that was probably a 19th-century joke: Llanfairpwllgwyngyllgogerychwyrndrobwllllantysiliogogogoch (literally, St. Mary's by the White Aspen over the Whirlpool and St. Tysilio's by the Red Cave). The old railway station sign is on display in Penrhyn Castle.

The name says a lot about **Beaumaris** (after the Norman French for "beautiful flat land"). This pleasant town is rich in fine old houses, and the **castle**, with a sea moat lapping at its outer walls, is one of the finest designs of Edward I's master builder, James of St. George.

Sadly, many travellers see little of Anglesey as they hurry to the ferry port of **Holyhead**. They might be surprised to hear that seaborne trade with Ireland has been going on by this route for 4,000 years, since gold and axe heads were first imported. The port is actually on **Holy Island** (reached by a causeway), the seat of Celtic saints. Try to make time to take the road to the western tip of the island, where South Stack is the site of a lighthouse, bird sanctuary and caves where grey seals breed.

Caernarfon
10 C2

The name means "the fort on the shore", rather an understatement for this last and most dominating of Edward I's castles in Wales. His son, the first English Prince of Wales, was born here in 1284. (The investiture at Caernarfon of the present prince in 1969 was televised to an audience of 500 million worldwide.)

The walled town was built for English merchants and settlers; it's intensely Welsh today, and you'll hear plenty of Welsh spoken. Take the dizzying walk around the battlements for some expansive views of Anglesey, across the Menai Strait, and mountainous Snowdonia.

Did Edward I know of the remains of the Roman fort of **Segontium,** only half a mile (less than a kilometre) away? Those earlier intruders arrived about A.D. 78 and stayed 300 years. Then the legions, led by Magnus Maximus, departed for Gaul and brief glory before disappearing into the darkness of disintegrating empire. Around this event, Welsh bards wove legends of the hero Macsen Wledig, second only to King Arthur in splendour.

The Lleyn Peninsula
10 B2

A coast of rocky coves, fishing harbours and sandy beaches; whitewashed slate-roofed cottages; low, windswept hills covered with heather and gorse; cliffs at "Land's End"—doesn't it all sound a bit like a miniature Devon and Cornwall? But it's very Welsh, though unlike any other part of Wales.

A dreamer who got results, Welsh architect Sir Clough Williams-Ellis hated mere "developments" and dull repetition and wanted to show that the new village of **Portmeirion** could be imaginative, beautiful and liveable at the same time. Although Portofino in Italy was his inspiration, Portmeirion took on a life of its own. Building started in 1926, around the nucleus of an old house, now a hotel. You'll see pieces of architectural treasure from all over the country that Williams-Ellis saved from destruction, interspersed with an eclectic mixture of building designs he happened to admire. An Italian campanile, elegant colonnades, Georgian houses and tiny cottages are all set amid exotic gardens. Somehow you keep discovering steps that invite climbing, with superb vistas as your reward.

Wales has never lacked visionaries, and another, William Madocks, saw the need for a port for the shipping of slate from local quarries and mines. In the early 19th century he had the twin Regency-style towns, **Tremadog** and **Porthmadog** built (the names derive from his own). As you'll see, the town plans anticipated an expansion that never quite happened. T.E. Lawrence ("Lawrence of Arabia") was born in Tremadog in 1888. Perhaps his early interest in castles was triggered by first-hand knowledge of some of the greatest here in North Wales.

Just along the coast, **Criccieth's** ruined fortress dominates the little town and beaches from its high headland. Walk up and around it for views of Snowdonia and the Lleyn.

Close by to the west, **Llanystumdwy** was the boyhood home of David Lloyd George—dubbed the "Welsh Wizard" for his oratory—statesman and British Prime Minister during World War I. His grave is here, along with a memorial and museum designed by Williams-Ellis.

Mention **Pwllheli** and many people will think of the huge holiday camp, but that's some way from the old town and harbour full of yachts and powerboats. From little **Abersoch** you can sail round St. Tudwal's Islands, which are bird sanctuaries.

The last bay on the south of the Lleyn Peninsula shelters **Aberdaron,** where countless pilgrims used to embark for **Bardsey Island,** across Bardsey Sound. The isle is site of ancient monasteries and the purported burial place of 20,000 "saints" (in the sense of "believers"). Less than one square mile (about 2 sq. km.) in area, it's another bird sanctuary—with the addition of a few sheep farms.

Nefyn is the main resort on the north coast of the Lleyn, but its popularity isn't new. Edward I organized a tournament here in 1284 to celebrate his successful Welsh campaign. Four miles (6 km.) north, there's an impressive Iron Age site with 100 hut-circles, but even earlier Bronze Age burial places show the peninsula to have been inhabited considerably earlier.

Snowdonia   *11 C2*

Snowdonia National Park covers about 800 square miles (over 2,000 sq. km.) of mountains, hills and coastline between Conwy, Bala, Aberdovey and Bangor. National Park Information offices in Llanberis and Betws-y-Coed, the main centres, sell maps and detailed guides and organize guided day walks.

Just because you can "climb" to the 3,560-foot (1,085-m.) peak of **Snowdon** on a Swiss-type rack railway, don't think these mountains are easy, or safe. There are plenty of challenging routes, and the first expedition to reach the top of Mount Everest did a lot of training here.

Llanberis is where you catch the Snowdon train—or start the most straightforward walk to the summit, which will give you 5 miles (8 km.) of aerobic exercise, plus a great feeling of superiority to the rail passengers. Either way, the views are worth the trip.

Back at Llanberis the narrow-gauge Lake Railway follows the shore of wildly scenic Llyn Padarn. The return (round) trip takes 45 minutes, leaving sightseers plenty of time for a visit to the Welsh Slate Museum on the site of the old Dinorwic quarry, where the workings rise in terraces to 1,800 feet (550 m.).

A dramatic road south-east over Llanberis Pass leads to **Pen-y-Gwryd**, the climbers' inn which is now a centre offering courses in all kinds of mountain activities. There's a similar centre at **Capel Curig**. The alpine nature reserve at **Crafnant** attracts specialists from all over.

Betws-y-Coed can be crowded, and the traffic brought to a standstill by the daily influx of tourists and excursion coaches attracted to this famous beauty spot. You'll do well to get away from the roads by walking the forest paths. Three valleys meet here, the Conwy, Lledr and Llugwy, all with waterfalls (including the celebrated Swallow Falls and Conwy Falls).

Everything seems to be made of slate at **Blaenau Ffestiniog,** a small town set splendidly in a steep horseshoe of moun-

213

This glacial valley in Snowdonia National Park is as green as a sheep's dream. The park attracts outdoorsmen and mountaineers. For those who are up to climbing it, Mount Snowdon is the summit of Wales, and England, too.

narrow-gauge line runs through a glorious section of Snowdonia National Park on its 13-mile (21-km.) journey from the market town of Ffestiniog to Porthmadog on the coast (see p. 213). Inaugurated in 1836, this is the oldest passenger-carrying light railway in the world, now restored by enthusiasts after a period of neglect.

On the eastern fringes of Snowdonia, Lake Bala, the largest natural lake in Wales, lies at the heart of some of the finest and wildest hill country. The town of **Bala,** quiet except in July and August, played an important role in the growth of Methodism. From here, too, came many of the Welsh who established a colony in Patagonia, in southern Argentina, where a few of their descendants still speak some Welsh today.

Harlech   *11 C2*
Every Welsh child, and plenty of English, could sing you the rousing song "Men of Harlech". It's practically a second national anthem, immortalizing the defence of Harlech's awe-inspiring castle by the Constable of Wales, Dfydd, at the end of the Wars of the Roses. Like so many heroes in Welsh history, he was on the losing side, but Harlech had been the last refuge of a lost cause before. Owain Glyndwr made the fortress his headquarters in 1408 and his family was captured here by the future Henry V of England. On the losing side again in 1647, Harlech was the last bastion to withstand Parliamentary attack in the Civil War. Consequently the fortress suffered some destructive "slighting" to ensure no repetition of such defiance.

The usual entrance is on the eastern side, where you can visualize the bridge that crossed the great ditch, then the drawbridge, three doors and three portcullises. On the west, the sea has receded, but imagine how it once lapped against the rocks below. Ships could actually unload supplies, and you can still climb the 200-foot (60-m.) fortified stairway to the castle.

tains that have been cut, sliced and mined by the slate quarriers. Dress up warmly—you'll be given lights and safety helmets—for a grim descent into the **Nyth y Gigfran** quarry. Or go the tourist route at **Llechwedd** slate mines. You can ride an electric train through the labyrinth of old tunnel workings and buy things you never imagined could be made from slate.

Most of the "Great Little Trains of Wales" began as industrial services, transporting slate. The **Ffestiniog Railway** is no exception. The steam-hauled,

Barmouth   *11 C2*

Sands and sheltered waters, plus count-less sights to see if the weather drove them off the beach, drew families to Barmouth when the railway arrived in the 19th century. The terraced Victorian town remains a popular holiday centre. If your travels have made you a supporter of the great work of the National Trust, you might like to walk up **Dinas Oleu**, the hill behind the harbour. It was the first piece of land ever acquired by the Trust, in 1895.

Up-river, **Dolgellau's** dark slate houses match the cliffs around. This is a rather tradition-minded area, and you'll hear a lot of Welsh spoken. Visitors use the town as a base for exploring and climbing in the **Cadair Idris** range of mountains that fill the southern horizon. You'll see the "Chair of Idris" in the outline of the peaks. (Legends disagree as to whether Idris was King Arthur or a giant.) By all means head for the hills—but don't miss the walks around Dolgellau itself. "Precipice Walk" is not at all hair-raising, despite the name, and there are some fine views.

Tywyn   *11 C2*

The **church** of Tywyn is part-Norman, but the famous St. Cadfan's Stone it shelters is much older, perhaps 7th or 8th century, and inscribed in Welsh. There's a lot of argument about what it actually says, but scholars agree that it's the oldest known example of the Welsh language.

You may have seen the Talyllyn narrow-gauge steam railway in half a dozen films and TV series. Opened in 1865 and in continuous operation ever since, the steep little line starts from Tywyn and doesn't quite reach the enchanting lake which gives the line its name. Disembark at Nant Gwernol and walk through forested country to the lake.

Aberdovey   *11 C2*

Aberdyfi in Welsh, the town didn't actually have any bells when an 18th-century

song "The Bells of Aberdovey" spread its name round the world. They were supposed to come from a drowned city under the waves, perhaps a folk memory from the distant past. Tree stumps thousands of years old are sometimes visible in the sand at low tide, so the sea has indeed risen. The port once built schooners, sending them around the world—have a look at the small museum of sailing—but the trade declined. Then the railway brought English holidaymakers, and Aberdovey even acquired a golf course.

216

The village looks unassuming enough now. But in 1404 Dolgellau was the chosen site of the last Welsh parliament of Owain Glyndwr. This romantic figure led a popular uprising against the English oppressors. Despite early successes, Owain's was a lost cause. Centuries later, however, Welsh nationalism is still a potent force.

217

O'er Vales and Hills to Rome's Frontier

Most European countries have a north-south divide: England is no different. Southerners can't help seeing the north in terms of smoke-blackened industrial cities. It was never true of more than a small fraction, and still less is it true in these post-industrial days of clean air and soot-free buildings.

Most of the north remains what it was, the most varied and beautiful, as well as the most rugged landscape in England. All over the north there are abbeys and fortresses with stirring tales to tell. There's an infectious warmth to the big cities, too, and a new pride in their industrial history.

Northern Cities

A swathe of great manufacturing cities runs across the north of England from Liverpool, Manchester and the mill towns of Lancashire to Sheffield, Bradford and Leeds in Yorkshire. Motorways link the cities and surrounding towns together into one immense industrial network. But splendid recreational tracts of open country, moorland and valley lie near at hand, on both sides of the Pennines.

*A*mong the bracken and heather of the Nidderdale moors, near Pateley Bridge, wind and rain carved out the fantastic shapes of Brimham Rocks.

Liverpool   II D1

Who hasn't heard of this rowdy, rebellious seaport city? Kids the world over can reel off the names of Liverpool's football (soccer) stars. For their parents' generation, Liverpool meant the Beatles. Earlier, emigrants to the New World sailed from here in their millions, and in World War II this was the landfall in Europe of many G.I.s. Since then, the Atlantic trade that made the city rich has mostly gone elsewhere, leaving miles of docks derelict and whole areas depressed. Now people are beginning to see the magnificence of some of the Victorian and Edwardian architecture on the waterfront. Imaginative schemes have restored quayside warehouses, as fine in their way as the palazzos of Venice. The town has a long way to go, but a start has been made.

The best view of the **waterfront** would be from a ship—not so easy to arrange now that most of the ferry services have been superseded by tunnels and bridges across the Mersey. (Ferries still operate to

219

the Isle of Man and Ireland from here.) You can't miss the two towers of the Royal Liver (pronounced "lyver") Building, with mythical "liver" birds on top— at 295 feet (90 m.) they're the tallest thing around.

A short walk south brings you to the showpiece of the docks renewal. The buildings around **Canning Dock** have been converted to house the **Merseyside Maritime Museum**, along with part of the magnificent colonnaded **Albert Dock**. Trendy shops, offices and restaurants fill the rest. Another warehouse here has been taken over by the **Tate Gallery, Liverpool,** for the display of modern art from the collections of the Tate in London.

From the waterfront, Water Street leads inland past the Georgian Town Hall, designed by John Wood the Elder of Bath fame. Almost a mile from the Mersey, you'll find the city's cultural centre of gravity, a cluster of 19th-century palaces near Lime Street railway station. Massive, classical **St. George's Hall**—law court and concert hall—is the grandest of the lot.

Liverpool Museum, strong on natural history and archaeology, doesn't stand up to the London competition, but the **Walker Art Gallery** is world class. Begin with the early Italian and North European section (Simone Martini to Cranach), or concentrate on the Flemish and Dutch masters. A memorable self-portrait of Rembrandt as a young man stands out. Gainsborough, Constable, Romney, Reynolds and Turner are well represented in a comprehensive British collection. And the gallery's Pre-Raphaelite and later Victorian works (Millais, Holman Hunt, Watts and many more), disparaged for decades, have come into their own—none more so than the celebrated *And When Did You Last See Your Father?* by the almost forgotten name of W.F. Yeames. Among British painters of the 20th century, don't miss that brilliant recorder of the industrial north, L.S. Lowry.

There's more Pre-Raphaelite and Victorian art on view across the Mersey at the model village of **Port Sunlight**, built for the workers of Lord Lever's Sunlight soap factory. The **Lady Lever Art Gallery** specializes in these dramatic, romantic, narrative pictures.

Two cathedrals crown Liverpool's skyline. The **Anglican Cathedral** by Sir Giles Gilbert Scott, completed in 1978, was seven decades in the building. It's one of the last—and among the biggest—ever constructed in Gothic style—rivalling Rome's St. Peter's Basilica in size. The 1960s Roman Catholic **Metropolitan Cathedral** could hardly be more different. Dubbed the "tea cosy" by the locals, it's circular, with a conical roof topped by a tower of coloured glass and slender pinnacles.

Beatles fans, of course, are more interested in the **"Beatles' Magical History Tour"**, leaving Lime Street Tourist Information Office daily at 2.30 p.m. You'll take in all the key places in the early lives of the quartet: where they were born, went to school, the Cavern nightclub where they got their start, Strawberry Fields... all against a background of Beatles hits. The itinerary doesn't miss a beat.

Manchester   8 A1

"What Manchester thinks today, London thinks tomorrow", self-confident cotton bosses used to declare. The textile industry has declined now, but Victorian pride survives. That was the quality which drove the Manchester Ship Canal 36 miles (58 km.) through to the sea in 1894, turning the inland city into a port for ocean-going vessels. The same attitude demanded that the self-proclaimed northern capital should have public buildings, educational institutions, museums, theatres and an orchestra (the Hallé) the equal of—or better than—London's.

World War II bombing, the demolition of mills and slums, and piecemeal modern development changed the character of the city, and not always for the better. But clean-air laws and the removal of decades of grime have certainly brightened things up. The financial sector burgeoned as cotton declined: Manchester still means business.

The Gothic-revival **Town Hall** (1877) on Albert Square sets the tone with its murals of commerce, industry and Christianity by Pre-Raphaelite painter Ford Madox Brown. A civic building on a grand scale, the massive **Central Library** opposite is one of the world's largest lending libraries.

Nearby in Brazenose Street you'll perhaps be surprised to find a statue of Abraham Lincoln, presented to the city in gratitude for the support the Lancashire cotton workers gave the Union in the Civil War, when self-interest might have led them to favour the South. You may want to continue across Deansgate to the **John Rylands Library** of rare books and manuscripts, with 4,000 books printed before 1500, including the oldest dated example of European block printing.

The **City Art Gallery** (Princess Street) displays a rich collection of the High Victorian painting that's returning to fashion after decades of disregard, and much more besides. Special emphasis is given to Manchester's own L.S. Lowry (1887–1976), painter of industrial and slum landscapes. There's a representative sampling of Lowry's work, as well as a reconstruction of his modest living-room and studio.

While Manchester boomed in the 19th century, the factory hands struggled in deplorable conditions. Friedrich Engels described their plight in his 1845 book *The Condition of the Working Class in England.* Engels did his writing in the library of **Chetham's Hospital** (a medieval charitable institution) on the north side of town near the 15th-century cathedral. You can see the desk he shared with Karl Marx when they teamed up to denounce the exploitation of the cotton workers.

The city's wealth of art seems limitless. In the university area south of the centre, the **Whitworth Art Gallery** has superb watercolours, modern art and historic textiles in a collection that would do credit to any international capital.

Castlefield was the site of the Roman fort of Mancunium (Manchester people are still called Mancunians), as well as the one-time terminus of the earliest canal and railway systems. Now it's home to the **Museum of Science and Industry**, the **Air and Space Museum** and an **Urban Heritage Park** with constantly changing exhibits. The **Granada TV Studios** let you stare at the stars and walk around the set of the oldest British "soap" of them all, *Coronation Street.*

Sheffield 8 A2

The name has been synonymous with cutlery since the Middle Ages. The miller in Chaucer's 14th-century *Canterbury Tales* was carrying a Sheffield knife (visit the City Museum in Weston Park to see implements like it). Unfortunately you can't manufacture steel without pollution, and by the 18th century Sheffield had become appallingly grimy. Horace Walpole declared it "the foulest town in England in the most charming situation". Today's prosperous city boasts clean air, a largely new centre and good shopping in traffic-free complexes. Look for Sheffield cutlery—they're still making it.

Leeds 13 C3

The bold commercial capital of Yorkshire can hardly be ignored, even if it isn't on many tourist routes. You might come here for the cricket at Headingley, scene of Yorkshire and England triumphs and as many disasters. Or for the music: the International Piano Competition is one of the most important in the world, though the local vote might be for the brass band championships.

The public buildings speak of Victorian self-confidence, led by the imposing classical **Town Hall**, opened by Queen Victoria herself in 1858. The **City Art Gallery** concentrates on English painting of the 19th and 20th centuries and on the work of English sculptors—two of the greatest, Henry Moore and Barbara Hepworth, both studied art here in Leeds.

Many of the Old Masters from the city's collection are on view at **Temple Newsam**, a severe Jacobean house on the eastern outskirts of Leeds, acquired by the municipality in the 1920s. The enormous park was designed by the indefatigable Capability Brown, though he might now be surprised by the golf courses. How that man got around!

Harewood House

Capability Brown laid out the park here, too, for Edwin Lascelles, whose family had grown rich on West Indian sugar. His descendant, the Earl of Harewood, cousin of the queen, lives on at Harewood. The interiors represent some of the best work of Robert Adam. Everything carries the Scotsman's stamp, from ceilings to carpets, chimneypieces to mirrors. He even designed furniture for Thomas Chippendale to make. The elegant **Gallery** is the best room in the house, perfectly setting off a formidable collection of pictures by Titian, El Greco, Bellini and Turner.

Bradford   13 C3

If, a few years ago, you had said you were including Bradford on a holiday itinerary, you would have been met with blank incomprehension. But the home of "worsted" (a type of tightly-woven wool) has made a major effort to attract visitors. The city is used to arrivals from overseas: so many came from India and Pakistan to work here that you might think you're on another continent—with the appropriate shopping and restaurant options.

Some of the mill buildings are models of industrial architecture. The slim Florentine chimney—smokeless now of course—at **Manningham Mill** rivals the campanile of the neo-Gothic **City Hall**. They've gone out of their way in Bradford to cater to the growing interest in industrial history. You can learn about wool and worsted at the **Bradford Industrial Museum**. There's a transport collection there, too, and another at the **West Yorkshire Transport Museum**.

Housed appropriately in a former cinema, the **National Museum of Photography, Film and Television** is compulsive viewing, with its lively displays and film shows on the stunning, several-storeyshigh IMAX screen.

Yorkshire Dales and Pennine Moors

First-timers here or elsewhere in the industrial north are invariably amazed by the proximity of open country to inner-city streets. Windswept moors and idyllic valleys, called dales in these parts, are never far away. No coincidence this, for it was water from the high Pennines, soft for washing and fast-flowing for power, that the mills needed. When steam power replaced the waterwheels, there was plenty of coal to generate it. The towns became smoke-blackened, but the countryside stayed pristine. Climbers, potholers and hikers head for the dales and hills, and some of the more accessible roads can become processions of traffic on summer weekends.

Brontë Country   12 C3

At the top of the steep, cobbled main street of **Haworth** stands the parsonage where the brilliant, tragic Brontë family settled in 1820. Here at the edge of the bleak moors that so often feature in the sisters' writing, Charlotte, Emily and Anne Brontë and their brother Branwell spent most of their lives. Charlotte published *Jane Eyre* in 1847, and Emily's *Wuthering Heights* soon followed. Anne's *The Tenant of Wildfell Hall* appeared in 1848, but within months, and before their worth was recognized, Emily and Anne had died. With Branwell dead, too, Charlotte was left alone with her father.

In 1854, Charlotte Brontë married the curate, Arthur Nicholls, in **Haworth Church**, where you can see the family vault in which all were buried except Anne. Charlotte herself died only nine months after her wedding. The church is largely a later reconstruction, but the **parsonage** has been restored to the way it was in the Brontës' time. It's filled with memorabilia—look out for Branwell's portraits of the family—and the **museum wing** has a fine collection of letters and manuscripts. In the village, which can be overrun by visitors in summer, you can still find the **Black Bull**, the inn where Branwell Brontë, already ill, drank away his days.

You'll escape most of the crowds if you take some of the sisters' favourite walks, perhaps to the Brontë Waterfall and on to the ruins at **Top Withens**, the possible site of *Wuthering Heights*. The sisters liked to walk to **Keighley** to borrow books, but you could take the steam-powered Worth Valley Railway.

Wharfedale   *12 C3*
One of the most attractive of the valleys which cut the eastern side of the Pennines, Wharfedale gets more scenic as you head up it. You can start at **Ilkley**, a one-time Victorian spa where "curists" treated every ill from rheumatism to melancholia with a freezing plunge bath. History goes back much further. **All Saints** parish church has the shafts of three Anglo-Saxon crosses, and the **Manor House Museum** displays Roman relics from its own back yard. The Panorama Stone in the public gardens dates from the same Bronze Age period as the Twelve Apostles stone circle on the moors above the town. South-west of Ilkley, on Addingham Moor, the unique **Swastika Stone** may be a religious relic of the Iron Age. The folksong, "On Ilkla Moor baht 'at" (i.e., without a hat) is practically Yorkshire's national anthem.

Both Turner and Landseer were inspired to paint the ruin of 12th-century **Bolton Priory** (near the village confusingly called Bolton Abbey). You hardly notice at first, but the nave is not a ruin: it was already in use as the parish church when the monastery was dissolved, and remains so still. Several beautiful walks begin here, either upstream or climbing to the moors above.

A diversion into Airedale, the next valley to the south, gives you a chance to see **Skipton Castle**, former stronghold of the powerful Cliffords. It was restored by the energetic Lady Anne Clifford after the Civil War and survives little changed since then. She planted the yew tree which dominates Conduit Court. In Skipton itself, the **Craven Museum** has Bronze Age relics, including cloth from a tomb, and tells the story of the lead boom of the 18th and 19th centuries.

The little streets of **Grassington** can be busy in summer. It was a centre for lead mining, and former miners' cottages now house the Upper Wharfedale Folk Museum. Over the river in the village of **Linton** you'll see the ancient packhorse bridge and tinkling "beck" (the local word for stream). A few miles west, **Malham** is set in rugged limestone country, and Malham Cove is a celebrated natural theatre of cliffs rising to 300 feet (90 m.). The little lake of Malham Tarn inspired Charles Kingsley to write *The Water Babies*. It's now the centre of a 4,000-acre (1,620-ha.) nature reserve owned by the National Trust.

Wensleydale   *12 C3*
Don't look for a river called the Wensley, though there is a sleepy village of that name with a fine old church. This green valley is watered by the River Ure. At **Aysgarth**, the river tumbles down a photogenic succession of falls crossed by an ancient bridge. In the hills to the north-east, **Bolton Castle** (not to be confused with Bolton Priory or Abbey) was one of the first fortresses to serve as a prison for Mary Queen of Scots after her flight to England in 1568. Climb the battlements for the same views she had, over Wensleydale and the high moors beyond.

Further downriver, the massive Norman keep survives at **Middleham Castle,** "Windsor of the North". Early each morning, see the stable lads (and lasses) taking the many racehorses trained near here for exercise on the moor near the castle. It was probably the monks of nearby **Jervaulx Abbey** who started horse-breeding in this area, and the tradition survived the dissolution of the abbey in 1537. Credit for producing the first Wensleydale cheese also goes to them. The ruins of Jervaulx (pronounced "jervo") are romantically overgrown, but you'll be able to work out the ground plan. The wall with fine high windows was once part of the monks' dormitory.

You'll share the little market town of **Hawes** in Upper Wensleydale with local farmers and their livestock every Tuesday. Any day it makes a good centre for touring and walking. The long-distance north-south trail called the Pennine Way funnels hikers through here. You can join them on a short walk to **Hardraw Force,** where water cascades 99 feet (30 m.) over a limestone ledge. In town, the **Upper Dales Folk Museum** occupies the station building of the defunct railway. A line that does still exist, after years of running battles between preservationists and accountants, sweeps over the famous **Ribblehead Viaduct** (9 mi. [14 km.] southwest) on its way across the high moors from Settle to Carlisle. Building the 24 soaring arches is said to have cost the lives of 100 men. The marshy ground beneath was supposedly stabilized with the fleece of sheep.

The best-known caves in the Pennines are reached through the village of **Clapham** (with a National Park Information Centre). It's a short walk to **Ingleborough Cave,** which goes half a mile into the hillside. Another mile up the hill you'll come to the mouth of **Gaping Ghyll**, most dramatic of Yorkshire's potholes, where a waterfall flings itself 360 feet (110 m.) to the ground. For cavers, that's just the start of one of the most exciting labyrinths in Europe. Claustrophobes will cringe

at the idea, and instead perhaps make the easy climb to the summit of **Ingleborough,** 2,373 feet (724 m.).

Upper Swaledale
12-13 C2

In deeper and wilder valleys than those to the south, the fast-flowing Swale and its tributaries burrow under windswept fells where hardy Swaledale sheep live out all winter. Remote villages here can be cut off by snow, and the farms are some of the loneliest in Britain.

You can join Upper Swaledale by the

*In the 18th century the Agricultural Revolution
changed the face of rural England. With the introduction of a four-year
crop rotation system, the fields were cut up into a patchwork of small
enclosures, and bounded by hawthorn hedges or dry stone walls to keep
cattle away from the crops. Conservationists violently oppose the
demolition of these walls, home to birds, insects... and hedgehogs.*

road from Hawes over Buttertubs Pass. Head for **Keld,** a pretty greystone village where footpaths follow the Swale as it tumbles down roaring cataracts. Downstream, at **Reeth,** the river is joined by Arkle Beck flowing out of Arkengarthdale—on a grey day as dark, mysterious and Nordic as its name. There's a National Park Information Centre here, as well as the Swaledale Folk Museum.

At **Richmond,** the Swale emerges from the hills and begins a gentler journey across the Vale of York. The fine old town is dominated by the Norman castle, with its 12th-century keep towering over the gatehouse. (Climb to the top for the views of the town and the moors.) Glastonbury's claims notwithstanding, northern tradition holds this is the last resting place of King Arthur and his Knights of the Round Table, and that they will rise again at the sound of the trumpet should the nation ever be in peril.

Eighteenth-century prosperity left the big, sloping, cobbled marketplace surrounded by good Georgian buildings, including the remarkable little **theatre** with its boxes and gallery. Built in 1788, it was closed in 1848 and became an auction room, warehouse and finally a rubbish tip, before restoration in 1962. It's one of only two theatres of the period left (the other being in Bristol).

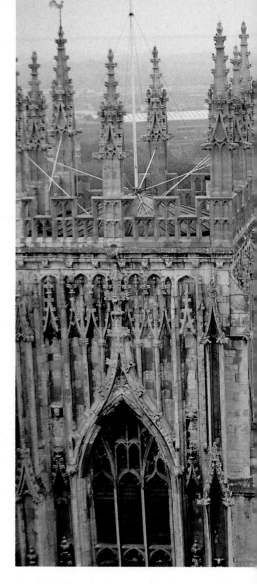

⚓ *York* 13 D3

History is packed into the ancient walls of this jewel of English cities. Narrow streets twist and turn like a maze around the medieval splendour of the Minster, perhaps the greatest medieval cathedral in northern Europe. As Eboracum, York was the headquarters of Roman emperors—Hadrian came here in 121, Septimius Severus, born in North Africa, died in York in 211 and Constantine the Great was proclaimed emperor here in 306.

After the Romans left, the city was for a time capital of Deira, kingdom of the Angles. Then it came under the sway of Saxon Northumbria. Invading Danes captured the city in 867, calling it Jorvik (whence is derived the name York). They stayed for a century, developing the town as a trading port on the River Ouse. The Normans, for their part, expanded the walls and built two castles. In the Middle Ages, York was England's second city, grown rich from the wool trade. For long periods the affairs of the north were run from here, scarcely influenced by king or Parliament in London.

226

*Y*ork's history is recounted in stone, in its museums, and in the medieval names of the little streets around the Minster. Most refer to the trades practised there: the Shambles was called Flesh-ammels, or slaughterhouses, and Colliergate was the street of the charcoal dealers. In the shortest street of all, Whip-ma-Whop-ma-gate, petty criminals were tied to a post and given a public thrashing.

York is an ideal place for sightseeing on foot, and the narrow streets, traffic and parking limitations make driving ill-advised anyway. You can orient yourself and enjoy the views by walking the **city walls**, a 3-mile (5-km.) circuit. If you only go part of the way, be sure to include the section nearest to the Minster, between Bootham Bar and Monk Bar. (No drinks at these "bars": they're the old city gates.)

York Minster, despite its vast size, has a warmth and beauty unsurpassed in English cathedrals. A wonderful harmony of style was achieved, although it took from 1220 until about 1475 to build. Make an early visit if you can, to enjoy the atmosphere before the crowds arrive, and hope for a sunny morning to see the stone glowing honey-gold.

The Minster's glory is its fabulous **stained glass**, which has somehow survived civil wars, religious turmoil and the ravages of several fires—including one in 1984 that destroyed part of the roof of the south transept. It's now rebuilt, and the 40,000 pieces of the rose window weakened in the blaze have been painstakingly remounted. The west window dates from 1338, while the great east window was completed 70 years after that. At 2,000 square feet (186 sq.m.), it's the largest expanse of such early stained glass in the world.

The 15th-century stone **rood screen** between the nave and choir supports a parade of stern statues of the English kings up to that time.

From the north transept, with its **Five Sisters Window** in grisaille, go through the vestibule to the 13th-century **Chapter House**—and look up. The vaulted wooden roof is original, and the stone carving incorporates amusing grotesques and grisly vignettes. In the **undercroft** and **crypts** you can see Norman and even Roman foundations, as well as fine displays of York silver.

Outside, take time to walk in the little streets around the Minster: Low Petergate, Stonegate, Goodramgate and The Shambles, where the medieval buildings seem almost to meet overhead.

Off the modern Coppergate shopping complex, the **Jorvik Viking Centre**, a Disney-style recreation of the 9th-century Viking settlement—complete with appropriate noises and smells—is one of those tourist attractions that people love or loathe. But it's not all ersatz: the actual excavations of Coppergate are on view, along with finds from the site.

The curators of the prize-winning **Castle Museum** in the former women's prison (opposite the Norman Clifford's Tower) use more orthodox methods to bring the past to life. Everyone finds some part of the folk collections fascinating, but the highlight is a 19th-century "street" with fully stocked shops, a prison, post office and fire station.

A million visitors a year descend on the **National Railway Museum** alone. Next to the railway station, former engine sheds house gleaming locomotives from the earliest days right up to the last mighty behemoths produced before boring diesel and electric power took over. A prize exhibit is the *Mallard*, world record-breaker at 126 mph (203 kph). Carriages on show include Queen Victoria's lush, plush saloon car.

Beverley 13 D3

They love their horse racing in these parts, and Beverley is no exception. This charming market town, predictably enough, has one of Yorkshire's most attractive courses. While you're here, be sure to see the **Minster,** bigger and more magnificent than some cathedrals. The stone carving of the **Percy tomb** is exceptionally beautiful, as is the wood carving of the **misericords**, all 68 of them—the greatest number in any English church.

Harrogate 13 C3

An elegant spa which is now a leading conference centre, this attractive town managed to make the change without losing its appeal. In fact, the extra vitality and facilities have added to Harrogate's advantages, both as a destination and as a touring base.

Parks and flower gardens everywhere, hosts of small shops both antique and boutique, restaurants and tearooms make it perfect for idling. The dignified **Royal Pump Room** (1842) now houses a museum of local history and dress. One of the many springs in the area is in the basement, and you can sample its sulphurous water: you may well feel that you have been cured—of ever trying it again.

Mystery queen Agatha Christie disappeared in 1926 and was found staying at the lovely Old Swan hotel (then called the Hydropathic). Now, they run "murder weekends" for would-be detectives.

Ripon   *13 C3*

One of England's smaller cities, Ripon has one of its smaller cathedrals, a 12th–15th-century edifice built on Saxon foundations. The local woodcarvers' guild created the Perpendicular choir stalls, a striking feature here. Notice the misericords under the seats, full of medieval humour, with portraits of Samson and Jonah and a fox and geese. Every night at 9 p.m. the City Hornblower in tricorn hat "sets the watch", as he has, so they say, for 1,000 years.

Fountains Abbey   *13 C3*

The poignantly beautiful ruins of what was once the greatest monastery in England stand in wooded Skelldale near Ripon: Fountains Abbey, begun in the 12th century, famous for wool. The profits enabled the Cistercian monks to buy more farms, employ farm workers— and to build on a noble scale. Their **church** extends for a considerable 360 feet (110 m.), its walls remarkably complete. At the east end, the remains of the soaring 13th-century **Chapel of the Nine Altars** make a tremendous impression.

Walk round the cloisters with a ground plan, to see how such a complex community lived. The **lay brothers' refectory** is amazingly preserved: their dormitory

would have been on the floor above. The sheer opulence of such religious houses was in the end to lead to their downfall, when Henry VIII dissolved them and sold their property.

A lot of the credit for the survival of so much of Fountains Abbey goes to 18th-century landowner William Aislabie, who bought the ruins—a convenient source of stone—and protected them from dispersal. (Some of the stone had already gone into Fountains Hall nearby.) His father John established the formal gardens of **Studley Royal**, diverting the River Skell into water gardens and building classical temples and follies. The gardens and deer park make a perfect approach to the abbey. They're now all in the care of the National Trust.

Castle Howard *(near Malton)*

If it looks familiar, that's probably because it *is* familiar as the setting for the TV production of *Brideshead Revisited*. In real life the Howard family, not the Marchmains, reside here.

Charles Howard, the 3rd Earl of Carlisle, chose Sir John Vanbrugh to design the place in 1699, which was curious, because Vanbrugh was a playwright, not an architect. But he in turn picked Nicholas Hawksmoor, pupil of Wren, as clerk of works and together they produced this colossal Baroque tour de force.

Everything is on a monumental scale, outside and in, from the aptly named Great Hall, with its painted dome, to the vaulted Antique Passage, a gallery of classical statuary.

Walk in the vast park and gardens to the haunting Mausoleum and Temple of The Four Winds. The stables house a notable **costume museum**.

The North York Moors   *13 D2-3*

North of York and the lush green Vale of Pickering, the land rises suddenly to a surprisingly wild plateau. There's a scattering of villages in the hills and deep valleys that cut through the heather-covered uplands. Bronze and Iron Age stone

*In 1132, thirteen Cistercian monks opted for a crash
programme of austerity. They settled on the banks of the Skell, in "a place
of horror and vast solitude". The aging Dean of York joined them
and contributed his fortune, enabling them to build Fountains Abbey.
Paradoxically, the community became one of the richest in the land.*

The Cistercians refused all superfluous ornament in their architecture, relying on simplicity to glorify God. Rievaulx was the first abbey to be built with pointed arches. The monastery has been abandoned since the 16th century.

moors, makes a possible starting point. It's a magnet in itself for fans of the writer-vet James Herriot, whose stories are set here and in the countryside around. You can follow trails that take in some of the locations in the TV series, *All Creatures Great and Small.*

The road east climbs to the top of **Sutton Bank**, a 700-foot (214-m.) escarpment irresistible to hang-glider aces, who leap off into the prevailing south-west wind. **Helmsley** is one of North Yorkshire's prettiest towns, with a big market square and ruined Norman castle. But connoisseurs of romantic ruins will travel on for a couple of miles to the glorious shell of **Rievaulx Abbey** (say "reevo") in Ryedale. Like Fountains, it was a rich Cistercian monastery dating from the 12th century and dissolved in the 16th. The lofty choir (1225) soars over a whole range of remains of the monastery's domestic buildings. For a heart-stopping view, climb to **Rievaulx Terrace**, above the ruins to the east. The gardens here were laid out in the 18th century, and one of the two classical temples houses an exhibition on period landscape design.

The market town of **Pickering** is a good base for exploring the eastern moors. Before heading off, you can get a drink or a snack in one of the friendly pubs. Take a look in the church to see the rare 15th-century wall paintings that were found beneath layers of whitewash. One scene shows the murder of 9th-century King Edward the Martyr. The **Beck Isle Museum** celebrates Victorian ingenuity with exhibits that run the gamut from a foot-powered lemon squeezer to "Moule's Automatic Earth Closet"—something of a contradiction in terms of sanitary technology.

The North Yorkshire Coast   13 D2

Scarborough enjoys a magnificent setting, on two bays separated by a headland crowned by a **Norman castle**. From its walls, you can look out over the old town and fishing harbour of **South Bay**, 300

circles suggest that people then may have preferred the vulnerability of the open moors to the dangers that lurked in lowland forests. This is good walking country: one of England's long-distance trails follows the western and northern heights for 90 miles (145 km.). The Romans marched this way too, and you can still trace sections of their road across Wheeldale Moor. Some more-recent roads are remarkably steep and a test for lungs and car engines alike.

Thirsk, below the western edge of the

The Great Navigator

Like many English sailors before and since, James Cook came from the Cleveland coast of north-east England. With eight years' experience aboard North Sea traders carrying Tyne coal to London and lumber from the Baltic, he volunteered for the Royal Navy. Rapidly recognized for superb seamanship, he was given his first command at the age of 29 and saw action with Wolfe at Quebec. When peace came, he made his name by accurately surveying the coasts of Newfoundland and Labrador.

In 1768, the Royal Society appointed him to carry some of their members to Tahiti, and then to establish whether there was a Terra Australis, a great southern continent. He sailed from the port of Whitby which he knew so well from his apprentice days, in the Whitby-built *Endeavour*. Not only was the expedition carried safely to Tahiti (where Cook appears to have been unique in resisting the attractions of free-loving Tahitian women), but the whole coast of New Zealand was charted for the first time. Then Cook made a landfall on the south-east coast of Australia and charted the east coast including the hazardous Great Barrier Reef.

Remarkably, through Cook's insistence on a varied diet, not a single member of his crew died of scurvy, which usually claimed a large fraction of the crews of such long voyages.

During a second amazing expedition, he sailed round the world further south than anyone had done before. On his third, in 1776–77, he explored the coasts of Oregon, Alaska and eastern Siberia before making a fatal landing on the island of Hawaii in 1779, when he was killed by the local Polynesians. He was 50, and he left a new map of the world.

feet (90 m.) below. Make your way there, down the steep streets and steps, and you'll find all the fun of the fair, from cockle stalls to bingo halls. Sea-bathing began in Scarborough in the mid-18th century, as early as anywhere in Britain. Quite a masochistic exercise, you may think, if you test the water temperature.

Northward up the coast, **Robin Hood's Bay** is a former fishing (and smuggling) village, now a popular and crowded resort. The houses squeeze into a picturesque cove and up its steep slopes, trying to avoid the fate of many along this shore which have been washed away by the encroaching sea.

Whitby is the gem of the north-east coast. Its pretty red-roofed houses are stacked up the steep sides of the busy harbour, where the River Esk reaches the sea. Walk through the old town and, if you have the energy, do as the parishioners have to, and climb the 199 Church Stairs to **St. Mary's Church** at the top of East Cliff. Up there on the breezy heights, you'll be drawn to the gaunt ruins of 13th-century **Whitby Abbey**,

Invisible from the road above, and sheltered from the North Sea by the twin cliffs Colburn Nab and Penny Nab, the little fishing community of Staithes lives almost in a time warp. James Cook was apprenticed here to a tradesman in a seafront shop, long since swept away in a storm. An atmosphere of secrecy pervades the narrow cobbled streets and alleys, once the haunt of smugglers.

235

founded in 657 by St. Hilda for both monks and nuns.

That great English navigator, Captain James Cook, served an apprenticeship in Whitby, and it was from here that he sailed for Tahiti in the locally built *Endeavour*. The house in Grape Lane where he lived is now the **Captain Cook Memorial Museum**. The municipal museum also displays memorabilia of Cook and other local sailors.

From Whitby, you can drive up the coast through Runswick to the charming fishing village of **Staithes** (pronounced "steers"). Park your car at the top of the cliff and make the precipitous descent on foot; although the road is paved, your car might never make it back up again. At the bottom, on the sea's edge, is the higgledy-piggledy cluster of stone cottages, beloved of local Sunday painters.

Further north still, **Saltburn** is an elegant Victorian resort, with a wide stretch of sand reaching as far as the mouth of the Tees.

Whitby also offers a glorious drive across the gorse- and heather-clad moors via Gromont and Castleton to **Guisborough,** a cheerful market town dominated by the ruins of an Augustinian priory.

⚑ Lake District

The most popular scenic region of England draws 12 million visitors a year. Only 35 miles (56 km.) across and scarcely more from north to south, its astonishingly varied landscapes and countless sights are so concentrated that you could spend a lifetime exploring them, and some people have. Glance at a map and you'll see that the lakes radiate roughly to the points of the compass. They formed at the end of the Ice Age when the rivers running off a dome of ancient rocks were blocked by glacial debris. Even the largest, Lake Windermere, is only 10 miles (16 km.) long, and the mountains are hardly on an alpine scale. Yet somehow the scenery can be just as awe-inspiring.

There are few roads, so weekend and summer traffic can be reduced to a crawl. In any case, the most beautiful parts of the Lake District can only be reached by walking. Fortunately, plenty of short walks suggest themselves: if you intend to make longer hikes you'll need to prepare for severe weather. This is, by the way, one of the wettest parts of England.

Kendal   *12 B3*

A gateway to the Lakes, the market town of Kendal made its name for woollen cloth, then shoes. Not much is left of the castle, birthplace of Catherine Parr, Henry VIII's last wife. The portrait painter George Romney (1734–1802) worked in Kendal before leaving for London, fame and fortune. The **Abbot Hall Art Gallery,** in a Georgian house by the river, displays several of his works, and fine watercolours by other artists who loved the Lakes. The stables of the house have been converted into a Museum of Lakeland Life.

Windermere   *12 B2*

On the long narrow lake of the same name, Windermere town merges with busy Bowness—two fixtures on the holiday circuit. The scenery is gentle rather than dramatic. Consequently, it's not too hard a climb up **Orrest Head** (754 ft./ 230 m.), the classic lookout view. Windermere's **Steamboat Museum** exhibits some fine old craft, but there are plenty still in action to take you for a cruise. At times there are so many boats on the water you'd think you could walk to the other side. In fact, there's a car ferry from Bowness, and if you were brought up on *Peter Rabbit* and the rest of the stories of Beatrix Potter (1866–1943), you might like to take it. From the landing stage on the west side of the lake, it's only a couple of miles to **Hill Top**, the farm cottage near the little lake of Esthwaite Water where the writer lived in the early 1900s.

Lakeland is for ever associated with the poet William Wordsworth. From 1779 until 1787 he went to school at **Hawkshead,** near the head of Esthwaite Water. Apart from the crowds of literary tourists on his trail, the village probably looks much as it did then, though the school is now a museum. You can still see the desk on which the poet carved his initials. There's a fine view to be had from Hawkshead Hill, and good walking in Grizedale Forest.

Coniston   *12 B2*

Set below the 2,635-foot (804-m.) Old Man of Coniston, this is a fine centre for climbing and walking, but take care if you go exploring in the old copper mines near the village. The little lake of **Tarn Hows,** 2 miles (3 km.) to the north-east, is a favourite with excursionists.

The writer and art historian John Ruskin is buried in Coniston churchyard, and if you take the road along the east side of Coniston Water you can visit his house, **Brantwood.** Ruskin lived here from 1871 until he died in 1900, preaching his gospel of beauty and of the value of hand-made things. He was a champion of the Pre-Raphaelites, and some of their work—and his own—is still in the house.

The children's writer Arthur Ransome based some of his stories on and around the lake; his admirers come to try to spot the references.

Ambleside   *12 B2*

Walkers and climbers always crowd the town, a natural centre for the southern Lakes. There's a Roman fort nearby: the east–west road of the Romans went through here on its way to Wrynose and the steep Hardknott Pass. Some would like to believe that the rush-bearing ceremony and floral procession held here in July has come down from Roman times, but a medieval origin is more likely.

Not quite so old, **Bridge House** is a curiosity built entirely over a river—not, as the joke goes, by a Scot to avoid ground rent, but as an 18th-century summerhouse. The building has the distinc-

tion of being the National Trust's oldest information centre and smallest shop.

It's a short walk to the waterfall of **Stock Ghyll Force,** but for the more energetic who want to forge on farther, there are no limits except time, equipment and weather. The truly fit locals go in for fell running, racing up and—even more hazardously—down the steep hill-sides.

Although Wordsworth lived just north of Ambleside at **Rydal Mount** from 1813 until his death in 1850, the crowds of literary pilgrims go on a little further, to **Grasmere.** Just outside the village and near Grasmere Lake lies their objective: white **Dove Cottage,** where the poet set up house with his sister, Dorothy, then with his wife and growing family, from 1799 to 1808. The little cottage shows how simply the penurious Wordsworths lived. In the barn opposite is housed a fascinating museum of the life and times of Wordsworth and his friend Samuel Taylor Coleridge.

Typical Lakeland events feature at Grasmere Sports festival, held in mid-August. Crowds pour in to see fell races, local styles of wrestling and "trailing", in which hounds follow a scent trail laid across open country.

Keswick   *12 B2*

The kingpin of the northern lakes lies below the towering mass of Skiddaw. Keswick retains its charm while pursuing a long-standing devotion to the tourist business. Here, as elsewhere in Lakeland, it started with the poets: first Coleridge, then Southey lived at **Greta Hall,** now part of the school. The quaint **Pencil Museum** recalls the much earlier industry of graphite mining, and **Fitz Park Museum** exhibits range from local geology to literary manuscripts by Keswick's famous residents, to paintings by Ruskin and Turner. Right in the centre, **Moot Hall** (1813), with its odd one-handed clock, now houses a useful information centre.

The walks near Keswick are superb. **Castle Head** just to the south gives a

glorious view of **Derwentwater**, where wooded slopes and rocky crags descend to the shore. The lakeside road leads to steep-sided **Borrowdale**, celebrated as one of the most beautiful valleys of them all. You can take the trail to the famous viewpoint of **Friar's Crag**, or make a side-trip over Ashness Bridge through woods and past grazing sheep to prospects that set the poets into rhapsodies.

The road through Borrowdale climbs steeply to the top of **Honister Pass**, where black-faced sheep pick their way through forbiddingly rocky terrain. From here, 1,176 feet (359 m.) up, it's a vigorous 3-mile (5-km.) walk south to the top of **Great Gable** (2,949 ft./899 m.), affording one of the most magnificent panoramas in England.

West of Honister Pass, the road drops into the green valley of **Buttermere**, passing wilder **Crummock Water** on its way to the beginning of the Wordsworth trail, the poet's birthplace at Cockermouth.

Cockermouth   *12 B2*

The handsome pink Georgian house in Main Street, **Wordsworth House**, was where William was born in 1770. The elegant furnishings, though not family originals, are typical of the time. While you're admiring the Turner painting, the Sheraton table and Hepplewhite chairs in the dining room, you may be drawn by appetizing smells to the copper-gleaming kitchen, where cooks in costume make cakes for the tearoom.

It's pleasant to walk through the town, with its colourfully painted houses, to the castle, largely in ruins. Cockermouth has more claims to fame than the Wordsworths. Fletcher Christian, leader of the mutiny on the *Bounty*, and John Dalton, who formulated the atomic theory, were born on the outskirts of Cockermouth. And the town gave its name to the cocker spaniel.

You can return to Keswick by way of the quite gentle Whinlatter Pass, which transits Thornthwaite Forest. The most direct route follows the west side of **Bas-**senthwaite Lake. The road was built despite the protests of conservationists who said it would destroy the atmosphere. They were right, and this most northerly of the lakes is best seen from the east side, at the foot of Skiddaw.

Ullswater   *12 B2*

The favourite lake of many, Ullswater snakes south between higher and higher fells. Boats crowd the water, and roads along the shore can be congested, too. The roads don't make a complete circuit,

How attitudes change. In the 1720s Daniel Defoe, writing of his travels around Britain, could call the Lake District scenery "the most barren and frightful of any that I have passed through in England". Yet by 1800, writers and artists were in raptures over the same landscape. Eventually almost every literary figure made the pilgrimage, or came and stayed.

239

so you'll get away from traffic if you walk the shore path between **Howtown** and **Glenridding**. If you don't want to undertake that 6-mile (10-km.) hike, take one of the motor launches that cruise the lake, touching at all the main points. From Glenridding or nearby Patterdale, hardy hikers set out to climb **Helvellyn**, at 3,118 feet (951 m.) not the highest, but arguably the most striking, of the Lakeland peaks. It's about 3 miles (5 km.) to the top, a trek that takes some two hours. No actual climbing is involved on this route, but you need to be equipped for fell walking, and to have a good head for heights on the mile-long, sharp Striding Edge which leads to the top. Check the weather forecast before you set out, and take advice from the National Park Information Centre at Glenridding.

At **Penrith**, a few miles north-east of Ullswater, you're practically out of the Lake District, though it can make a useful base. The historic market town is within striking distance of Scotland—as Scots raiders proved whenever they sacked it in the Middle Ages. The view from **Penrith Beacon** west to the lakes is worth the walk up, whether it's your first or last look.

Carlisle   *12 B2*

Capital of Cumbria and railway junction, this busy industrial centre was England's fortress at the western end of the border. Before that it was Rome's—Hadrian's Wall passes nearby. Such a frontier position meant that Carlisle had 17 of the most violent centuries of any English city, right up to 1745 when Bonnie Prince Charlie's army captured the town and held it for a few weeks.

The **castle** has a suitably grim look, especially the massive Norman keep where you'll be shown marks cut in the walls by some of the many prisoners held here. But not by the most famous, Mary Queen of Scots, who had her own quarters in another tower when she was confined here in 1568. Carlisle's **cathedral** dates in part from the 12th century, but much of it was in ruins by the time a Scottish army tore a large part down during the Civil War. So now, though restored, it's England's smallest cathedral, but there's fine wood-carving to be seen, and original painting on the backs of the 15th-century choir stalls.

The North-East

Nothing happened by halves up here in a part of England much nearer Edinburgh than London. There was almost perpetual war or raiding across the Scottish border, from Roman times until the Union of the Crowns. Dukes and prince-bishops reigned like kings with scarcely a glance to the south. When industry came, it came in an extreme form, but most of the land was left as

*N*o *cathedral in Britain is more magnificently sited than Durham, towering over the Wear. The monks seeking a place to lay St. Cuthbert's bones were guided to the spot by a woman looking for her lost cow—the figure of a cow was sculpted on the cathedral's north-east façade as a reminder of the tale. The architecture is a fine example of Norman and Gothic; the rose window in the Chapel of the Nine Altars was remodelled in the 18th century.*

*In 1829, six Quakers set up the coal-exporting
community of Middlesbrough. Two years later iron was discovered in the
Cleveland Hills, and the city boomed. An industrial wasteland by day,
with smouldering heaps of slag, rusting blast furnaces and coke ovens,
the scene takes on an almost mystical quality by night, as clouds billow
from cooling towers and flames leap from tall chimneys.*

242

across Palace Green. It's a sight worth gazing on from every direction.

Monks fleeing from Viking raids on Lindisfarne eventually ended up in Durham in 995, carrying the coffin and remains of St. Cuthbert. The church they built as his shrine was replaced by the present Norman **cathedral,** begun in 1093. It's a masterpiece which creates an impression of enormous strength and antiquity. The bronze Sanctuary Knocker on the North Door is a replica of the one (in the Treasury) to which criminals once clung to claim immunity from pursuers. Inside, there are several architectural "firsts": the ribbed stone vaulting of the choir roof, the first in northern Europe, and the pointed transverse arches of the nave, the first suggestion of Gothic in England. The nave itself is lined with massive columns deeply cut with geometric designs.

St. Cuthbert's shrine lies behind the high altar, but parts of his wooden coffin, carved in the 7th century, are in the **Treasury,** off the fine 14th-century cloisters. The tomb of the equally revered Venerable Bede, 8th-century historian, is in the wonderfully light, 12th-century **Galilee Chapel.** You're reminded that the Washington family came from these parts, too, by a plaque in the cloisters to Prior John Washington (1416–46), "whose family has won an everlasting name in lands to him unknown".

The bishops of Durham were so powerful that they ruled not only the church but the county, as prince-bishops. Granted the right to keep an army, they ran a kind of buffer state against the Scots. The headquarters of these potentates, the Norman **castle,** stands on the peninsula, completing its defences. Now restored, it belongs to Durham University, but the chapel, Norman gallery, Great Hall and huge kitchens are open to the public.

To see how modern architects meet the challenge, stroll onto **Kingsgate** footbridge (1962) from Palace Green. From the bridge itself, you'll see the univer-

wild and remote as ever. The economic wind can blow as cold as the one off the North Sea, but there's a sense of humour second to none—if you can understand the accent.

Durham   *13 C2*

The setting is one of the most thrilling in Britain. The River Wear makes such a great bend that it almost cuts off a steep bluff of sandstone, like a moat. Crowning its wooded banks, the magnificent cathedral and the castle face each other sity's modern Dunelm House. Five minutes from the centre of the city on Elvet Hill, the **Oriental Museum** is also part of the university. It's modern, pleasant and small enough for you to take in most of the outstanding pieces, from the Near and Far East, that are on display.

Beamish

The **Open Air Museum** here has won many awards for its re-creation of the town and country scene at the end of the 19th century. There's a working farm, a drift mine and miners' cottages and the whole street scene with horse-drawn vehicles, a pub, a bakery and shops of the period.

Tees Valley   *12-13 C2*

If you like contrasts, travel up the valley of the Tees, south of Durham. Near the coast, industry at its heaviest dominates: Billingham has a main plant of mighty I.C.I.; Middlesbrough, on the opposite bank, was an important centre of shipbuilding and the steel industry. The history of transport was changed in 1825 when George Stephenson's *Locomotion* pulled the first-ever passenger train from Stockton-on-Tees to **Darlington** at the hair-raising speed of 12 miles per hour (19 kph). That actual locomotive is on show, with many more relics, in Darlington's **Railway Centre and Museum**.

At **Barnard Castle,** the land begins to rise towards the High Pennines. At the west end of town stands a huge 19th-century French château, the **Bowes Museum.** John Bowes and his wife, a French actress, formed a superb collection of art works, ceramics and furniture, but sadly died before they could see their dream museum completed. Don't miss the paintings by El Greco, Goya and Boucher, and the magnificent tapestries.

Further up the Tees valley you'll reach the picturesque little town of **Middleton-in-Teesdale**, a centre for walking. Head especially for some of the most spectacular waterfalls in England, **High Force** and **Caldron Snout.**

Newcastle-upon-Tyne   *13 C2*

The bridges over the Tyne gorge are a fine sight as you approach from the south. Newcastle has come a long way since it was a fort near the end of Hadrian's Wall. The "new" castle in the name is the one the Normans built in 1080. For centuries Newcastle was engaged in warfare with the Scots. A port for coal exports (hence the expression "coals to Newcastle"), the town experienced explosive growth as a shipbuilding and engineering centre. It's been hard-hit by the decline of heavy industry, but the "Geordies" with their sing-song accent are irrepressible.

You can still find vestiges of the medieval town near the quayside, and the Victorians gave Newcastle a fine city centre. Queen Victoria opened the vast central railway station in 1850. The **Laing Art Gallery** has good collections of the decorative arts and of British painting from the 18th-century portraitists to modern times.

Hadrian's Wall   *12 B–C2*

The greatest testimony to the Roman presence in Britain snakes for 73 miles (118 km.) across the width of northern England. Still as much as 14 feet (4 m.) high in places, and faced with dressed square stones, the wall once stood 21 feet (over 6 m.) high, including its battlements. Add to that a ditch on the north side and you have an impressive barrier. The Emperor Hadrian had the wall built to mark and defend the north-west extremity of Rome's empire. He actually came to Britain himself in the year 122 and seems to have decided on a strategy of active defence, not so much using the wall as if it were a castle but sending cavalry out from its forts to cut off any attackers.

There was a "milecastle" every Roman mile (1,620 yards), and 17 larger forts stood 3 to 7 miles (5 to 11 km.) apart. The garrisons ranged from 500 to 1,000 men. Each fort had its bath house and steam rooms, which may have gone some way

to make up for the harsh climate. Strange to think of soldiers from the Mediterranean serving on these bleak moors—it can't have been a popular assignment.

You can walk along the line of the wall today, and roads follow quite near it for most of the way for those without the time or energy. The best-preserved parts are in the middle, near **Winshields Crags,** where the wall climbs to 1,230 feet (375 m.) above sea level. The most impressive of the forts, **Housesteads,** is here, too: you can see the outline of storehouses, hospital, even latrines. The model in the museum gives a still clearer idea. East, at **Chesters,** are the elaborate bath houses used by the cavalry who were stationed here on and off until the wall was finally abandoned in about 383.

The Northumberland Coast   *15 B3*

The north-east has its seaside resorts, though sea bathing is only for the hardy. The coast is visually impressive and marked by formidable fortresses like the dramatic ruin of **Warkworth.** Most were built, or at some time held, by the powerful Percy family, which wrote its own rules in these remote lands for most of the Middle Ages.

Alnwick (say "annick") is a picturesque old town dominated by a huge castle, seat of the Percys, earls and later dukes of Northumberland. It fell into ruin before 1600, so today's fine sight is a restoration. The 19th-century Italian Renaissance-style interior is worth a look for curiosity value and paintings by Titian, Canaletto, Van Dyck and Turner. There's an archaeological museum in the Postern Tower, with Roman objects that will be of interest if you've been visiting Hadrian's Wall.

Up the coast at Seahouses, you can vary the diet of castles with a boat ride out to the **Farne Islands,** a couple of dozen rocky islets that were once the haunt of hermits, and now of seals and seabirds. The Victorian heroine Grace Darling was 23 when she rowed out with her father, then keeper of the Longstone Lighthouse on one of the remoter islands, to rescue the survivors from a shipwreck. The boat is now in a little museum in **Bamburgh,** where another massive Norman castle dominates the shore. You have a fine view of the Farne Islands from its upper terraces.

It was Newcastle industrialist Lord Armstrong who paid for the late 19th-century restoration of Bamburgh Castle. His remarkable house, **Cragside,** lies inland near the little market town of Rothbury. It's a triumph of Pre-Raphaelite decoration allied to Victorian technology. This was the first house in the world to be lit by electricity, and it's got central heating and a lift. The fascinating powerhouses which provided the energy for all this have been restored.

Off the coast north of Bamburgh, low-lying **Lindisfarne,** or Holy Island, was one of the cradles of Christianity in Britain. A 3-mile (5-km.) causeway connects the isle to the mainland, but you'll have to consult the tide tables at either end; you can't cross from two hours before high tide to at least three hours after. St. Aidan came here from Iona in 635 to convert the people of Northumbria. St. Cuthbert, Lindisfarne's bishop, was buried here until Viking raiders forced the monks to flee, carrying his coffin with them (see p. 243). You can see the ruins of the later Norman priory and a church, and visit the castle, built in 1550 and restored by Lutyens in 1902.

The border town of **Berwick-upon-Tweed** looks well worn within its walls. They're 16th century, unusually late, in fact. This place was long a bone of contention between England and Scotland. In fact it was sold, sacked, ransomed or captured by one side or other at least 13 times in the Middle Ages. Finally accepted as English, it was still looked on as separate and used to be listed specially in Acts of Parliament. Berwick claims, bizarrely enough, to be at war with Russia, having been listed in the declaration of the Crimean War but not in the peace treaty!

Bagpipes and Oil Rigs

Scotland's economy is booming along with the North Sea oil industry. In the Britain of the 1990s, the rigs and drilling platforms signify Scotland as much as bagpipes ever did.

Constitutionally entwined with England for nearly three centuries, Scotland in certain respects is still a place unto itself. The Scots print their own banknotes and postage stamps (British money and stamps circulate as well), maintain independent educational and judicial systems and their own church, and quite often speak in ways even the English find hard to decipher.

✦ Edinburgh   15 A3

Proud, cultured and increasingly lively, Scotland's capital surprises and pleases—particularly when the sun shines. National attention focuses on the city for three weeks every summer, when the August–September Edinburgh Festival showcases innovative dance, opera, theatre and music from around the world—fringe events, too—with performances in every possible venue, including in the street.

Most of Edinburgh's principal sights are within easy walking distance of each other.

In the romantic loneliness of Scotland's far north, the ruins of Varrich Castle overlook the Kyle of Tongue.

Edinburgh Castle

The castle dominates the city from its great crag, the stump of an extinct volcano. It was a royal residence from the 11th century, and medieval Edinburgh grew up along the ridge that runs from here to Holyrood. Kilted guards from the Royal Scots Regiment are posted by the gate at the end of the Esplanade, the parade ground where the Military Tattoo is held in festival time. On **Half-Moon Battery** you'll see the cannon which is fired every weekday at 1 p.m. Why not at noon? "Remember where you are", quip the guides. "One shot at one o'clock is much cheaper than 12 at noon."

Tiny **St. Margaret's Chapel**, only 26 feet (8 m.) by 10 feet (3 m.), may well be the oldest building in Edinburgh. Honouring the saintly Queen Margaret who died in 1093, it has survived every assault on the fortress. And it was the only structure spared when Robert Bruce captured the castle from the English in 1313. The terrace in front of the chapel commands one of the best views over the symmetrical crescents and squares of the Georgian New Town.

The residential section of the castle fronts onto Crown Square. On the east side, the **royal apartments** include the claustrophobic little chamber where Mary Queen of Scots gave birth to the future James VI (James I of England) in 1566. The Crown Chamber in the same building houses the **Honours of Scotland**—the ancient crown, sceptre and sword. Among the oldest crown jewels in Europe, they were successfully hidden from Cromwell, who destroyed all the royal regalia he could lay his hands on.

On the south side of Crown Square, the **Great Hall** of 1502, still used for official functions, claims one of Britain's finest hammerbeam roofs, while the military museums to the west highlight the history of Scotland's regiments. Another relic of the military past can be seen in the old prisons below the Crown Square building: **Mons Meg**, a massive cannon given to James II of Scotland in the 15th century. He was killed by an exploding cannon, and this one burst too, when firing a royal salute in 1680.

The Royal Mile

A bit more than a mile—Scottish miles were longer—it's a gentle downhill stroll along the Old Town's famous main street from the castle to Holyroodhouse. Start near the top with a visit to the **Camera Obscura**, in the Outlook Tower. This fascinating piece of Victorian technology projects a 360-degree view of the living, moving city onto a white table—provided the weather is bright enough.

The street and the wynds (alleys) and courtyards leading off the Mile must have been smelly and hazardous in the days when the citizens threw the contents of their chamber pots out of the windows. Some of the 17th-century tenements were a surprising six storeys high. One such, **Gladstone's Land**, has been beautifully

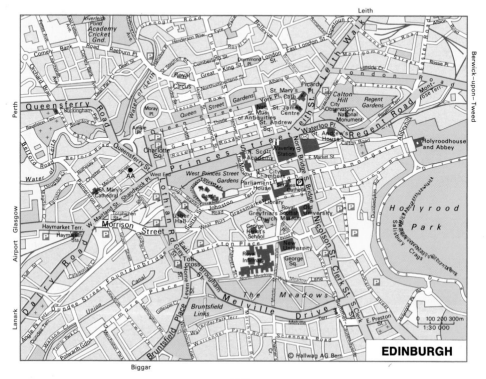

EDINBURGH

restored as a shop, with living quarters (open to view) on the first floor. The painted ceilings are original and the furniture is typical of the period.

Take a detour down across George IV Bridge to see the statue of **Greyfriars Bobby.** This Skye terrier waited faithfully by his master's graveside in Greyfriars Churchyard for 14 years, until he died of old age himself in 1872. In adjoining Chambers Street, the **Royal Scottish Museum** features world arts and crafts, science and the history of transport.

Back on the Royal Mile, **St. Giles Cathedral** doesn't look its age (15th century). Refaced in the 19th century, the High Kirk of Scotland retains its famous spire, the **Crown of St. Giles,** a replica in stone of the Scottish crown. The present church is probably the third on the site. Elements survive from the previous, Norman, structure—notably the piers supporting the central tower. But most of the side chapels were destroyed in the Reformation, along with the relic and statue of St. Giles. The Reformer John Knox was minister of St. Giles. Look for his statue inside the church. The 1911 **Thistle Chapel** contains a stall for the sovereign and one for each of the 16 Knights of the Thistle, Scotland's oldest order of chivalry.

Further down the Royal Mile, here called High Street, the **Museum of Childhood** displays all kinds of toys and games. The 15th-century **John Knox House,** now a museum of Knox's life and times, may not itself have had much to do with the great reformer.

The **Palace of Holyroodhouse** began life as a guest residence for the adjacent abbey. Around 1500, James IV began the alterations that transformed the residence into a royal palace. The Reformation and Civil War took their toll, and Charles II gave the order to rebuild. His architect, Sir William Bruce, incorporated part of James IV's building into a new Palladian design. The so-called **Historic Apartments** include the rooms occupied by Mary Queen of Scots. A plaque marks the spot where her secretary, Rizzio, was stabbed to death at the instigation of her husband, Lord Darnley.

New Town

As old Edinburgh became increasingly crowded and unhealthy, pressure for expansion mounted. Architect James Craig was still in his twenties when he won a competition to design a new residential area in 1767. He proposed a rectangular grid of streets, with spacious terraces linking two squares (Charlotte and St. Andrew). It was Craig's idea to build on only one side of Princes and Queen streets, the outer streets of the grid.

A fetid stretch of water called Nor' Loch was drained and turned into **Princes Street Gardens,** the city's attractive centrepiece for more than two centuries now. The pinnacled **Scott Monument** was added to the cityscape in the 1840s. You can climb to the top—287 narrow steps wind their way up—for a wide-angle view of the gardens (see the huge floral clock).

A sloping road called the Mound crosses the gardens. The **National Gallery of Scotland,** to one side, boasts a distinguished collection of Old Masters. A pleasure to visit, the museum is manageable in size, with works laid out in chronological order. Look for Velázquez's striking *Old Woman Cooking Eggs,* Rubens' gory *The Feast of Herod,* the Rembrandt portraits and Van Dyck's early *Lomellini Family,* with its superb detail of costume. Gainsborough's ravishing *The Honourable Mrs. Graham,* Reynolds' *Ladies Waldegrave* and several works by Edinburgh's own Sir Henry Raeburn take pride of place among the British portraits.

At first the New Town began to grow piecemeal, but Robert Adam set an example of unified development in his designs for noble **Charlotte Square.** The Georgian house at **No. 7** has been restored and furnished in the style of the period. See the marvellous old medicine chest and antique sanitary arrangements in the bedchamber, and the kitchens, wine cellar and National Trust for Scotland shop downstairs.

Along Inverleith Row, the 75-acre (30-ha.) **Royal Botanic Gardens** have one of the world's best rhododendron collections, huge plant houses and a great, meticulously tended rock garden.

At the famous **Zoo** in the western suburb of Corstorphine, the park setting and lack of bars allow visitors and animals to get a good look at each other.

Firth of Forth   *15 A3*

Hopetoun House, an outstanding country manor on the south shore of the Forth, preserves its original furnishings and paintings. The core of the building, completed in 1703 to Sir William Bruce's design, was expanded and altered by William Adam, beginning around 1720. After William's death in 1748, the work went forward under the talented supervision of his sons Robert and James, who had already begun to decorate the interior. The **Yellow** and **Red Drawing Rooms,** with gilded plasterwork and specially commissioned furniture, are fine early examples of the Adam style.

It's not far from here to the huge spans of the Forth Bridges, road and rail, that lead to the north. Cross over, if you've time, to the lovely little town of **Culross,** with its steep cobbled streets and 16th-century houses.

Border Country   *15 A3*

South in the Borders region, the River Tweed and the streams that feed it cut picturesque valleys through the green hills. Sheep wander nonchalantly across the minor roads, and their wool still goes into the local knitwear and—naturally—tweed.

Peebles is a wool town, but its coat of arms shows three salmon: this is prime fishing country. **Traquair House** near Innerleithen claims to have sheltered 27 Scottish and English monarchs in its 1,000-year history. It's full of intriguing things from secret stairs and a private

brewery to family needlework, 400 years old but in brilliant original colours.

Abbotsford, on the Tweed near Galashiels, was the home of Sir Walter Scott for the last 20 years of his life. The novelist personally designed the study where he worked, as well as many other features of this Scottish Baronial-style house—as romantic as any of the novels. Scott was buried at **Dryburgh Abbey** nearby, his favourite of the four great 12th-century Border abbeys, the others being **Jedburgh** (roofless but complete), **Melrose**

*E*dinburgh bows to no city in vivacity and elegance. Scotland's ancient capital, occupying seven hills, keeps up to date with the latest trends in the arts, especially at its annual festival.

(famous for the decorative sculpture around the outside) and **Kelso,** once the largest, now largely in ruins. Jedburgh and Kelso were destroyed in English raids during the 1500s; Melrose gradually decayed.

Two generations of Adams worked on **Mellerstain,** near Kelso. Father William designed the simple, square wings in 1725, while his son, Robert, planned the palatial main block 45 years later. A sophisticated simplicity characterizes Robert's contribution, the greater in every way, though his father's has a certain provincial charm. The Neoclassical interiors show Robert Adam at his most accomplished. Especially fine is the beautifully detailed **library,** in which the same theme recurs again and again, in the bookcases, fireplaces, door cases and friezes, like the leitmotif in a classical symphony.

⚑ Glasgow *17 D3*

There's no denying the eternal rivalry between Scotland's two great cities and near neighbours. With almost a million people, Victorian Glasgow is twice the size of Georgian Edinburgh. It has much more industry, too, despite the decline of the once-mighty shipyards. For a long time people perceived Edinburgh as Scotland's cultural centre. Now Glasgow has struck back, by providing a home for the Scottish Opera and Ballet, and for the world-class Burrell Collection. Recognized by the European Community as a City of Culture, "Glasgow's Miles Better", the ad men proclaim.

Urban motorways and expressways slash through the city, and the major sights are scattered. But you can get around easily enough by bus or the small underground railway (subway), nicknamed the "Clockwork Orange" for its colour.

The heart of Glasgow today is pleasant **George Square,** surrounded by the grand stone buildings of Glasgow's 19th-cen-

tury prime. The Tourist Information Centre lies nearby in St. Vincent Place. For orientation, you might take a city bus tour from here. Cathedral Street leads to the Gothic **cathedral,** a rare medieval survival among so much Victoriana. The crypt holds the tomb of 6th-century St. Mungo, the city's patron. See also the Early English choir, with its crisply carved capitals and corbels.

Head west along pedestrian-only Sauchiehall Street and you come to the **Glasgow School of Art,** a milestone in the

*N*ear the River Clyde in central Glasgow, Victorian brick buildings cheerfully coexist with the imaginative superstructure of a vast modern shopping centre. On-the-move Glasgow and stately Edinburgh form two very different but complimentary aspects of urban Scotland.

history of modern architecture by Glasgow-born Charles Rennie Mackintosh (1862–1928). Tours of the interior are on offer mornings and afternoons.

West again, beyond the centre, the eclectic collections of the **Art Gallery and Museum** in Kelvingrove Park grew with the bequests of Glasgow's 19th-century magnates. Exhibits include items of scientific and historic, as well as artistic interest. But the Old Masters steal the show: Rembrandt's powerful *Man in Armour,* the Ruisdael landscapes, Van Gogh's 1887 portrait of Glasgow art dealer Alexander Reid, some penetrating Raeburn portraits... Don't overlook the work of Scotland's own artists, the late 19th-century Glasgow Boys and early 20th-century Colourists.

As if this were not enough, a stone's throw away stands the university's **Hunterian Art Gallery** with more fine Old Masters, English portraits by Romney and Reynolds, and the highly original works of Scotland's own William McTaggart (1835–1910). Above all, the Hunterian boasts a definitive James McNeill Whistler collection. An entire wing is devoted to Charles Rennie Mackintosh. Glasgow-style furniture and objects are displayed in rooms reconstructed from the pioneer designer's Glasgow home.

The event that crowned the cultural renaissance of this city was the opening in 1983 of the **Burrell Collection,** in a purpose-built gallery in Pollok Park, south of the River Clyde. Scottish shipping magnate Sir William Burrell spent the half-century up to his death in 1958 amassing thousands of works of fine and decorative art with the intention of presenting them to the City. After years in packing cases, they're now on display, to universal acclaim. Burrell collected widely but concentrated on certain fields: Chinese bronzes, jade and ceramics (notably the Ming Dynasty figure of a *Lohan*), European tapestries (like the Flemish *Peasants Hunting Rabbits with Ferrets),* stained glass (including the superb 12th-century *Prophet Jeremiah*

window from St.-Denis), and French 19th-century painting (*The Rehearsal* by Degas, *The Ham* by Manet). The works are so compelling and the displays so attractive that you'll find yourself developing an interest in things you've never considered before. What better accolade for a museum?

Loch Lomond   *17 D3*
Britain's largest freshwater lake runs about 23 miles (37 km.) north to south. It's so near to Glasgow that traffic can be heavy at weekends. To get off the roads, take one of the steamers that cruise the loch, starting from Balloch. They'll take you to the north end, past majestic Ben Lomond, 3,192 feet (974 m.).

Ayrshire Coast   *17 C3*
Famous golf links (Troon, Turnberry) and breezy resorts line the coast southwest of Glasgow, a traditional playground for the crowded metropolis.

This is Burns Country, too, where the beloved national poet Robert Burns was born, lived most of his very full 37 years and died in 1796. In **Alloway**, near Ayr, you can visit Burns's birthplace, a whitewashed cottage with thatched roof. You'll see the little box bed where Burns and three of his brothers slept as small children. The original of *Auld Lang Syne* and many other Burns documents are on display in the adjacent museum.

After you finish at the birthplace, wander down to the River Doon and the 13th-century **Auld Brig o' Doon**, the bridge mentioned by Burns in his narrative poem *Tam o' Shanter.* Nearby in the **Land o' Burns Centre** you can decide how much more of the Burns Heritage Trail to follow.

Further up the coast, **Culzean Castle** (pronounced "culeen"), a National Trust of Scotland property, towers above the sea. The present structure dates mostly from the 18th century, when it was rebuilt by Robert Adam, whose elegant classical designs grace the interior. Dwight D. Eisenhower had the use of an upstairs apartment for his lifetime, a mark of Scotland's gratitude for his contribution to the Allied victory in World War II. An Eisenhower exhibition details the general's wartime career as Allied Supreme Commander in Europe.

Unjustly neglected by most visitors, the south-western corner of Scotland has beautiful shorelines, moors and forests and a mild climate. That helps to make the **Logan Botanic Garden,** on the peninsula called the Rhinns of Galloway, one of the best collections in the country, with palms, tree ferns and rare magnolias.

On a hill half-way down the peninsula, a chapel houses the ancient Christian **Kirkmadrine Stones:** three tombstones with Latin inscriptions dating back to the 5th century. A string of peaceful old fishing villages leads to the tip of the next peninsula to the west. Here, at **Whithorn,** is the true cradle of Scottish Christianity. The ruins of a 13th-century priory adjoin the probable site of St. Ninian's 4th-century chapel.

Robert Burns lived his last five years in **Dumfries,** the most important town in the south-west, and it was here that he wrote some of his best-known verses. Burns tourism focuses on the bard's house, in Burns Street, a shrine and museum of manuscripts and mementoes. The Burns Mausoleum in nearby St. Michael's churchyard contains his tomb. There's also a Burns Centre in Mill Road.

It's worth the brief detour north just for a look at the dashing, turreted roofline of **Drumlanrig Castle** (open to the public in summer). This 17th-century residence still has the feel of a family home—which it is—that of the dukes of Buccleuch. But it's a palatial one, furnished with outstanding French and Flemish pieces as old as the house. Among the paintings, look for Holbein's wonderfully detailed portraits and Rembrandt's *Old Woman Reading.* Pictures of the Buccleuch family's ancestors include the unlucky, or misguided, Duke of Monmouth.

Arran
16–17 C3

Offshore in the Firth of Clyde, the Isle of Arran offers a little bit of the loveliest things in Scotland: mountains, glens and lochs, a rugged coastline... This is preeminently hill walkers' country. An amazing ten summits rise to over 2,000 feet (600 m.), headed by 2,866-foot (874-m.) Goat Fell. Car ferries link Ardrossan on the Ayrshire coast to Brodick; in summer services connect Claonaig on the Kintyre peninsula with the north of Arran.

Brodick, the "capital", is just a little village, and all Arran's inhabitants together number only about 3,500. Almost as many red deer roam wild on this unspoiled isle. Apart from the natural attractions, the chief sight to see is **Brodick Castle,** a 19th-century baronial residence housing priceless silver, porcelain and paintings by Watteau and Turner. Thousands of rhododendrons bloom in a magnificent garden that covers 65 woodland acres (26 ha.) between the castle and Brodick Bay.

The main sightseeing route takes you right around the coast—a distance of 50 miles (80 km.). You may spot seals basking on the rocks offshore, as well as herons, gannets and the like.

Central Scotland

This scenic area of lakes, hills and fertile fields lies on Glasgow's northern doorstep. It's also within minutes of Edinburgh, via the M90 and M9 motorways.

Bannockburn
17 D3

The epic victory here in 1314 confirmed Scotland's independence. Hero of the hour, Robert Bruce routed an English army three times the size of his own. Shown in chain mail and on horseback, his statue stands on the field today.

The National Trust for Scotland's centre on the site features a clear explanation of the complex Wars of Independence. "We fight not for glory nor for wealth nor for honour, but only and alone we fight for freedom, which no good man surrenders but with his life," declared Bruce.

Legend recounts that while in hiding on the Irish island of Rathlin, he watched a spider try six times to affix its web; on the seventh attempt, it succeeded. Impressed by the spider's perseverance, Robert Bruce was encouraged to resume his fight for Scottish independence.

Stirling   *17 D3*

The town commands the main route between the Lowlands and the Highlands. Consequently, Stirling for centuries saw some of Scotland's most savage warfare. The strategic **castle** on a 250-foot (76-m.) crag was a prize worth fighting for. Guides tell of sieges, betrayals and dastardly murders within the massive walls. Call in at the Visitor Centre for an audiovisual outline of local history before, climbing to the clustered buildings of the fortress itself.

There are no architectural remains from early times. James V built the **palace** in the early 16th century, and he made it the most sumptuous in Scotland. An early example of the Renaissance style, it's decorated with rather strange classical carvings outside and in. (Local workmen probably copied the motifs from pattern books.) Look out for the "Stirling Venus", cherubs and demons on the Upper Square façade and, inside the palace, in the Queen's Outer and Own Halls, the "Stirling Medallions", a series of portrait medallions that depict historical and mythological personages.

The **Great Hall** was once Scotland's grandest Gothic chamber, fit for sessions of parliament, but later it suffered two centuries as a military barracks. Now this section of the castle is being restored.

The Trossachs   *17 D2*

Romanticized by Sir Walter Scott in *The Lady of the Lake* and *Rob Roy*, the Trossachs is a region of lovely glens, lochs and lochans. The word "trossachs" probably means "bristly places", after all its

wooded crags. It's easy to get off the beaten track here, since beaten tracks are few. Try the road past Loch Arklet to Inversnaid on Loch Lomond (such a memorable dead end that you won't mind retracing your route). It's reached via the wild ravine country between Loch Katrine and Loch Achray, in the heart of the Trossachs. Salmon may be leaping up the falls of Leny near Callander. (See also p. 60.)

Argyll   *16–17 C2*

There's a storybook quality to **Inveraray Castle,** near Loch Fyne, home to the dukes of Argyll, chiefs of Clan Campbell and "uncrowned kings of the Highlands". The present edifice, with its decorative towers and keep, dates from the 18th century, when the Campbells felt secure enough to dispense with fortifications. They held on to the old armoury, though, just for show—enough axes, broadswords, halberds and ancient firearms to equip a small army.

To the west, near Kilmartin, among many Stone Age and Bronze Age remains, stands **Nether Largie North Cairn,** a ritual stone chamber used nearly 3,000 years ago. Clambering down, you'll make out dozens of cup marks and carved axeheads.

West again, on the coast, lies **Oban,** a busy ferry port with connections to several islands.

Glen Coe   *17 C2*

The spectacular scenery of Glen Coe, complete with red deer, even golden eagles, attracts thousands of hikers and climbers. In the steep valley, a memorial commemorates the 1692 massacre of over 40 Macdonalds by Campbell soldiery.

More often than not, clouds obscure the rounded and not very dramatic summit of **Ben Nevis,** at 4,406 feet (1,344 m.) the highest mountain in the British Isles. It's best seen from the north, but the easiest climb is from the bustling touring centre of Fort William. Caution is advised: bad weather can close in quickly.

Glen Garry
17 C-D2

East–west roads are few when you get this far north, and from Fort William to Blair Atholl there's really only one route. How fortunate then, that it follows beautiful Glen Garry down to Robert Burns' favourite **Falls of Bruar.**

Not far beyond, **Blair Castle** is the seat of the Duke of Atholl, who commands the last "private army" of Highlanders— most of them in reality his peaceable estate workers. Brussels tapestries, Sèvres porcelain and some fine period furniture decorate the castle, built in the 13th century, renovated in the 18th and "baronialized" in the 19th. Don't miss the portrait of Lord George Murray, the member of the family who, as Bonnie Prince Charlie's lieutenant general, found himself having to besiege this, his own home, in 1746.

Pitlochry
17 D2

The main road now bypasses the picturesque **Pass of Killiecrankie,** so make a diversion to learn about the battle that took place near here in 1689, when Jacobite Highlanders fought a successful holding action. The crowded riverside resort of Pitlochry also lies off the main road. The Pitlochry Festival Theatre runs a long summer season of plays and music. On stage, too, in a manner of speaking, are the thousands of salmon that leap up special ladders by the local power station (the fish observation room gives you a ringside view) to reach their spawning grounds upriver.

Dunkeld
17 D2

Notice the splendidly restored little houses from the 17th century, on the way to the grand old cathedral. It stands, part ruined, part restored, by the River Tay. From the grounds, you can see Thomas Telford's fine 1809 stone arched bridge.

Scone Palace

The Scots call the palace "Skoon". This ancestral home of the earls of Mansfield stands at or near the site of the abbey where once was kept the Stone of Destiny or Stone of Scone, on which the Scottish kings were crowned—until Edward I of England appropriated it in 1296. (Some people say the stone now in the Coronation Chair in Westminster Abbey is only a replica, and that the real one remains hidden somewhere in Scotland.)

The baronial residence you see today contains fine, mostly French, furniture acquired by the 2nd Earl, who served as Britain's ambassador to the court of Louis XVI. In the **Long Gallery**, notice the rare Vernis Martin objects, which look like china but are actually varnished papier-mâché, made in Paris in the 18th century by the Martin brothers.

Vast grounds surround the palace. With stately cedars, California sequoias, Japanese silver firs and other conifers, the Pinetum alone covers 50 acres (20 ha.).

St. Andrews
15 A2

Out on the Fife coast, St. Andrews is known worldwide as the home of golf. The game, or something like it, has been played here for over 500 years; in 1457 an Act of Scottish Parliament utterly condemned it as a threat to church attendance. Today, anyone can tee off on the Old Course at the **Royal and Ancient Golf Club,** where so many epic championships have been held.

Charming seaside St. Andrews also claims Scotland's oldest university (1411), as well as the great ruin of the country's largest-ever cathedral. The old castle features a blood-chilling, escape-proof "bottle dungeon" cut 24 feet (7 m.) down into the rock.

East Neuk
15 A3

Picturesque fishing villages with little harbours and red-tiled cottages are strung like beads along Fife's south-east coast. The locals call the area the East "Neuk", or corner. On two levels, **Crail** comprises the quaint port still used by lobster boats and the upper town, with its marketplace and 16th-century tolbooth (courthouse-

jail). The weathervane on the belfry takes the form of a gilded copper haddock.

Learn about the history of the fishing industry at the Scottish Fisheries Museum in **Anstruther** (pronounced "anster"). You'll see how the fisherfolk lived and worked—displays illustrate traditional and modern fishing methods—and there are some magnificent model ships. These days most fishing boats sail from **Pittenweem** and bring in enticing catches to the quayside market.

In good weather, take a boat excursion to the **Isle of May**, a seabird sanctuary with 250-foot (76-m.) cliffs.

North-East Scotland

If it's north of Perth and east of the A9 motorway, it's in the North-East. The region claims Aberdeen, the Grampian castles (including Balmoral) and Aviemore, Scotland's premier ski resort. Here, too, is the Whisky Trail, featuring tours and tastings.

Aberdeen   *19 D3*

The title "Granite City" is explained when you see the grey stone buildings and houses of Aberdeen. Yet the effect is anything but sombre when the crystalline granite sparkles in the sunshine. Aberdeen may lie farther north than Moscow, but a million roses and countless other flowers planted along the roads and in the parks discount the latitude. Aberdeen has won the Britain in Bloom award so many times that it's no longer eligible to enter the competition.

The Fife fishing village of Crail is popular for its stony charm and, more tangibly, the fresh crab and lobster caught by the local fishermen.

Scotland's third city (pop. 210,000) is still a great fishing port, though the emphasis has changed from the North Sea and herring to more distant waters, white fish and modern methods. The **fish market** down at Commercial Quay is the best show in town. To see it in full swing, try to get there any weekday soon after the 7 a.m. opening. Battered trawlers land fish by the ton for inspection by canny buyers. Halibut, skate, dogfish, cod, haddock and the rest—it's not long before the day's catch has been auctioned off to nationwide retailers and to local processors for freezing, smoking or canning.

But fishing is only one of Aberdeen's vocations, and not the most important, either. The "Offshore Capital of Europe" has struck it rich servicing all the oil rigs that extend out across the North Sea, half-way to Norway. The influx of oil people has brought a surprising cosmopolitanism to Aberdeen: the Texans you hear on Union Street are probably local residents.

In medieval Shiprow, not far from the harbour, the **Maritime Museum** occupies two 16th-century town houses. A series of exhibits honour the Aberdeen builders of some of the fastest tea clippers afloat, before steam, while the fascinating survey of offshire oil technology brings you right up to date.

Where Union Street widens into Castlegate, see the 1686 **mercat cross** (as market crosses are called in Scotland), topped by the Scottish unicorn and decorated with portrait medallions of ten Stuart monarchs, from James I to James VII (James II of England). The impressively austere walls of 17th-century **Provost Skene's House** (in Guestrow, off Broad Street) hide rather elegant rooms, which probably appealed to the Duke of Cumberland when he stayed here (before Culloden, where he defeated Bonnie Prince Charlie).

In Broad Street itself, the 1905 **Marischal College** is claimed by some to be the finest granite building in the world:

259

it's certainly one of the biggest and most elaborate. For a long time a separate foundation, it's now part of Aberdeen University. Another and even older part, King's College, stands a few hundred yards away in **Old Aberdeen**, a separate burgh until 1891. Have a look at the Gothic **King's College Chapel:** the superb carved wood rood screen and stalls are medieval originals. But the famous Crown Tower had to be rebuilt after a storm in 1633.

High Street leads to Aberdeen's **Cathedral of St. Machar.** The fortified, undecorated exterior, especially the stern west front, reflects a time when religion and war were two sides of a coin. Inside, the brightly painted heraldic ceiling of around 1520 contains a lesson in ecclesiastical power politics. The arms of the pope, prince of the Church, take precedence over those of mere kings, while the arms of the King of Scots are placed higher than those of the King of England.

Before you leave town, it's worth stopping by the **Aberdeen Art Gallery,** housing a notable collection of contemporary British paintings.

Grampian Highlands *19 C2*

This is the name given to the area north and west of Aberdeen. If you like castles, ruined or perfectly preserved, you'll have about 70 to choose from here.

Crathes Castle, on the River Dee, has dramatic gardens with giant yew hedges centuries old. Within the 16th-century tower house you'll spend half the time looking up at the painted ceilings, which include vigorous representations of the Nine Nobles (Alexander the Great to Charlemagne), and Seven Virtues. Robert Bruce gave the ivory **Horn of Leys** in the Hall to an ancestor of the Burnett family in 1322 to symbolize his tenure of the property. (Burnetts lived at Crathes until 1951, when they donated the castle to the National Trust for Scotland.)

The A980 leads on to **Craigievar Castle,** a fairy-tale extravaganza finished in 1625 and little changed since. The clustered six- and seven-storey castellated towers and conical-roofed turrets are the last word in the Scottish baronial style. Inside, ornate plaster ceilings and pine panelling grace the Great Hall and many of the other rooms. Among the unusual objects you'll see: the "scold's bridle", a metal collar used to silence nagging wives, and three rare long "Craigievar tables" for gaming.

Alternatively, you can follow the long, picturesque valley of the River Dee west from Crathes. Queen Victoria loved the Deeside area and often came to stay at **Balmoral Castle**, which her consort Prince Albert bought and rather ponderously refashioned in a Germanic version of Scottish baronial style. In summer, you can visit the grounds provided royalty are not in residence. When they are, crowds gather at little **Crathie Church,** where the queen and her family attend Sunday service.

North near Udny, **Pitmedden Garden** is a re-creation of a 17th-century formal sunken garden in elaborate geometric designs. Some 37,000 annuals are planted out each summer, so the optimum time to view is in July and August; but the subtle colours at other seasons have their own appeal.

In contrast to this disciplined version of nature, the often stormy coastal waters crash against plunging cliffs south of Peterhead. Don't go too near the edge at the **Bullers of Buchan**, caverns and clefts where the waves seem to boil and the screams of gulls cut through the roar of the sea. Visiting Scotland with Dr. Johnson in the 18th century, Boswell called this sight a "monstrous cauldron".

Speyside *19 C2*

Along the lovely valley of the River Spey fishermen cast their lines into the rushing waters to entice the elusive salmon. The slate-roofed houses with pagoda-like chimneys, almost hidden in the trees, are the old distilleries, generating some of the finest of Scotch whiskies. Enthusiasts will soon notice familiar names on the signposts: Glenlivet, Glenfiddich, Balvenie, Knockando and the rest. Some of the larger companies open their doors to tourists. Around Keith and Dufftown they've actually organized a **Whisky Trail**, a 70-mile (112-km.) circuit that takes in seven distilleries (see p. 65 in our Leisure Routes section for the complete itinerary). You'll be shown the time-honoured methods of malting and mashing and can observe the subtle processes of fermentation and distillation, which go on as they have for at least 500 years. Then you'll very likely be invited to taste a wee dram.

Cairngorms   *18 B2*
Up the Spey at **Aviemore**, one of Scotland's ski centres has turned into a year-round resort with sports and entertainment, day and night. On a clear day, take the chairlift ride into the high Cairngorms. The view from the terminal, 3,600 feet (1,100 m.) up, is superb, but the footpath to the summit of Cairn

---

Kilts and Tartans

For the Scotsman, Highland dress is not just an item of folklore to be brought out of mothballs on ceremonial occasions. It's everyday wear for some and the standard uniform of certain Scottish regiments. You'll see at least one pipe and drum band arrayed in kilted splendour.

Daytime Highland dress consists of knee-length kilt, matching vest and tweed jacket, long knitted hose (with a knife stuck in the right stocking) and garters. The kilt is held up by a belt, and a sporran (purse) hangs from the waist. Sometimes a plaid, a sort of tartan rug, is flung over the shoulder.

Authentic tartans are registered designs. Each clan—originally a loose organization based on a family—had its own pattern. As the years went by and the clans subdivided, many variations (setts) of the tartans were produced. Today, it's estimated that there are more than a thousand setts.

While a certain amount of commercial gimmickry surrounds the tartan business, you may in fact have a genuine clan association—even if your family name seems far removed from Campbell, Macdonald or Stewart.

Gorm, 4,084 feet (1,246 m.), puts you on top of the world. At **Carrbridge**, the Landmark Visitor Centre features a multi-screen film about the life and landscape of the Highlands.

At the excellent **Highland Wildlife Park** further upriver near Kincraig you can drive through, just like an African game park—except for the animals you'll spot. Herds of red deer, European bison, wild horses, ibex, shaggy Highland cattle and mouflons (wild ancestors of domestic sheep) roam free. In the walk-through areas you'll see wildcats, badgers, arctic foxes and wolves and many of the native birds.

The Highlands

Scotland's mountains might not stand up in size to the Andes or the Alps, but they contrive to be just as awe-inspiring. Snow-capped peaks and hills purple with heather reflect in deep, silent lochs. The moors and forests are home to birds and mammals found nowhere else in Britain: the wildcat, pine marten, golden eagle and turkey-like capercaillie. Ruined crofts and castles are reminders that the population was once larger than today's small numbers. Roads are few, though this means that summer traffic is concentrated on them: you really need to walk or climb to experience the solitude of Britain's northern wilderness.

Inverness   *18 B2*
The town has been known as capital of the Highlands since ancient times. For a useful introduction to Highland history, visit the **Museum and Art Gallery** in Castle Wynd. Road and rail links from the south funnel through here, so it's hard to avoid in any case.

So, too, are all the souvenirs of the local submarine celebrity presumed to inhabit the deeps of **Loch Ness** to the south-west. The Loch Ness Monster (dubbed "Nessie" on the T-shirts) has a long history of sightings, as well as

261

some persuasive photographs that experts have accepted as genuine. Murkiness caused by peat particles washed in by the rivers that feed the loch has defeated underwater cameras. Submarine-tracking sonar equipment has picked up some echoes that could be anything. If there *are* descendants of the dinosaurs or giant eels down there, they've got lots of room to hide: the water is 1,000 feet (300 m.) deep in some parts. Excursion boats make regular monster-spotting cruises down the loch.

Loch Ness is only the beginning of the **Great Glen**, a fissure that cuts right across Scotland. The lochs that stretch along it were linked up in the early 19th century (by one of Britain's greatest engineers, Thomas Telford) to form the Caledonian Canal. You can go through on an excursion boat, or take the time to hire one yourself and make the trip, working your way through the 29 locks on the canal. (No need to go all the way back; you can start from either end and drop the boat off at the other.)

Culloden Moor

Bleak Culloden Moor saw the defeat of Bonnie Prince Charlie's Highlanders in 1746. The victorious Duke of Cumberland's army lost only 76 men, compared to the Highlanders' 1,200 dead. His treatment of the injured, the prisoners and captured fugitives earned him the title of "Butcher" Cumberland. A stirring film at the battlefield Visitor Centre recounts the story of the '45.

Cawdor Castle *18 B2*

You might feel the presence of ghosts at Cawdor Castle if you took all the legends seriously. But here, you're not really expected to. If you recall your Shakespeare, Macbeth was promised by the witches that he would be Thane of Cawdor and a king. Some say that it was at this castle that he had King Duncan murdered, but the historical Macbeth lived much earlier than the 14th-century date of the castle, and the whole story

owes more to Shakespeare's imagination than Scottish history.

Today, the grounds have fine gardens and a nature trail. Inside the castle, the walls are hung with wonderful 17th-century tapestries. Beautiful, but they had a practical advantage, too, in keeping rooms a bit less cold and draughty. The **Thorn Tree Room** encloses a 600-year-old hawthorn, the legendary reason for choosing this spot for the building.

West of Inverness *18 A2*

A narrow road, or one of the most dramatic railway lines in Britain, can take you through the mountains to the west coast. The train journey ends at Kyle of Lochalsh, where you can cross to the Isle of Skye (see p. 265). Minor roads lead north around the dramatic shores of remote sea lochs: **Loch Carron, Loch Torridon** and **Loch Gairloch**. The diversion inland to mountain-girt **Loch Maree** will bring you to some breathtaking views. But most of this wild land is accessible only to well-equipped walkers (carrying tents if they want to penetrate far).

At Loch Ewe, the Gulf Stream works its magic in the luxuriant **Inverewe Gardens**, a riot of colour in spring and early summer when azaleas, magnolias and rhododendrons bloom. The founder, Osgood Mackenzie, clearly relished a challenge. Frost-free it may be, but salt-laden gales blasted the rocky site when he started the gardens in 1862, and this is the same latitude as Juneau, Alaska.

Ullapool *18 A2*

Near the seaward end of Loch Broom, Ullapool is a picturesque fishing port and the terminal of the car ferry to Stornoway

*U*rquhart Castle is the vantage point for seeking a glimpse of Nessiteras Rhombopterix, alias the elusive Loch Ness Monster.

in the Outer Hebrides. Boats will take you deep-sea fishing, too, or out to the lovely **Summer Isles,** once the home of fisherfolk, now abandoned to countless birds. At the head of Loch Broom, the **Falls of Measach** plunge 200 feet (60 m.) into the awesome chasm called Corrieshalloch Gorge.

The Far North *18 A–B1*
Scotland's most memorable scenery is probably the north-west coast above Ullapool. Whenever you can, take the secondary road closest to the shore, winding past lochs and tiny lochans. The rare little fishing villages of no more than a handful of houses have been given a new lease of life by the fish-farming industry. You can reach the north-western tip of the mainland, **Cape Wrath,** by ferry and minibus in summer. You need a clear day: then the cliffs, the seascapes and the bird-watching are superb.

Smoo Cave near Durness is a set of limestone caverns, the outer one reached from the seaward side through a huge arch (the inner ones being for serious potholers only). Having come so far, you'll probably want to make the journey along the north coast, via the glorious scenery of the **Kyle of Tongue.** An exhibition in Farr Church, at Bettyhill, tells the story of the vicious "Highland Clearances" of the 18th and 19th centuries, when crofters were turned off their land to make way for sheep.

Dunnet Head, the northernmost point in mainland Scotland, is less famous than **John O'Groats**, which is as far as you can get (874 miles, the sign says) from Land's End by road. If you like making these geographical points, **Duncansby Head** is the furthest north-east you can go without getting your feet wet, and it's quite impressive, too. Should you hanker for still more northern latitudes, the Orkney Isles are in view on a clear day; the Shetlands are quite a bit further. Car ferries sail for both from Scrabster (and from Aberdeen).

Islands

Scotland's islands are counted in hundreds—great and small, legendary and unknown. A complex network of steamers, car ferries, little fishing boats, even some planes can get you to a surprising number of them.

Skye *20 B2*
Extravagantly beautiful, Skye is rich in history and myth, and it's harder here than anywhere to tell which is which. There's no disagreement about the size: 50 miles (80 km.) long, with a coastline so indented that nowhere is more than 6 miles (9½ km.) from the sea. Or the weather—when the rain and mists clear, make the most of it. It can be magical.

The rugged **Cuillins** in the south are a hikers' and climbers' paradise, with a string of peaks over 3,000 feet (900 m.). Getting to the hills involves a well-prepared expedition and a trek, or a boat from Elgol. Some call **Loch Coruisk**, ringed by peaks, the prettiest lake in Britain. The hills of the north are more accessible: inland from the precipitous coast near Staffin, the road crosses them on the way to Uig, ferry terminal for the Outer Hebrides.

No castle in Scotland has been lived in

A Highlands variation on the javelin throw, tossing the caber involves a tapered fir pole 17 feet (5 m.) long, weighing 90 pounds (40 kg.). By ancient tradition, competitors in the caber caper must wear the kilt. Grunting is optional.

N̄orth-easternmost extremity of mainland Scotland, Duncansby Head is too exposed and vertiginous for settlement, but sheep thrive on the cliffside grass. Exotic northern seabirds inhabit perches on the face of the precipice.

by the same family for as long as **Dunvegan Castle**, stronghold of the chiefs of Clan MacLeod for more than seven centuries. One of their treasures, a faded square of spotted silk, is the fabled Fairy Flag, said to have been given to the 4th chief in the 14th century. It saved the MacLeods in clan battles twice, they say, and has the power to do it once more.

At **Kilmuir**, you can visit the grave and monument of Skye's heroine, Flora Macdonald, who smuggled the fugitive Bonnie Prince Charlie to safety dressed as her maid. And anywhere in the north you're likely to hear the lilting Gaelic language spoken. Portree and Broadford are the main touring centres, but you'll easily find somewhere quieter and more atmospheric to stay.

Mull   16 B–C2
Peaceful moorland glens and dramatic peaks, forests and little crofting villages, and a coastline as varied as any in Scotland combine to make Mull an ideal island. It's a stepping stone, too, to Iona

267

and Staffa. Ferries from Oban sail to Craignure on Mull, and if you want to continue north by a different route, cross the Sound of Mull from Fishnish.

Tobermory, the charming "capital" (pop. 700), clusters round its harbour, ringed by wooded hills. Small it may be, but this is Scotland, so it has its own golf course, and the bay is often filled with sailing boats. Somewhere deep in the mud of the sea bottom lies the wreck of one of the greatest galleons of the Armada, said of course to be laden with treasure when it blew up and sank in 1588. Salvage attempts ever since have failed to produce more than a tantalizing doubloon or so.

Little **Calgary**, to the south-west, with one of the best of Mull's sandy beaches, inspired the name of the Canadian city about a century ago. If you have the time, take the winding coast road bordering **Loch Na Keal**, perhaps returning through Glen More. It's single track and slow going, and dozing sheep only reluctantly get up and out of your way.

Two of Mull's castles, both visible from the Oban ferryboat, are open to visitors. **Duart** on its promontory is the restored home of the chiefs of Clan Maclean; parts date back to the 13th century. **Torosay Castle** was built in the 19th, with showpiece gardens of different styles: Italian, Japanese and the water garden.

Iona 16 B2

Precious to Scots and revered by Christians worldwide, this tiny island lies off the south-west tip of Mull. Here from Ireland in 563 came St. Columba and a handful of followers to establish a mon-astery, with the ultimate mission of converting all Scotland.

It takes seven minutes by sometimes bumpy passenger ferry (no cars are allowed on Iona) from Mull, and excursion boats make the journey from Oban. All the main sights are within an easy walk of the pier. The entire island measures less than 2 miles (3 km.) across and 4 miles (6 km.) long.

Nearest the pier, the early nunnery was restored in the 19th century. The mostly 15th-century abbey doubtless stands on the site of St. Columba's original. **St. Oran's Chapel** is the oldest surviving building on the island, with a notable Norman west door, and next to it, a graveyard said to be the burial place of many early Scottish kings and lords of the Isles. The carved stone Celtic St. Martin's Cross near the abbey dates from as early as the year 800.

Most of Iona's 100 or so inhabitants live near the ferry landing. They raise a few sheep or cattle, but in summer most of their time is taken up with the throngs of visitors and pilgrims. Religious scholars come too, to spend time with the active abbey community.

Staffa 16 B2

From Iona you can take an hour's boat trip around Staffa, the small uninhabited island whose dramatic **Fingal's Cave** inspired Mendelssohn to write his "Hebrides" overture. Columns of smooth black basalt stand out of the sea like organ pipes as the sound of the waves echoes in the cave. (Excursion boats usually circle Staffa. Only in very calm weather is it possible to land there.)

On the sacred isle of Iona, a seagull pauses atop a richly decorated ancient Celtic cross. The Benedictine Abbey is supposed to be built on the site of the original community established by St. Columba 14 centuries ago.

Never a Dull Moment

Monuments and museums are only the beginning of a holiday in Britain. Along with the sightseeing, you'll want to participate in the nation's rich cultural life. Innovative theatre, opera and ballet (pop music, too) flourish in London and northern cities from Manchester to Edinburgh. Elsewhere country pursuits come into their own—from active sports to leisurely walks.

Sports

The sporting British invented just about every game worth playing. There's not much in the way of sports you can't do, or see, during a stay in the country.

For Spectators

Major events are always televised, something to bear in mind if you can't get tickets for Wimbledon or Wembley.

Cricket was born at a place called, quaintly enough, Broadhalfpenny Down near Hambledon in Hampshire, and even today much of England's cricketing strength is drawn from the south. The game, described as "chess on grass", is bound to mystify the uninitiated at first, but the rules aren't hard to pick up. Just remember that there are two teams of 11 players, both wearing the same white trousers and shirts. The two players on the field holding bats belong to one team, all the others to the second, whose object is to remove the batsmen. The cricket season runs from late April to the end of September. Important county and test (international) matches are played in London at Lord's Cricket Ground and The Oval.

The most unlikely people get excited about **football** (soccer). Professional clubs belonging to the Football League (92 clubs) play each Saturday between August and May to sell-out crowds of chanting supporters. Cup Finals take place at London's Wembley Stadium. The violence of a small proportion of fans has given British football a bad name, but the game itself as played here is admired the world over, and British clubs regularly come out the winner in European competitions. If you'd like to see a match, but are worried about violence, avoid the standing room areas on the terraces, where trouble is more likely to occur.

Rugby. This popular game originated when a soccer player at Rugby School in Warwickshire picked up the ball and ran with it. Rather than disqualifying him,

Unlike the leviathans of American football, rugby players wear no armour in spite of the perils. The game involves violence, but the fans, unlike some soccer vandals, wouldn't think of it.

271

those present heralded the beginning of a new sport. There are two variants of "rugger" as played in Britain: Rugby League (13-a-side) and Rugby Union (15-a-side), each with slightly differing rules. Rugby League is mostly played by professionals and has the largest following in the north of England. Rugby Union, the amateur version and the one that attracts most international attention, has its English headquarters at Twickenham, near London, the place to see major matches, including internationals. Scottish rugby fans have their mecca at Murrayfield in Edinburgh, and the Welsh at Cardiff Arms Park. The Five Nations Tournament between England, Scotland, Wales, Ireland and France is the culmination of the rugby year.

Horse events. Racing is the sport of kings—and Britain's Queen, a knowledgeable horse breeder. Watch the thoroughbreds run at Epsom (Surrey), Ascot (Berkshire), Goodwood (Sussex), Newmarket (Suffolk), Doncaster (Yorkshire) and other courses around the country. The Epsom Derby and Royal Ascot in June are just two highlights of the long and eventful flat racing season (March to early November). National Hunt steeplechasing events are scheduled from late August to early June. Cheltenham is the venue for the National Hunt Festival Meeting in February or March, while the most famous of steeplechases, the Grand National, takes place at Aintree near Liverpool.

The major show jumping events of the year are held at Wembley: the Royal International Horse Show in July and the Horse of the Year Show in October.

Polo can be exciting to watch—especially should Prince Charles be playing. Matches are held weekends between April and August at some 20 clubs across the country, including Windsor (Berkshire), Cowdray Park (Sussex) and Cirencester Park (Warwickshire).

Motor Racing. Silverstone in Northamptonshire hosts the British Grand Prix for Formula One racing in July. The circuit is also used most weekends for motorcycle or car races, as is Brands Hatch in Kent.

Tennis fans descend on London at the end of June for the Wimbledon Lawn Tennis Championships, the most prestigious tournament on the international circuit. Tickets for Centre Court matches are hard to come by, especially for the final, but you may be able to see some young hopeful take on one of the greats in an earlier round.

Rowing events take place on the Thames: the hotly contested Oxford and Cambridge University Boat Race (between the London suburbs of Putney and Mortlake) and the Head of the River race, the largest assembly of river craft in the world. Of the 250 regattas held each year, the most important is the Henley Royal Regatta in July; crews from all over the world compete.

The **Scottish Highland Games** are a summer tradition, especially the Braemar Gathering, attended by the Royal Family. Watch the kilted titans grunting through tugs-of-war and tossing the famous caber.

Active Sports

Walking. You can get away from traffic and people on canal and river towpaths and long-distance footpaths. Walkers often have legal right of way over privately owned property, provided they respect the laws against trespassing, damage or misuse. Local and regional tourist offices publish suggestions for short walks and cross-country jaunts. You can also get information and advice from the Ramblers Association, 1–5 Wandsworth Road, London SW8 2XX.

Hiking. Combine physical challenge with scenic thrills in England's Peak District or Lake District, the Snowdonia region of Wales or the Scottish Highlands. You'd be well advised to join one of the excursions conducted by trained naturalists familiar with the terrain: week-long treks over moors and glens include food and accommodation, as well as the services of a guide.

Mountain climbing. British professionals train for Everest on the slopes of Mt. Snowdon in North Wales, on the peaked ridges of Arran in Scotland and the Cuillins on Skye. Information centres in mountain regions have a stock of maps and guide books for sale. For advance information, contact the British Mountaineering Council, Crawford House, Precinct Centre, Booth Street East, Manchester M13 9RZ.

Despite safety campaigns, significant numbers of climbers continue to get into trouble, many having to be brought down by mountain rescue teams. Always get local advice on weather and conditions and plan your route so as to be back before dark. And never go alone.

Cycling. Join a tour (for beginners or advanced riders, according to your stamina) or go it alone. The flatlands of Essex and Suffolk are ideal for gentle cycling in rural surroundings. More demanding routes follow the contours of the Downs, the Cotswolds, the Dorset hills, the dales and moors of Yorkshire, and the Scottish Borders. Keep to the unclassified roads and cycleways—cross-country paths designated as bridleways—and you'll avoid traffic.

Horse riding and **pony trekking.** You can ride by the hour, half-day or full day at centres across Britain. Instruction is often available. Many centres also organize pony trekking holidays (touring at a walk or gentle trot)—a great way to explore the countryside, whatever your level of skill. Choose from a variety of weekend and week-long tours in different parts of the country. Or opt for a weekly package programme with accommodation, setting out from the same base on a different ride each day. Establishments affiliated to the British Horse Society have been inspected and approved. For details write to British Horse Society, British Equestrian Centre, Stoneleigh, Kenilworth, Warwickshire.

Golf. Top professionals agree that Britain has some of the finest courses in the world—1,800 in all. The surprise is that it's cheaper and easier to play here than in most countries. Scotland, where the game was devised, claims some historic greens: the St. Andrews Royal and Ancient Golf Club's Old Course, where an open championship is held every year, Carnoustie, Royal Troon, Turnberry and Gleneagles.

Hunting. The sport arouses strong feelings, pro and con. Most popular in Britain is **fox hunting** on horseback with a pack of hounds. A lot of people follow the hunts on Saturdays in autumn, circling the fields on foot or in cars. Shooting for grouse, black-grouse, partridge, pheasant and ptarmigan is practised on specially supervised estates, with a closed season. You will need a licence to shoot game and a certificate for your shotgun, issued by the police.

Fishing. Second only to darts in popularity, it's one of the favourite sports in the land. England's most famous trout river, the Trent, flows through Hampshire—an old haunt of Izaak Walton, author of that 17th-century classic, *The Compleat Angler*. The best salmon and trout rivers in Wales are the Severn, Usk and Wye, matched by Scotland's Spey, Tay and Tweed. In Scotland you need only a local permit to fish, but in England and Wales a general licence is required. Apply to the regional water authority, the nearest tackle shop or hotel.

Most fishing is fly, though occasional spinner or bait may be used. Closed season for salmon or trout runs from early October to mid-March; for salmon net fishing, it's from late August into February; for salmon rod fishing from sometime in October until January or February. Coarse fishing for perch, pike and the like is allowed year round and can be very good, particularly in southern waters.

Deep-sea fishermen land dogfish, mackerel, conger eel, pollack and shark. Trips run from many ports in South-West England, on the Scottish mainland and in the islands. The fishing can be good from beaches and shoreline perches as well.

273

*S*ome say the fish bite more enthusiastically in the rain. To prove the theory, these Cotswolds anglers settle down under umbrellas for a long wait. If true, the proposition would seem to give British fishermen a big advantage.

cruise the inland waterways of the Norfolk Broads in East Anglia. Bookings can be made through Boat Enquiries Ltd., 7 Walton Well Road, Oxford.

Sailing. Opportunities abound in maritime Britain, notably in the South-West. Chichester (Sussex), Poole (Dorset), Salcombe and Plymouth in Devon, and Falmouth (Cornwall) are the big yachting centres, not forgetting Cowes on the Isle of Wight. The Cowes Week races at the beginning of August attract international participation. Also popular for sailing are the Norfolk Broads.

For information about all aspects of sailing and a list of the recognized teaching centres in Britain, contact the Royal Yachting Association (RYA) headquarters at Victoria Way, Woking, Surrey GU21 1EQ.

Swimming. Quite a few of the better country hotels have pools, many of them heated and under cover. Pools in the large urban hotels often belong to an indoor fitness centre. Leisure complexes with pools, slides and wave machines have opened up in some of the old seaside resorts. There's swimming, too, at beaches around the coast, though the traditional resorts like Brighton, Blackpool and Clacton aren't likely to have a magnetic appeal for a tourist. The remoter West Country beaches are attractive, but currents here can be treacherous. And nowhere is the water warm.

Surfing. The Cornish coast is the ideal place, especially Newquay. Boards can be hired here and at various other resorts. There's also year-round surfing off the west coast of Wales. Bring your wet suit.

Windsurfing (boardsailing). You'll never be far from a suitable stretch of water, be it the sea, a lake or reservoir. Equipment is available for hire in larger towns and resorts.

Skiing. You'll find instructors, chairlifts, tows and mushrooming accommodation at Scotland's three developed ski areas: Aviemore, Glenshee and Glen Coe. There's usually snow on the slopes from December to May.

You don't need a licence unless you're going after sea trout in tidal estuaries.

Boating. Britain's extensive network of inland waterways, developed during the early days of the Industrial Revolution, now serves a purely recreational purpose. Charter a traditional narrowboat (barge) and cruise the rivers and canals of England, Wales and Scotland at a leisurely pace (average speed 4 mph/6 kph). The rental company will show you how to steer and operate the locks along the way. Or hire a motorboat or houseboat and

Shopping

None of the provincial centres even approach the selection available in London. If you're planning to do some serious shopping, set aside a couple of days at the end of your trip for an assault on the capital's shops. It probably won't be cheaper to go to the source for most items—to Stoke-on-Trent for Wedgwood, or Scotland for cashmere. London's discount outlets offer bargains equal to any you'll find on the spot. A notable exception is antiques. London dealers do their own buying at country fairs and auctions where prices are appreciably lower.

In many cases visitors from abroad can be reimbursed for value-added tax (VAT) paid on goods purchased in the United Kingdom for export. For details, see page 314.

When to Shop

Most shops open from 9 or 9.30 a.m. to 5.30 or 6 p.m., Monday to Saturday. Department stores tend to stay open late— till 7 or 8 p.m.—one day a week. Conversely, small-town shops usually close one midweek afternoon.

British Shopping From A to Z

Antiques. From classical antiquities to Beatles memorabilia, the British market caters to the most diverse interests. The weekly *Antiques Trade Gazette* announces all the auctions and shows in London and around the country. The better dealers display the seal of the professional associations: LAPADA and BADA.

Books. The best all-round booksellers in London are Foyles (Charing Cross Road); Dillons, London University's bookshop (Malet St., London WC1); and the efficient Hatchard's (Piccadilly and branches). For antiquarian books, roam the area between Charing Cross Road and the British Museum. In Oxford, Blackwell's is the traditional haunt of the bibliophile. The Welsh town of Hay-on-Wye is a national centre of the book trade and a famous source of secondhand titles.

Cars. Inspect this year's crop of bold British cars: Lotuses and TVRs for the sporty look; Aston-Martins and Jaguars for luxury and speed; or the ultimate in status symbols, a brand-new Bentley or Rolls-Royce.

China. Spode, Wedgwood, Minton and Royal Doulton are some of the names to look for. The department stores carry a wide selection of patterns and makes. London's Reject Shops stock seconds and ends of series at bargain prices.

Clothing. Made-to-measure elegance is a British speciality. London's Savile Row and Jermyn Street fill most masculine requirements from head (Locke, the hatters) to toe (Lobb, the cobblers). King's Road and Covent Garden suit the trendy. For women, the choice ranges from couture classics (Jean Muir, Jaspar Conran) to King's Road fads.

Fabrics. The selection ranges from tweeds, cashmeres and Viyella to Liberty lawn, fine cotton cloth in garden party prints. John Lewis and Liberty's in London have the largest stock.

Fine Foods. Take home a taste of Britain: handmade jams and marmalade (flavoured with whisky in Scotland), cheese (Stilton sealed in stoneware jars, or some farmhouse Cheddar), biscuits, mustards and traditional Christmas puddings.

Glassware. Several lines of handmade glassware are manufactured in Scotland: Edinburgh and Stuart Crystal and Caithness Glass, with distinctive thistle or star designs. Other names in British glass: Royal Brierley and Webb.

Artisan at work designing textiles. Overleaf: new, angular variations on traditional porcelain products play a rhapsody in blue.

Perfumes and potpourri. The British go in for traditional scents like lavender, rose, English bluebell and Scottish heather. Penhaligon's and Floris are the specialists.

Pottery. Craftsmen around the country work in traditional and contemporary styles. The West Country, Wales and Scotland seem to attract the most creative talents.

Rainwear. The British, who know more about rain than anybody, gave the world the umbrella, the trenchcoat and Wellington (rubber) boots. You'll still find the best selection of all-weather clothing here.

Scottish Souvenirs. Look for the heraldic shield or tartan that denotes your clan. Other Scottish ideas include "heather gems", silver jewellery—even bagpipes. There are half a dozen suppliers in Edinburgh alone.

Sports equipment. The hunting, riding and fishing gear can't be bettered, nor can the equipment. The British produce everything from golf clubs to badminton racquets. Cricket sweaters are popular on and off the playing field.

Teas. An inexpensive souvenir of the British way of life, and easily portable. Specialized merchants sell the widest range of blends in the western world.

Tobacco. Connoisseurs far and wide know two famous London shops—Dunhill and Fribourg & Treyer, both in St. James's. They carry notable pipe mixtures and the best imported cigars.

Toys. Britain is the home of Paddington Bear, Peter Rabbit—and Hamleys, London's superstore for toys.

Whisky. Although Scotch is probably no cheaper in Scotland, you'll find far more brands than you ever thought existed; experts rave about the best Highland malts.

Woollens. Cardigans, shawls and scarves come in cashmere, Shetland and lambswool. Harris tweed (from the Outer Hebrides) is hand loomed. Other fine tweeds are from mainland Scottish and Welsh sources.

Shopping in London

The West End is the obvious place to start. Bond Street, Piccadilly, Regent and Jermyn streets offer the best in antiques, fine art, jewellery, leather goods and clothing. Oxford Street has the chain stores and the crowds. It's worth battling through to the busy main branch of Marks and Spencer for well-styled woollens at popular prices. The comprehensive Selfridges is convenient for one-stop shopping.

Knightsbridge sends up a big challenge to the West End. The emphasis is on high fashion along Sloane Street and Beauchamp Place, while Harvey Nichols and Harrods, one of the world's great department stores, dominate the Brompton Road scene. Chelsea offers the contrasts of King's Road excess and Fulham Road chic, and Walton Street has some very attractive small shops for home furnishings and clothes. Over in Kensington, the High Street proves only slightly less frenetic than Oxford Street. Veer off into Kensington Church Street and have a look at the antique shops.

London Street Markets

Market traders set up their stalls year-round, fair weather or foul. The main markets:

Portobello Road (W11), Saturday. General antiques, collectibles. Begin at the Notting Hill end in the covered arcades.

Bermondsey (New Caledonian Market), south of the river off Tower Bridge Road (SE1), Fridays. General antiques, collectibles.

Camden Passage (Islington, N1), Wednesdays and Saturdays. General antiques, collectibles.

Camden Lock, by Regent's Canal (Chalk Farm, NW1), Thursdays, and especially Sundays. Crafts and collectibles.

There's not much of interest at Petticoat Lane, the Sunday market in the East End, nor at Club Row nearby, now that the animal market has closed.

279

The bright lights of London's West End. There are half a dozen theatres in Shaftesbury Avenue; neighbouring Soho streets traditionally offer some less legitimate entertainment. The heart of London's Chinatown is a few steps to the south.

into three categories: repertory, commercial West End, and "fringe" (experimental). The National Theatre (South Bank Arts Centre) stages innovative productions of the classics and the best contemporary pieces. At the modern Barbican Centre, the highly respected Royal Shakespeare Company puts the accent on England's greatest playwright. For both venues, some tickets are available from 10 in the morning for performances the same day. And if it's avant-garde or alternative, you'll see it at the Royal Court (SW3) or Riverside Studios (Hammersmith W6).

West End theatres—including the distinguished Theatre Royal in Haymarket and that old London institution, the Palladium—feature comedies and musicals, as well as some drama. In many theatres, drinks are served during the interval (intermission). To avoid the crush at the bar, order and pay before the performance begins.

Most towns in Britain have at least one legitimate theatre; there are hundreds nationwide. Some, like the Palace Theatre in Manchester and the Theatre Royal, Nottingham, are historically important buildings. National touring companies and local professionals keep audiences across the country entertained. The regional repertory companies take their most successful productions to London's West End.

In tourist circles the best known theatre outside London is the Royal Shakespeare in Stratford-upon-Avon. Tickets can be hard to come by, but returns are sometimes available at the box office on the day of a performance. The company also performs plays by authors classical and modern in a small experimental theatre, a former warehouse called The Other Place.

Opera. The Royal Opera House, in London's ever-lively Covent Garden, is the home of the prestigious Royal Opera Company. Over at the Coliseum, just off Trafalgar Square, the excellent English National Opera sings in English.

Entertainment

London dominates the nation's entertainment but doesn't monopolize it. Theatre, opera, concerts, even nightclubs prosper in the provinces as well as the capital. In London the choice is so great you'd do well to consult one of the events magazines like *What's On, Time Out* or *City Limits* to plan your entertainment for the week ahead.

Theatre. For many London visitors, the theatre comes first. It can be divided

A night at the opera might also feature the Scottish Opera, based in Glasgow but often on the road. The New Theatre in Cardiff is home for the Welsh National Opera, known as the most adventurous of Britain's opera companies.

Choral groups such as the Royal Choral Society and the Bach Choir give frequent concerts, often in conjunction with the big symphony orchestras. Regionally, the human voice probably reaches its highest note in Wales, where there are dozens of community choirs worth listening to.

Ballet. Be it classical or contemporary, ballet in London is superb. The Royal Ballet appears at the Royal Opera House, alternating with the opera company. Tickets may be out of the question unless you're willing to queue (sometimes overnight) for a seat the same day. One ticket per caller is available from 10 a.m. If that fails, try to see the Royal Ballet's sister company, the Sadler's Wells Royal Ballet, or perhaps the English National Ballet.

When it comes to modern repertory, you can't do better than the London Contemporary Dance Theatre or the Ballet Rambert, founded in 1926 by the visionary Marie Rambert.

Concerts. London enjoys Europe's busiest concert scene. Local orchestras of international repute, such as the Royal Philharmonic, the London Symphony Orchestra, the Philharmonia and the BBC Symphony, all perform here, as do guest orchestras, chamber groups and soloists from around the world. The prime concert halls are at the South Bank Arts Centre (Royal Festival Hall and two smaller houses), the Barbican, Royal Albert Hall (South Kensington) and intimate Wigmore Hall (W1). If you're in London between July and September, try for the informal Henry Wood Promenade Concerts, the Proms. Holders of cheap tickets (on sale one hour beforehand) sit, stand, even walk around while the orchestra plays. Another London tradition is the lunchtime concert—perhaps a chamber orchestra or an or-

gan recital in St. Martin-in-the-Fields (Trafalgar Square) or St. John's (Smith Square, SW1).

An unusually vigorous concert life goes on around the rest of the country, too. Among world-class orchestras based beyond London: The City of Birmingham Symphony, the Hallé Orchestra of Manchester and the Scottish National Orchestra. And thanks to TV licence fees, the BBC can afford to run its worthy regional orchestras.

Jazz. The great showcase in London is Ronnie Scott's (Frith Street in Soho), where the biggest names in the business let loose. There are other clubs, big and small. And look for jazz events in less intimate but more prominent places like the Festival Hall, Royal Albert Hall and Hammersmith Odeon. Elsewhere in London and beyond, jazz is performed in many a pub.

Folk and rock. Big halls like the Wembley Arena and Hammersmith Odeon in West London host the big names. But countless pubs and clubs around Britain showcase other groups. You may "discover" the next David Bowie, Paul McCartney or Elton John. All over Scotland, *Ceilidhs* or folk nights are held, featuring dancers, pipers and fiddlers.

Nightclubs. The more exclusive London clubs, like Annabel's and Tramps, restrict admission to members. At other night spots, entrance is at the discretion of the management. Nightclubs and discos in all the provincial cities offer late night entertainment, or at least some music and company.

Cinema. The London film scene includes the big West End houses, featuring first-run films; the neighbourhoods, showing movies on release; and the art cinemas, screening classic and foreign films. Things are quieter in the provinces, where television and video have conspired to wipe out many cinemas. Still, the British Film Institute and related organizations subsidize film-makers and regional movie theatres.

282

CALENDAR OF EVENTS

Most of the traditional festivals and celebrations coincide with the tourist season, though there's bound to be something going on, no matter when you visit. Local festivals feature some or all of the following cultural offerings: classical music, jazz, opera, drama, exhibitions, fringe events. A sample of annual events:

January. *London International Boat Show* (Earl's Court Exhibition Centre, London SW5).

February. *Cruft's Dog Show* (Earl's Court Exhibition Centre, London SW5).

March. *Chelsea Antiques Fair* (Chelsea Old Town Hall, London SW3), *Cheltenham Gold Cup Meeting* (horse racing; Cheltenham).

March–April. *Oxford and Cambridge University Boat Race* (River Thames, Putney to Mortlake), *Grand National Meeting* (horse racing; Aintree Racecourse, Liverpool). *Edinburgh International Folk Festival* (Edinburgh).

March–January. *Shakespeare Theatre Season* (Stratford-upon-Avon).

April. *London Marathon* (Greenwich to Westminster). *Newport Drama Festival* (Newport).

May. *Brighton International Festival* (Brighton), *Chelsea Flower Show* (Royal Hospital, London SW3), *Guineas Stakes* (horse racing; Newmarket), *Newbury Spring Festival* (Newbury), *Sheffield Chamber Music Festival* (Sheffield). *Mayfest* (Glasgow), *Perth Festival of the Arts* (Perth).

May–June. *Bath International Festival* (Bath), *Exeter Festival* (Exeter), *Malvern Festival* (Malvern), *Nottingham Festival* (Nottingham).

May–August. *Glyndebourne Festival Opera Season* (Glyndebourne).

May–October. *Pitlochry Festival Theatre Season* (Pitlochry).

June. *The Derby* (horse racing; Epsom), *Trooping the Colour* (Horse Guards Parade, Whitehall, London SW1), *Greenwich Festival* (Greenwich, London SE10), *Royal Ascot* (horse racing; Ascot), *Aldeburgh Festival of Music and the Arts* (Aldeburgh), *Sevenoaks Summer Festival* (Sevenoaks). *Royal Scottish Automobile Club International Scottish Rally* (start and finish in Glasgow).

June–July. *Wimbledon Lawn Tennis Championships* (Wimbledon, London SW19), *Henley Royal Regatta* (Henley-on-Thames), *Ludlow Festival* (Ludlow).

July. *City of London Festival* (London), *Birmingham International Jazz Festival* (Birmingham), *British Grand Prix* (Silverstone), *Cambridge Festival* (Cambridge), *Cheltenham International Festival of Music* (Cheltenham), *Chester Summer Music Festival* (Chester), *Chichester Festivities* (Chichester), *King's Lynn Festival of Music and the Arts* (King's Lynn), *Lichfield Festival and Fringe* (Lichfield), *Warwick Arts Festival* (Warwick), *York Early Music Festival* (York). *Open Championship* (Royal Troon Golf Club). *Fishguard Music Festival* (Fishguard), *Llangollen International Musical Eisteddfod* (Llangollen).

July–August. *Buxton International Festival* (Buxton), *Harrogate International Festival* (Harrogate).

July–September. *Henry Wood Promenade Concerts* (Royal Albert Hall, London SW7), *Summerscope on the South Bank* (South Bank Centre, London SE1).

August. *Three Choirs Festival* (Gloucester). *Edinburgh International Jazz Festival* (Edinburgh), *Keith Agricultural Show* (Keith). *Vale of Glamorgan Festival* (Vale of Glamorgan), *Royal National Eisteddfod of Wales*.

August–September. *Arundel Festival* (Arundel). *Edinburgh International Festival* (Edinburgh), *Edinburgh Military Tattoo* (Edinburgh Castle).

September. *Salisbury Festival* (Salisbury), *St. Leger Festival Meeting* (horse racing; Doncaster). *Braemar Royal Highland Gathering* (Braemar), *Pitlochry Highland Games* (Pitlochry). *North Wales Music Festival* (St. Asaph).

September–October. *Cheltenham Festival of Literature* (Cheltenham), *Windsor Festival* (Windsor).

October. *Horse of the Year Show* (Wembley Arena, Wembley), *Canterbury Festival* (Canterbury), *Norfolk and Norwich French Festival* (Norwich). *Swansea Musical Festival* (Swansea).

November. *Lord Mayor's Procession and Show* (City of London), *London to Brighton Veteran Car Run* (from Hyde Park, London, to Brighton).

November–December. *Cardiff Festival of Music* (St. David's Hall, Cardiff).

December. *Olympia International Showjumping Championships* (Olympia, London W14).

BRITISH POP CULTURE

"I hope I die before I get old." In 1965 Pete Townsend of The Who issued a manifesto for every post-war generation of British teenagers. Called "My Generation", it expressed all the frustration and excitement of being young in a society that was caught between tradition and the rising social expectations of the welfare state. It was both an anthem for the frenzied hedonism of "Mod" life and a rejection of the values of parents and authority.

In Britain the most exciting (and usually the most commercially successful) pop music has always been associated with a particular youth culture. Music is the means by which a group carves out an identity for itself in opposition not only to the Establishment, but also to the fashion that has immediately preceded it. Hippies rejected the Mods, Glitter Rock was a reaction to flower power, and Punks rejected everything in sight. Since the 1960s, social fashions and musical tastes have been a rapidly swinging pendulum between opposing poles. But this time-honoured tradition seems in danger of demise, as the changing economic environment has made conformity more fashionable with young people than rebellion.

It all began in the '60s with the fresh Mersey Beat sound of the Beatles. Only one of hundreds of similar groups that had sprung up around the country, they owed their success not only to their own original talent, but also to the shrewd marketing skills of their manager, an ex-Liverpool shopkeeper named Brian Epstein. The string of hits that started with "Please Please Me" was sustained by careful packaging of the Fab Four, making them acceptable to all ages, first in Britain, then around the world. The Beatles had longish hair, but they were at pains to stress that they washed it every day.

Elton John in concert

They wore suits on stage, and were eventually rewarded with the Order of the British Empire by the Queen, as much for their contribution to Britain's invisible earnings as for their musical achievements.

If the Beatles were the acceptable face of pop music in the early '60s, there were plenty of other groups to remind British teenagers (and their parents) that pop music could also be dangerous, subversive and anti-social. The Rolling Stones, The Who, The Kinks and The Pretty Things produced a much harder and more aggressive music that was the perfect accompaniment to Mod culture. A fetishistic concern with the details of personal appearance was the main criterion for entry into the Mod peer group. The Mods stressed a minimalistic approach to fashion, favouring Italian boots and parkas. A customized Lambretta or Vespa scooter and a manic facial expression completed the Mod image, the latter the result of an excessive consumption of amphetamines. Aggression was an important part of Mod life. It found expression in the pitched battles that took place between Mods and Rockers (the other tribal entity of the time) and in the ritual violence of groups like The Who, who destroyed their instruments at the end of every performance.

Fashions changed again at the end of the '60s. A sudden interest in love, peace and happiness blew in on a warm wind from California, and new fashions emerged in drugs (LSD and cannabis), clothes (flared trousers, Indian prints, caftans), hairstyles (as long as possible), perfume (patchouli oil) and, of course, music, which now aspired to profundity where before commercial success had been sufficient. In most cases the existing British groups embraced the new "lifestyle" with open arms. The Beatles went to visit the Maharishi in India, Mick Jagger was arrested on a drugs charge, and another generation of pop groups emerged to satisfy the new taste in music. The Cream and Pink Floyd played long, meaningful solos. Youth culture became imbued with self-importance and convinced itself that it was not just a passing phase but a serious alternative to the ageing process.

The '60s were the golden age of pop culture in Britain. Musicians, artists, writers, film makers, photographers and fashion designers produced the vibrant cultural scene described by *Time* magazine as "Swinging London". But the feeling of optimism that had been sustained by growing prosperity and economic freedom for young people eventually came to an end, and by 1970 the party was over.

The '70s saw increasingly bitter reactions to the stylistic and musical legacies of the '60s. The first of these was Glitter Rock—the collective description for bands such as T Rex, Gary Glitter and The Sweet, and the stars who flirted with it, notably David Bowie and Elton John. The inspiration for Glitter Rock came from a disgust for the portentous seriousness of so much of '60s music. The bands accordingly plastered themselves with make-up, wore outrageously glamorous (or silly) clothes and platform boots, sprinkled themselves with glitter and presented a deliberately androgynous image to their huge following of thirteen-year-old fans, dubbed "teeny-boppers". Glitter Rock faded quickly from the scene, but it did have the beneficial effect of injecting camp humour and theatricality into pop music. David Bowie and Elton John took off their make-up and continued their careers. The others simply disappeared.

By the mid-'70s more radical measures were needed to express the growing reality of unemployment and disenchantment for young people. Punk grew out of the activities of a small number of bands (The Sex Pistols, The Clash and Generation X) that aimed to jolt society out of complacency. Their example was rapidly followed by others around the country and amplified by Malcolm McLaren, the manager of the Sex Pistols and co-owner with Vivienne Westwood of a shop in the Kings Road which specialized in clothing and T-shirts designed to give offence. Punk regenerated pop music and created the first genuinely British youth culture since the Mods. However, it, too, had a short life span, and died with Sid Vicious's overdose.

The '80s was a period in which no special culture emerged to challenge orthodoxies, and no musical style predominated. Mass events such as the Live Aid and Nelson Mandela concerts characterized the decade. These orgies of self-congratulation consciously brought together musicians and stars who previously wouldn't have been seen dead in the same place. A number of stars emerged—Duran Duran, Boy George, Frankie Goes To Hollywood and Sade—accompanied by enough imitators and acolytes to give the impression of some greater movement. But the contemporary teenager seems to be a more careful consumer than his or her predecessor and doesn't succumb so easily to the lure of a rebellious pop culture.

Food, Glorious Food

The British may not live to eat, as the French and Italians do, but they know how to eat well. The best of British food is traditionally based on top-quality ingredients uncomplicated by fancy sauces. But it's no secret that eating habits are changing, and food is getting more varied all the time. The ethnic influence has been decisive, introducing flavours and spices from the Far East and the Caribbean. And the lifting of frontier barriers in the European Community has brought an influx of Continental products, from French cheeses, pâtés and wines to Greek yoghurt.

Where to Eat

The proliferating fast food chains need no introduction. More typically British are the sandwich bars and working men's cafés, open for breakfast (the best bet), lunch and dinner, where food is sustaining and cheap. At fish and chip shops, you can take food away or, in some cases, eat on the premises.

Pubs, many of them historic and architectural landmarks, are everywhere to be found. In addition to snacks and drinks, you can have a hot meal at most of them—usually meat and two vegetables.

*I*n the Tudor atmosphere of Stratford-upon-Avon, a toque-hatted chef presides over the British answer to smorgasbord.

Sunday lunch at a country pub is a British tradition.

Wine bars provide hot and cold food along with wine by the bottle or glass. More prevalent in London than elsewhere, they've overtaken the pubs in popularity, at least with young professionals.

Restaurants range from rustic inns to elegant Michelin-starred gourmet spots (especially in the London area). But beware: pricey menus don't always guarantee quality.

Carveries, often attached to hotels or pubs, specialize in roast meat carved from the joint, with potatoes, vegetables and salads.

Ethnic Restaurants

Chinese and Indian restaurants and takeaways proliferate in London and other big cities, but there is hardly a group or nationality that isn't represented: French, Italian, Turkish, Greek, West Indian, African, Malaysian, Hungarian, kosher, Indian vegetarian... the choice is all-encompassing. And the price is right.

287

Breakfast

A Continental-style start to the day may keep you going until "elevenses", mid-morning tea break. But a true British breakfast is a more serious proposition. You'll typically be served cold cereal or porridge (oatmeal), followed by bacon and eggs, sausages and fried tomatoes, or kippers (smoked herrings), toast, jam and tea or coffee. The Scots cook their porridge with salt, not sugar, and serve it with cream and milk.

Lunch

Lunchtime pub fare includes the "ploughman's lunch"—a plateful of Cheddar cheese, bread, salad and pickle (a kind of spicy relish). Other pub staples served cold: English meat pies (pork or game); Scotch eggs (hard-boiled eggs wrapped in sausage meat and deep fried); and Cornish pasties (pronounced PAS-tea), pastries filled with a mixture of beef, potato and onion.

By way of hot food, there's the traditional "shepherd's pie" (minced beef or lamb with herbs and onions, topped with mashed potatoes); steak and kidney pie; chicken and mushroom pie; "bubble and squeak" (a mixture of corned beef, cabbage and mashed potatoes fried until crisp); "bangers and mash" (sausages and mashed potatoes); or "toad-in-the-hole" (sausages in a batter base).

"Fish 'n chips" is a national institution. Batter-dipped fillets of cod, plaice or haddock are deep fried and served with chips (French fries), traditionally sprinkled with vinegar—or doused with ketchup—but rarely nowadays wrapped in the traditional newspaper.

Tea

It is no longer quite the rule that "everything stops for tea", but the ritual still holds sway in restaurants and hotels across the land. A "cream tea" involves the sinfully good combination of scones spread with jam and a lavish helping of whipped or "clotted" cream. Otherwise, cakes and thinly sliced sandwiches of egg,

cucumber, tomato, cress and smoked salmon are served. In Scotland and Yorkshire "high tea" means a complete evening meal of grilled ham and freshly baked bread buns.

All this, of course, accompanied by strong Indian or Ceylon teas, smoky Lapsang Souchong, scented Earl Grey or, more rarely, Chinese green teas. The English, by the way, drink their tea with milk and sugar, but serve lemon when asked, though you may see a raised eyebrow.

*The setting is simple, the food unfussed, the view
superb, what more could London restaurant-goers ask for? A preview of
the dishes on offer (overleaf) in London's Chinatown.*

Dinner

A more elaborate restaurant meal may start with smoked salmon, a prawn (shrimp) cocktail, terrine or fish mousse. In season you may find melon with smoked game or ham, and green asparagus, hot with hollandaise sauce or cold with vinaigrette. Rainy, raw weather calls for heart-warming soups—cream of tomato or chicken, oxtail or a light consommé laced with sherry.

Dover sole comes grilled (broiled) or meunière. Trout is usually sautéed with butter and served with almonds. Salmon can be hot with melted butter or cold with mayonnaise.

For the main course, roast beef is invariably accompanied by Yorkshire pudding, puffed-up portions of batter (like American popovers). Leg or saddle of lamb (medium to well-done, never rare or pink) is served with new potatoes, peas and tangy mint sauce or red currant jelly. Lamb or pork chops and fillet steaks are at their best simply grilled. Chicken is usually roasted and served with bread

low) or crumbles (with a top crust of crumbly pastry). "Fool" is a confection of cream and raspberries, strawberries or gooseberries. "Summer" or "paradise" pudding lives up to its name: a mouth-watering concoction of stewed raspberries and redcurrants poured into a bread-lined mould, chilled and dished up with whipped cream. English trifle is no trifling matter, but a complex compilation of sponge cake soaked in sherry or brandy, topped with layers of fruit or jam, custard or cream. A winter treat is the seasonal plum pudding or Christmas pudding, studded with almonds, raisins, sultanas, and candied fruit, doused in brandy and flamed at the table.

Cheeses follow dessert and are eaten with biscuits (crackers) rather than bread. Among the best: blue-veined Stilton (often enriched with port), tangy Cheddar, red or white Cheshire, full-flavoured Gloucester and crumbly white Wensleydale.

Regional Specialities
You'll find the main dishes are much the same throughout the country. But each region has a few local favourites:

England
London food is generally too cosmopolitan to favour any speciality, but if you have a taste for eels, head for the East End markets where they're served stewed or jellied.

The **South** excels in steak and kidney pudding: the meat is stuffed into a suet-crust pastry and steamed. Here you'll also find that homey dessert, bread-and-butter pudding (baked with sugar, cream, vanilla, sultanas and apricot jam), or its first cousin, queen of puddings (bread crumbs mixed with milk and egg, flavoured with lemon or chocolate and baked with a meringue topping).

In the seafaring **West Country**, you can't go wrong with fish: lobster, crab, Torbay sole, Tamar salmon or smoked mackerel. Pilchards or herrings appear in "stargazy pie", their heads peeping out

sauce. In the game season, wild duck, partridge, grouse and pheasant are added to the list.

With main courses come a garnish of seasonal vegetables—grean beans, peas, Brussels sprouts, carrots, courgettes (zucchini), parsnips or cauliflower—and potatoes, perhaps roasted, "creamed" (mashed) or "jacket potatoes" (baked).

Dessert
Fruit of all kinds appears in tarts (with pastry below), pies (pastry above and be-

from a blanket of piecrust. Cornish pasties, pastry folded over a filling of beef, onions, swedes (rutabaga) and potatoes, started out as a tin miner's lunch just the right size to fit in his pocket—but are now a popular snack all over.

The fertile soil of **East Anglia**'s reclaimed fens yields a wealth of vegetables and fruit—strawberries, asparagus, peas, parsnips and young potatoes. Geese and turkeys are raised by the million. Seafood is equally plentiful: herrings and whitebait from Yarmouth and Lowestoft, or flat round oysters from Colchester, considered among the world's finest. Savoury eel pie is a typical local dish. But also look out for parsley-stuffed "chine" or salt pork, a Lincolnshire speciality. For dessert, try the quince or greengage tart.

In the **Midlands**, Melton Mowbray is famed as the home of the pork pie—cuts of pork, veal, ox-tongue and hard-boiled egg baked in a pastry crust. Elvers (baby eels that look like soya sprouts) are served fried with onions and herbs as a spring delicacy. Derbyshire has its Bakewell tart: a rich almond-flavoured custard cooked in a deep-dish crust spread with raspberry jam. You can try Shrewsbury cakes, flavoured with caraway seeds, and Banbury cakes, stuffed with candied peel and currants. And don't miss brandy snaps, a speciality of Nottinghamshire: lacy little cylinders of sugar and butter, filled with whipped cream.

The **North** is the home of potted seafood, preserved by a covering of clarified butter and eaten cold. Potted Tweed salmon or potted shrimps from Morecambe Bay are delicious spread on wholemeal bread or toast. Yorkshire pudding has been adopted by the whole country, and so has the dry-salted York ham. But Lancashire hot-pot is still at its best around Bolton or Liverpool, where the beef and onion casserole topped with sliced potatoes is slowly oven-simmered. The Lake District is famed for rich and sticky gingerbread, eaten warm or cold with whipped cream.

Wales

The Welsh thought of it first, but it's now universal: cheese melted with ale and mustard, piled on hot buttered toast and browned under the grill. It's known as a Welsh rabbit or rarebit.

Welsh cawl (pronounced "cowl") is a hearty hotpot of mutton and smoked gammon (a kind of bacon), simmered with potatoes, leeks and carrots. Welsh lamb is excellent and prepared inventively—barbecued or stuffed with apricots or walnuts and roasted.

Cockles, famous around the coast near Penclawdd, are fried quickly in browned breadcrumbs and spring onion.

The leek is the national symbol of Wales. It crops up in soups (cream of leek), in pancakes, and in "flans" (first cousin of the quiche) with cheese. Leeks also feature in a Welsh version of the pasty.

Soft, unripened Caerphilly is the main Welsh cheese.

Tea time might bring on traditional oat cakes with butter, Welsh cakes with currants or raisins cooked on a griddle or grilled, or cinnamon cakes. Bara brith is a tantalizing Welsh currant bread, best eaten warm from the oven. Welsh apple flan, a kind of pie with apple baked in an egg mixture, and a similar but smoother dish, Welsh apple delight, do wonders with the humble apple. Snowdon pudding, served with a lemon-sherry sauce, contains eggs and raisins.

Scotland

Soups are particularly welcome in Scotland's temperamental weather. Cock-a-leekie, Scotland's national soup, is a hearty brew of chicken, leeks and prunes, and a good Scotch broth is a consistent soup-stew made with vegetables, mutton or beef and a thickening of barley.

Don't expect a game bird if you see Scotch woodcock on a menu. This delicious "savoury" consists of toast spread with anchovy butter and topped with a creamy sauce.

King of the rivers, Scotch salmon is legendary, best prepared as simply as possible: simmered (not boiled) and served with hollandaise sauce; grilled (broiled) with lemon; served cold with mayonnaise; or smoked. And there are also marvellous trout, oysters, langoustine (comparable to scampi) and scallops from Loch Fyne.

Beef is a firm favourite in the land of Aberdeen Angus cattle. The preferred variation is Gaelic steak, flavoured with garlic, onions and whisky.

Game is fairly abundant in Scotland, especially after the "glorious 12th" (of August), when the grouse season opens. You'll also get pheasant, guinea fowl, quail and hare, served with a counterpoint of fruit or sweet-sour sauce. Venison is marinated and spiced with brandy, mushrooms, wine vinegar, and salt pork.

If you've never tasted haggis, you should—before you consider what's in it. Scotland's most famous dish contains chopped sheep's innards, onions, beef suet and seasoning, stuffed into a sheep's stomach bag and boiled. Eat it as the Scots do, with "chappit tatties and bashed neeps"—mashed potatoes and turnips—and wash it down with a tot of whisky.

Potatoes are Scotland's pride. There's much ado about "stovies", sliced potatoes and onions stewed together, sometimes with meat scraps. A mixture of boiled cabbage and mashed potatoes, possibly with onions or chives, goes by the name of "Rumbledethumps".

Scots delight in home-made crusty bread, scones, bannocks, pancakes and baps. Old-fashioned oatcakes are eaten with butter, pâté, jam or crowdie, Scotland's centuries-old version of cottage cheese. The renowned buttery shortbread keeps so well it's exported all over the world.

Cheeses to watch for: "Caboc", a Highland cream cheese coated in oatmeal; "Hramsa", a cream cheese with herbs and garlic.

"Crannachan" is a Scottish dessert of raspberries folded into a mixture of whipped cream and lightly toasted oat-

meal, sweetened with honey and a generous tot of whisky. Dundee, birthplace of bitter-orange marmalade, also contributes a popular fruit cake ("Dundee cake") and a crumble.

Drinks

A casual pub crawl might convince you that beer is *the* national drink. But there's much more to lift the spirits, including excellent English gin and Scotch whisky.

Sherry is a popular apéritif, a civilized prelude to a good meal. Some of the greatest brands are a legacy of the enterprising British families who emigrated to Jerez de la Frontera in southern Spain nearly two centuries ago.

Port was created in the 17th century when a heavy tax on French wines forced the British to turn to a Portuguese variety. But it proved too harsh for their palates, and was eventually "fortified" with brandy and then aged. Port is often served with the cheese course after dinner, but in restaurants you can ask for it as an apéritif, Continental-style.

Gin evolved about the same time as port, and for the same reason—the prohibitive wine tax. Originally a medicinal brew from Holland, it became such a rage by the mid-18th century that desperate addicts were killing themselves, swilling spurious substitutes containing sulfuric acid or turpentine. Today English gins are clear and pure spirits, with various secret-formula flavourings from such ingredients as coriander, cassia bark, liquorice, orange peel and—above all—juniper. Specify your proportions of gin to Vermouth if you want that all-American cocktail, the dry martini.

Beer is the overwhelming favourite. There's a bewildering variety of brews, depending on what region, town or pub you happen to be in. The preferred English beer is "bitter", clear and light amber-coloured, with body and distinctive flavour given by the malted barley, hops and yeast. Its alcoholic content is higher than American beers, and it's drunk at cellar temperature, which can

"Last orders, please!" Pub regulars recognize the familiar signal that time is running out. Britain's arcane and highly restrictive licensing laws have frustrated drinkers and mystified foreigners since they were introduced in World War I. Curtailed hours of operation, devised to keep the workers sober, have recently been relaxed, but pubs must still close relatively early.

Whisky comes from a Gaelic word meaning "water of life". If you hit Scotland's whisky trail (see p. 65), you'll be regaled with all the folklore and flavours involved in true whisky production: pure mountain water is used in the distillation of whisky, and even the terrain it flows through is important, as is the peat fire used for drying the malted barley.

It's generally conceded that the Irish invented whisky and set up distilleries in Scotland and Wales in the 16th century. The Scots, of course, did it their own way, producing spirits with such finesse that Scotch became the world's most famous whisky.

Scotch is most often a blend of two kinds: malt whisky, meaning the barley is malted or germinated before fermentation, and whiskies from other unmalted grains. While there are excellent blends well worth trying, the purists and especially Highlanders recognize unblended malt whisky as the only one for discerning drinkers.

A speciality of the West Country, English **cider** is not only deliciously thirst-quenching but can pack a terrific punch. Beautifully golden-amber, clear and sometimes sparkling, it can contain up to 8 per cent alcohol.

A few intrepid English **wine**-growers are making progress with their vintages, but their output is just a drop in the barrel compared to the enormous quantity needed to satisfy the growing British taste for wine. You probably won't have any trouble finding a decent claret, as the British call Bordeaux; you'll also come across Burgundy and Beaujolais, Alsace and even lesser-known wines from France, plus honourable wines from Germany, Italy, Spain, Yugoslavia and even Australia.

Post-prandial **brandy** used to be offered with cigars to men at dinner parties, while women sipped their coffee in another room, but that custom is dying out; and in any case, restaurants now offer a choice of digestifs from cognac to Grand Marnier—to both women and men.

also be disconcerting to Americans. It must not be pressurized or carbonated, but rather pulled from the keg by a pump handle, used gently. Another type of beer known as "mild" is reddish in colour and tastes somewhat sweeter than bitter. "Stout" is heavier, due to its high hops content. The brew known to Americans and Europeans as beer is "lager" to the British. Nowadays, with stiff drink-driving laws and health concerns, you can get bottled low-alcohol and no-alcohol beers in most pubs.

HOTELS AND RESTAURANTS

The Right Place
at the Right Price

Broadly, it has to be said, Britain's hotels are expensive. They can be superb; take the famous luxury establishments of London or those great country house hotels. Smaller establishments may be prized for their historical associations, or for their charm, character—and, on occasions, cuisine.

To help you choose, we have made a selection of hotels and restaurants in London and strategic points around the country, based on price, attraction and location and listed alphabetically by town. We have not, however, included bed-and-breakfast houses (B&Bs), a possibility well worth exploring (for more details, see p. 307). By the same token, we do not cover pizzerias, fast-food outlets, snack bars and "takeaways" which offer meals at more modest rates. Most restaurants advertise a lower-priced menu at lunchtime.

Map coordinates at the end of each hotel entry refer to the Road Atlas section.

KEY

🛏 **Hotel**   🍴 **Restaurant**

Hotels *(for double room with bath)*

🍴🍴🍴 Higher-priced: above £120
🍴🍴 Medium-priced: £60–120
🍴 Lower-priced: below £60

Restaurants
(for a three-course gourmet meal)

🍴🍴🍴 Higher-priced: above £25
🍴🍴 Medium-priced: £15–25
🍴 Lower-priced: below £15

Caledonian Thistle   🛏🍴🍴
10 Union Terrace
Aberdeen, Grampian AB9 1HE
Tel. (0224) 640233; tlx. 73758
80 rooms. Victorian building with modern facilities.
Sauna, solarium.   *19 D3*

New Marcliffe   🛏🍴🍴
51–53 Queen's Road
Aberdeen, Grampian AB9 2PE
Tel. (0224) 321371; tlx. 73225
28 rooms. Tasteful decor.   *19 D3*

Plas Penhelig   🛏🍴🍴
Aberdovey, Gwynedd LL35 0NA
Tel. (065472) 676
12 rooms. Edwardian country house in terraced gardens.
View. Tennis, croquet.
Closed Jan. and Feb.   *11 C2*

Kirkstone Foot   🛏🍴🍴
Country House
Kirkstone Pass Road
Ambleside, Cumbria LA22 9EH
Tel. (05394) 32232
15 rooms. Attractive 17th-century manor house.
Traditional English cuisine.
Closed Dec. and Jan.   *12 B2*

Rothay Manor   🛏🍴🍴
Rothay Bridge
Ambleside, Cumbria LA22 0EH
Tel. (05394) 33605
15 rooms. Elegant late-Georgian house. Attractive interior. Croquet.
Closed Jan. to mid-Feb.   *12 B2*

Arisaig House   🛏🍴🍴🍴
Beasdale
Arisaig, Highland PH39 4NR
(3 mi./5 km. south-east on A 830)
Tel. (06875) 622; tlx. 777279

14 rooms. Pleasant hotel in old mansion. Magnificent setting above Loch nan Uamh. Good cuisine.
Closed Nov. to end-March.   *18 A3*

Norfolk Arms   🛏🍴🍴
22 High Street
Arundel, West Sussex BN18 9AD
Tel. (0903) 882101; tlx. 878436
34 rooms. 18th-century coaching inn.   *6 B2*

Bell Inn   🛏🍴🍴🍴
Aston Clinton, Buckinghamshire
HP22 5HP
(Aylesbury 4 mi./6 km.)
Tel. (0296) 630252; tlx. 83252
21 rooms. Charming old coaching inn. Converted stables. Rose gardens. Good cuisine. Croquet.   *6 B1*

Tullich Lodge   🛏🍴🍴
Ballater, Grampian AB3 5SB
Tel. (0338) 55406
10 rooms. Pleasant hotel in country house. View of the Dee Valley.
Closed Nov. to March.   *19 C3*

Lord Crewe Arms   🛏🍴🍴
Front Street
Bamburgh, Northumberland
NE69 7BL
Tel. (06684) 243
24 rooms. Peaceful location.
Closed Nov. to March.   *15 B3*

Downrew House   🛏🍴🍴
Bishop's Tawton
Barnstaple, Devon EX32 0DY
(2 mi./3 km. south on A 377)
Tel. (0271) 42497
13 rooms. 18th-century country house. Golf, tennis, swimming pool, solarium. Closed Dec. 28 to mid-March.   *4-5 C2*

Pratts 🖼 ➡ ▯▯
South Parade
Bath, Avon BA2 4AB
Tel. (0225) 60441; tlx. 444827
46 rooms. Pleasant
Georgian house. 5 D2

The Priory 🖼 ➡ ▯▯▯
Weston Road
Bath, Avon BA1 2XT
Tel. (0225) 331922; tlx. 44612
21 rooms. Attractive, elegant hotel.
Good cuisine. View. Garden,
swimming pool. 5 D2

Royal Crescent 🖼 ➡ ▯▯▯
16 Royal Crescent
Bath, Avon BA1 2LS
Tel. (0225) 319090; tlx. 444251
45 rooms. Pleasant luxury hotel in
exquisite 18th-century town house.
Good cuisine. View. Garden, spa
pools, croquet. 5 D2

King's Arms 🖼 ➡ ▯▯
43 Hide Hill
Berwick-upon-Tweed,
Northumberland TD15 1EJ
Tel. (0289) 307454; tlx. 848608
36 rooms. Impressive
stone building. 15 B3

Durrant House 🖼 ➡ ▯▯
Heywood Road, Northam
Bideford, Devon EX39 3QB
(1 mi./1.6 km. north on A 386)
Tel. (02372) 72361; tlx. 46740
85 rooms. Georgian and modern.
Swimming pool,
sauna, solarium. 4-5 B2

Yeoldon House 🖼 ➡ ▯▯
Durrant Lane, Northam
Bideford, Devon EX39 2RL
(1 mi./1.6 km. north on A 386)
Tel. (02372) 74400; tlx. 46410
10 rooms. Country house overlooking
the River Torridge.
Sauna, solarium. 4-5 B2

Copthorne 🖼 ➡ ▯▯▯
Paradise Circus
Birmingham, West Midlands
B3 3HJ
Tel. (021) 200 2727; tlx. 339026
215 rooms. Indoor swimming pool,
sauna, solarium.
Central location. 8 A2-3

Plough & Harrow 🖼 ➡ ▯▯
135 Hagley Road, Edgbaston
Birmingham, West Midlands
B16 8LS
Tel. (021) 454 4111; tlx. 338074
44 rooms. Prestigious hotel.
Sauna. 8 A2-3

Sloan's ➡ ▯▯
Chad Square, Hawthorne Road,
Edgbaston
Birmingham, West Midlands
B15 3TQ
Tel. (021) 455 6697
Good cuisine. Well-known
French-style restaurant.
Closed Sat. lunch, Sun. evening,
Bank Holidays, Xmas
and New Year. 8 A2-3

White Hart 🖼 ➡ ▯
Bridge Foot
Boston, Lincolnshire PE21 8SH
Tel. (0205) 64877
23 rooms. Regency-style
building. 9 C2

Chinehead 🖼 ➡ ▯
31 Alumhurst Road
Bournemouth, Dorset BH4 8EN
Tel. (0202) 752777
24 rooms. Friendly atmosphere.
Good home cooking. 6 A2

Cliffeside 🖼 ➡ ▯▯
32 East Overcliff Drive
Bournemouth, Dorset BH1 3AQ
Tel. (0202) 25724; tlx. 418297
62 rooms. Panoramic view.
Swimming pool. 6 A2

Highcliff 🖼 ➡ ▯▯▯
105 St. Michael's Road, West Cliff
Bournemouth, Dorset BH2 5DU
Tel. (0202) 27702; tlx. 417153
111 rooms. Clifftop location. Tennis,
croquet, swimming pool, sauna,
solarium. 6 A2

Mason's Arms 🖼 ➡ ▯▯
Branscombe, **Devon EX12 3DJ**
(Lyme Regis 11 mi./18 km.)
Tel. (029780) 300
21 rooms. 14th-century thatched inn.
Renowned restaurant. 5 C2

Waterside Inn ➡ ▯▯▯
Ferry Road
Bray-on-Thames, Berkshire
SL6 2AT
(Reading 13 mi./21 km.)
Tel. (0628) 20691; tlx. 8813079
Outstanding French cuisine.
Elegant riverside restaurant.
Closed Tues. lunch, Sun. evening,
Mon. and 7 weeks
from Dec. 26. 6 B2

Wellington 🖼 ➡ ▯
The Bulwark
Brecon, Powys LD3 7AD
Tel. (0874) 5225
21 rooms. Pleasant Georgian
hotel. 11 C3

Old Ship 🖼 ➡ ▯▯
King's Road
Brighton and Hove, East Sussex
BN1 1NR
Tel. (0273) 29001; tlx. 877101
153 rooms.
Pleasant hotel with view.
Traditional services. 6 B2

St. Catherine's Lodge 🖼 ➡ ▯▯
Kingsway, Hove
Brighton and Hove, East Sussex
BN3 2RZ
Tel. (0273) 778181; tlx. 877073
52 rooms. Well-established
seafront hotel opposite King Alfred
Leisure Centre. 6 B2

Whitehaven 🖼 ➡ ▯▯
34 Wilbury Road, Hove
Brighton and Hove, East Sussex
BN3 3JP
Tel. (0273) 778355; tlx. 877159
17 rooms. Friendly
hotel in quiet residential area.
Solarium. 6 B2

Barbizon ➡ ▯▯
43–45 Corn Street
Bristol, Avon BS1 1HT
Tel. (0272) 262658
French cuisine. Stylish restaurant.
Closed Sat. lunch, Sun.,
Bank Holidays and 3 weeks
in Aug. 5 D2

Clifton 🖼 ➡ ▯
St. Paul's Road, Clifton
Bristol, Avon BS8 1LX
Tel. (0272) 736882; tlx 449075
64 rooms. Attractive
restaurant and bar.
Close to city centre. 5 D2

Holiday Inn 🖼 ➡ ▯▯▯
2 Lower Castle Street, Old Market
Bristol, Avon BS1 3AD
Tel. (0272) 294281; tlx. 449720
284 rooms. Indoor swimming pool,
sauna, solarium, gymnasium.
Central location. 5 D2

Unicorn 🖼 ➡ ▯▯
Prince Street
Bristol, Avon BS1 4QF
Tel. (0272) 230333; tlx. 44315
194 rooms. Modern. Central
location. 5 D2

Quayside 🖼 ➡ ▯▯
41–49 King Street
Brixham, Devon TQ5 9TJ
Tel. (08045) 55751; tlx. 946240
30 rooms. Old hotel
overlooking the harbour.
Sailing. 5 C3

Buckland Manor ⌂ ⌸ ▯▯▯
Buckland
**Broadway, Hereford and
Worcester WR12 7LY**
(2 mi./3 km. south-west by B 4632)
Tel. (0386) 852626
*11 rooms. Pleasant hotel in ancient
Cotswold country house. Good
cuisine. Tennis, swimming pool.
Closed mid-Jan. to mid-Feb.*   *8 A3*

Lygon Arms ⌂ ⌸ ▯▯▯
High Street
**Broadway, Hereford and
Worcester WR12 7DU**
Tel. (0386) 852255; tlx. 338260
*64 rooms. Pleasant hotel. Part
15th-century inn. Tennis.*   *8 A3*

Carey's Manor ⌂ ⌸ ▯▯
Lyndhurst Road
**Brockenhurst, Hampshire
SO42 7RH**
Tel. (0590) 23551; tlx. 47442
*80 rooms. Gardens. Indoor swimming
pool, sauna, solarium.*   *6 A2*

Hartland ⌂ ⌸ ▯
Hartland Terrace
Bude, Cornwall EX23 8JY
Tel. (0288) 55661
*29 rooms. Overlooking the beach.
Swimming pool.
Closed Nov. to Easter.*   *4 B2*

Angel ⌂ ⌸ ▯▯
3 Angel Hill
**Bury St. Edmunds, Suffolk
IP33 1LT**
Tel. (0284) 753926; tlx. 81630
*41 rooms. A coaching inn since 1482.
Period atmosphere. Central.*   *9 C3*

Portland ⌂ ⌸ ▯
32 St. John's Road
Buxton, Derbyshire SK17 6XQ
Tel. (0298) 2462
*26 rooms. Converted Victorian
houses.*   *8 A2*

Arundel House ⌂ ⌸ ▯
53 Chesterton Road
**Cambridge, Cambridgeshire
CB4 3AN**
Tel. (0223) 67701; tlx. 817936
*88 rooms. Overlooking the river.
Central location.
Closed Dec. 25 and 26.*   *9 C3*

Garden House ⌂ ⌸ ▯▯▯
Granta Place
**Cambridge, Cambridgeshire
CB2 1RT**
Tel. (0223) 63421; tlx. 81463
*117 rooms. Modern. Riverside
gardens. Central location.*   *9 C3*

Falstaff ⌂ ⌸ ▯
8–12 St. Dunstan's Street
Canterbury, Kent CT2 8AF
Tel. (0227) 462138; tlx. 96394
*25 rooms. 15th-century
coaching inn.*   *7 D2*

Angel ⌂ ⌸ ▯▯
Castle Street
**Cardiff, South Glamorgan
CF1 2QZ**
Tel. (0222) 232633; tlx. 498132
*91 rooms. Elegant.
Central location.*   *5 C2*

La Chaumiere ⌸ ▯▯
44 Cardiff Road, Llandaff
**Cardiff, South Glamorgan
CF5 2XX**
Tel. (0222) 555319
*Good French cuisine. Closed Sat.
lunch, Sun. evening, Mon.
and Jan. 1 to 14.*   *5 C2*

Royal ⌂ ⌸ ▯
St. Mary Street
**Cardiff, South Glamorgan
CF1 1LL**
Tel. (0222) 383321; tlx. 498062
*63 rooms. Victorian. Central
location.*   *5 C2*

Central ⌂ ⌸ ▯
Victoria Viaduct
Carlisle, Cumbria CA3 8AL
Tel. (0228) 20256
70 rooms. Central location.   *12 B2*

Swallow Hilltop ⌂ ⌸ ▯▯
London Road
Carlisle, Cumbria CA1 2PQ
Tel. (0228) 29255; tlx. 64292
*97 rooms. Modern. Golf, indoor
swimming pool, sauna, solarium,
gymnasium.*   *12 B2*

De La Bere ⌂ ⌸ ▯▯
Southam
**Cheltenham, Gloucestershire
GL52 3NH**
(3 mi./5 km. north-east on A 46)
Tel. (0242) 37771; tlx. 43232
*60 rooms. Tudor manor house. Good
restaurants. Tennis, squash,
sauna, solarium.*   *8 A3*

Greenway ⌂ ⌸ ▯▯▯
Shurdington
**Cheltenham, Gloucestershire
GL51 5UG**
(4 mi./6 km. south-west on A 46)
Tel. (0242) 862352; tlx. 437216
*19 rooms. Tastefully furnished
Cotswold manor house. Good
cuisine. Croquet. Closed Dec. 28
to mid-Jan.*   *8 A3*

The Chester ⌂ ⌸ ▯▯▯
Grosvenor
Eastgate Street
Chester, Cheshire CH1 1LT
Tel. (0244) 324024; tlx. 61240
*87 rooms. Luxury hotel.
Friendly atmosphere.
Sauna, solarium.*   *11 D2*

Crabwall Manor ⌂ ⌸ ▯▯
Parkgate Road, Mollington
Chester, Cheshire CH1 6NE
(2 mi./3 km. north-west on A 540)
Tel. (0244) 851666; tlx. 61220
*32 rooms. Luxurious
countryside hotel with 16th-century
origins.*   *11 D2*

Green Bough ⌂ ⌸ ▯
60 Hoole Road
Chester, Cheshire CH2 3NL
Tel. (0244) 326241
*11 rooms. Pleasant, family-run
hotel. Closed Xmas.*   *11 D2*

The Dolphin & Anchor ⌂ ⌸ ▯▯
West Street
Chichester, West Sussex PO19 1QE
Tel. (0243) 785121
*54 rooms.
Combination of two old inns.
Central location opposite
the cathedral.*   *6 B2*

Cotswold House ⌂ ⌸ ▯▯
The Square
**Chipping Campden, Gloucester-
shire GL55 6AN**
Tel. (0386) 840330; tlx. 336810
*15 rooms. Attractive Regency
town house. Croquet.*   *8 A3*

Fleece ⌂ ⌸ ▯▯
Market Place
**Cirencester, Gloucestershire
GL7 4NZ**
Tel. (0285) 68507; tlx. 437287
*25 rooms. Tudor inn.
Closed Dec. 24 and 25.*   *8 A3*

De Vere ⌂ ⌸ ▯▯
Cathedral Square
**Coventry, West Midlands
CV1 5RP**
Tel. (0203) 633733; tlx. 31380
*190 rooms. Modern. Central
location.*   *8 A3*

Old Mill ⌂ ⌸ ▯
Mill Hill, Baginton
**Coventry, West Midlands
CV8 2BS**
(3 mi./5 km. south by A444 off A45)
Tel. (0203) 303588
*20 rooms. Attractively
converted mill.*   *8 A3*

Carved Angel ═▬ 🛏🛏🛏
2 South Embankment
Dartmouth, Devon TQ6 9BH
Tel. (08043) 2465
Good cuisine. Quayside location.
Closed Sun. evening, Mon.,
Xmas and Jan. 5 C3

Royal Castle 🛁═▬🛏🛏
11 The Quay
Dartmouth, Devon TQ6 9PS
Tel. (08043) 4004
21 rooms. Former coaching inn of
historic interest. View. 5 C3

Maison Talbooth 🛁🛏🛏🛏
Stratford Road
Dedham, Essex CO7 6HN
(Colchester 8 mi./13 km.)
Tel. (0206) 322367; tlx. 987083
10 rooms. Luxuriously converted
Victorian house. Garden. 9 D3

Le Talbooth ═▬🛏🛏🛏
Gun Hill
Dedham, Essex CO7 6HP
(Colchester 8 mi./13 km.)
Tel. (0206) 323150; tlx. 987083
English and French cuisine.
Charming cottage on the banks
of the River Stour. 9 D3

Midland 🛁═▬🛏🛏
Midland Road
Derby, Derbyshire DE1 2SQ
Tel. (0332) 45894; tlx 378373
60 rooms. Pleasant old railway hotel.
Closed Dec. 25, 26 and
Jan. 1. 8 A2

Pennine 🛁═▬🛏🛏
Macklin Street
Derby, Derbyshire DE1 1LF
Tel. (0332) 41741; tlx. 377545
100 rooms. Modern. Central. 8 A2

Cliffe Court 🛁═▬🛏
25–26 Marine Parade
Dover, Kent CT16 1LU
Tel. (0304) 211001
25 rooms. Central location on the
seafront. Friendly. 7 D2

White Cliffs 🛁═▬🛏
Sea Front
Dover, Kent CT17 9BW
Tel. (0304) 203633; tlx. 965422
54 rooms. Good view of the harbour.
Closed Dec. 24 to 26. 7 D2

Royal County 🛁═▬🛏🛏🛏
Old Elvet
Durham, Durham DH1 3JN
Tel. (091) 386 6821; tlx. 538238
118 rooms. Historic hotel overlook-
ing the river. Sauna. 13 C2

Downland 🛁═▬🛏
37 Lewes Road
Eastbourne, East Sussex BN21 2BU
Tel. (0323) 32689
16 rooms. Warm atmosphere.
Simple home cooking. 7 C2

Grand 🛁═▬🛏🛏🛏
King Edward's Parade
Eastbourne, East Sussex
BN21 4EQ
Tel. (0323) 412345; tlx. 87332
178 rooms. Victorian seafront hotel.
Swimming pools, sauna. 7 C2

Lansdowne 🛁═▬🛏🛏
King Edward's Parade
Eastbourne, East Sussex BN21 4EE
Tel. (0323) 25174; tlx. 878624
134 rooms. Seafront hotel close to
theatres and shops.
Closed Jan. 1 to 14. 7 C2

Cairn 🛁═▬🛏🛏
10–18 Windsor Street
Edinburgh, Lothian EH7 5JR
Tel. (031) 557 0175
52 rooms. Friendly atmosphere.
East of the city centre. 15 A3

Caledonian 🛁═▬🛏🛏🛏
Princes Street
Edinburgh, Lothian EH1 2AB
Tel. (031) 225 2433; tlx. 72179
238 rooms. Distinguished luxury
hotel. Central location near
Edinburgh Castle. 15 A3

Handsel's ═▬🛏🛏🛏
22 Stafford Street
Edinburgh, Lothian EH3 7BD
Tel. (031) 225 5521
Good cuisine. Closed Sat. lunch,
Sun. and 1 week in Jan. 15 A3

King James Thistle 🛁═▬🛏🛏
107 St. James Centre
Edinburgh, Lothian EH1 3SW
Tel. (031) 556 0111; tlx. 727200
147 rooms. Smart. Central
location. 15 A3

Martins ═▬🛏🛏
70 Rose Street, North Lane
Edinburgh, Lothian EH2 3DX
Tel. (031) 225 3106
Inventive menu. Cheerful.
Closed Sat. lunch, Sun., Mon.,
Xmas and New Year. 15 A3

Roxburghe 🛁═▬🛏🛏
38 Charlotte Square
Edinburgh, Lothian EH2 4HG
Tel. (031) 225 3921; tlx. 727054
75 rooms. Traditional. Elegant.
Close to Princes Street. 15 A3

Barton Cross 🛁═▬🛏🛏
Huxham
Exeter, Devon EX5 4EJ
(5 mi./8 km. north by A 377)
Tel. (039284) 245; tlx. 42603
6 rooms. Part 16th- and 17th-century
cottage. 5 C2

Buckerell Lodge 🛁═▬🛏🛏
Topsham Road
Exeter, Devon EX2 4SQ
Tel. (0392) 52451; tlx. 42410
54 rooms. Part 12th-century
buildings. 5 C2

St. Olaves Court 🛁═▬🛏🛏
Mary Arches Street
Exeter, Devon EX4 3AZ
Tel. (0392) 217736
53 rooms. Attractive, centrally
located Georgian hotel with good
restaurant. Closed Xmas and
New Year. 5 C2

White Hart 🛁═▬🛏
65–66 South Street
Exeter, Devon EX1 1EE
Tel. (0392) 79897; tlx. 42521
61 rooms. Part 14th-century
inn with 15th-century
wine room and bars.
Closed Dec. 25 and 26. 5 C2

Royal Beacon 🛁═▬🛏🛏
The Beacon
Exmouth, Devon EX8 2AF
Tel. (0395) 264886; tlx. 94016961
35 rooms. Georgian
posting house
overlooking the sea. 5 C2

Penmere Manor 🛁═▬🛏🛏
Mongleath Road
Falmouth, Cornwall TR11 4PN
Tel. (0326) 314545; tlx. 45608
32 rooms. Overlooking Falmouth
Bay. Swimming pools, sauna,
solarium. 4 A3

Garden House 🛁═▬🛏
142 Sandgate Road
Folkestone, Kent CT20 2BL
Tel. (0303) 52278
42 rooms. Refurbished
Victorian house.
Central location. 7 D2

Inverlochy Castle 🛁═▬🛏🛏🛏
Fort William, Highland PH33 6BN
(3 mi./5 km. north-east on A 82)
Tel. (0397) 2177; tlx. 776229
16 rooms. Attractive luxury hotel in
Victorian castle. Splendid view of the
loch and mountains. Good food.
Tennis, fishing. Closed mid-Nov.
to mid-March. 18 A3

The Albany 🖼️═▯▯
Bothwell Street
Glasgow, Strathclyde G2 7EN
Tel. (041) 248 2656; tlx. 77440
254 rooms. Modern hotel with view.
Central location. *17 D3*

Holiday Inn 🖼️═▯▯
500 Argyle Street, Anderston
Glasgow, Strathclyde G3 8RR
Tel. (041) 226 5577; tlx. 776355
304 rooms. High-rise. Central
location. Indoor swimming pool,
sauna, solarium, squash. *17 D3*

One Devonshire 🖼️═▯▯▯
Gardens
1 Devonshire Gardens
Glasgow, Strathclyde G12 0UX
Tel. (041) 339 2001
8 rooms. Victorian mansion house.
Elegant and comfortable. *17 D3*

George & Pilgrims 🖼️═▯▯
1 High Street
Glastonbury, Somerset BA6 9DP
Tel. (0458) 31146
14 rooms.
Part 15th-century inn. *5 D2*

Hatton Court 🖼️═▯▯
Upton St. Leonards
Gloucester, Gloucestershire
GL4 8DE
(3 mi./5 km. south-east on B 4073)
Tel. (0452) 617412; tlx. 437334
46 rooms. View across the Severn
Valley. Swimming pool. *11 D3*

Michael's Nook 🖼️═▯▯▯
Grasmere, Cumbria LA22 9RP
Tel. (09665) 496; tlx. 65329
11 rooms. Pleasant hotel in peaceful
Lakeland country house. Antique
furnishing. Good cuisine. *12 B2*

Ayton Hall 🖼️═▯▯
Low Green
Great Ayton, North Yorkshire
TS9 6BW
Tel. (0642) 723595
9 rooms. Historic countryside house.
Antique furnishing. Tennis. *13 D2*

Le Manoir aux 🖼️═▯▯▯
Quat' Saisons
Church Road
Great Milton, Oxfordshire
OX9 7PD
(Oxford 12 mi./19 km.)
Tel. (08446) 8881; tlx. 837552
10 rooms. Attractive, elegant 15th-
and 16th-century manor house.
Outstanding cuisine. Riding, tennis,
croquet, swimming pool. View.
Closed Dec. 24 to Jan. 20. *6 B1*

Greywalls 🖼️═▯▯
Duncar Road
Gullane, Lothian EH31 2EG
Tel. (0620) 842144; tlx. 72294
23 rooms. Attractive country house.
Magnificent view.
Golf, tennis, croquet.
Closed Nov. to mid-April. *15 A3*

Gables 🖼️═▯
2 West Grove Road
Harrogate, North Yorkshire
HG1 2AD
Tel. (0423) 505625
9 rooms. Converted
Victorian house.
Central location. *13 C3*

Studley 🖼️═▯▯
28 Swan Road
Harrogate, North Yorkshire
HG1 2SE
Tel. (0423) 60425; tlx. 57506
40 rooms. Attractive hotel
near Valley Gardens.
Good cuisine. *13 C3*

Cliff 🖼️═▯
Marine Parade, Dovercourt
Harwich, Essex CO12 3RE
Tel. (0255) 503345; tlx. 98372
30 rooms. Seafront. *9 D3*

Beauport Park 🖼️═▯▯
Battle Road
Hastings, East Sussex TN38 8EA
Tel. (0424) 51222; tlx. 957126
23 rooms. Georgian house in
formal gardens.
Riding, golf, tennis, squash,
croquet, swimming pool. *7 C2*

Black Swan 🖼️═▯▯
Market Place
Helmsley, North Yorkshire
YO6 5BJ
Tel. (0439) 70466; tlx. 57538
38 rooms. Picturesque 16th-century
inn. Comfortable. *13 D3*

The Green Dragon 🖼️═▯▯
Broad Street
Hereford, Hereford and Worcester
HR4 9BG
Tel. (0432) 272506; tlx. 35491
88 rooms. Traditional. Central
location. *11 D3*

Imperial 🖼️═▯▯
Princes Parade
Hythe, Kent CT21 6AE
Tel. (0303) 67441; tlx. 965082
83 rooms. Seafront hotel.
Golf, tennis, squash, croquet,
swimming pool, sauna,
solarium, gymnasium. *7 D2*

Langleigh 🖼️═▯
Langleigh Road
Ilfracombe, Devon EX34 8EA
Tel. (0271) 62629
8 rooms. Georgian country
house. Garden. *4-5 C2*

Culloden House 🖼️═▯▯▯
Culloden
Inverness, Highland IV1 2NZ
(3 mi./5 km. east on A 82)
Tel. (0463) 790461; tlx. 75402
20 rooms. Near site of the 1746
battle. Period decorations. Tennis,
sauna, solarium. *18 B2*

Kingsmills 🖼️═▯▯
Culcabock Road
Inverness, Highland IV2 3LP
Tel. (0463) 237166; tlx. 75566
68 rooms. Landscaped gardens.
Squash, indoor swimming pool,
sauna, gymnasium. *18 B2*

Hintlesham Hall 🖼️═▯▯▯
Hintlesham
Ipswich, Suffolk IP8 3NS
(5 mi./8 km. west by A 1214 on
A 1071)
Tel. (047387) 268; tlx. 98340
24 rooms. Pleasant hotel.
16th-century country house in
a park. Good cuisine. Tennis,
fishing, riding, croquet. *9 D3*

Sunlaws House 🖼️═▯▯
Heiton
Kelso, Borders TD5 8JZ
(3 mi./5 km. south-west by A 698)
Tel. (0573) 331; tlx. 728147
21 rooms. Charming Victorian
country mansion. View. Tennis,
croquet, fishing. *15 A3*

Garden House 🖼️═▯
Fowling Lane
Kendal, Cumbria LA9 6PH
Tel. (0539) 31131
10 rooms. Pleasant hotel in garden.
Closed Xmas. *12 B3*

Ardsheal House 🖼️═▯▯▯
Kentallen, **Highland PA38 4BX**
(Fort William 17 mi./27 km.)
Tel. (063174) 227
13 rooms. Historic house in lochside
setting. View. Good cuisine. Tennis.
Closed Nov. to Easter. *16-17 C2*

Grange 🖼️═▯
Country House
Manor Brow, Ambleside Road
Keswick, Cumbria CA12 4BA
Tel. (07687) 72500
11 rooms. Pleasant hotel with
panoramic view. *12 B2*

Congham Hall ⌂⇔🍽🍽
Lynn Road, Grimston
King's Lynn, Norfolk PE32 1AH
(6 mi./10 km. north-east by A 148)
Tel. (0485) 600250; tlx. 81508
11 rooms. Charming hotel.
Handsome Georgian country house.
View. Good cuisine. Tennis, croquet,
swimming pool. 9 C2

The Swan ⌂⇔🍽🍽
High Street
Lavenham, Suffolk CO10 9QA
(Colchester 22 mi./35 km.)
Tel. (0787) 247477; tlx. 987198
48 rooms. Picturesque Tudor
houses. 9 C3

The Metropole ⌂⇔🍽🍽
King Street
Leeds, West Yorkshire LS1 2HQ
Tel. (0532) 450841; tlx. 557755
110 rooms. Victorian and modern.
Central Carvery restaurant. 13 C3

The Queen's ⌂⇔🍽🍽
City Square
Leeds, West Yorkshire LS1 1PL
Tel. (0532) 431323; tlx. 55161
198 rooms. Impressive building.
Central location. Sauna. 13 C3

Belmont ⌂⇔🍽🍽
De Montfort Street
Leicester, Leicestershire LE1 7GR
Tel. (0533) 544773; tlx. 34619
56 rooms. Victorian. 8 A-B2

Hillcrest ⌂⇔🍽
15 Lindum Terrace
Lincoln, Lincolnshire LN2 5RT
Tel. (0522) 510182
17 rooms. Former Victorian rectory.
View, garden. Closed Xmas and
New Year. 8 B2

The White Hart ⌂⇔🍽🍽
Bailgate
Lincoln, Lincolnshire LN1 3AR
Tel. (0522) 26222; tlx. 56304
49 rooms. Early Georgian house
near the cathedral. 8 B2

Liverpool Moat House ⌂⇔🍽🍽
Paradise Street
Liverpool, Merseyside L1 8JD
Tel. (051) 709 0181; tlx. 627270
258 rooms. Modern. Central. Indoor
swimming pool, sauna. 11 D1

St. George's ⌂⇔🍽🍽
St. John's Precinct, Lime Street
Liverpool, Merseyside L1 1NQ
Tel. (051) 709 7090; tlx. 627630
155 rooms. Modern. Opposite
Lime Street Station. 11 D1

Housel Bay ⌂⇔🍽🍽
Housel Cove
The Lizard, Cornwall TR12 7PG
Tel. (0326) 290417
25 rooms. Breathtaking view.
Quiet location.
Closed Jan. 4 A3

The Metropole ⌂⇔🍽
Temple Street
Llandrindod Wells, Powys
LD1 5DY
Tel. (0597) 2881; tlx. 35237
121 rooms. Town-centre hotel.
Relaxed atmosphere.
Indoor swimming pool, sauna,
solarium. 11 C3

Bodysgallen Hall ⌂⇔🍽🍽
Llandudno, Gwynedd LL30 1RS
Tel. (0492) 584466; tlx. 617163
28 rooms. Pleasant hotel.
17th-century house in
terraced gardens. View.
Elegant comfort. Tennis,
croquet. 11 C2

Dunoon ⌂⇔🍽
Gloddaeth Street
Llandudno, Gwynedd LL30 2DW
Tel. (0492) 860787
56 rooms. Friendly atmosphere.
Solarium. Central location. Closed
Nov. to mid-March. 11 C2

Amsterdam ⌂🍽
7 Trebovir Road, Earl's Court
London SW5 9LS
Tel. (01) 370 2814; tlx. 8952387
20 rooms. Pleasant bed-and-
breakfast hotel.

L'Arlequin ⇔🍽🍽🍽
123 Queenstown Road, Battersea
London SW8 3RH
Tel. (01) 622 0555
Good French cuisine. Relaxed
atmosphere. Closed Sat., Sun.,
3 weeks in Aug.–Sept. and 1 week
at Xmas.

Athenaeum ⌂⇔🍽🍽🍽
116 Piccadilly, Mayfair
London W1V 0BJ
Tel. (01) 499 3464; tlx. 261589
112 rooms. Luxury hotel overlooking
Green Park. High-quality French
cuisine.

The Berkeley ⌂⇔🍽🍽🍽
Wilton Place, Knightsbridge
London SW1X 7RL
Tel. (01) 235 6000; tlx. 919252
160 rooms. Fairly modern luxury
hotel with traditional standards.
Indoor swimming pool.

Bloomsbury Crest ⌂⇔🍽🍽
Coram Street, Bloomsbury
London WC1N 1HT
Tel. (01) 837 1200; tlx. 22113
175 rooms. Modern. Carvery
restaurant.

Bombay Brasserie ⇔🍽🍽
Courtfield Close, 140 Gloucester
Road, South Kensington
London SW7 4QH
Tel. (01) 370 4040
Indian cuisine. Authentic
regional dishes.

Brown's ⌂⇔🍽🍽🍽
29–34 Albermarle Street, Mayfair
London W1A 4SW
Tel. (01) 493 6020; tlx. 28686
130 rooms. Traditional British hotel.

Capital ⌂⇔🍽🍽🍽
22–24 Basil Street, Knightsbridge
London SW3 1AT
Tel. (01) 589 5171; tlx. 919042
60 rooms. Elegant modern hotel with
atmosphere. Good cuisine.

Central Park ⌂⇔🍽🍽
Queensborough Terrace, Bayswater
London W2 3SS
Tel. (01) 229 2424; tlx. 27342
241 rooms. Contemporary hotel with
attractive restaurant.

Claridge's ⌂⇔🍽🍽🍽
Brook Street, Mayfair
London W1A 2JQ
Tel. (01) 629 8860; tlx. 21872
190 rooms. Distinguished luxury
hotel favoured by royalty
and VIPs.

Connaught ⌂⇔🍽🍽🍽
16 Carlos Place, Mayfair
London W1Y 6AL
Tel. (01) 499 7070
90 rooms. Pleasant luxury hotel
with traditional comfort and
excellent cuisine.

Dan's ⇔🍽
119 Sidney Street, Chelsea
London SW3 6NR
Tel. (01) 352 2718
English and French. Cheerful.
Simple, good-quality food. Closed
Sat. lunch, Sun., Bank Holidays and
1 week at Xmas.

Duke's ⌂⇔🍽🍽🍽
35 St. James's Place, St. James's
London SW1A 1NY
Tel. (01) 491 4840; tlx. 28283
58 rooms. Pleasant hotel. Charming
Edwardian house. Good cuisine.

Durrants 📖 ═ ▯▯
26–32 George Street, Marylebone
London W1H 6BJ
Tel. (01) 935 8131; tlx. 894919
96 rooms. Converted Georgian
house.

Ebury Court 📖 ═ ▯▯
26 Ebury Street, Victoria
London SW1W 0LU
Tel. (01) 730 8147
38 rooms. Old-fashioned, homey
hotel near Victoria Coach Station.

Edward Lear 📖 ═ ▯
30 Seymour Street, Marylebone
London W1H 5WD
Tel. (01) 402 5401
30 rooms. Georgian town house with
informal atmosphere.

Elizabeth 📖 ▯
37 Eccleston Square, Victoria
London SW1V 1PB
Tel. (01) 828 6812
23 rooms. Quiet hotel behind Victoria
Station. Friendly atmosphere.

Le Gavroche ═ ▯▯▯
43 Upper Brook Street, Mayfair
London W1P 1PF
Tel. (01) 408 0881
Outstanding French cuisine.
Closed Sat., Sun., Bank Holidays
and Dec. 23 to Jan. 2.

Gore 📖 ═ ▯▯▯
189 Queen's Gate, South Kensington
London SW7 5EX
Tel. (01) 584 6601; tlx. 296244
54 rooms. Attractive decor.

Goring 📖 ═ ▯▯▯
15 Beeston Place, Grosvenor
Gardens, Victoria
London SW1W 0JW
Tel. (01) 834 8211; tlx. 919166
90 rooms. Traditional English hotel
with pleasant restaurant.

Hilaire ═ ▯▯
68 Old Brompton Road, South
Kensington
London SW7 3LQ
Tel. (01) 584 8993
Good French cuisine. Smart.
Unpretentious. Closed Sat. lunch,
Sun., Xmas and Bank Holidays.

Kensington Close 📖 ═ ▯▯
Wright's Lane, Kensington
London W8 5SP
Tel. (01) 937 8170; tlx. 23914
524 rooms. Large and busy. Indoor
swimming pool, sauna, solarium,
squash, fitness centre.

London Ryan 📖 ═ ▯▯
Gwynne Place, Kings Cross Road,
Finsbury
London WC1X 9QN
Tel. (01) 278 2480; tlx. 27728
211 rooms. Modern hotel with well-
equipped rooms.

London Tara 📖 ═ ▯▯
Scarsdale Place, Wrights Lane,
Kensington
London W8 5SR
Tel. (01) 937 7211; tlx. 918834
831 rooms. Lively, modern hotel.

Ma Cuisine ═ ▯▯
113 Walton Street, Brompton
London SW3 2EP
Tel. (01) 584 7585
Good French cuisine. Small, well
appointed. Closed Sat. lunch, Sun.
and Bank Holidays.

Martin's ═ ▯▯
239 Baker Street, Marylebone
London NW1 6XE
Tel. (01) 935 3130
English cuisine. Smart.
Contemporary decor.
Closed Sat. lunch, Sun., Easter
and Bank Holidays.

Novotel London 📖 ═ ▯▯
1 Shortlands, Hammersmith
London W6 8DR
Tel. (01) 741 1555; tlx. 934539
640 rooms. Modern facilities.

Odin's ═ ▯▯
27 Devonshire Street, Marylebone
London W1N 1RJ
Tel. (01) 935 7296
Good English cuisine. Comfortable,
interesting. Closed Sat. lunch, Sun.
and Public Holidays.

Poon's of Russell Square ═ ▯
50 Woburn Place, Bloomsbury
London WC1H 0JZ
Tel. (01) 580 1188
Chinese cuisine. Authentic dishes.
Closed Xmas.

Red Fort ═ ▯▯
77 Dean Street, Soho
London W1V 5HA
Tel. (01) 437 2525
Indian cuisine.
Genuine regional dishes.
Closed Dec. 25 and 26.

Regent Palace 📖 ═ ▯▯
Glasshouse Street, Piccadilly Circus
London W1A 4BZ
Tel. (01) 734 7000; tlx. 23740
879 rooms. Good value-for-money.

Rue St. Jacques ═ ▯▯▯
5 Charlotte Street, Bloomsbury
London W1P 1HD
Tel. (01) 637 0222
Good French cuisine. Closed Sat.
lunch, Sun., Bank Holidays and
Xmas–New Year.

Santini ═ ▯▯▯
29 Ebury Street, Victoria
London SW1W 0NZ
Tel. (01) 730 4094
Italian cuisine. Comfortable.
Closed Sat. lunch, Sun. and Bank
Holidays.

The Savoy 📖 ═ ▯▯▯
Strand, Covent Garden
London WC2R 0EU
Tel. (01) 836 4343; tlx. 24234
200 rooms. Attractive, impressive
luxury hotel with relaxed
atmosphere, famous for its excellent
restaurants.

Sutherlands ═ ▯▯▯
45 Lexington Street, Soho
London W1R 3LG
Tel. (01) 434 3401
English and French. Good cuisine.
Stylish restaurant.
Closed Sat. lunch, Sun. and Bank
Holidays.

La Tante Claire ═ ▯▯▯
68 Royal Hospital Road, Chelsea
London SW3 4HP
Tel. (01) 352 6045
Excellent French cuisine. Closed
Sat., Sun., 10 days at Easter, 3 weeks
in Aug.–Sept., 10 days at Xmas, and
Bank Holidays.

Alexandra 📖 ═ ▯▯
Pound Street
Lyme Regis, Dorset DT7 3HZ
Tel. (02974) 2010
24 rooms. 18th-century residence.
Panoramic view over Lyme Bay.
Garden. Closed Dec. 18
to Feb. 3. 5 D2

Parkhill 📖 ═ ▯▯
Beaulieu Road
Lyndhurst, Hampshire SO43 7FZ
Tel. (042128) 2944; tlx. 477930
22 rooms. Tastefully furnished
Georgian mansion. View.
Swimming pool. 6 A2

Hewitt's 📖 ═ ▯▯
North Walk
Lynton, Devon EX35 6HJ
Tel. (0598) 52293
12 rooms. Victorian country house.
View. Quiet location. 5 C2

Mitre 🖼 ══ 🍴
Cathedral Gates
Manchester M3 1SW
Tel. (061) 834 4128; tlx. 669581
30 rooms. Family-run hotel near
the cathedral. 8 A1

Portland Thistle 🖼 ══ 🍴🍴
3–5 Portland Street,
Piccadilly Gardens
Manchester M1 6DP
Tel. (061) 228 3400; tlx. 669157
219 rooms. Modern hotel with
restored warehouse façade. Indoor
swimming pool, sauna. 8 A1

Riber Hall 🖼 ══ 🍴🍴
Riber
Matlock, Derbyshire DE4 5JU
(3 mi./5 km. south-east by A 615)
Tel. (0629) 582795
11 rooms. Attractive Elizabethan
house. Peaceful. Tennis. 8 A2

Teesdale 🖼 ══ 🍴
Market Place
Middleton-in-Teesdale, Durham
DL12 0QG
Tel. (0833) 40264
14 rooms. Friendly. 12-13 C2

Benares 🖼 ══ 🍴
Northfield Road
Minehead, Somerset TA24 5PT
Tel. (0643) 4911
20 rooms. Gardens. Closed end-Nov.
to end-Feb., except Xmas. 5 C2

Kings Arms 🖼 ══ 🍴
Bishopston
Montacute, Somerset TA15 6UU
(Yeovil 5 mi./8 km.)
Tel. (0935) 822513
11 rooms. Attractive
16th-century inn. 5 D2

Fisherman's Lodge ══ 🍴🍴🍴
Jesmond Dene, Jesmond
Newcastle-upon-Tyne, Tyne and
Wear NE7 7BQ
Tel. (091) 281 3281
Good cuisine. Seafood. 13 C2

Gosforth Park Thistle 🖼 ══ 🍴🍴
High Gosforth Park
Newcastle-upon-Tyne, Tyne and
Wear NE3 5HN
Tel. (091) 236 4111; tlx. 53655
178 rooms. Modern hotel in
woodland setting. Indoor swimming
pool, sauna, squash. 13 C2

Trebarwith 🖼 ══ 🍴🍴
Trebarwith Crescent
Newquay, Cornwall TR7 1BZ
Tel. (06373) 872288

44 rooms. View of bay and coast.
Fishing, indoor swimming pool,
sauna, solarium. Closed Oct.
to Easter. 4 A-B3

Lime Trees 🖼 ══ 🍴
8 Langham Place, Barrack Road
Northampton, Northamptonshire
NN2 6AA
Tel. (0604) 32188
20 rooms. Friendly, family-run hotel.
Closed Dec. 25 and 26. 8 B3

Swallow 🖼 ══ 🍴🍴
Eagle Drive
Northampton, Northamptonshire
NN4 0HW
Tel. (0604) 768700; tlx. 31562
122 rooms. Modern. Indoor
swimming pool, sauna. 8 B3

Arlington 🖼 ══ 🍴🍴
Newmarket Road
Norwich, Norfolk NR2 2DA
Tel. (0603) 617841; tlx. 975392
42 rooms. In residential area. 9 D2

Maids Head 🖼 ══ 🍴🍴
Tombland
Norwich, Norfolk NR3 1LB
Tel. (0603) 761111; tlx. 975080
80 rooms. Part 13th-century house
opposite the cathedral. Good
restaurant. 9 D2

Bestwood Lodge 🖼 ══ 🍴🍴
Bestwood Lodge Drive, Arnold
Nottingham, Nottinghamshire
NG5 8NE
(3 mi./5 km. north off A 60)
Tel. (0602) 203011; tlx. 57515
36 rooms. 19th-century
hunting lodge. 8 A2

Stakis Victoria 🖼 ══ 🍴🍴
Milton Street
Nottingham, Nottinghamshire
NG1 3PZ
Tel. (0602) 419561; tlx. 37401
167 rooms. Former railway hotel.
Central location. 8 A2

The Randolph 🖼 ══ 🍴🍴
Beaumont Street
Oxford, Oxfordshire OX1 2LN
Tel. (0865) 247481; tlx. 83446
109 rooms. Gothic-style. Central
location. 8 A3

Welcome Lodge 🖼 ══ 🍴🍴
Peartree Roundabout,
Woodstock Road
Oxford, Oxfordshire OX2 8JZ
Tel. (0865) 54301; tlx. 83202
100 rooms. Modern. Carvery
restaurant. Swimming pool. 8 A3

Old Custom House 🖼 ══ 🍴
South Quay
Padstow, Cornwall PL28 8ED
Tel. (0841) 532359
26 rooms. Pleasant
harbourside inn.
Closed Jan. and Feb. 4 B2

Tarbert 🖼 ══ 🍴
11–12 Clarence Street
Penzance, Cornwall TR18 2NU
Tel. (0736) 63758
12 rooms. Central location.
Closed Xmas and
New Year. 4 A3

Green Park 🖼 ══ 🍴
Clunie Bridge Road
Pitlochry, Tayside PH16 5JY
Tel. (0796) 3248
37 rooms. Charming country-house
hotel. View of Loch Faskally
and the mountains.
Fishing. Closed Nov.
to end-March. 17 D2

Copthorne 🖼 ══ 🍴🍴
Armada Centre, Armada Way
Plymouth, Devon PL1 1AR
Tel. (0752) 224161; tlx. 45756
135 rooms. Modern. Good
restaurants. Indoor swimming pool,
sauna, solarium.
Central location. 4 B3

Novotel Plymouth 🖼 ══ 🍴
270 Plymouth Road
Plymouth, Devon PL6 8NH
Tel. (0752) 221422; tlx. 45711
101 rooms. Modern. Pleasant atmos-
phere. Swimming pool. 4 B3

Mansion House 🖼 ══ 🍴🍴🍴
11 Thames Street
Poole, Dorset BH15 1JN
Tel. (0202) 685666; tlx. 41495
19 rooms. Attractive
18th-century town house.
Central location. 6 A2

Knockinaam Lodge 🖼 ══ 🍴🍴🍴
Portpatrick, Dumfries and
Galloway DG9 9AD
Tel. (077681) 471
10 rooms. Pleasant hotel.
Victorian lodge in a park.
Exceptional sea view. Quiet location.
Excellent cuisine. Fishing.
Closed Jan. to Easter. 14 B2

Holiday Inn 🖼 ══ 🍴🍴
Southampton Road, North Harbour
Portsmouth, Hampshire PO6 4SH
Tel. (0705) 383151; tlx. 86611
170 rooms. Indoor swimming pool,
sauna, solarium, squash. 6 B2

303

Ruthin Castle 🛏️ ⇌ 🍴🍷
Corwen Road
Ruthin, Clwyd LL15 2NU
Tel. (08242) 2664; tlx. 61169
58 rooms. 15th-century castle.
View. Fishing. 11 C2

Mermaid Inn 🛏️ ⇌ 🍴🍷
Mermaid Street
Rye, East Sussex TN31 7EU
Tel. (0797) 223065; tlx. 957141
29 rooms. Famous inn rebuilt
in 1420. Attractively
furnished rooms. 7 C2

Rufflets 🛏️ ⇌ 🍴🍷
Strathkinness Low Road
St. Andrews, Fife KY16 9TX
Tel. (0334) 72594
21 rooms. Attractive country house
in splendid gardens. View.
Closed Jan. 15 A2

Boscundle Manor 🛏️ ⇌ 🍴🍷
Tregrehan
St. Austell, Cornwall PL25 3RL
(2 mi./3 km. east by A 390)
Tel. (0726) 3557
11 rooms. 18th-century manor
in a park. Golf, croquet,
swimming pool. Closed
mid-Oct. to mid-April. 4 B3

Tides Reach 🛏️ ⇌ 🍴🍷
South Sands
Salcombe, Devon TQ8 8LJ
Tel. (054884) 3466
42 rooms. Splendid view of
the estuary. Indoor swimming
pool, squash, sauna,
solarium, gymnasium. Closed
Dec. to March. 5 C3

King's Arms 🛏️ ⇌ 🍴
9 St. John's Street
Salisbury, Wiltshire SP1 2SB
Tel. (0722) 27629
12 rooms. Part 13th- and part 15th-
century inn. Friendly. 6 A2

Rose & Crown 🛏️ ⇌ 🍴🍷
Harnham Road, Harnham
Salisbury, Wiltshire SP2 8JQ
Tel. (0722) 27908; tlx. 47224
28 rooms. Characterful 13th-century
inn on the banks of the
River Avon. 6 A2

St. Brides 🛏️ ⇌ 🍴🍷
St. Brides Hill
Saundersfoot, Dyfed SA69 9NH
(Tenby 3 mi./5 km.)
Tel. (0834) 812304; tlx. 48350
46 rooms. Good sea view. Swimming
pool, sauna, solarium, sailing.
Closed Jan. 1 to 14. 10 B3

Holbeck Hall 🛏️ ⇌ 🍴🍷
Seacliff Road, South Cliff
Scarborough, North Yorkshire
YO11 2XX
Tel. (0723) 374374
30 rooms. Victorian house.
Panoramic view.
Good cuisine. 13 D3

Red Lea 🛏️ ⇌ 🍴
Prince of Wales Terrace, South Cliff
Scarborough, North Yorkshire
YO11 2AJ
Tel. (0723) 362431
67 rooms. Traditional. Sea view.
Swimming pool, sauna. 13 D3

Wrea Head 🛏️ ⇌ 🍴🍷
Scalby
Scarborough, North Yorkshire
YO13 0PB
(3 mi./5 km. north-west by A 171)
Tel. (0723) 378211
21 rooms. Victorian country house.
Landscaped gardens. View. Quiet
location. Good English food. 13 D3

Beauchief 🛏️ ⇌ 🍴🍷
161 Abbeydale Road
Sheffield, South Yorkshire S7 2QW
Tel. (0742) 620500; tlx. 54164
41 rooms. Part old inn,
part modern. Riverside setting.
Sauna, solarium. 8 A2

St. George 🛏️ ⇌ 🍴🍷
Kenwood Road
Sheffield, South Yorkshire S7 1NQ
Tel. (0742) 583811; tlx. 547030
119 rooms. Pleasant, modern hotel in
a park. Indoor swimming pool,
spa bath, sauna, solarium. 8 A2

The Lion 🛏️ ⇌ 🍴🍷
Wyle Cop
Shrewsbury, Shropshire SY1 1UY
Tel. (0743) 53107
59 rooms. Modernized
Georgian inn. 11 D2

Littlecourt 🛏️ ⇌ 🍴🍷
Seafield Road
Sidmouth, Devon EX10 8HF
Tel. (0395) 5279
21 rooms. Regency house in a
garden. Central location. Swimming
pool. Closed mid-Jan.
to mid-Feb. 5 C2

Victoria 🛏️ ⇌ 🍴🍷🍷
The Esplanade, Peak Hill
Sidmouth, Devon EX10 8RY
Tel. (0395) 512651; tlx. 42551
61 rooms. Elevated gardens. Superb
view. Spa bath, swimming pools,
tennis, beach, sauna. 5 C2

Post House 🛏️ ⇌ 🍴🍷
Herbert Walker Avenue
Southampton, Hampshire SO1 0HJ
Tel. (0703) 330777; tlx. 477368
133 rooms. Modern. Panoramic
view. Swimming pool.
Central location. 6 A2

Star 🛏️ ⇌ 🍴
26–27 High Street
Southampton, Hampshire
SO9 4ZA
Tel. (0703) 339939
45 rooms. Friendly, family-run hotel.
Central location. Closed Dec. 24
to Jan. 3. 6 A2

George 🛏️ ⇌ 🍴🍷🍷
of Stamford
71 St. Martin's
Stamford, Lincolnshire PE9 2LB
Tel. (0780) 55171; tlx. 32578
47 rooms. Characterful historic
coaching inn.
Friendly service. 8-9 B2

Terraces 🛏️ ⇌ 🍴
4 Melville Terrace
Stirling, Central FK8 2ND
Tel. (0786) 72268; tlx. 778025
15 rooms. Georgian town house.
Close to the shopping centre. 17 D3

The North Stafford 🛏️ ⇌ 🍴🍷
Station Road
Stoke-on-Trent, Staffordshire
ST4 2AE
Tel. (0782) 744477; tlx. 36287
70 rooms. Friendly. Opposite
the railway station. 8 A2

Grapewine 🛏️ ⇌ 🍴🍷
Sheep Street
Stow-on-the-Wold, Gloucestershire
GL54 1AU
Tel. (0451) 3044; tlx. 43423
17 rooms. Charming. Friendly.
Closed Xmas and New Year. 8 A3

The Shakespeare 🛏️ ⇌ 🍴🍷
Chapel Street
Stratford-upon-Avon,
Warwickshire CV37 6ER
Tel. (0789) 294771; tlx. 311181
70 rooms. Famous 16th-century
timbered inn. 8 A3

Welcombe 🛏️ ⇌ 🍴🍷🍷
Warwick Road
Stratford-upon-Avon,
Warwickshire CV37 0NR
Tel. (0789) 295252; tlx. 31347
79 rooms. Superb 19th-century
mansion. View, park.
Quiet location.
Golf, croquet. 8 A3

The White Swan 📷 🍴 ⏸️⏸️
Rother Street
Stratford-upon-Avon,
Warwickshire CV37 6NH
Tel. (0789) 297022
35 rooms. 15th-century inn.
Central location. 8 A3

Windsor Lodge 📷 🍴 ⏸️
15 Mount Pleasant
Swansea, West Glamorgan
SA1 6EG
Tel. (0792) 42158
19 rooms. Georgian town house.
Sauna. Closed Dec. 25
and 26. 5 C1

Castle 📷 🍴 ⏸️⏸️⏸️
Castle Green
Taunton, Somerset TA1 1NF
Tel. (0823) 272671; tlx. 46488
35 rooms. Attractive hotel. Part 12th-
century building with Norman garden
and castle keep. Warm atmosphere.
Good cuisine. 5 D2

Homers 📷 🍴 ⏸️⏸️
Warren Road
Torquay, Devon TQ2 5TN
Tel. (0803) 213456
15 rooms. Panoramic view.
Closed Jan. 5 C3

Kistor 📷 🍴 ⏸️⏸️
Belgrave Road
Torquay, Devon TQ2 5HF
Tel. (0803) 212632
59 rooms. Central location close to
the beach. Indoor swimming pool,
sauna, solarium. 5 C3

Orestone Manor House 📷 🍴 ⏸️⏸️
Rockhouse Lane, Maidencombe
Torquay, Devon TQ1 4SX
(3 mi./5 km. north by A 379)
Tel. (0803) 38098
20 rooms. Georgian house in
peaceful countryside.
Sea view. Swimming pool.
Closed Jan. and Feb. 5 C3

Ceilidh Place 📷 🍴 ⏸️⏸️
14 West Argyle Street
Ullapool, Highland IV26 2TY
Tel. (0854) 2103
15 rooms. Friendly atmosphere.
Popular restaurant. 18 A2

Sharrow Bay 📷 🍴 ⏸️⏸️⏸️
Pooley Bridge
Ullswater, Cumbria CA10 2LZ
Tel. (08536) 301
30 rooms. Attractive hotel in country
house with lakeside setting. View.
Tasteful decor. Excellent cuisine.
Closed Dec. to March. 12 B2

Crown 📷 🍴 ⏸️
Market Place
Wells, Somerset BA5 2RF
Tel. (0749) 73457
21 rooms. 15th-century inn.
Pleasant restaurant. 5 D2

Streamside 📷 🍴 ⏸️
29 Preston Road, Overcombe
Weymouth, Dorset DT3 6PX
Tel. (0305) 833121
15 rooms. Charming mock-Tudor
hotel and restaurant. 5 D2

Lainston House 📷 🍴 ⏸️⏸️⏸️
Sparsholt
Winchester, Hampshire SO21 2LT
(3 mi./5 km. north-west by A 272)
Tel. (0962) 63588; tlx. 477375
32 rooms. Pleasant, elegantly
furnished Georgian manor house
in a park. View.
Good cuisine.
Riding, croquet, squash. 6 A2

Langdale Chase 📷 🍴 ⏸️⏸️
Windermere, Cumbria LA23 1LW
(3 mi./5 km. north-west on A 591)
Tel. (05394) 32201
28 rooms. Fine old house in
landscaped gardens. Exceptional
view of lake and mountains.
Tennis, rowing boats. 12 B2

Miller Howe 📷 🍴 ⏸️⏸️
Rayrigg Road
Windermere, Cumbria LA23 1EY
Tel. (09662) 2536
13 rooms. Exceptional view of
lake and mountains.
Good cuisine. Closed mid-Dec.
to mid-Feb. 12 B2

Willowsmere 📷 🍴 ⏸️
Ambleside Road
Windermere, Cumbria LA23 1ES
Tel. (09662) 3575
13 rooms. Family-run hotel. Friendly
atmosphere. Home cooking. Closed
Dec. to Easter. 12 B2

Oakley Court 📷 🍴 ⏸️⏸️⏸️
Windsor Road, Water Oakley
Windsor, Berkshire SL4 5UR
(2 mi./3 km. west on A 308)
Tel. (0628) 74141; tlx. 849958
91 rooms. Part Gothic manor house
on bank of the Thames. 6 B2

Feathers 📷 🍴 ⏸️⏸️
Market Street
Woodstock, Oxfordshire OX7 1SX
Tel. (0993) 812291; tlx. 83138
16 rooms. Tastefully furnished
17th-century house.
Good cuisine. 8 A3

Watersmeet 📷 🍴 ⏸️⏸️
Mortehoe
Woolacombe, Devon EX34 7EB
Tel. (0271) 87033
24 rooms. Country-house
atmosphere. Panoramic view.
Swimming pool, tennis.
Closed mid-Dec.
to mid-Feb. 4 B2

Brown's 🍴 ⏸️⏸️
South Quay
Worcester, Hereford and
Worcester WR1 2JN
Tel. (0905) 26263
Pleasant restaurant in converted
riverside cornmill. Good cuisine.
Closed Sat. lunch, Sun. evening,
Bank Holidays and Xmas. 11 D3

Fownes 📷 🍴 ⏸️⏸️
City Walls Road
Worcester, Hereford and
Worcester WR1 2AP
Tel. (0905) 613151; tlx. 335021
61 rooms. Converted glove
factory. Sauna. 11 D3

Ye Olde Talbot 📷 🍴 ⏸️
Friar Street
Worcester, Hereford and
Worcester WR1 2NA
Tel. (0905) 23573; tlx. 333315
29 rooms. 13th-century inn.
Traditional standards. Central
location. 11 D3

Crest 📷 🍴 ⏸️⏸️
Clifford Tower, 1 Tower Street
York, North Yorkshire YO1 1SB
Tel. (0904) 648111; tlx. 57566
128 rooms. Elegant and comfortable.
Golf, riding. 13 D3

Kilima 📷 🍴 ⏸️
129 Holgate Road
York, North Yorkshire YO2 4DE
Tel. (0904) 625787; tlx. 57928
15 rooms. Restored Victorian
rectory. Garden. 13 D3

Middlethorpe Hall 📷 🍴 ⏸️⏸️
Bishopthorpe Road
York, North Yorkshire YO2 1QP
Tel. (0904) 641241; tlx. 57802
31 rooms. Pleasant 17th-century
house. Charming interior design.
Gardens. Croquet. View. 13 D3

Savages 📷 🍴 ⏸️
15 St. Peters Grove
York, North Yorkshire YO3 6AQ
Tel. (0904) 610818
18 rooms. Victorian house. Quiet.
Solarium, gymnasium.
Closed Dec 25. 13 D3

All the Nuts and Bolts for a Successful Journey

CONTENTS

306	Accommodation	318	Language
308	Airports	319	Lost Property
310	Bicycle Hire	319	Maps
310	Camping and Caravanning	319	Medical Care
310	Car Hire	319	Money Matters
311	Children	320	Newspapers and Magazines
311	Climate and Clothing	320	Opening Hours
312	Communications	320	Prices
313	Complaints	321	Public (Legal) Holidays
313	Crime and Theft	321	Radio and TV
313	Customs and Entry Regulations	321	Religious Services
314	Disabled Visitors	321	Restaurants
315	Driving in Britain	322	Time Differences
316	Electric Current	322	Tipping
316	Embassies and Consulates	322	Toilets
316	Emergencies	322	Tourist Information Offices
316	Entertainment Booking		
317	Getting to Britain	323	Travelling in Britain
318	Guides and Tours	325	Travel Tickets
318	Hitch-hiking	326	Weights and Measures

ACCOMMODATION

See also CAMPING AND CARAVANNING.

Stay in a castle or a caravan, a friendly bed-and-breakfast house, farmhouse or country house hotel: the choice of accommodation couldn't be wider.

Hotels vary tremendously in character and price. The discreet service in London's grand traditional establishments is matched by the elegant informality of certain country house hotels and the convenience of the national and international chains.

Classification. Hotels, guesthouses, inns, bed-and-breakfast establishments and farmhouses that participate in the British Tourist Authority's (BTA) standards scheme are inspected regularly by the national tourist boards. Those that pass muster are classified according to facilities and services provided, from "Listed" through one to five crowns. A few exceptional hotels in England are awarded five *gold* crowns. A low crown classification does not imply low standards, but indicates, rather, that the facilities and services provided meet an acceptable minimum.

Some establishments in the countryside (mostly privately owned and with less than 50 bedrooms) have been "commended" by the BTA for outstanding service and cuisine. Other, "commended special", hotels offer special-interest packages including anything from heritage and literary tours to ballooning excursions. Ask for the publication *BTA Commended Country Hotels, Guesthouses and Restaurants,* available free of charge from BTA offices abroad (see TOURIST INFORMATION OFFICES).

Rates. Establishments (except those belonging to organizations like the Youth Hostels Association) with four or more bedrooms are required to display a notice at the entrance or in the reception area showing minimum and maximum overnight rates and whether they include service charges and value added tax (VAT). Advantageous full- or half-board terms may be available, especially in the country. Breakfast (English or continental) is usually included in the quoted overnight rate; in addition, most hotels provide tea- and coffee-making facilities for an early morning "cuppa". A service charge of 10 to 12½% (15% in some larger hotels) is usually added to the bill. If not, you should give a 10 to 15% tip to the dining room staff and about 50p per day to the maid.

Reservations. It might be difficult to book rooms in summer and at Easter and Bank Holiday weekends. Try to reserve well in advance, either through your local travel agent or by contacting individual hotels or hotel chains. In autumn, winter and spring, hotels all over Britain offer off-peak bargain rates and short-break deals. See the BTA's free booklet *Let's Go: Short Breaks in Britain* for details.

The list of selected hotels and restaurants on p. 296 will help you choose a hotel in your price range. For a comprehensive listing, consult the English Tourist Board's accommodation guidebook *Where to Stay in England.* The Scottish Tourist Board publishes *Scotland: Where to Stay;* and the Wales Tourist Board *Wales: Where to Stay.* For full details of accommodation in London, refer to the official London Tourist Board (LTB) guide *Where to Stay in London.* All these books can be ordered through BTA-nominated agents abroad; for addresses and procedure, contact the BTA office in your home country.

Accommodation in London may be reserved in advance through the London Tourist Board. Your request must reach London at least six weeks prior to your date of arrival. Address:

26 Grosvenor Gardens,
London SW1W 0DU (telex 919041 LTBG)

Many local Tourist Information Centres (TIC) can make reservations on the spot. Most have lists of the types of accommodation available in the area. Centres displaying a "Local Bed-Booking Service" sticker make reservations at local establishments for the same day (book before 4 p.m.) or next night, while those with the sign "Book-a-Bed-Ahead" (BABA) also reserve in any other locality with a centre offering this facility. TICs in Scotland and Wales ask for a deposit. In London, the British Travel Centre at 12 Regent Street, a two-minute walk south of Piccadilly Circus, provides a national reservation service.

A number of organizations and hotel groups offer an accommodation voucher scheme called "Go-as-you-please", "Welcome to Wales" or "Welcome to Scotland". Travel agents sell the books of vouchers that entitle you to stay at any of the participating hotels.

Inns, small country hotels and pubs with rooms, are listed in BTA's booklet *Britain: Stay at an Inn.* Many inns and pubs offer a traditional or historic ambience and all the amenities, including full restaurant service ranging from reasonably priced to top class.

You'll find bargain **bed-and-breakfast (B&B) houses** in towns and villages throughout Britain. They can be small, family-operated, budget hotels, private homes or farmhouses, and usually have a warm, friendly atmosphere. A private bath is the exception, rather than the rule. In general, you don't need a reservation. Just look for a sign saying "B&B" and ring the doorbell.

LTB's free *London Budget Hotels* lists a selection of inexpensive classified establishments.

Guesthouses have more rooms and better bathroom facilities than B&Bs, and many serve an evening meal. They are slightly more expensive, but still cheaper than most hotels. The Automobile Association's book *Bed & Breakfast in Britain* recommends both guesthouses and B&Bs.

Working **farms** that accept paying guests appear in BTA's free booklet *Britain: Stay on a Farm.* Some offer bed and breakfast, while others give you the option of taking an evening meal—and the possibility of staying for longer periods to get a feel for life in the British countryside. In Wales, walkers and hikers can spend the night in converted **barns** which provide dormitory accommodation for up to 25 people.

Self-catering accommodation ranges from furnished flats (apartments) and houses to country cottages. Refer to two free BTA booklets, *Britain: Holiday Homes* and *Apartments in London,* for details of properties, rates and agencies.

The National Trust and the National Trust for Scotland are charitable foundations that let (rent) cottages and country houses of historic interest. From two to ten people can be accommodated. The Landmark Trust specializes in restored monuments—forts, medieval towers, mills, industrial buildings and manor houses. Early reservation is essential. For further information, write (enclosing a stamped, self-addressed envelope or, if writing from abroad, an international reply coupon):

National Trust,
36 Queen Anne's Gate, London SW1H 9AS

National Trust for Scotland,
5 Charlotte Square, Edinburgh EH2 4DU

Landmark Trust,
Shottesbrooke, Maidenhead,
Berkshire SL6 3SW

Stay in a **private home** with a local family and gain an insider's knowledge of British life. Yet another free booklet from BTA, *Britain: Stay with a British Family,* tells you how to go about it. Or participate in a **home-exchange scheme** and experience British family life, minus the family. BTA will be happy to advise.

Youth and **student accommodation** includes youth hostels, YMCA/YWCAs and college and university halls of residence. These last offer both B&B and self-catering arrangements during student holiday periods. Britain's 260 youth hostels are open to everyone. Many have dormitories with four to eight beds which can be booked as private rooms for families with children up to the age of 16 (some stipulate a minimum age of 5). To stay in a youth hostel, you need either a national or international membership card, or a guest card that you can buy on arrival in Britain. For information about locations and facilities, contact one of the following youth hostel associations:

England and Wales:

Youth Hostels Association (YHA),
Trevelyan House, 8 St. Stephen's Hill,
St. Albans, Hertfordshire AL1 2DY;
tel. (0727) 55215

Scotland:

Scottish Youth Hostels Association
(SYHA),
7 Glebe Crescent, Stirling FK8 2JA;
tel. (0786) 51181

YMCAs and YWCAs:

YMCA of Great Britain,
640 Forest Road, Walthamstow,
London E17 3DZ

YWCA of Great Britain, Clarendon House,
52 Cornmarket Street, Oxford OX1 3EJ

Universities, colleges and schools:

British Universities Accommodation
Consortium,
Box 391, University Park,
Nottingham NG7 2RD

Higher Education Accommodation
Consortium,
36 Collegiate Crescent,
Sheffield S10 2BP

AIRPORTS

Though London is the principal gateway to Britain, many direct intercontinental flights land in Manchester and Glasgow (Prestwick). There are also international airports at Aberdeen, Birmingham, Cardiff and Edinburgh.

England

London is served by Heathrow and Gatwick airports. Stansted and Luton, two smaller and more distant airports, specialize in charter traffic. They also handle an increasing number of scheduled domestic and continental flights. London City Airport is geared to business people commuting between the City of London and British and continental centres.

National Express airport coaches (buses) link most of the major towns of England

and Wales to one or more of the international airports.

London Heathrow, mainly used for scheduled air traffic, is 15 miles (24 km.) west of central London. Terminal 1 serves mostly British and Irish airlines; Terminal 2, other European airlines; Terminal 3, intercontinental traffic; and Terminal 4, mainly British Airways intercontinental flights.

The Piccadilly underground line links Heathrow to central London in about 45 minutes. The Green Line Flightline bus runs direct from the airport to Victoria Coach Station in about 40 minutes (depending on the traffic). London Transport Airbuses, routes A1 (to Victoria) and A2 (to Euston Station), stop at all the main hotel areas and take from 50 to 85 minutes, according to area. Taxis can be expensive: consider sharing to keep costs down.

For connections to other parts of southern England, take the Railair Link bus from Heathrow to the railway station in Woking. To reach towns in the far west of England and Wales, take the Railair Link bus to Reading station.

Coaches link Heathrow and Gatwick in approximately 60 minutes and Heathrow and Stansted in about 80 minutes.

London Gatwick, handling both scheduled and charter flights, is in West Sussex, 28 miles (45 km.) south of central London. The North Terminal handles British Airways and many British Caledonian flights; other airlines use the South Terminal. The rail journey to or from Victoria Station in the air-conditioned Gatwick Express takes 30 minutes. Trains leave every 15 minutes during the day and once an hour at night. There's also an hourly rail connection (35 minutes) to London Bridge Station. Green Line Flightline buses travel from Gatwick to Victoria in about 70 minutes.

London City Airport lies 6 miles (10 km.) east of the City of London in the Docklands area. Green Line London City Flightline buses run every 30 minutes between the airport and Victoria Station. Trains from Silvertown Station, about 300 yards from the airport terminal, link up with the underground at West Ham and Stratford. A rapid Thames riverbus service operates between London City Airport Pier and the City and West End.

London Stansted in Essex is about 37 miles (60 km.) north-east of central London. Regular bus service operates to London

Victoria Coach Station, about 75 minutes away. There's also a rail connection from nearby Bishop's Stortford to London's Liverpool Street Station (journey time 45–50 minutes).

Luton International Airport in Bedfordshire is 35 miles (56 km.) north-west of central London. The Luton Flyer bus connects the airport to Luton Station, 35 minutes by train from London's St. Pancras.

Manchester International Airport lies some 10 miles (16 km.) south of the city centre. Airport shuttle buses leave the international arrivals hall every 30–45 minutes for Chorlton Street Coach Station and to Manchester Piccadilly and Victoria mainline stations, from where InterCity trains will take you to other destinations in the north.

Birmingham International Airport is situated 9 miles (14 km.) south-east of the city centre. From the airport railway station there's a train connection every 10–15 minutes to Birmingham New Street Station (journey time 10–15 minutes). Buses also make the journey into town.

Scotland

Edinburgh Airport, 8 miles (13 km.) west of the city centre, is linked to the city terminal at Waverley Bridge by Airlink buses. Travel time is about 30 minutes.

Glasgow is served by two airports, *Abbotsinch,* 8 miles (13 km.) to the west, and *Prestwick,* Scotland's main transatlantic airport, 32 miles (51 km.) to the south-west. A bus leaves Abbotsinch every 20–30 minutes for the 20-minute ride to Glasgow Anderston Cross Bus Station. From Prestwick Airport, there are Citylink bus connections to Glasgow centre (Buchanan Street Station, journey time approximately 1 hour) and to Edinburgh, as well as airport coach services to central Glasgow. Courtesy buses take passengers from the airport to Prestwick railway station, where a train leaves for Glasgow about every 30 minutes.

Aberdeen Airport lies 6 miles (10 km.) north-west of the city centre. There's a half-hourly airport bus service to the terminal at Guild Street.

Wales

Cardiff-Wales Airport, about 10 miles (16 km.) south-west of the city centre, is linked by city buses to Cardiff centre. There are also rail connections to London Heathrow, London Gatwick, Birmingham and Manchester airports.

BICYCLE HIRE

Britain counts as one of Europe's most popular areas for cycling. The Cyclists' Touring Club, Britain's national cycling association, organizes cycling holiday tours and provides information on individual bicycle routes. For further details, write to the CTC (enclosing a stamped self-addressed envelope/international reply coupon):

Cyclists' Touring Club, Cotterell House, 69 Meadrow, Godalming, Surrey GU7 3HS

The booklet *Britain: Cycling,* obtainable from BTA offices, tells you all you need to know about itineraries and bicycle hire. Several organizations, both in Britain and overseas, arrange package tours for cyclists. Brochures and leaflets are available from BTA offices.

You might prefer to take your own bike. Trains will carry them free of charge. Most airlines accept them as part of the luggage allowance—check when you book your ticket. You might have to pay a small charge on ferries.

CAMPING AND CARAVANNING

Britain has thousands of campsites generally termed "caravan and camping parks" or "holiday parks". Many have stationary caravans (trailers) or lodges for rent. Details of licensed sites, their charges and amenities—graded from one to five—as well as information on how to get there, are given in the publication *Camping & Caravan Parks in Britain,* available free from BTA offices. The best holiday caravan parks are awarded symbols by the tourist boards: a rose in England, a thistle in Scotland, a dragon in Wales. Most campsites are open from end-March to October. During July, August and September, the more popular ones tend to fill up early in the day, so it's best to reserve a space in advance. If you want to camp outside official sites, you'll need the permission of the landowner or tenant.

The International Camping Carnet (normally available from automobile associa-tions) is rarely required in Britain. However, Carnet holders have access to some 100 private sites belonging to the Camping and Caravanning Club. This club publishes a biannual guide to more than 2,000 sites in Britain and Eire. Temporary membership is available.

The Camping and Caravanning Club, 11 Lower Grosvenor Place, London SW1W 0EY

The Caravan Club gives information on caravanning and camping and publishes a directory listing its own parks and some 4,000 farm campsites. Temporary membership can be arranged for members of affiliated overseas automobile associations.

The Caravan Club, East Grinstead House, London Road, East Grinstead, West Sussex RH19 1UA

Some of the most scenic locations come under the jurisdiction of the Forestry Commission. See the free leaflet *Come Camping in the Forest,* available from:

Forestry Commission, 231 Corstorphine Road, Edinburgh EH12 7AT

You can hire a minibus or camper from most car-hire companies. BTA's booklet *Britain: Vehicle Hire* lists a selection of firms by location.

For a holiday out of the ordinary, hire a traditional canal narrowboat (a kind of houseboat) and cruise Britain's inland waterways. No special permits, licences or previous experience are required, but the "skipper" must be at least 21 years of age. The minimum rental period is normally one week. Narrowboats have from two to eight berths. You could cover about 100 miles (160 km.) in a week at a leisurely pace, depending on how many stops you make and the number of locks you'll have to negotiate. Local TICs can direct you to rental agencies. However, for the July–August holiday period, you should reserve in advance; the BTA office in your home country will have all the brochures.

CAR HIRE

See also DRIVING IN BRITAIN.

Numerous local firms compete with the international rental companies, so it's worth shopping around for the best deal.

Weekend and weekly unlimited-mileage rates are usually available, as well as various seasonal deals. It's usually more economical to book your car at the same time as your travel tickets, or to order it in advance through your automobile association or a company in your home country. Some rental agencies offer packages that include unlimited mileage. VAT, full insurance coverage, 24-hour emergency assistance service and emergency car replacement in case of a breakdown. Chauffeur-driven cars are available through most major companies.

To hire a car in Britain, you'll have to show your passport and driving licence. Generally the licence must have been held for at least one year. The minimum age varies from 21 to 25, depending on the value of the car. A maximum age of 70 or 75 may be stipulated. A substantial deposit is required unless you pay with a recognized credit card. Third-party liability insurance is included in the rental charge; an additional collision-damage waiver covers your liability towards the rental company in case of an accident.

CHILDREN

Donkey rides, funfairs and Punch and Judy at the seaside, cave exploring at Cheddar and Wookey Hole, zoos and safari parks—there's plenty for children to see and do on holiday in Britain. Here are some ideas for fun things to do with the kids to help vary the cultural programme:

In London
In addition to the perennial attractions of a ride on a double-decker bus, a boat trip down the Thames, Egyptian mummies at the British Museum, dinosaurs at the Natural History Museum, and a visit to the Regent's Park home of London Zoo, there are endless other possibilities: Madame Tussaud's famous waxworks museum (Marylebone Road, NW1); the Bethnal Green Museum of Childhood (Cambridge Heath Road, E2); the London Toy and Model Museum (23 Craven Hill, W2); and Pollock's Toy Museum (1 Scala Street, W1). Older children might enjoy the London Dungeon, a horror museum (28/34 Tooley Street, SE1), or Rock Circus, the world of rock and pop in wax at the London Pavilion, Piccadilly Circus.

A number of puppet theatres stage reg-ular performances, including Little Angel Marionette Theatre (14 Dagmar Passage, Islington, N1) and the Polka Children's Theatre (240 Broadway, SW19).

Around Britain
Beaconsfield, Buckinghamshire. Bekonscot Model Village and railway.

Beaulieu, Hampshire. National Motor Museum of vintage cars, Disneyesque "Wheels" attraction, mini-car and motorbike race circuit.

Beltring, Kent. Whitbread Hop Farm. Oast houses contain rural museum, crafts centre, shire horses, nature trail.

Bourton-on-the-Water, Gloucestershire. Model village built of Cotswold stone.

Chatham, Kent. Chatham Historic Dockyard. Tours for children. Traditional rope-, sail- and flag-making demonstrations. Carriage rides.

Chertsey, Surrey. Thorpe Park—Space Station Zero and Thunder River rides.

Chessington, World of Adventures, a 65-acre (26-ha.) theme park that promises a "whole day of adventures and thrills".

Edinburgh. Museum of Childhood, High Street. Books, toys, clothes.

Rugely, Staffordshire. Blithfield Hall, Museum of Childhood and Costume.

Torquay. Babbacombe Model Village.

Warwick. Doll Museum, Oken's House, Castle Street.

Baby-sitting
Maybe *you'd* like to get away from the kids for a few hours? Many hotels, guesthouses and bed-and-breakfast places provide babysitters. Otherwise local TICs will know of someone reliable. For referenced babysitters in London, contact:

Universal Aunts Ltd.,
tel. (01) 3515767

CLIMATE AND CLOTHING

The butt of endless jokes, Britain's weather will probably be wetter, milder and more capricious than you'd expected. Rain falls in every season, and the humidity is generally high, especially in autumn and winter. But come prepared with your raincoat and umbrella, as every good tourist should, and a heat wave may ensue. Britain's weather is nothing if not fickle. There's considerable regional variation, too, from the relatively warm and sunny South-West (the "British

Temperature Chart

°F		Jan	Feb	Mar	Apr	May	Jun	Jul	Aug	Sep	Oct	Nov	Dec
Cardiff	max	45	45	50	55	61	66	68	70	64	57	50	46
	min	36	36	37	41	46	52	54	57	52	46	41	37
Edinburgh	max	43	43	46	52	57	63	64	64	61	54	48	45
	min	34	34	36	39	43	48	52	52	48	45	39	36
London	max	43	45	50	55	63	68	72	70	66	57	50	45
	min	36	36	37	43	46	54	57	55	52	46	41	39
°C		Jan	Feb	Mar	Apr	May	Jun	Jul	Aug	Sep	Oct	Nov	Dec
Cardiff	max	7	7	10	13	16	19	20	21	18	14	10	8
	min	2	2	3	5	8	11	12	13	11	8	5	3
Edinburgh	max	6	6	8	11	14	17	18	18	16	12	9	7
	min	1	1	2	4	6	9	11	11	9	7	4	2
London	max	6	7	10	13	17	20	22	21	19	14	10	7
	min	2	2	3	6	8	12	14	13	11	8	5	4

Minimum temperatures are measured just before sunrise, maximum temperatures in the afternoon.

Riviera'') to the damp Highlands and islands of Scotland. The chart above gives maximum and minimum daily temperatures for the three national capitals.

So what to pack, apart from the raingear? Woollens, even in summer, a pair of good, comfortable walking shoes, a few lightweight things for a hot spell and a heavy coat for the depths of winter.

When it comes to style of dress, anything goes in Britain. Informality is the rule, apart from the better hotels and restaurants.

COMMUNICATIONS

Post offices. Main post offices are open from 9 a.m. to 5, 5.30 or 6 p.m., Monday to Friday, and from 9 a.m. to noon or 12.30 p.m. on Saturdays. Smaller district offices have shorter hours. Stamps can be bought at post-office counters and from vending machines outside post offices.

Poste Restante/General Delivery. You can have your mail addressed to you in any town c/o Poste Restante. In municipalities with more than one post office, it will be sent to the main branch. You'll have to show identification to retrieve mail.

Telegram, telex, fax. Telegrams within Britain and from abroad are communicated via the telephone (telemessage); the actual telegram is sent by mail the following day. Telegrams from Britain can be sent from post offices or over the phone—dial 190. Telex and facsimile companies are listed in the *Yellow Pages* under "Telex" and "Fax".

Telephone. There are several types of public telephones. For some you need coins, while others accept only telephone cards.

Coin-operated payphones can be used for direct domestic (minimum charge 10p) and international calls (you're recommended to deposit 30p). Unused coins are returned.

Phonecard phones accept British Telecom Phonecards only. Available in anything from 10 to 200 units, cards are on sale at post offices and in shops displaying the green sign "Phonecards sold here".

"Pay-on-answer" payphones are being phased out. They take 10p coins only; push the money into the slot when your party answers (not suited to international direct dialling).

CreditCall payphones accept Visa, MasterCard (Access), Diners Club and American Express cards, as well as British Telecom's Phonecards. The charge of 10p per unit applies, but there's minimum purchase of five call units.

Cheap-rate calls can be made from private telephones only. Reduced rates are in effect from 6 p.m. to 8 a.m., Monday to Friday, for local and long-distance calls, and from 8 p.m. to 8 a.m. for international calls. The cheap rate also applies all day Saturday and Sunday.

Hotel telephone surcharges. With very few exceptions, you will be charged at a much higher rate when calling from a hotel telephone. Ask about the surcharge rate before calling from a hotel or use a public payphone—or dial 155 from any phone and ask the British Telecom International operator for a reverse-charge (collect) call. U.S. citizens can call home from Britain at lower U.S. rates via AT&T's USADIRECT service for collect and AT&T-card calls; dial 0800 89 00 11 and you'll be connected to an AT&T operator in the U.S.

To make a direct international call from Britain, dial 010 (Britain's international prefix), then the country code, the area code and the subscriber's number. Some country codes:

Australia	(010) 61
Austria	(010) 43
Belgium	(010) 32
Canada	(010) 1
Denmark	(010) 45
Eire	(010) 353
Finland	(010) 358
India	(010) 91
Japan	(010) 81
Netherlands	(010) 31
New Zealand	(010) 64
Norway	(010) 47
Singapore	(010) 65
South Africa	(010) 27
Sweden	(010) 46
Switzerland	(010) 41
United States	(010) 1
West Germany	(010) 49

To call a subscriber in Britain from abroad, dial the international prefix used in your country followed by 44.

COMPLAINTS

In hotels and restaurants, address any complaint to the manager or proprietor. If there is something you can't sort out with the owner, report it to the British Tourist Authority. They'll investigate the matter or suggest what action to take.

The British Consumers' Association guarantees that a defective article or one which doesn't correspond to its description may be returned or exchanged providing you've kept the sales receipt. You may be offered credit, but you always have the right to ask for a cash refund.

If you need further help, contact the local Citizens' Advice Bureau (listed in the *Yellow Pages*) or apply directly to the Consumers' Association:

*2 Marylebone Road,
London NW1; tel. (01) 486 5544*

CRIME AND THEFT

While Britain remains a relatively safe country, crime is on the rise here as elsewhere. Be on your guard after dark in the cities, and watch out for pickpockets in crowds—especially at street markets, in cinema and theatre lines, in department stores and on public transport. Deposit items of value in your hotel safe. Lock your car (and caravan) when you park it and remove all property from view.

Keep photocopies of your tickets, driving licence, passport and other vital documents in case you have to report a theft and obtain replacements. For insurance purposes, any loss or theft should be reported at once to the nearest police station; your insurance company will need to see a copy of the police report.

CUSTOMS AND ENTRY REGULATIONS

See also DRIVING IN BRITAIN.

Nationals of European Community countries need only a valid national identity card to enter Britain. For nationals of other Western European countries, as well as North America, Australia, New Zealand, Japan and South Africa, a valid passport is required. Visitors from other countries may need a visa; check with your travel agent or the nearest British consulate before you leave home. No vaccinations are required to enter Britain from any country. Citizens of countries outside the EEC usually have to fill in a landing card.

At most British ports and airports, Customs Control is divided into two channels, green for "nothing to declare" and red for "goods to declare". Green channels are subject to spot checks.

The table below shows what you can carry into Britain duty free.

	Cigarettes		Cigars		Tobacco	Spirits		Wine	Perfume		Toilet water
1)	400	or	100	or	500 g.	1 l.	and	2 l.	50 g.	and	¼ l.
2)	300	or	75	or	400 g.	1½ l.	and	5 l.	75 g.	and	⅜ l.
3)	200	or	50	or	50 g.	1 l.	and	2 l.	50 g.	and	¼ l.

1) Goods obtained outside Europe.
2) Goods obtained duty and tax paid in the European Community.
3) Goods obtained duty and tax free in the European Community or duty and tax free on a ship or an aircraft, or goods obtained in another European country.
Other goods/gifts: 1) and 3) £32 worth; 2) £250 worth

The chart below shows the goods you can take into Britain duty- and tax-free. (Allowances are subject to change at short notice.) Travellers under 17 are not entitled to the wine, spirits or tobacco allowance. As for what you can bring back home, ask before departure for the appropriate customs notice.

Currency. There are no restrictions on the import or export of pounds sterling or foreign currencies.

Pets. To keep out rabies, very stringent regulations, including lengthy quarantines (up to six months), are in force for the import of dogs, cats and other animals to Britain. The smuggling of pets is penalized with heavy fines, imprisonment and perhaps the confiscation of the animal. If you intend to take your pet with you, permission must be obtained at least six weeks in advance from the British Ministry of Agriculture, Fisheries and Food:

Hook Rise South, Tolworth,
Surbiton, Surrey KT6 7NF

Other restrictions. There are severe penalties for drug smuggling. Travellers are warned never to carry baggage or packages through customs for someone else. Items subject to import control include firearms, fireworks, flick knives, horror or pornographic material, plants, meats, etc. For further customs regulations and details of import and export licences, contact H.M. Customs and Excise:

Dorset House, Stamford Street,
London SE1 9PS; tel. (01) 928 0533

Reimbursement of VAT/sales tax. Most department stores and many quality and specialist shops can help you avoid paying VAT if your purchases exceed a stipulated amount. Special rules apply to European Community travellers. Take your passport or national identity card to the shop as proof of foreign citizenship.

There are three ways to avoid paying VAT. 1) Major stores will send goods directly to your home address free of VAT. 2) When you make your purchases, ask for the VAT 407 form. This will be completed and stamped by the shop; you must present it together with the goods to the customs officer on duty at the airport or point of departure within three months of purchase. After the officer has certified the form, seal it in the envelope provided and deposit it in the letter box at the customs desk. In due course, the shop will forward you the VAT reimbursement (minus a small administration fee). The amount will be refunded by sterling cheque, or, if you wish to avoid bank charges, transferred to your credit card account. 3) Make your purchase in a shop displaying the "Tax Free For Tourists" sign. You'll be given a voucher for validation by the customs officer on leaving the country. Return it in the prepaid envelope issued by the shop, addressed to Tourist Tax Free Shopping. The company will refund the VAT in your own currency by international banker's draft (minus a service charge) or directly into your credit card account. Tourist Tax Free Shopping, a part of Europe Tax Free Shopping, has an advisory service at the British Travel Centre, 12 Regent Street, London.

DISABLED VISITORS

Free information on accommodation and facilities for disabled visitors to Britain is available from the Holiday Care Service:

2 Old Bank Chambers,
Station Road, Horley, Surrey RH6 9HW;
tel. (0293) 774535

DRIVING IN BRITAIN

To bring a car to Britain, you'll need:

● a valid driving licence or a current International Driving Permit
● vehicle registration document
● insurance coverage (the green card is recommended but not obligatory for vehicles registered in Western Europe; drivers of vehicles registered in other countries must show proof of public-liability and property-damage insurance)
● a nationality sticker for both cars and caravans (trailers)

Drivers and front-seat passengers are required by law to fasten their seat belts; offenders are penalized by heavy fines. Dipped (low-beam) headlights should be used whenever daytime visibility is reduced by rain or fog.

Motorcycle drivers and passengers must wear crash helmets. A driving licence is required even for mopeds under 55 cc. The minimum age for operating a moped is 16, for motorcycles, scooters and cars 17.

Whether you bring your own vehicle or hire one, you should buy a copy of the *Highway Code,* which gives detailed information on the rules of the road. It's available at most ports of entry and from book shops in Britain.

Roads and regulations. Remember that traffic keeps to the left, overtaking (passing) on the right. Think twice every time you set off, and pay special attention at junctions and roundabouts (traffic circles). After a few days it feels natural to drive on the "wrong" side—simply keep in mind that the middle of the road is to your right.

Cars already in a roundabout have priority; when entering, precedence must be given to vehicles coming from the right. At junctions, signs and markings indicate who has priority. Pedestrians have priority on zebra crossings—broad white stripes painted across the road, marked by flashing orange Belisha beacons.

Motorways (expressways, marked "M") are toll-free. Main trunk roads, often dual carriageways (divided highways) are marked "A". "B" stands for paved secondary roads and "C" for other roads.

Speed limits are, unless otherwise indicated, 30 mph (48 kph) in towns and built-up areas, 70 mph (112 kph) on motorways and dual carriageways and 60 mph (96 kph) on other roads. For cars towing a caravan or camping trailer, the maximum speed limit on motorways and dual carriageways is 60 mph and on other roads 50 mph (80 kph). These vehicles are banned from the fast lane of motorways with three lanes in each direction.

Fuel. Petrol (gas) is sold in Imperial gallons (the equivalent of 1.2 U.S. gallons) and litres, and the price is shown for both. Fuel is graded according to stars—two stars mean minimum 90 octane, three stars minimum 94 octane and four stars minimum 97 octane. Unleaded 95-octane petrol is widely available.

Few petrol stations stay open at night. On the motorways, the distance between stations can be up to 50 miles (80 km.), so remember to keep an eye on the fuel gauge.

Alcohol. If you plan to drink more than half a pint of beer or a tot of whisky, you had better leave the car behind. Penalties for drunken driving are severe: loss of driving licence, heavy fines, even imprisonment in some cases.

Parking. The international sign with a white "P" on a blue background indicates public parking. Never park on white zigzag lines along the kerb (which indicate pedestrian crossings), on a double yellow line, on a single yellow line during working days (times are given on nearby signboards), on spaces marked "Permit Holders Only", in a "Control Zone" or in "No Unattended Parking" areas.

Infringement of parking regulations may result in heavy fines. In some places, offending cars are towed away; in central London, the police clamp the wheels of cars parked illegally.

Repairs. Most major international car manufacturers are represented in Britain. Members of motoring organizations affiliated with the British Automobile Association (AA) or the Royal Automobile Club (RAC) can take advantage of speedy, efficient assistance in case of a breakdown. Both associations offer information and advice to overseas motorists at Dover, Portsmouth and other principal ports of entry. They also maintain touring departments in a number of towns.

Before leaving home, check with your own automobile association concerning procedure and documentation, or contact the AA or RAC head office:

AA, Fanum House, Basing View,
Basingstoke, Hampshire RG21 2EA;
tel. (0256) 20123

RAC, 49 Pall Mall, London SW1Y 5JG;
tel. (01) 839 7050

ELECTRIC CURRENT

The standard current is 240-volt, 50-cycle A.C. Most hotels have sockets for shavers that operate on 240 or 110 volts. Voltage transformers and adaptors for the British three-prong sockets are available at hardware stores.

EMBASSIES AND CONSULATES

Contact the embassy or consulate of your home country when in trouble (loss of passport, serious accident). All embassies, many with consular offices, are in London. Many countries also maintain consulates in other cities in Britain.

In London (telephone code 01), diplomatic and consular representatives are listed in the *Yellow Pages* under the heading "Embassies, Consulates, High Commissions and Legations":

Australia. High Commission,
Australia House, Strand, WC2B 4LA;
tel. 379 4334

Canada. High Commission,
1 Grosvenor Square, W1X 0AB;
tel. 629 9492

Denmark. Embassy,
55 Sloane Street, SW1X 9S; tel. 235 1255

Eire. Embassy,
17 Grosvenor Place, SW1X 7HR;
tel. 235 2171

Finland. Embassy and consulate,
38 Chesham Place, SW1X 8HW;
tel. 235 9531

India. High Commission, India House,
Aldwych, WC2B 4NA; tel. 836 8484

Japan. Embassy and consulate,
46 Grosvenor Street, W1X 0BA;
Information Centre, 9 Grosvenor Square,
W1X 9LB; tel. 493 6030

The Netherlands. Embassy,
38 Hyde Park Gate, SW7 5DP; tel. 584 5040

New Zealand. High Commission,
New Zealand House, Haymarket,
SW1Y 4TQ; tel. 930 8422

Norway. Embassy,
25 Belgrave Square, SW1X 8QD;
tel. 235 7151

South Africa. Embassy and Consulate,
South Africa House, Trafalgar Square,
WC2N 5DP; tel. 930 4488

Sweden. Embassy,
11 Montagu Place, W1H 2AL; tel. 724 2101

U.S.A. Embassy,
24 Grosvenor Square, W1A 1AE;
tel. 499 9000

EMERGENCIES

For police, fire brigade or ambulance service, dial 999 from any telephone (no coin required). Tell the operator what you need and give the telephone number shown on the phone. Wait on the line. When the emergency service replies, give the address where help is needed and any other vital information.

ENTERTAINMENT BOOKING

For some productions it's possible to buy tickets at the box office just before the performance. But to be sure of a seat at the more popular shows and events, especially in London, you should book in advance through British Airways offices abroad, travel agencies abroad with representatives in Britain, or through a booking agency (the commission normally amounts to 10 or 15%). Some addresses:

Edwards & Edwards (for theatre and shows),
156 Shaftesbury Avenue,
London WC2H 8HL; tel. (01) 379 5822.
Offices also in British Travel Centres
of London, New York, and many overseas
countries.

First Call (for theatre, cinema, concerts),
73–75 Endell Street, London WC2H 9AJ;
tel. (01) 240 7200.
Also: London Showline Inc.,
130 Skylin Drive, Suite 103, Ringwood,
NJ 07456; tel. 1-800-962-9246

Keith Prowse Theatre Sport and Co. Ltd.
(for theatre, classical and pop concerts,
sports events throughout the country),
Banda House, Cambridge Grove,
London W6 0LE; tel. 0800 262 142
(toll free).
Also: Keith Prowse & Co.
(USA) Ltd., 200 Galleria Parkway,
Suite 720, Atlanta, GA 30339;
tel. 1-800-669-8687, telex 239797

In London, theatre tickets priced at £5 or
more can be purchased at half price (plus
a service charge) *on the day of perfor-*
mance from the Half-Price Ticket Booth in
Leicester Square (open Monday to Saturday
from noon to 2 p.m. for matinee tickets and
from 2.30 to 6.30 p.m. for evening performances).

GETTING TO BRITAIN

See your travel agent well before departure
for help with timetables, budget and personal requirements.

By air
London's airports at Heathrow and Gatwick are the main gateways to Britain,
though many direct, scheduled international flights operate to other cities and
towns (see p. 308).

The average journey time between London and New York is 7 hours (about 3½
hours by Concorde), Toronto 9 hours, Sydney 25 hours and Johannesburg 15 hours.

Apart from the first-, business- and econ-
omy-class tickets, there's a complex series
of special fares (APEX, Midweek, Weekend, Standby), discounts for families, children and students, as well as charter services, package tours, and others of which
only a travel agent familiar with the latest
changes can give up-to-date information.

Tour operators offer a wealth of packages (with air fare, accommodation and
sightseeing tours), as well as hiking, biking,
boating, riding, golfing, language and other
special-interest holidays. BTA offices supply lists of tour operators and a free booklet
entitled *Britain: Special Interest Tours &*
Holidays.

By sea
From mainland Europe and Eire. All the
main North Sea and cross-Channel ferries

apart from jetfoils carry cars. Vehicle space
should be booked in advance, especially
during the high season (July–August and
Christmas). Cross-Channel operators offer
several special deals at competitive prices.
From southern Scandinavia, the main
ferry link is the Esbjerg–Harwich stretch
(19 hours), with daily departures in summer
(train connections to London Liverpool
Street Station in 80 minutes). Other crossings include Bergen/Stavanger/Gothen-
burg/Esbjerg–Newcastle-upon-Tyne; Rot-
terdam/Zeebrugge–Kingston-upon-Hull;
Hamburg/Hook of Holland–Harwich;
Ostend/Calais–Dover (about 35 minutes
by hovercraft, 75 to 105 minutes by ferry);
Boulogne–Dover/Folkestone; Dieppe–
Newhaven; Le Havre–Portsmouth; Cherbourg–Weymouth; Roscoff/Santander–
Plymouth.

Travellers crossing the Irish Sea have a
choice of several routes, including Rosslare–Fishguard (about 3½ hours), Dun
Laoghaire–Holyhead (3½ hours), Dublin–Holyhead (4 hours), Dublin–Liverpool
(7–9 hours). Ferry services from Northern Ireland connect Belfast to Liverpool
(about 9 hours) and Larne to Cairnryan and
Stranraer (2–2¼ hours).

You can also buy special through-tickets
and travel by train/ship/train to London
or any British railway station from Amsterdam (ferry from Hook of Holland to
Harwich or jetfoil from Ostend to Dover),
from Brussels (ferry or jetfoil from Ostend
to Dover) or from Paris (ferry or hovercraft
from Calais to Dover or ferry from Boulogne to Folkestone), as well as from Dublin, Rosslare, Belfast or Larne.

Non-European residents who plan to
travel around Western Europe by train
before or after their visit to Britain should
inquire at a travel agent before departure
about the *Eurailpass* (not valid in Britain).
For *BritRail Pass,* see TRAVEL TICKETS.

From North America. The *Queen Eliza-*
beth 2 makes about a dozen return trips a
year Southampton–New York, a journey of
five days each way, certain return trips
calling at Cherbourg, Cork, Baltimore or
Boston. Fares are high, but less expensive
packages, enabling you to travel one
way on *QE2* and return by air (economy
class), are available, as are return trips by
Concorde.

A number of freight-carrying ships take
passengers across the Atlantic to ports in
Britain and continental Europe.

GUIDES AND TOURS

First-time visitors to London will get the best introduction to the capital's principal sights on a guided panoramic tour bus. London Transport runs the classic 90-minute *Original London Transport Sightseeing Tour* (frequent daily departures except on Christmas Day). You see the sights from the top deck of a red London bus (open-deckers in fine weather). London Transport and other companies also organize half- and full-day bus tours of London and environs. Guided walking tours of London are advertised in the newspapers and what's on magazines. You can also see the city from the water—Thames cruises are organized up- and downriver; more offbeat are the narrowboat tours of Regent's Canal. Inquire at the London Tourist Board (see TOURIST INFORMATION OFFICES) for details of sightseeing possibilities in the London area.

Packages available from London include *Britainshrinkers*—fully escorted round-trip tours by express train and coach (entrance fees included). They can be booked through travel agencies and BritRail Travel International offices (see TRAVEL TICKETS). Other tours offered by British Rail include the *Silver Arrow,* the *Great Britain Express* and the *Great Wales Express.*

The national bus companies and a range of private tour operators also offer escorted tours of the country, usually starting in London. Most of these can be booked through local travel agencies in Britain. Local Tourist Information Centres will tell you which tours are available, and they can also arrange personally conducted tours.

The *Great British Heritage Pass,* valid for 15 days or one month, admits visitors from abroad to more than 600 stately homes, castles and gardens. Seven or eight visits cover the cost of the card, available from the British Travel Centre in London and from certain TICs in Britain, as well as from agents abroad; ask at your local BTA office.

HITCH-HIKING

In theory you can thumb a ride anywhere in Britain except on motorways, but don't depend on it as a method of travelling around the country. If you must hitch-hike, do it in pairs.

LANGUAGE

You may not catch the quick, slick cockney of a London cabbie, but neither does the average Yorkshireman. Quite apart from problems of accent, which varies in every region of Great Britain, even beautifully enunciated words may mean something quite different from what you'd expect. Transatlantic differences, for instance, are so numerous that full-scale British-American dictionaries have been published.

A sampler of the more flagrant differences:

British	American
bill	*check (restaurant)*
bonnet	*hood (of car)*
boot	*trunk (of car)*
caravan	*trailer*
chemist	*druggist, pharmacy*
fag	*cigarette*
first floor	*second floor*
flat	*apartment*
ground floor	*first floor*
lay-by	*roadside parking spot*
lift	*elevator*
lorry	*truck*
nappy	*diaper*
off-licence	*liquor store*
pants	*shorts (underwear)*
pavement	*sidewalk*
pram	*baby carriage*
pushchair	*stroller*
petrol	*gasoline*
public school	*private school*
to queue	*to stand in line*
reception	*front desk*
return	*round-trip (ticket)*
rubber	*eraser*
single	*one-way (ticket)*
surgery	*doctor's or dentist's office*
sweet	*candy*
torch	*flashlight*
underground	*subway*

318

LOST PROPERTY

Finding a lost object depends on where you lost it. Check with officials at the relevant train or bus station, airport or store, or at your hotel. For property left behind on London's underground or buses, go, or write to, the London Transport Lost Property Office (forms are available at bus and underground stations):

200 Baker Street, London NW1 5RZ

Report the loss of your passport or identity card to your embassy or consulate. Any other major loss or theft should be reported to the nearest police station; unless you do, and demand a certificate while you're at it, your insurance company at home may not pay up.

If you lose a credit card, call:

American Express, London: (01) 222 9633
(0800 521313 for traveller's cheques)

Diners Club, Farnborough: (0252) 516261

MasterCard/Access, Southend-on-Sea:
(0702) 352211, ext. 2522

Visa/Barclaycard, Northampton: (0604) 230230

MAPS

You can pick up basic local maps and street plans at any Tourist Information Centre. Bookshops, service stations and some newsagents carry a range of detailed maps. If you're driving, ask for a copy of BTA's *Britain: A Map for Travellers,* which includes practical information for anyone touring by car. One of the best atlases of Britain is the Automobile Association's *Big Road Atlas of Britain* (1:250,000). For hikers and cyclists, the most detailed maps are Bartholomews (1:100,000) and Ordnance Survey (1:50,000).

The maps in this book were prepared by Hallwag A.G., Bern.

MEDICAL CARE

Visitors from EEC countries or those with which Britain has a reciprocal health agreement (including New Zealand, Norway and Sweden) are eligible for free emergency medical and hospital treatment through the National Health Service. Visitors from other countries can benefit from free emergency treatment but will have to pay for overnight stays in hospitals. If your general health insurance policy does not cover foreign travel, it is advisable to take out supplementary insurance before travelling to Britain.

In an emergency dial 999 for an ambulance (no coins needed). If the situation does not warrant emergency assistance, you can get the address of a local doctor or hospital from the telephone operator by dialling 100 (free).

Pharmacies. In every large town, at least one pharmacy (called chemist's) stays open until 7.30 or 8 p.m., and 24-hour prescription service may be available. Look in the local newspaper or the window of any pharmacy for the name and address of the shop open after hours. If you have a minor ailment, a pharmacist can advise about treatment.

MONEY MATTERS

Currency. The *pound sterling* (symbolized £) is divided into 100 *pence* (p).
Coins: 1p, 2p, 5p, 10p, 20p, 50p; £1, £2 (rare)
Banknotes: £5, £10, £20, £50
Scotland issues its own banknotes but English notes are interchangeable. The Channel Islands and the Isle of Man issue their own currency, not accepted elsewhere as legal tender. English coins and notes can be used on these islands.

Banks and currency exchange offices. Exchange rates can vary considerably. Banks give a better rate than most exchange offices, many of which also charge a hefty commission. Always choose a firm that displays the BTA code of conduct plaque.

Credit cards, traveller's cheques, Eurocheques (see also LOST PROPERTY). Most hotels and many shops and restaurants honour the major international credit cards. Symbols of those accepted are usually displayed on the doors or windows. Even the police honour credit cards to bail out cars impounded for illegal parking.

Traveller's cheques are readily accepted by hotels, B&Bs, restaurants and stores, but banks usually give a better rate of exchange. Eurocheques can be used anywhere, up to the set limit. Take your passport or national identity card along when you go to cash a cheque.

VAT. Practically all merchandise and services (hotels, restaurants, car hire, car repairs, etc.) in Britain—except for the Channel Islands—are subject to a 15% value added tax. Foreign visitors can avoid some of the VAT on goods bought in shops (see CUSTOMS AND ENTRY REGULATIONS).

Shopping hours are normally from 9 a.m. to 6 p.m., Monday to Saturday. Shops in smaller towns generally close for an hour during lunchtime and some are closed on Saturday afternoons. Newsagents also open on Sunday mornings.

In London, the shopping area in Covent Garden is open until 8 p.m. Shops in Knightsbridge and Chelsea close at 7 p.m. on Wednesdays, while those in the West End and Kensington High Street stay open till 7 p.m. on Thursdays.

NEWSPAPERS AND MAGAZINES

In addition to the large variety of national and local publications, newsagents sell newspapers and magazines from Europe, the U.S. and Middle East. In big towns you'll find the *International Herald Tribune* and *USA Today*. Entertainment and special events are publicized in the daily papers. In London, happenings are listed in magazines such as *What's On in London, Time Out* and *Where to Go in London*.

OPENING HOURS

Banks are normally open from 9.30 a.m. to 3.30 p.m. Some open on Saturday mornings. Branches in Scotland generally close for one hour at lunchtime.

Museums, art galleries, castles, sites. Standard hours are from 9 or 10 a.m. to 5 or 6 p.m. on weekdays, and from approximately 2 p.m. on Sundays. Sites in the open air usually close at sundown. Off season, many tourist attractions observe a severely reduced schedule. Hours do vary, so check with the local Tourist Information Centre before you set out.

Offices and **businesses** operate from 9 or 9.30 a.m. to 5 or 5.30 p.m., Monday to Friday. Some open on Saturday morning as well.

Post office hours are generally from 9 a.m. to about 5.30 p.m., Monday to Friday, and from 9 to noon or 12.30 p.m. on Saturdays.

Pub licensing hours are from 11 a.m. to 11 p.m., Monday to Saturday, and from noon to 3 p.m. and 7 to 10.30 p.m. on Sundays. Some establishments keep shorter hours.

PRICES

To give you an idea of what to expect, here are some average prices in pounds sterling (£). As annual inflation and other factors can cause sudden changes, they must be considered approximate.

Car Hire (international company). *Ford Escort 1.3 L* £21 per day, 22p per mile, £222.25 per week with unlimited mileage. *Ford Granada 2.8/2.8 L* £52.75 per day, 55p per mile, £549.50 per week with unlimited mileage. Add 15% tax, insurance and petrol.

Cigarettes. £1.10 and up per packet of 20.

Entertainment. Cinema £3.50 and up, discotheque £4–6, musical £6–18, night club £8–12, theatre £4–15.

Hairdressers. *Woman's* shampoo and set £6–10, permanent wave £20 and up, manicure £4 and up. *Man's* wash, cut and blow-dry £5.50 and up, trim £3, shave £2.50.

Meals and drinks. English breakfast £2.75 and up, continental breakfast £1.50 and up, lunch £7.50 in fairly good establishment (£2.50 and up in cafeterias, snack bars and pubs), dinner £13 in fairly good establishment, aperitif from 75p, pint of beer 89–95p, whisky 88–90p, soft drink 45p.

Taxi (London). Approximately £1 for the first mile, and about 90p for every following mile. Luggage 10p per piece. Extra charge after 8 p.m., after midnight and on Saturdays, Sundays and holidays, and for extra passengers.

Underground. Outer zone 40p, central zone 50p, two zones 70p, three zones £1. One-day Travelcard £1.70 (£2 including outer London).

PUBLIC (LEGAL) HOLIDAYS

Banks, most shops and many museums close on the following holidays.

January 1	New Year's Day
January 2	Bank Holiday (Scotland)
March/April	Good Friday
	Easter Monday (except Scotland)
First Monday in May	May Day Bank Holiday
Last Monday in May	Spring Bank Holiday
First Monday in August	Bank Holiday (Scotland)
Last Monday in August	Summer Bank Holiday (except Scotland)
December 25	Christmas Day
December 26	Boxing Day

If any of these holidays falls on a Saturday or Sunday, the usual practice is to take the following Monday off.

RADIO AND TV

On radio, you have the choice between five BBC stations—everything from pop music on Radio 1 to classical on Radio 3—and a range of local commercial stations. The BBC World Service provides excellent international news coverage.

British television broadcasts programmes of a consistently high standard on its four main channels. The two BBC channels are state-owned and financed by a yearly licence-fee paid per television set. There are thus no advertisements (commercials) between programmes. The independent channels, ITV and Channel 4, have advertising, as do the several satellite and cable channels. Newspapers carry details of the day's viewing.

RELIGIOUS SERVICES

The Church of England is the established state church. In Scotland, the leading religious denomination is the Presbyterian Church of Scotland, while Methodists and Baptists predominate in Wales. Virtually every major religious grouping in the world has a place of worship somewhere in Britain. Local Tourist Information Centres have the addresses.

RESTAURANTS

See also p. 287.

The revival of traditional British culinary arts inspired Britain's National Tourist Boards to create schemes promoting regional foods. Look for the "Taste of England", "Taste of Scotland" and "Taste of Wales" signs displayed outside restaurants. Many establishments offer fixed-price menus.

In the countryside as in the city, the local pub (Britain has more than 70,000) is the centre of social life, and many serve good, inexpensive lunches. Children under 14 are not permitted in public houses or bars unless there is a family room or garden on the premises. Only people 18 years or older can buy or consume alcoholic drinks in a bar or pub. However, where a special dining room has been set aside, young people 16 years and older may drink beer, wine or cider with their meals.

All restaurants and cafés are obliged to display prices outside and to indicate whether service charges are included. Even where service is included it is customary to leave something more. Otherwise tip 15% of the bill.

Breakfast is usually served between 8 and 9.30 a.m. (sometimes from 7 to 10.30 a.m. in hotels), and lunch from noon to 2 or 2.30 p.m. Teatime may extend from 3 to 6 p.m. and dinner from 7 to 9.30 or 10.30 p.m.

Many foods have different names in British and American English. Here are some that can cause confusion.

British	U.S.
aubergine	eggplant
banger	sausage
bilberries	blueberries
biscuit	cookie/cracker
black pudding	blood sausage
brawn	headcheese
chips	french fries
courgettes	zucchini
crisps	potato chips
endives	chicory
fillet of beef	tenderloin steak
fizzy/still	sparkling/plain
jacket potato	baked potato
main course	entree

marrow	squash
minced	ground
neat	straight (alcoholic drink)
pudding	dessert
spirits	liquor
starter	appetizer
sweet	dessert
tunny	tuna
wholemeal bread	whole wheat bread

TIME DIFFERENCES

In winter, Britain is on Greenwich Mean Time (GMT). From the last Sunday in March to the last Sunday in October, clocks are put ahead one hour (GMT+1).

Northern Hemisphere summer time chart:

Honolulu	1 a.m.
Los Angeles	4 a.m.
New York	7 a.m.
London	**noon**
Copenhagen	1 p.m.
Johannesburg	1 p.m.
Athens	2 p.m.
Delhi	4.30 p.m.
Singapore	7 p.m.
Tokyo	8 p.m.
Sydney	9 p.m.
Auckland	11 p.m.

For the correct time, dial 123 from telephone numbers with the area code 01 (London and surroundings), 9801 from numbers with other area codes.

TIPPING

A service charge of 10 to 15% is included in most hotel bills. Most restaurants also add a service charge, but it's customary to leave something extra for the waiter. The chart below will give you some guidelines.

Hotel porter	50p per bag
Maid	about 50p per day (optional)
Waiter	15% if service not included; otherwise a small amount
Taxi driver	10–15%
Tour guide	10% (optional)
Hairdresser	15%, plus 5% to the assistant

TOILETS

Look for the sign "Public Conveniences" or "WC" in railway stations and in museums and parks. If you're asking directions, simply inquire about the "toilets" or the "lavatory" (pronounced *lav*-a-tree). In Britain a bathroom is a room with a bathtub in it; a restroom means nothing at all; and if you should ask to "wash up", your hostess will refuse to permit it—"washing up" in Britain means washing the dishes.

TOURIST INFORMATION OFFICES

The British Tourist Authority (BTA) office in your country will provide information before you leave home:

Australia. Midland House, 4th floor, 171 Clarence Street, Sydney N.S.W. 2000; tel. (02) 29-8627

Canada. 94 Cumberland Street, Suite 600, Toronto, Ont. M5R 3N3; tel. (416) 925-6326

Denmark. Møntergade 3, 1116 København K; tel. (01) 12 07 93

Eire. 123 Lower Baggot Street, Dublin 2; tel. (01) 614188

Hong Kong. 1 Hysan Avenue, Suite 903, Causeway Bay; tel. (5) 76 43 66

Japan and **Korea.** 246 Tokyo Club Building, 3-2-6 Kasumigaseki, Chiyoda KU, Tokyo 100; tel. (03) 581-3603

The Netherlands. Aurora Gebouw, 5. e., Stadhouderskade 2, 1054 ES Amsterdam; tel. (020) 85 50 51

New Zealand. Dilworth Building, 3rd floor, Suite 305, corner Queen and Customs streets, Auckland 1; tel. (09) 3031-446

Norway. Fridtjof Nansens plass 9, 0160 Oslo 1. Mailing address: Postboks 1554, Vika, 0117 Oslo 1; tel. (02) 41 18 49

Singapore. 24 Raffles Place, 17-04 Clifford Centre, Singapore 0104; tel. 535-2966/7

Sweden. Malmskillnadsgatan 42, Stockholm. Mailing address: Box 293, 10390 Stockholm; tel. (08) 21 24 44

U.S.A. John Hancock Center, Suite 3320, 875 North Michigan Avenue, Chicago, IL 60611; tel. (312) 787-0490

Cedar Maple Plaza, Suite 210, 2305 Cedar Springs Road, Dallas, TX 75201-1814; tel. (214) 720-4040

World Trade Center, Suite 450, 350 South Figueroa Street, Los Angeles, CA 90071; tel. (213) 628-3525

40 West 57th Street, New York, NY 10019-4001; tel. (212) 581-4700

In Britain, more than 700 Tourist Information Centres provide information about what to do and see and where to go and stay. England's 12 regional tourist boards are administrative offices only.

Tourist offices in **London** (telephone area code 01):

British Travel Centre, 12 Regent Street, Piccadilly Circus, SW1Y 4PQ
Open seven days a week, 9 a.m. to 6.30 p.m. Monday to Friday, 10 a.m. to 4 p.m. Saturdays and Sundays (9 a.m.–5 p.m. from mid-May to September). All major agencies represented. Information and reservations for the whole of Britain. Telephone information service: 730 3400 during Centre opening times except Sundays.

British Tourist Authority, Thames Tower, Black's Road, Hammersmith, W6 9EL

Scottish Tourist Board's Travel Centre, 19 Cockspur Street, SW1Y 5BL; tel. 930 8661

Wales Tourist Board, Wales Centre, 34 Piccadilly, W1V 9PB; tel. 409 0969

London Tourist Board and Convention Bureau, 26 Grosvenor Gardens, SW1W 0DU. Telephone information service: 730 3488, Monday to Saturday 9 a.m. to 6 p.m. Artsline telephone information service for the disabled: 388 2227

The London Tourist Board maintains TICs at the following addresses:

Victoria Station Forecourt, SW1
Open daily from 9 a.m. to 8.30 p.m., from Easter to end October; from 9 a.m. to 7 p.m. Monday to Saturday, and 9 a.m.

to 5 p.m. on Sundays in November and December and from January to Easter.

Harrods department store, Brompton Road, Knightsbridge, SW1
Open store hours.

Selfridges department store, Oxford Street, W1
Open store hours.

Tower of London, West Gate, EC3
Open Easter to end-October.

Heathrow Airport, terminals 1, 2 and 3, underground station concourse
Open daily from 9 a.m. to 6 p.m.

Heathrow Airport, Terminal 2, arrivals concourse
Open daily from 9 a.m. to 7 p.m.

Isle of Man
Isle of Man Tourist Board, 13 Victoria Street, Douglas; tel. (0624) 74323

Scotland
Scottish Tourist Board's Travel Centre, 14 South St. Andrews Street, Edinburgh EH2 2AZ; tel. (031) 332 2433

Wales
Wales Tourist Board, Brunel House, 2 Fitzalan Road, Cardiff CF2 1UY; tel. (0222) 499909.
Telephone and written inquiries only.

TRAVELLING IN BRITAIN

See also BICYCLE HIRE, CAR HIRE, DRIVING IN BRITAIN, GUIDES AND TOURS and TRAVEL TICKETS.

It's easy to get around, and the choice of bargain travel tickets permits substantial savings. On most public transport, senior citizens (women over 60 and men over 65) and children aged 5 through 15 travel at reduced fares (half or one third off normal fare), while children up to 5 travel free.

London Transport
London is served by single- and double-decker buses, under- and overground trains, taxis and boats. London Transport has its own Travel Information Centres at Oxford Circus, Piccadilly Circus, King's Cross, Heathrow and at Victoria and Euston mainline stations. Dial (01) 222 1234 for travel information (24 hours).

The **underground** (or "tube") is the quickest means of public transport in London. ("Subway" in Britain means an underground pedestrian passage.) Maps in the stations and trains show the various lines, colour-coded for easy reference. Buy your ticket in the station entrance hall, either from a vending machine or at the cashier's window. As you go through the turnstile to your platform, insert your ticket in the slot and retrieve it when it pops out. You have to hand in your ticket when you get out at your destination. Trains run from 5.30 a.m. to midnight on weekdays, from 7.30 a.m. to 11.30 p.m. on Sundays.

London Transport maintains a dense and somewhat complicated **bus** network. Free route maps and timetables are available at underground stations. Buses run from early morning to around midnight. On the red double-deckers, the conductor circulates round the bus collecting fares (tell him your destination); on single-decker Red Arrow buses, insert the exact fare into the slot of the entry gate. At "Request" stops, you must wave down your bus; at all others, every bus must stop (unless it's full).

Ticket prices increase with the number of zones to be travelled. A standard fare is charged for all routes within one zone. London Transport offers a selection of money-saving cards (*Visitor Travelcard*, see p. 325), available from underground ticket offices and from any London Transport Travel Information Centre (see above).

Green Line buses connect central London with the surrounding countryside. The main terminal is at Eccleston Bridge, behind Victoria Station; tel. (01) 668 7261 for information. Special rover tickets are available.

You can also travel between certain points by **boat**. On Regent's Canal, there's a waterbus service between Camden Lock and Little Venice (buy the ticket on board). On the Thames, a catamaran service operates regularly between Chelsea Harbour Pier and the Docklands, with stops at both banks. Travel time from Charing Cross Pier to West India Pier on the Isle of Dogs is about 20 minutes.

You can hail a **taxi** on the street when the yellow "For Hire" or "Taxi" sign is on. They can also be ordered by telephone—look in the *Yellow Pages* for the numbers. Taxi ranks are found at main rail stations, ports and airports. Should the cab have no meter, ask the fare to your destination before setting off.

Coach/Long-distance Bus

National Express (England and Wales) and Citylink (Scotland), Britain's two largest motorcoach companies, account for more than 80% of intercity connections. Tickets and information can be obtained from any local coach station. In London, you can book tickets at the British Travel Centre (12 Regent Street), at the National Express Coach Travel Centre across the street (13 Regent Street) and at Victoria Coach Station, the terminal for express motorcoach services. For information, contact:

National Express Central Enquiry Bureau, Victoria Coach Station, Buckingham Palace Road, London SW1W 9TP; tel. (01) 730 0202

Open Monday to Saturday 8 a.m. to 10 p.m., Sundays 10 a.m. to 8 p.m.

Train

British Rail's trains are comfortable and punctual; most have first- and standard-class compartments. Main routes are served by high-speed Intercity trains travelling at up to 125 miles (200 km.) per hour. Best time from London to Cardiff 1 hour 47 minutes; to Edinburgh 4 hours 23 minutes. Seat reservations on long-distance trains are not normally necessary, except at rush hour and on some popular routes during holiday periods. On night trains, sleeping-car berths must be booked in advance. In some parts of the country, an old-fashioned type of carriage is still used on local trains; they are marked round the outside with a bold red stripe. The doors of these carriages open directly into individual compartments, with no corridor or access to other carriages. Women travelling alone are advised to avoid them.

If you don't have a *BritRail Pass* (see TRAVEL TICKETS), the most reasonable way to travel is with rail rover tickets, available at any British Rail station or Travel Centre. There are also various travelcards and cheap day-return (round-trip) tickets.

London has about a dozen railway stations. The principal ones (24-hour telephone service, prefix 01 if dialling from outside London):

Paddington (for South-West England, West Midlands and South Wales); tel. 262 6767

Euston/St. Pancras (for Midlands, North Wales, North-West England and West Scotland); tel. 387 7070

King's Cross (for West Yorkshire, North-East England and East Scotland); tel. 278 2477

Liverpool Street/Fenchurch Street/ Victoria/Charing Cross/Waterloo (for South and South-East England, Essex and East Anglia); tel. 928 5100

Plane

British Airways and about a dozen independent airlines fly to some 60 domestic airports and heliports, linking the major towns and connecting the mainland with Orkney and Shetland, the north-western islands, Northern Ireland, the Isle of Man, Isles of Scilly and Channel Islands. From London, there are shuttle flights to Belfast, Edinburgh, Glasgow and Manchester. Check-in time is 30 minutes before departure.

TRAVEL TICKETS

Buy the appropriate reduced-rate tickets, passes and cards and you'll cut costs substantially. Here are the main bargains for anyone who plans to travel widely in Britain.

The *BritRail Pass* (British Rail's equivalent of the *Eurailpass,* which is not valid in Great Britain) offers unlimited rail travel in England, Scotland and Wales for periods of 4, 8, 15 or 22 days, or one month in first class *(Gold Pass)* or standard class *(Silver Pass).* Passes for children aged 5 through 15 are available at half price. Men and women over 60 can buy first-class passes at reduced rates. For young people 16 through 25, there's a *BritRail Youth Pass* (standard class only). A *BritRail Flexipass,* valid for 4 days' travel within a period of 8 days or 8 days within a period of 15 days, is on offer in certain countries and with BritRail/Drive packages. A special *BritFrance Railpass* offers similar conditions to the Flexipass, but covers France, too, including the Channel crossing.

These passes are sold in Europe at accredited travel agents, main railway stations and BritRail Travel International offices (Amsterdam, Basle, Brussels, Copenhagen, Dublin, Frankfurt, Milan, Paris); in North America, at BritRail accredited travel agents and BritRail Travel International offices (see below); in other countries at appointed travel agencies—a list is available from your local BTA office. They cannot be bought in Britain.

BritRail Travel International:

Canada. 94 Cumberland Street, Toronto, Ont. M5R 1A3; tel. (416) 929-3333

409 Granville Street, Vancouver, BC V6C 1T2; tel. (604) 683-6896

U.S.A. Cedar Maple Plaza, Suite 210, 2305 Cedar Springs Road, Dallas, TX 75201-1814; tel. (214) 748-0860

Suite 603, 800 South Hope Street, Los Angeles, CA 90017-4697; tel. (213) 624-8787

630 Third Avenue, New York, NY 10017; tel. (212) 599-5400

In the Highlands and islands of Scotland, the *Travelpass* is good for travel on Caledonian MacBrayne ferries, P&O Ferries to Orkney, Scottish Bus Group coaches, Scottish Citylink coaches and on Scotrail. The pass is valid for 7 days' travel in 8 days or 13 days' travel in 15 days between March 1 and October 31. It's on sale at principal British Rail stations, the British Travel Centre in London, Scottish Citylink and Scottish Bus Group offices. When buying a *Travelpass,* ask for the free *Scotpass,* good for discounts at certain shops, hôtels, restaurants and attractions.

The *Britexpress Card* gives a reduction of up to one-third on every journey by bus made in any 30-day period on all National Express coaches in England and Wales and most Citylink coaches in Scotland. The *Tourist Trail Pass* (available to all age groups) is valid for unlimited travel by bus for any 5-, 8-, 15-, 22- or 30-day period. Both passes are on sale at National Express and Citylink Travel Centres in Britain.

British Airways' *Highland Rover* offers eight separate flights within a 21-day period on the Highlands Division network. The ticket must be obtained seven days before the first flight and is only good for one return journey between any two points. Available from all British Airways offices.

The London *Visitor Travelcard* gives 1, 3, 4 or 7 days' unlimited travel on London Transport buses (except the Heathrow Airbus service) and most of the underground railway network (including the Piccadilly line to Heathrow). The ticket—which comes with discount vouchers for various museums and shops in London—is not available in Britain. You have to buy one through a travel agent or BritRail Travel International office abroad.

325

WEIGHTS AND MEASURES

The metric system is slowly inching its way into every walk of life, though people still prefer the old Imperial weights and measures. Decimalization was adopted in 1971 for British currency, and young people, who were brought up with the system, generally don't know what a shilling is. Cloth is sold by the metre and wine by the litre, but you always ask for beer in pints or "halves". Temperatures are officially quoted in Centigrade, but understood in Fahrenheit. Foodstuffs are generally marketed in metric packs, painstakingly converted into exact equivalents in pounds (lbs) and ounces (oz). The famous gallon is disappearing, being replaced by the litre.

Temperature

Length

Weight

Fluid measures

Distance

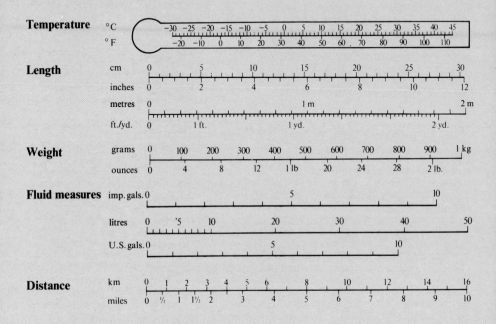

Road Atlas

GROSSBRITANNIEN IRLAND

GRAND-BRETAGNE IRLANDE

GREAT BRITAIN IRELAND

GRAN BRETAGNA IRLANDA

Autobahn mit Anschlussstelle Tankstelle, Restaurant, Motel Motorway with interchange Filling station, restaurant, motel		Autoroute avec échangeur Station-service, restaurant, motel Autostrada con svincolo Stazione di servizio, ristorante, motel
Autobahn im Bau mit Eröffnungsdatum Motorway under construction with opening date	1990　1991	Autoroute en construction avec date de mise en service Autostrada in construzione con data d'apertura
Autostrasse (international, regional) Dual carriageway (international, regional)		Route rapide à chaussées séparées (internationale, régionale) Superstrada a carreggiate separate (internazionale/regionale)
Grosse internationale Durchgangsstrasse Major international throughroute		Route de grand transit internationale Strada di gran transito internazionale
Sonstige internationale Fernverkehrsstrasse Other International throughroute		Autre route de transit internationale Altra strada di transito internazionale
Interregionale Verbindungsstrasse Interregional throughroute		Route de transit interrégionale Strada di transito interregionale
Regionale Verbindungsstrasse Regional connecting road		Route de liaison régionale Strada di collegamento regionale
Lokale Verbindungsstrasse Local road		Route de liaison locale Strada di collegamento locale
Strassen im Bau Roads under construction		Routes en construction Strade in construzione
Entfernungen in Meilen Distances in miles	10 3 3 4 2 5 7 2 3 5 10	Distances en miles Distanze in miglia
Strassennummern: Europastrasse, Autobahn, Nationalstrasse Road classification: European road, motorway, national road	E7　M9　60	Numéros des routes: route européenne, autoroute, route nationale Numerazione stradale: strada europea, autostrada, strada nazionale
Berg mit Höhenangabe Summit with altitude	▲ 2941 (in feet, 1 ft = 0,3 m)	Sommet avec altitude Vetta con altitudine
Eisenbahn, Berg-/ Luftseilbahn Railway, mountain/ cable railway		Voie ferrée, téléphérique/ funiculaire Ferrovia, funivia/ funicolare
Autoverlad: per Fähre Car transport:by ferry	2h	Transport des autos: par bac Trasporto automobili: su chiatta
Internationaler Flughafen, Flugplatz International airport, airfield	✈　✈	Aéroport international, aérodrome Aeroporto internazionale, aerodromo
Schloss/Burg, Kirche/Kloster, Ruine Castle, church/monastery, ruin		Château/fort, église/couvent, ruine Castello/fortezza, chiesa/convento, rudero
Höhle, Leuchtturm, Campingplatz Cave, lighthouse, camping site		Grotte, phare, camping Grotta, faro, campeggio
Bemerkenswerter Ort, Nationalpark Place of interest, National Park	★	Localité intéressante, parc national Località interessante, parco nazionale
Staatsgrenze National boundary		Frontière d'Etat Confine di Stato

1 : 1 000 000

0	10	20	40	60	80 km

0	10	20	30	40	50 miles

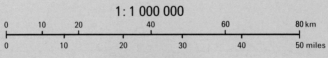

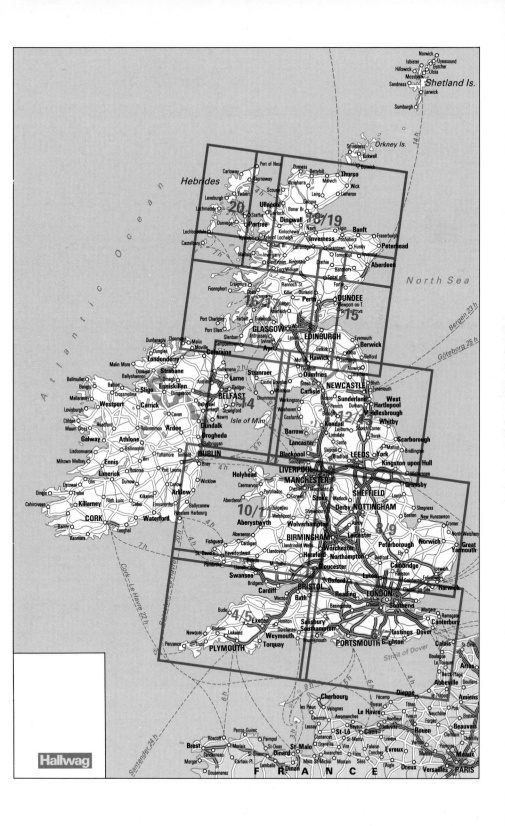

10

yboghil
1
Rush

E1

Donabate

Lambay

Malahide

D U B L
Santry
Howth

DUBLIN
BAILE ÁTHA CLIATH
Dún Laoghaire

3h30'

7h

Cemaes

Carmel Hd.
Llanfaethlu
Llanerchym

Holyhead
E22

Angles

Foxrock
Dalkey
116
Bray
(Brí Chualann)
Greystones

Holy Island

Holy Island
Valley
Gwalchmai
Llanfairp

The
Scalp
Enniskerry

2384

Newtown
Mt. Kennedy
Roundwood
11
Kilcoole
Newcastle

Caernarf

*Caernarfon
Bay*

5

25

E20
Talla
Brittas
Kilbride
ington

ulaphous
Reservoir

Laragh
K L
755
Rathnew
O W
Ballinalea

Wicklow

499

Clynnogfaw

Llanaelhaearn

Rathdrum
103
Beehive
Wicklow Hd.

Nefyn

Aughrim
752
12
Avoca
E1

*Brittas
Bay*
Mizen Hd.

Sarn Meyllteyrn

7

Pwllheli

Woodenbridge
4

roghan 1993
ountain
Inch
11
Arklow

499
Aberdaron
St Tudwa
Islands

Absersoch

Gorey
6

Kilmichael Pt.

Bardsey
Trwyn Cilan

Courtown Harbour
Ballycanew
Kilena
R
D
Cahore Pt.

C a r d i g a n

741
Ford
Blackwater
bridge

B a y

W e x f o r d
d
B a y

slare
Rosslare Harbour
hurchtown
ore Pt.

3h30'

A b

G *e* *o* *r* *g* *e* *'s* *C h a n n e l*

Aberaeron
New Quay

3h30'
4h

Brynhoffnant
Synod
486
487
487
Gwbert-on-Sea
10
Cardigan
475
Ffostrasol
Drefa
475

Pembrokeshire Coast

484
11

Strumble Hd.
Goodwick
Newport
487
Eglwyswrw
Newcastle
Emlyn
Llandyssul

Mathry
Fishguard
478
485
Cwmduad
Alltw

3

E30
40
Crymmych
Trelech
484

St David's
Ramsey
Croesgoch
Wolf's Castle
The
Kell
1759
Tufton
Cynwyl
Elfed

487
Newgale
Llandissilio
Whitland
61
St Clears
Carmar

*St Brides
Bay*
Haverfordwest
40
Narberth
477
4066
40
48

Broad Haven
St Brides
4076
477
4075
478
Laugharne
484
Cross
Kidwelly

Skomer
Pendine

Skokholm
Dale
4
Milford Haven
Burry Por

Angle
Pembroke
Dock
477
Kilgetty
Tenby

A
Pembroke

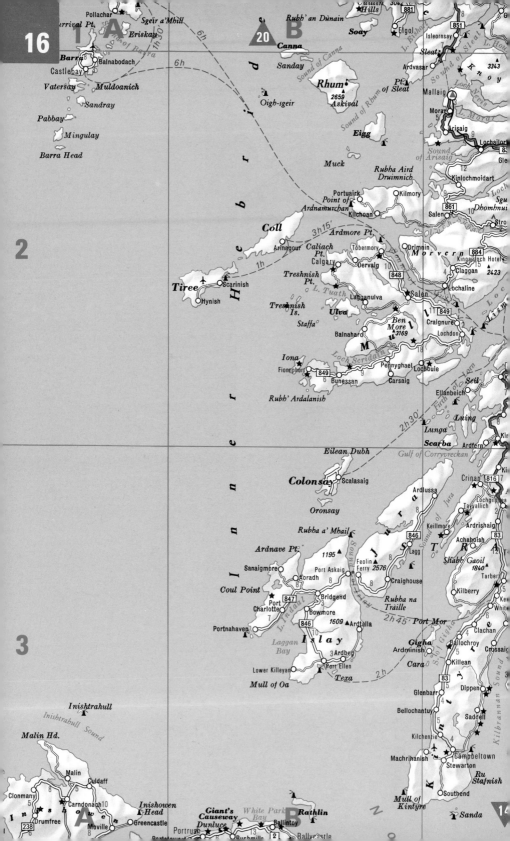

1

For Ness
Swona
Burwick
Brough Ness
Rohalasay

Dunnet
Head
Pentland
Stroma
Firth
Pentland
Skerries
Duncansby Head
John o' Groats

C

Thurso
836 Mey
Castletown
882
Roadside
Klrk
9
Nybster
Kelss
Reiss
Sinclair's
Bay
Watten
Watten
Noss Head
Mybster
882
Wick
895
Thrumster
avanich
5
Latheron
9
Clyth
Lybster
Dunbeath
Berrledale

F i r t h

Lossiemouth
Spey Bay
Portknockie
Elgin
96
Spey Bay Buckie
6
Cullen
Portsoy
98 3
Banff
Macduff
Troup
Head
Rosehearty
Fraserburgh
941
6
98
Longmanhill
St. Combs
Crook of
Alves
Longmorn
Fochabers
Gordonstown
12
Plaidy
92
Crimond
941
Aberchirder
New Pitsligo
98
Strichen
13
St Fergus
Mulben
105
95
Turriff
950 Mintlaw
952
Rothes
Keith
11 Milltown
97
Cuminestown
Peterhead
Craigellachie
13
Darra
New Deer
Clola
Burnhaven
Cardow
Charlestown of Aberlour 14
Fortrie
Auchnagatt
Hatton
Buchan Ness
95
Dufftown
920
Huntly
Fyvie
948
12
Cruden Bay
Dalnashaugh
Inn
Ardwell
10
Methlick
975
The Skares
Auchbreck
941
11
Insch
920
Ellon
Kirktown of Slains
Knockandhu
2366
Rhynie
Pitcaple
96
Oldmeldrum
Newburgh
Carn Mor
The Buck
G R A M P I A N
Tomintoul
2639
Mossat
944
Inverurie
947
Balmedie
939
Alford
Kintore
Dyce
92
Cock Bridge
97
Tornaveen
11
Blackburn
ABERDEEN
Corgarff
Tarland
Dunecht
944
Torry
Girdle Ness
Newkirk
980
Lumphanan
Echt
Petercutter
Crathie
Aboyne
Torphins
Banchory
Cammachmore
Ballater
12
93
Kirkton
Balmoral
93
Tombae
Dee
of Durris
92
Muchalls
Castle
Strachan Kerloch
957
Braemar
3080
1754
13
Lochnagar
3791
Mount Keen
Stonehaven
L. Muick
Dunnottar
Castle
Tarfside
L. Lee
Ben Tirran
Fettercairn
94
14
Roadside
Clova
2941
15
of Kinneff
D
Inverbervie
Forter
Edzell
Marykirk

© Hallwag AG, Bern

DISTANCE CHART

(miles)

	Aberdeen	Bath	Birmingham	Bristol	Cambridge	Canterbury	Cardiff	Dover	Edinburgh	Exeter	Glasgow	Inverness	Liverpool	London	Manchester	Oxford	Penzance	Plymouth	Southampton	Stratford-upon-Avon	York
Aberdeen		523	430	511	468	610	532	626	127	584	149	105	361	537	354	498	690	624	567	461	332
Bath	523		97	13	174	177	56	200	384	157	384	544	195	116	181	66	213	141	64	71	236
Birmingham	430	97		85	101	186	107	203	293	81	291	453	98	117	88	63	278	199	128	24	128
Bristol	511	13	85		178	187	45	198	373	81	372	532	178	119	167	74	195	125	75	75	221
Cambridge	468	174	101	178		114	213	121	337	255	349	500	205	60	153	80	368	297	132	131	157
Canterbury	610	177	186	187	114		218	16	451	233	472	632	281	61	268	131	345	275	131	171	258
Cardiff	532	56	107	45	213	218		233	393	120	393	558	205	155	188	109	232	164	122	99	241
Dover	626	200	203	198	121	16	233		457	246	490	648	281	77	283	148	365	287	155	188	274
Edinburgh	127	384	293	373	337	451	393	457		446	45	159	225	401	218	362	488	275	433	324	195
Exeter	584	157	81	81	255	233	120	246	446		444	610	250	199	239	152	56	45	121	150	291
Glasgow	149	384	291	372	349	472	393	490	45	444		171	221	400	214	355	486	429	478	319	208
Inverness	105	544	453	532	500	632	558	648	159	610	171		385	569	378	518	651	596	596	478	360
Liverpool	361	195	98	178	205	281	205	281	225	250	221	385		210	34	165	370	237	237	124	101
London	537	116	117	119	60	61	155	77	401	199	400	569	210		197	56	312	244	78	95	209
Manchester	354	181	88	167	153	268	188	283	218	239	214	378	34	197		154	358	281	224	116	71
Oxford	498	66	63	74	80	131	109	148	362	152	355	518	165	56	154		265	193	65	48	185
Penzance	690	213	278	195	368	345	232	365	488	56	486	651	370	312	358	265		80	227	264	406
Plymouth	624	141	199	125	297	275	164	287	275	45	429	596	237	244	281	193	80		149	192	340
Southampton	567	64	128	75	132	131	122	155	433	121	478	596	237	78	224	65	227	149		107	252
Stratford-upon-Avon	461	71	24	75	131	171	99	188	324	150	319	478	124	95	116	48	264	192	107		154
York	332	236	128	221	157	258	241	274	195	291	208	360	101	209	71	185	406	340	252	154	

INDEX

Where there is more than one set of page references, page numbers in **bold face** refer to the main entry. Those in *italics* refer to the hotel and restaurant section.

Abbotsbury 126
Abbotsford 250
Aberaeron 206
Aberdaron 213
Aberdeen **259–260**, 265, *296,* 309
Aberdovey 216, *296*
Abergavenny 194
Abersoch 213
Aberystwyth 202–205
Agen Allwedd 194
Aldeburgh **155–157**, 283
Alfriston 103
Alloway 254
Alnwick 245
Alton Barnes Horse 47
Althrop 182
Amberley 108
Ambleside 237, *296*
American Museum in Britain, see Claverton Manor
Anglesey 56, 208, **212**
Anglesey Abbey 54, **155**
Anne of Cleves 25
Anstruther 259
Antony House 146
Appledore 139
Arisaig 65, *296*
Arran, Isle of **255**, 273
Arthur, King 16, 17, 43, 58, 137, 150, 195, 226
Arundel 52, 53, **108**, 283, *296*
Ashbourne 185
Ashburton 62
Ashridge 51
Aston Cantlow 59
Aston Clinton *296*
Audley End 51, **155**
Austen, Jane 114, 116, 126, 131
Austerfield 66
Avebury 15, 45
Aviemore 259, **261**, 275
Aysgarth 223

Bakewell **186**, 189
Bala 213, **215**
Ballater *296*
Balmoral 259, **260**
Bamburgh 245, *296*
Bangor **208–211**, 213
Bannockburn 22, 37, **255–256**
Bardsey Island 213
Barmouth 216
Barnard Castle 244
Barnstaple 139, *296*
Barrington Court 138
Bassenthwaite Lake 238
Bath 29, 39, 43, 44, 45, 46, 66, 69, 128, **131–134**, 283, *297*

Battle 43, 48, **102–103**
Battle Abbey 10, 20, 48, **102–103**
Beachy Head 103
Beaconsfield 311
Beamish Open Air Museum 67, **244**
Beaulieu **113**, 311
Beaumaris 56, **212**
Becket, St. Thomas 20, 22, 36, 97, 98, 99
Beer **142**, 143
Beltring 311
Belvoir Castle 183
Ben Nevis 13, **256**
Bere Regis 63
Berkeley Castle 178
Berwick-upon-Tweed 245, *297*
Bethesda 211
Betws-y-Coed 213
Beverley 228
Bickleigh 142
Biddenden 101
Bideford 139, *297*
Birmingham 13, 40, 66, 165, **181**, 282, 283, *297,* 309
Black Mountains 194
Blaenau Ffestiniog 213–215
Blaenavon 66, **194**
Blair Castle 257
Blackpool 275
Blake, William 88, 94, 165
Blenheim Palace 28, 52, 128, 129, **167**
Blickling Hall 160–161
Blidworth 59
Bluebell Railway 67
Bodiam 101
Bodmin 150
Bodmin Moor 58, **150**
Bodnant 54
Boleyn, Anne 24, 25, 37, 52, 80, 102, 161
Bolton Abbey 57
Bolton Castle 223
Bolton Priory 223
Bonnie Prince Charlie 29, 37, 64–65, 183, 240, 259, 262, 267
Borrowdale 238
Boscastle 150
Boscaswell 150
Bosham 108
Boston 66, **162**, *297*
Bournemouth 120, *297*
Bourton-on-the-Water **175**, 311
Bovey Tracey 146
Bradford 13, 66, 219, **222**
Bradford-on-Avon 134
Bramber 108
Branscombe 142, *297*
Brantwood 237
Bratton Down 48
Bray-on-Thames *297*
Brecon 195, *297*
Brecon Beacons National Park 67, **195**
Brecon Mountain Railway 67
Breydon Water 65
Bridport 126
Brighton 43, 102, **104–106**, 107, 128, 275, 283, *297*
Bristol 13, 43, 128, **134**, *297*
Brixham 144, *298*

Broadlands 113
Broadlands Conservation Centre 161
Broads, Norfolk 65, **161**, 275
Broadstairs 62, **98**
Broadway 43, **176**, *297–298*
Brockenhurst *298*
Brodick 255
Brontës 189, 222, 223
Brownsea Island 122
Bruar, Falls of 257
Bruce, Robert 22, 37, 247, 255, 256, 260
Buckfast Abbey 62
Buckfastleigh 62, 67
Buckland Abbey 54, **146**
Buckland-in-the-Moor 62
Buckler's Hard 113
Bude 150, *298*
Budleigh Salterton 144
Builth 204, **206**
Bullers of Buchan 260
Burnham-on-Sea 138
Burns, Robert 254, 255, 257
Burton Agnes Hall 52
Burton Constable 52
Burton-on-Trent 66
Bury St. Edmunds 160, *298*
Buttermere 238
Buxton 60, **189**, 283, *298*
Byland Abbey 58

Cadair Idris 216
Cadbury Castle 137
Caerleon 46, 55, **195**
Caesar, Julius 16, 36, 99
Caernarfon 22, 43, 47, 55, 208, 210, **212**
Caerphilly 55, 197, **198**
Cairngorms 261
Caldey Island 199
Calgary 268
Callander 60
Cambridge 23, 43, **153–155**, 283, *298*
Canterbury 17, 22, 36, 43, 56, 96, **97–98**, 128, 283, *298*
Cape Wrath 265
Capel Curig 213
Cardiff 13, 40, 55, **195**, 272, 282, 283, *298*, 309–310, 312, 324
Cardigan 202
Carlisle 47, 224, **240**, *298*
Carmarthen 198–199
Carrbridge 261
Carreg Cennen 198
Castell Coch 55, **198**
Castle Drogo 147
Castle Head 237–238
Castle Howard 34, 52, 128, **229**
Castleton 60, **189**
Catherine of Aragon 23, 37, 90, 184
Cawdor Castle 262
Cerne Abbas 48, **123**
Chalk 62
Channel Tunnel 7, 37, 98, 99
Channel, English 97, 98, 99, 111, 131, 325
Charlecote Park 59
Charles I 27–28, 37, 49, 56, 72, 92, 176, 184, 185

Charles II 28, 37, 73, 102, 155, 184, 249
Charles Edward Stuart, see Bonnie Prince Charlie
Charleston Farmhouse 103
Chartwell 51, **102**
Chatham 62, 311
Chatsworth House 60, **186–189**
Chaucer, Geoffrey 23, 73, 97, 98, 221
Chawton 116
Cheddar Gorge **135**, 311
Chedworth Roman Villa 46, **174**
Cheltenham 29, **175**, 272, 283, *298*
Chepstow 55, **194**
Chertsey 311
Chesil Bank 126
Chessington 311
Chester 47, **184–185**, 283, *298*
Chichester 45, **108**, 275, 283, *298*
Chipping Campden 176, *298*
Chirk Castle 207
Churchill, Sir Winston 33, 35, 51, 52, 73, 102
Cilgerran 202
Cinque Ports 98–99
Cirencester 46, **174**, 272, *298*
Clapham 224
Claverton Manor 134
Cley and Salthouse 65
Climate 13, 311
Clovelly 139
Cobham 62
Cockermouth 238
Colchester 16, 292
Colwyn Bay 208
Compton Acres 54, **122**
Compton Wynyates 52
Coniston 237
Constable Country 43, 63, 69, **157**
Constable, John 10, 43, 63, 88, 94–95, 157, 159, 220
Conwy Castle 22, 56, **208**, 213
Cook, Captain James 144, 234, 235, 236
Cooling 62
Corfe Castle 118, **122**
Cotehele House 52, **146**
Coton Manor 54
Cotswolds 23, 43, 165, **174–176**, 273, 274
Countisbury 139
Coventry 13, **182**, *298*
Cowes 112, 275
Crafnant 213
Cragside 245
Craigievar Castle 260
Crail 257–259
Crarae Gardens 55
Crathes Castle 260
Criccieth 22, **213**
Crickhowell 194
Cromwell, Oliver 28, 176, 184, 248
Crummock Water 238
Culloden Moor 65, **262**
Culross 250
Culross Palace 56
Culzean Castle 254–255

Dale 200
Darlington 244

Dartmeet 147
Dartmoor 60–62, 131, **146–147**
Dartmouth 144, *299*
Dart Valley Railway 67
Deal 99
Dedham 63, **157**, 159, *299*
Denbigh 208
Derby 60, **165**, 183, *299*
Derwentwater 238
Devil's Dyke 106–108
Dickens, Charles 33, 62, 73, 98, 168, 181
Dolaucothi 206
Dolgellau **216**, 217
Dolbadarn Castle 56
Dorchester 62, **122–123**
Dorset Coast Path 122
Dovedale Gorge 60
Dover 99, *299*
Drake, Sir Francis 25, 54, 142, 144, 146
Drinks 293–295
Drumlanrig Castle 255
Dryburgh Abbey 250
Duart 268
Dudley 181
Dulverton 139
Dumfries 255
Duncansby Head **265**, 266
Dunkeld 257
Dunnet Head 265
Dunster 139
Dunvegan Castle 267
Durdle Door 122
Durham 20, 57, 128, 240 **243–244**, *299*

East Bergholt 63, **157**
East Lambrook Manor 54
East Neuk 257–259
Eastbourne 103, *299*
Eating Out 40, 146, 287–295, 321–322
Ebbor Gorge 135
Edale 189
Edinburgh 12, 13, 39, 40, 43, 56, 65, **247–250**, 251, 253, 272, 283, *299*, 309, 311, 312, 324, 325
Edward I 22, 36, 55, 56, 73, 98, 193, 205, 208, 212, 213, 257
Edwinstowe 59, **182**
Elan Valley 205
Elizabeth I 24, 25–27, 37, 54, 73, 93, 102, 109, 124, 171, 176
Ely 20, 43, 56, **155**, 156, 157
Entertainment 281–283, 306
Erddig 207
Eton College 92
Exeter 20, 56, 140, **142**, 283, *299*
Exmoor 136, **139**
Exmouth 144, *299*

Falkirk 65
Falkland Palace 56
Falmouth **147**, 275, *299*
Farne Islands 245
Fishbourne 16, 45, **109**
Fishguard **200**, 283
Flatford 63, **157**, 159
Fleet Lagoon 126

Folkestone 98, **99**, *299*
Food, see Eating Out
Forde Abbey 54
Fort William *299*
Fountains Abbey 43, 58, **229**, 231
Fowey 43, 58, **147**
Friar's Crag 238

Gad's Hill Place 62
Gainsborough 66
Gaping Ghyll 224
Glasgow 12, 13, 35, 43, 66, 129, **252–254**, 282, 283, *300*, 309, 325
Glastonbury 43, **135–137**, *300*
Glen Coe 43, **256**, 275
Glen Garry 257
Glenfinnan 64
Glenridding 240
Gloucester 16, 57, **178**, 180, 283, *300*
Glyndebourne **103**, 283
Glyndwr Owain 55, 193, 207, 208, 215, 217
Goodwood House 109
Goudhurst 101
Gower Peninsula 198
Grampian Mountains 13, 65, **260**
Grantchester 155
Grantham 183
Grasmere 237, *300*
Grassholm 200
Grassington 223
Great Ayton *300*
Great Glen 262
Great Milton *300*
Great Orme Head 208
Greenwich 49, 81, **89**, 128, 283
Grimsborough 146
Guildford 109
Guisborough 236
Gullane *300*
Gwyllt Gardens 54

Hacpen Horse 47
Haddon Hall 60, **189**
Hadleigh 157
Hadrian's Wall 10, 14, 16, 36, 43, 47, 240, **244–245**
Ham House 51
Hampton Court Palace 43, 49, **90–92**, 128
Hardraw Force 224
Hardwick Hall 183
Hardy, Thomas 10, 62–63, 73, 120, 122, 123, 124
Harewood House 52, 128, **222**
Harlech 22, 55, **215**
Harold, King 20, 48, 102, 103, 206
Harrogate **228–229**, 283, *300*
Hartland Point 139
Harwich *300*
Hastings 10, 48, **102–103**, *300*
Hatfield House 51, 54, **93**
Haverfordwest 199–200
Hawes 224
Hawkshead 237
Haworth 67, **222–223**
Hay-on-Wye **206**, 276
Heathersage 189
Heights of Abraham 186
Helmsley 233, *300*

Helvellyn 240
Henry II 20, 22, 36
Henry VII 24, 72, 73, 193, 199, 200
Henry VIII 20, 22, 24–25, 37, 43,
    49, 51, 57, 90, 92, 98, 102, 154,
    184, 194
Hereford 184, *300*
Hever Castle 52, **102**
Hidcote Manor 54
Higher Bockhampton 63
Highland Wildlife Park 261
Highlands, Scottish 10, 12, 64,
    261–265, 272
Hockney, David 95
Hogarth, William 88, 94
Holbein, Hans the Younger 88, 94
Holkham Hall 161
Holme Nature Reserve 65
Holy Island 212
Holyhead 212
Honister Pass 238
Hopetoun House 56, **250**
Horning 161
Horsted Keynes 67
House of Pipes 108
Howard, Catherine 25, 92
Howtown 240
Hythe 67, **99**, *300*

Ightham Mote 52
Ilfracombe 139, *300*
Ilkley 223
Ingleborough Cave 224
Inveraray Castle 256
Inverewe Gardens 262
Inverness 261, *300*
Iona 17, 267, **268**
Ipswich *300*
Iron-Bridge Gorge 66, **181–182**
Isle of Portland 124
Isle of Purbeck 122
Isleworth 51

James I (VI of Scotland) 25, 27, 37,
    73, 155, 248
Jedburgh **250**, 252
Jervaulx Abbey 224
John O'Groats 265
John, King 20, 22, 36, 59, 161, 183,
    184
Jonson, Ben 26, 27, 117

Kedleston Hall 183
Keighley 67, **223**
Keighley and Worth Valley Light
    Railway 67
Keld 226
Kelso 252, *300*
Kendal 236, *300*
Kenilworth Castle 174
Kent & East Sussex Railway 101
Kentallen *300*
Kersey 157
Keswick 237, *300*
Killiecrankie, Pass of 257
Kilmuir 267
King's Lynn **161**, 283, *301*
Kingston Lacy House 54, 122
Kinlochmoidart 64
Kirkmadrine Stones 255
Knightshayes Court 54, **142**

Knole Park 52, **102**
Kyle of Lochalsh 262
Kyle of Tongue 247, **265**
Kynance Cove 149

Lake District 10, 43, **236–240**,
    272, 292
Lampeter 206
Land's End 17, 58, **149**, 151
Laugharne 199
Launceston 150
Lavenham 157, *301*
Leeds 13, 219, **221–222**, *301*
Leeds Castle 52, **101**
Leicester 46, *301*
Levens Hall 54
Lewes 103
Lincoln 43, 46, 57, 66, 128, **162**,
    301
Lindisfarne 17, 243, **245**
Linton 223
Little Orme Head 208
Littlecote House 54
Liverpool 13, **219–220**, 272, 283,
    292, *301*
Lizard 149, *301*
Llandeilo 198
Llandovery 206
LLandrindod Wells 206, *301*
Llandudno 208, *301*
LLanfair P.G. 212
Llangammarch Wells 206
Llangollen **207**, 209, 283
Llanwrtyd Wells 206
Llanystumdwy 213
Lleyn Peninsula 212–213
Loch Achray 60
Loch Ard Forest 60
Loch Carron 262
Loch Gairloch 262
Loch Katrine 60
Loch Lomond 43, **254**, 256
Loch Maree 262
Loch Na Keal 268
Loch Nan Uamh 64
Loch Ness 43, **261–262**
Loch Torridon 262
Loch Venachar 60
Logan Botanic Garden 255
London 10, 13, 16, 29, 39, 40, 43,
    45, 49, 51, **69–89**, 97, 271, 276,
    279, 280, 281, 282, 283, 287, 289,
    291, *301–302*, 307, 308, 310, 311,
    312, 315, 316, 317, 318, 319, 320,
    323, 324, 325
    Admiralty 73
    Apsley House 51, **82**
    Bank, the 80
    Banqueting House 49, **73**
    Barbican 76, **80**, 281, 282
    Beauchamp Place **85**, 279
    Belgravia 82
    Big Ben 68, 69, **72**
    Bloomsbury 85
    Bond Street **82**, 279
    British Museum 43, 45, 85, **88**,
        129, 276, 311
    Buckingham Palace 43, 49,
        70–72, 84
    Burlington Arcade 82
    Carnaby Street 85

London (cont.)
    Chelsea 86, **87**, 279, 283, 320
    Chinatown 70, **84**, 289
    Chiswick House 51
    City, The 70, **76–81**, 129, 283
    Courtauld Institute 49, **76**
    Covent Garden **85**, 128, 276,
        281, 320
    Docklands 77, **81**, 324
    Downing Street 73
    Eltham Palace 49
    Fleet Street 51, 76, **78**
    Green Park 49, **82**
    Guildhall 78, **80**
    Harrods 85
    Highgate Cemetery 89
    Horse Guards 72, **73**
    Houses of Parliament,
        see Westminster, Palace of
    Hyde Park 49, 83, **84**, 85, 283
    Kensington **87**, 279
    Kensington Church Street **87**,
        279
    Kensington High Street **87**, 279,
        320
    Kensington Gardens 49, **87**
    Kensington Palace 49, **87**
    Kenwood House 51, 128
    Kew Gardens 49, **89–90**, 91, 129
    King's Road **87**, 276, 279
    Knightsbridge **85**, 279, 320
    Leicester Square 81
    Lloyd's 80
    London Pavilion **81**, 311
    London Transport Museum 85
    Madame Tussaud's **89**, 311
    Mall, The 70
    Mansion House 80
    Marble Arch 84
    Markets 279
    Marlborough House 49
    Mayfair 70, **82–84**
    Monument, the 51
    Museum of Mankind 82
    National Army Museum 87
    National Gallery 43, 70, **88**, 94,
        95, 129
    Oxford Street **84**, 279
    Park Lane 84
    Piccadilly **81–82**, 279
    Piccadilly Circus 81
    Regent's Park 49, **84**, 89
    Regent Street 84
    Richmond Park 49
    Royal Academy of Arts 81
    Royal Hospital 87
    Royal Opera House **85**, 281, 282
    St. Andrew-by-the-Wardrobe 51
    St. Anne's 85
    St. Bride's 51, **78**
    St. Clement Danes 51
    St. James Garlickhythe 51
    St. James's 70, 73, **84**
    St. James's, Piccadilly 81
    St. James's Palace 49, **70**
    St. James's Park 49, **70**
    St. Mary-le-Bow 51
    St. Paul's Cathedral 43, 51, 70,
        78–80, 128
    St. Paul's Church 85
    St. Peter-upon-Cornhill 51

London (cont.)
St. Stephen Walbrook 51
Savile Row 82
Shepherd Market 84
Sir John Soane's Museum 51
Soho 70, **84–85**, 280
Somerset House 49, **76**
South Bank Arts Centre **76**, 281, 282
Speaker's Corner 84
Stock Exchange 80
Strand, The 49, 51, **73–76**
Tate Gallery **88–89**, 95
Temple 76–78
Theatre Museum 85
Tower Bridge 77, **81**
Tower of London 23, 43, 45, 49, 70, 76, **80–81**, 124, 128
Trafalgar Square 70
Trocadero 81
Victoria and Albert Museum 87
West End 70, **81–85**, 279, 280, 281, 282, 320
Westminster **70–76**, 283
Westminster, Palace of 43, 49, 70, **72**, 73, 129
Westminster Abbey 20, 43, **72–73**, 85, 92, 257
Whitehall 28, 49, 72, **73–76**, 128, 283
Zoo 49, 84, **89**, 311
Long Melford 157–160
Longleat House 12, 32, 34, 43, 54, **119**, 128
Looe 147
Loseley Park 109
Lower Slaughter 175
Lullingstone 16, 46
Lulworth Cove 63, 120, **122**
Lundy Island 139
Luton Hoo 93
Lyme Regis 126, *302*
Lyndhurst 112, *302*
Lynmouth 139
Lynton 139, *302*

Machynlleth 206–207
Maiden Castle 111, **123**, 125
Malham 223
Manaton 62
Manchester 13, 35, 60, 66, 219, **220–221**, 281, 282, *303*, 309, 325
Manorbier 199
Marble Hill House 51
Marches, the 20, 23, 178, **184**
Margate 98
Marlborough Horse 47
Marloes 200
Marnhull 63
Mary Stuart, Queen of Scots 25, 56, 73, 89, 223, 240, 248, 249
Marx, Karl 30, 88, 89, 221
Matlock 186, *303*
Matlock Bath 60
May, Isle of 259
Measach, Falls of 265
Mellerstain 252
Melrose 250–252
Menai Bridge 212
Mevagissey 147
Middleham Castle 224

Middlesbrough 242, **244**
Middleton-in-Teesdale 244, *303*
Midlands 10, 35, 165, **178–185**
Milford Haven 199
Milton Manor 52
Minehead 138, *303*
Monk's House 103
Monmouth 55, **194**
Montacute *303*
Montacute House 54, **137–138**
Moore, Henry 95, 222
More, Sir Thomas 24, 80, 109
Mousehole 58, **149**
Muchelney 138
Mull 267–268
Mullion Cove 149
Mumbles, The 198
Mynach Falls 205
Mynydd Preseli 200

Nefyn 213
Nelson, Lord Horatio 29, 37, 70, 80, 89, 111, 112, 194, 199
Nether Largie North Cairn 256
Nether Stowey 138
New Forest 112–113
New Quay 206
New Radnor 206
New Romney 67, **99**
Newby Hall 52, 55
Newcastle-upon-Tyne 47, 66, **244**, *303*
Newport 55, **195**, 283
Newquay 148, **150**, 275, *303*
Newstead Abbey 182–183
Norfolk Wildlife Park and Ornamental Pheasant Trust 65
North York Moors 10, 43, **229–233**, 273
Northampton 182, *303*
Northleach 174
Norwich 160, 283, *303*
Nottingham 59, 67, 165, **182**, 281, 283, *303*
Nymans Gardens 54

Oban **256**, 268
Offa's Dyke 184, 193, 207
Okehampton 146
Old Sarum 45
Osterley Park House 51
Oxenholme 67
Oxford 10, 23, 39, 43, 52, 53, 153, **165–167**, 276, *303*
Oxwich 198
Oystermouth 198

Padstow 150, *303*
Paignton 144
Parnham 126
Parr, Catherine 25, 117, 175–176, 236
Peak District 43, 60, 165, **185–189**, 272
Peebles 250
Pembroke Castle 199
Pembroke Dock 199
Pembrokeshire Coast 40, 43, **199–200**, 201
Pen-y-Gwryd 213
Pencarrow 54

Pendennis Castle 147
Pennine Way 40, 189, 224
Pennines 10, 13, 188, 219, 222
Penrhyn Castle **211**, 212
Penrhyn Slate Quarries 211
Penrith 240
Penshurst Place 52, **101–102**
Penzance 66, **149**, *303*
Petworth 108
Pevensey Bay 48, **103**
Peveril Castle 60, **189**
Pewsey 47
Pewsey New Horse 48
Pickering 233
Pilgrim Country 66
Pilgrim Fathers 27, 37, 66, 144–146, 155, 162
Pitlochry **257**, 283, *303*
Pitmedden Garden 260
Pittenweem 259
Plymouth 27, 40, 43, **144–146**, 275, *303*
Plynlimon 205
Polesden Lacey 54
Polperro 147
Pool 150
Poole **122**, 275, *304*
Porlock 139
Porthmadog 213
Portmeirion 54, **212**
Portpatrick *303*
Portsmouth 43, **111–112**, *303*
Postbridge 62
Powis Castle 207
Prestatyn 208
Prestonpans 65
Princetown 147
Pubs 11, 12, 40, 191, 288, 294, 307, 320, 321
Puddletown 62
Puddletown Heath 63
Purbecks 122
Pusey House 54
Pwllheli 213

Raglan 55, **194**
Raleigh, Sir Walter 80, 124, 142, 144, 150
Ramsey Island 200
Ranworth 161
Reculver 98
Reeth 226
Restaurants, see Eating Out
Restormel 147
Rhayader 205
Rheidol, Vale of the 205
Rhuddlan Castle 208
Rhyl 208
Riber Castle Fauna Reserve and Wildlife Park 186
Richard the Lionheart 20–22, 59, 199
Richborough 99
Richmond 226
Rievaulx Abbey 58, 232, **233**
Ripley 109
Ripon 229
Robin Hood's Bay 234
Rochester 62
Rodmell 103
Romney Marsh 99

Romsey 113
Roseland 147
Rousham House 52, 54
Royal Tunbridge Wells 29, **101**
Rufus Stone 113
Rugely 311
Ruthin 208, *304*
Rydal Mount 237
Rye **99**, 100–101, *304*

Saffron Walden 51, **155**
St. Albans 45
St. Andrews **257**, 273, *304*
St. Asaph **208**, 283
St. Austell 147, *304*
St. David's **200**, 203
St. Ives 43, **150**
St. Just 149–150
St. Margaret's Bay 99
St. Michael's Mount 149
St. Tudwal's Islands 213
Salcombe **144**, 275, *304*
Salisbury 43, 45, 56, 111, **116**, 128, 283, *304*
Salisbury Plain 15, 115, 116, 117
Saltburn 236
Saltram House 54, **146**
Sandringham House 161
Sandwich 98
Sarre 62
Saundersfoot *304*
Scarborough 233–234, *304*
Scilly, Isles of 54, 58, **149**, 325
Scolt Head Island 65
Scone Palace 56, **257**
Scotney Castle 101
Scrooby 66
Seahouses 245
Segontium 212
Selworthy 138–139
Seven Sisters **103**, 105
Seymour, Jane 25
Shaftesbury 63
Shakespeare, William 23, 26, 27, 43, 59, 88, 117, 167, 168, 172, 262
Sheffield 13, 60, 219, **221**, 283, *304*
Sherborne 63, **123–124**, 126, 127
Sherwood Forest 59, **182**
Shopping 276–279, 320
Shottery 59, **172**
Shrewsbury 184, *304*
Sidmouth 142, *304*
Silbury Hill 45
Sissinghurst Castle 54, **101**
Skipton 223
Skokholm 200
Skomer 200
Skye, Isle of 65, 262, **265–267**, 273
Slimbridge 178
Smarden 101
Smoo Cave 265
Snowdon, Mount 13, 55, 56, 213, 214, 273
Snowdonia 43, 55, 207, 208, 212, **213–215**, 272
Snowshill Manor 176
South Downs Way 40, **103**
Southampton 111, **112**, *304*
Sports 12–13, 271–275
Staffa 268
Staithes 235, **236**

Stamford *304*
Stanley 67
Stinsford 62
Stirling 256, *304*
Stoke-by-Nayland 63
Stoke-on-Trent 165, **183**, 276, *304*
Stonehenge 15, 18–19, 43, 45, 69, 111, **117–119**, 200
Stoney Cross Plain 113
Stonor Park 52
Stourbridge 67
Stourhead 43, 54, **119–120**
Stow-on-the-Wold 175, *304*
Stratford St. Mary 63
Stratford-upon-Avon 10, 26, 39, 43, 59, **167–172**, 281, 283, 287, *304*
Studley Royal 54, **229**
Sudbury 160
Sudeley Castle **175–176**, 177
Sulgrave Manor 172
Summer Isles 265
Sutton Bank 233
Swanage 122
Swansea 67, **198**, 283, *305*
Syon House 51

Talley Abbey 206
Talyllyn Railway 67, **216**
Tarn Hows 237
Taunton 138, *305*
Tavistock 146
Teignmouth 144
Tenby **199**, 201
Tenterden 101
Thames, River 10, 13, 76, 81, 92, 165, 272, 283, 311, 318, 324
Thatcher, Margaret 35, 37, 183
Thirsk 233
Tideswell 60
Tintagel 43, 58, **150**
Tintern Abbey 43, 55, 193, **194**
Tissington 185–186
Tiverton 142
Tobermory 268
Top Withens 223
Torosay Castle 268
Torquay **144**, *305*, 311
Totnes 144
Traquair House 250
Tregaron 206
Tremadog 213
Tresco Abbey 54
Tretower 195
Trossachs, the 43, 60, **256**
Truro 147
Tunbridge Wells, see Royal Tunbridge Wells
Turner, J.M.W. 88, 89, 94, 95, 108, 220, 223, 237
Two Bridges 62
Tywyn 67, **216**

Uffington White Horse 47
Ullapool 262–265, *305*
Ullswater 238–240, *305*
Upper Slaughter 175
Upper Swaledale 224–226
Urquhart Castle 262

Veryan 147
Victoria, Queen 30–33, 37, 49, 70, 87, 90, 93, 142, 161, 182, 211, 221, 228, 244
Vyrnwy, Lake 207

Waddesdon Manor 93
Walmer Castle 99
Wardour Castle 54
Wareham 122
Warkworth 245
Warwick 168, **172**, 283, 311
Warwick Castle 171, **172**
Watersmeet 139
Weald and Downland Open Air Museum 109
Wellington, Duke of 30, 37, 51, 80, 82, 175, 207
Wells 8, 43, 56, 128, **135**, *305*
Welshpool 207
Wendron 66
Wensleydale 223–224
West Kennet Long Barrow 45
West Stafford 63
Westbury White Horse 48
Weston-super-Mare 138
Weymouth 29, 63, **124**, *305*
Wharfedale 223
Whipsnade Park Zoo 92
Whisky Trail 65, 259, **261**
Whitby 58, **234–236**
White Castle 55
Whithorn 255
Whitstable 98
Wicken Fen 155
Widecombe-in-the-Moor 62, **146**
Wight, Isle of **112**, 275
William Rufus 20, 113, 114
William the Conqueror 10, 20, 48, 49, 102, 103, 155, 162, 184, 193
Wilmcote 59
Wilmington Long Man 103
Wilton House 54, **117**
Winchcombe 175
Winchelsea 99
Winchester 43, 56, 97, 111, **113–114**, 128, 191, *305*
Windermere 236, *305*
Windsor **92**, 272, 283, *305*
Windsor Castle 43, **92**, 128
Wisley Garden 109
Woburn Abbey 51, **92–93**
Wolverhampton 67
Woodstock *305*
Wookey Hole **135**, 311
Wool 63
Woolacombe 139, *305*
Worcester 184, *305*
Wordsworth, William 10, 43, 94, 138, 154, 194, 207, 236–237, 238
Wren, Sir Christopher 43, 49, 51, 78, 81, 87, 90, 128, 154, 155, 166
Wroxeter 46
Wroxham 161

York 16, 20, 39, 40, 43, 47, 57, **226–228**, 283, *305*
Yorkshire Dales 43, **222–226**, 273
Ystradfellte 195